FORGING ROMANTIC CHINA

The first major cultural study to focus exclusively on this decisive period in modern British–Chinese relations. Based on extensive archival investigations, Peter J. Kitson shows how British knowledge of China was constructed from the writings and translations of a diverse range of missionaries, diplomats, travelers, traders, and literary men and women during the Romantic period. The new perceptions of China that it gave rise to were mediated via a dynamic print culture to a diverse range of poets, novelists, essayists, dramatists, and reviewers, including Jane Austen, Thomas Percy, William Jones, S. T. Coleridge, George Colman, Robert Southey, Charles Lamb, William and Dorothy Wordsworth, and others, informing new British understandings and imaginings of China on the eve of the Opium War of 1839–42. Kitson aims to restore China to its true global presence in our understandings of the culture and literature of Britain in the late eighteenth and early nineteenth centuries.

PETER J. KITSON is Professor of English at the University of East Anglia. He is the author of *Romantic Literature, Race and Colonial Encounter* (2007).

CAMBRIDGE STUDIES IN ROMANTICISM

This series aims to foster the best new work in one of the most challenging fields within English literary studies. From the early 1780s to the early 1830s a formidable array of talented men and women took to literary composition, not just in poetry, which some of them famously transformed, but in many modes of writing. The expansion of publishing created new opportunities for writers, and the political stakes of what they wrote were raised again by what Wordsworth called those "great national events" that were "almost daily taking place": the French Revolution, the Napoleonic and American wars, urbanization, industrialization, religious revival, an expanded empire abroad and the reform movement at home. This was an enormous ambition, even when it pretended otherwise. The relations between science, philosophy, religion, and literature were reworked in texts such as *Frankenstein* and *Biographia Literaria*; gender relations in *A Vindication of the Rights of Woman* and *Don Juan*; journalism by Cobbett and Hazlitt; poetic form, content and style by the Lake School and the Cockney School. Outside Shakespeare studies, probably no body of writing has produced such a wealth of comment or done so much to shape the responses of modern criticism. This indeed is the period that saw the emergence of those notions of "literature" and of literary history, especially national literary history, on which modern scholarship in English has been founded.

The categories produced by Romanticism have also been challenged by recent historicist arguments. The task of the series is to engage both with a challenging corpus of Romantic writings and with the changing field of criticism they have helped to shape. As with other literary series published by Cambridge, this one will represent the work of both younger and more established scholars, on either side of the Atlantic and elsewhere.

For a complete list of titles published see end of book.

FORGING
ROMANTIC CHINA

Sino-British Cultural Exchange 1760–1840

PETER J. KITSON

CAMBRIDGE
UNIVERSITY PRESS

CAMBRIDGE
UNIVERSITY PRESS

University Printing House, Cambridge CB2 8BS, United Kingdom

Published in the United States of America by Cambridge University Press, New York

Cambridge University Press is part of the University of Cambridge.

It furthers the University's mission by disseminating knowledge in the pursuit of education, learning and research at the highest international levels of excellence.

1007089719

www.cambridge.org

Information on this title: www.cambridge.org/9781107045613

© Peter J. Kitson 2013

First published 2013

Printed in the United Kingdom by CPI Group Ltd, Croydon CR0 4YY

A catalogue record for this publication is available from the British Library

Library of Congress Cataloguing in Publication data
Kitson, Peter J.
Forging romantic China : Sino-British cultural exchange, 1760–1840 / Peter J. Kitson.
pages cm. – (Cambridge studies in Romanticism ; 105)
Includes bibliographical references and index.
ISBN 978-1-107-04561-3 (hardback)
1. English literature–18th century–History and criticism. 2. English literature–19th century–History and criticism. 3. China–In literature. 4. China–Civilization. 5. Great Britain–Civilization–Chinese influences. 6. Great Britain–Civilization–18th century. 7. Great Britain–Civilization–19th century. 8. Romanticism–Great Britain. I. Title.
PR447.K55 2013
303.48'241051–dc23
2013023417

ISBN 978-1-107-04561-3 Hardback

Contents

Illustrations

Acknowledgments

I would like to thank the Trustees of the Leverhulme Trust for their generous support in awarding me a major research fellowship for two years to allow me to undertake the researching and writing of this book. The University of Dundee also granted me generous research leave to see this book through to completion. I would also like to thank both the British Academy and the Carnegie Trust for the Universities of Scotland for a series of Fellowships allowing me to undertake the primary research for this book. The Academy and the Huntington Library also provided me with generous support to spend a month in the Huntington researching the Larpent Collection of play scripts for Chapter 8 of this study. I would like to thank the staff of the following libraries for allowing me to use their collections and assisting me in my researches: the British Library; the National Library of Scotland; the Huntington Library; the library of SOAS, University of London; the Angus Library, Oxford; the Linnaean Society; St. Andrews University Library; and the University of Dundee. I would also like to thank the following colleagues who have read parts of this book or contributed in other ways to its completion with their generous help and advice: Nicholas Roe, Michael O'Neill, Tim Fulford, Michael Franklin, Marilyn Gaull, Neil Chambers, Peter Cochran, David Worrall, Bruce Graver, Frederick Burwick, Jeff Cox, Daniel White, and Zeng Li. The manuscript was improved considerably thanks to the thoughtful comments of the two anonymous readers for Cambridge University Press, and Jim Chandler the Series Editor. I would like to thank Linda Bree for her continued encouragement and support, and Anna Bond for seeing this work through the press. Earlier versions of parts of two chapters of this book appeared in *The Wordsworth Circle*, Cian Duffy, ed., *Romantic Adaptations* (Ashgate, 2013), and Seamus Perry, David Vallins, and Kaz Oishi, eds., *Coleridge, Romanticism, and the Orient* (Continuum, 2013). I am grateful to the publishers for permission to use this material.

Introduction

Forging Romantic China is a cultural study focusing on one of the most decisive periods in the history of modern British and Chinese relations. It argues that Qing China was a central, though problematic, referent in the culture and literature of what we know of as the British Romantic period, demarcated generously in this study as *c.* 1760–*c.* 1840, and that this crucial presence has been oddly evaded in much of the literary writing of the period and its criticism. The idea of China, as Eric Hayot, David Porter, and Chi-ming Yang have reminded us, was central to the making of modernity and the formation of the modern Western human self.[1] A. O. Lovejoy, many years ago, put forward the thesis that one of the key origins of Romanticism signified a Chinese source, the preference for a form of wildness and irregularity in the eighteenth-century British landscape garden.[2] Other scholars of British literature and culture in the long eighteenth century, such as Robert Markley and Ros Ballaster, have addressed such issues placing British cultural responses to China in the context of a sinocentric global economy up until around 1800. Such criticism has demonstrated the sustained allure that Chinese commodities, tea, silk, porcelain, furniture, lacquerware, and Chinese designs in gardening and interior decoration held throughout the long eighteenth century.[3] Yet this British desire for Chinese forms and products was always balanced with either anxiety or an ambivalence for what David Porter describes as "an aesthetic monstrosity" underpinning this allure.[4] This study argues that the Chinese contribution to "Romanticism" or the literature of the British Romantic period was in fact substantial and just as important as the later, more discussed, nineteenth-century influence of Chinese aesthetics on European aestheticism and modernism.[5]

This study is cognate with such recent exemplary scholarship, but it attempts to address the specific question of how British knowledge of

China, its cultures, products, and its peoples, was constructed or forged from the writings and translations of a diverse range of missionaries, diplomats, travelers, East India Company employees, and literary personalities in certain key sites, notably Bengal, Canton (Guangzhou), and Malacca. Such knowledge was constructed from texts, cultural commodities, and physical artifacts, including Chinese export art and porcelain as well as plants and flowers, governed by long-established (and some newer) global flows of trade and existing networks of collaboration. The new perceptions and understandings of China that this body of knowledge gave rise to were mediated via a dynamic print and visual culture to a diverse range of poets, novelists, essayists, dramatists, and reviewers, including Jane Austen, S. T. Coleridge, Charles Lamb, the Wordsworths, and others, and subsequently informed British understandings and imaginings of China on the eve of the first Opium War of 1839–42. *Forging Romantic China* thus aims to restore China as a topos as well as a geographical place to its truly global presence in our understandings of the culture and literature of the late eighteenth and early nineteenth centuries, and to speculate about the kind of cultural landscape this assertion presents.

China is predicted to overtake the US and become the world's leading economy by 2016. In recent years, commentators and scholars in the West have become increasingly engaged in a whole range of enquiry, historical, political, economic, linguistic, and cultural, relating to China's global presence and its relationship with the West. China looms large in the consciousness of the twenty-first century but it also loomed quite as large in the minds of the late eighteenth and early nineteenth centuries. Political scientists such as Martin Jacques and William A. Callahan have persuasively argued for the crucial importance of the period of what is known by the Chinese as "the Century of National Humiliation" (*bainian guochi*) (1840–1940) to their understandings of their history and their proper role and place in the modern world.[6] The period prior to this century, *c.* 1760–1842, is thus the crucial watershed in which many modern British attitudes to China were established and explored. It was during this time that a new view of China was established in the anglophone world by the development of a body of work, that I provisionally describe as a "Romantic Sinology," which provided the underpinning for Britain's policies towards China and for the imaginings of Romantic period writers and artists about China, prior to the Opium Wars. This book explores this crucial process, examining a substantial number of textual and cultural artifacts that created a form of new British knowledge about China that enabled (and sometimes critiqued) British power in the "Far East."

Forging Romantic China thus seeks to write a new study of the cultural history of Romantic-period anglophone representation of, and exchange with, the Qing empire, informed by those changes in our understanding occasioned by current historical and postcolonial scholarship on the "East," that has adopting a "China-centered" approach.[7] This school of historical enquiry has rejected the conventional historical notion of a rich but stationary and largely unchanging Qing China confronted by a dynamic and modern Britain, a narrative largely inspired by a partial reading and misunderstanding of the economic analysis of Adam Smith's *Wealth of Nations* (1776) as mediated by the key accounts of the British Macartney embassy to China of 1792–94 and later developed by J. S. Mill, Hegel, Marx, and Weber. I will thus attempt to bring together several strands of recent scholarship combining literary studies of Romantic-period colonialism and imperialism with new research on the history and culture of the late Qing empire. Combining Linda Colley's influential use of "forge" in the context of the creation of national identity to symbolize a process of both construction and fabrication, and Lionel Jensen's notion of "manufacturing," this study seeks to demonstrate the processes by which Britons and their collaborators constructed a "new" idea of China in the period and the ways in which this process was inflected by their own increasingly national concerns.[8] This book also argues that such knowledge was a part of a process of "co-constitution" and intercultural encounter by which both Georgian Britain and Qing China, mirrors and inversions of each other, were formed in an already "globalized" eighteenth-century world order.[9] Rather than imposing a fully formed notion of British science and modernity on Southeast Asia, Britain was at this crucial time forging its own sense of national identity informed by its encounters with other cultures such as China's. This study argues that Qing China is an under-explored and crucial, possibly *the* crucial, informing context for this process of identity formation.

I am thus primarily concerned with the cultural transmission of knowledge about China to Britain in the late eighteenth and early nineteenth centuries. Adapting Mary Louise Pratt's concept of "transculturation" by which Europeans transmit indigenous non-European knowledge from the "contact zone" and produce "European knowledge infiltrated by non-European ones," this study argues that such European understandings were never simply a colonial mirror or inversion of the Western self, but neither were they the objective empirical enquiries that they claimed.[10] In this regard the new body of translations of key Chinese texts assumes a major significance. Though still largely ignored in recent influential theorizations of world literature, Chinese writings exerted a substantial cultural impact in the nineteenth century.[11] Such translations are usually dismissed by modern sinologists because they lack scholarly accuracy and were arrived at before the Chinese language was professionally mastered. Conventionally, the major British Sinologist and first professor of Chinese at Oxford in 1876, James Legge, is perceived as the first such person to deserve serious and extensive critical scrutiny.[12] Yet there was a range of Britons in the period, including Thomas Percy, William Jones, George Thomas Staunton, Robert Morrison, William Milne, John Francis Davis, and Walter Henry Medhurst, who were involved in producing key translations of Chinese writings and accounts of Chinese customs. My study is not concerned with the accuracy or authenticity of these translated texts *per se*, but rather with the "knowledge" that they contained about China, and the ways in which that knowledge was acquired, constructed, framed, and then mediated and transmitted to early nineteenth-century Britain in both orientalist institutional and more popular forms.

Translation studies have, in recent years, moved markedly in the direction of emphasizing the complex processes of the transmission of texts and ideas from one culture to another, rather than focusing on the formal importance of accurate translation. Translation, in this context, becomes less of a linguistic activity, and more of a cultural practice. Lydia H. Liu, for instance, poses the crucial questions about how "signs and meaning travel from place to place in global circulations," and whether or not "translatability" is a value in itself "or a product of repeated exchange and negotiation in the translation process."[13] Translation from and into Chinese involves extra levels of complexity due to the ideogrammatic and non-alphabetical nature of the language. The essays recently collected in *Sinographies: Writing China* (2008) have explored such issues, identifying the "distortions wrought by translation," but not presuming to correct such "misperceptions by asserting that their own perceptions are authentic." The editors conclude that "the intricacies of the relationship between various written Chinas—the texts—and the nation/culture known simply as 'China'—their main shared context—are so complex as to be nearly unspeakable."[14] The vexed question as to whether there is something known as a "Chinese aesthetic" that resists translation is also a complicating factor. Although the visual aesthetic properties of the Chinese character are not, to my knowledge, exploited by Romantic-period writers and translators in the ways that they would later be by Ezra Pound and other modernist writers, the status of the character as picture and word was often commented upon.[15] Yet, by and large, the period's concern with Chinese aesthetics is confined to the visual, to paintings, ceramic designs, architecture, and landscapes, rather than the aesthetic properties of the Chinese character. Mindful of the extraordinary complexity of this linguistic intercultural encounter, the conclusions I draw regarding the knowledge transmitted by the translations of Romantic Sinology remain hesitant, provisional, but I hope suggestive for other enquirers.

From the perspective of Said's powerful theorization of orientalism, all such translations would be viewed as a merely a "textual attitude" and part of a colonialist discourse by which source texts are appropriated and anything authentically Chinese lost.[16] We know that the English East India Company in Bengal was able to facilitate and reinforce its rule by translating and interpreting classical Indian texts, and that the orientalist William Jones, a Bengal judge, was the leading figure in this process.[17] Yet like Liu, Lawrence Venuti has shown how problematic the act of translation can be, arguing that at least two forms of translation strategy exist, one that seeks to "domesticate" the translated text and the other to "foreignize it."[18] The intercultural encounter between Britain and China in the nineteenth century is thus extremely complex and sophisticated, incapable of being constrained within conventional orientalist boundaries of "East" and "West" and "self" and "other." Increasingly, Chinese cultural critics are moving beyond such horizons. Wang Ning, in a series of publications, has argued that there is no longer any need to decry the contemporary Western impact on Chinese culture, or to accentuate those familiar, well-recorded orientalist misunderstandings perpetuated by Western sinology. He argues that such phenomena constitute the necessary stages in the process of the integration of Chinese culture into a global culture, in which Chinese literature and philosophy will become more accessible around the globe. Wang's insight is that, as "Oriental culture and Occidental culture usually influence each other, when one of these is in the state of temporary forcefulness, it might well influence the other, but even so, such influence is mutual and largely depends on the other's dynamic and creative reception."[19] Similarly Xiaomei Chen, in her challenging study of Occidentalism in post-Mao China, argues that this appropriation of Western discourse – what she calls "Occidentalism" – can have a politically and ideologically liberating effect on contemporary non-Western cultures. Chen refutes the connections that Said established between European power and orientalism, claiming that European representations of China mean very different things in different contexts. She argues that an official form of "occidentalism" has been used as a justification for political repression in China, whereas an anti-official version can be used to validate resistance against such oppression.

Wang and Chen are both largely concerned with modern China and the impact of contemporary Western culture and ideas, yet their differing critiques of orientalism in a twenty-first-century global context indicate that what is important are the ways in which Chinese and British ideas have been received in different historical and political contexts, and that their reception was never singular or homogenous.[20] This is especially so if we are discussing the response of a mixed and large audience to a nineteenth-century play about China as I do in the final chapter of this study. I will attempt to negotiate the complex cross-cultural encounter between Qing China and Georgian Britain in a way that respects the shifting allegiances of power and authority (economic, military, and cultural) between the two empires in the period restoring, I hope, a sense of the complexity to that fascinating cultural encounter, fashioned as it was from multiple poles of engagement and recognition produced from on-the-ground collaborations and negotiations between Chinese, British, and other peoples in the multi-ethnic and cosmopolitan cities of Southeast Asia: Canton, Calcutta, Malacca, Penang, and Singapore.[21]

SINICIZING ROMANTIC-PERIOD WRITING

According to the OED the term "sinology" was not coined until 1816, and scholars often date the birth of the modern academic discipline to the establishment of Jean-Pierre Abel-Rémusat as the first professor of Chinese at the Collège de France in 1814 and the subsequent publication of his *Elémens de la grammaire chinoise* of 1822. Abel-Rémusat and his successor, Stanislas Julien, were both sophisticated academics. This book, however, argues that British or Romantic Sinology begins at least as early as the 1760s, a decade marked by the publication of Thomas Percy's key writings on China and the direct translation of the first Chinese novel form (*xiaoshuo*) into English or any other European language. It thus covers roughly eighty years, to the abolition of the East India Company's monopoly at Canton of the China trade in 1833 (in many ways the crucial date) and the eve of the Opium Wars in 1839. In this respect it is coincident with the Romantic period in British letters and culture, especially if one accepts Percy as an important precursor of Romantic literary concerns. The period includes the arrival of the Macartney embassy to China in 1793 and its important successor led by Lord Amherst in 1816, as well as of the first British Protestant missionary, Robert Morrison, in Canton in 1807. It contains the establishment of the first institution dedicated to the study and teaching of the Chinese language, the Anglo-Chinese College, at Malacca in 1818, as well as the founding of the Royal Asiatic Society in 1823. The first English chairs in Chinese were established at the new University of London in 1837 (Samuel Kidd) and at King's College London in 1845 (Samuel Turner Fearon). During this period key translations of Chinese writings appeared, including the first direct translation of the Confucian *Lunyu* or *Analects* (1809) and the first complete translation of the classic Four Books (*Sishu*) (1828).

One of the key historical events during this period was the ending of the Company's monopoly of the China trade in 1833, which marked a watershed in British attitudes to a China that henceforth resisted newly invigorated attempts to impose Western ideologies of free trade and national sovereignty upon it. The Treaty of Nanjing (1842), which concluded the first Opium War, marked an end of the old "Canton system" where that city was the only and crucial point of contact with mainland China, and the removal, by the second-generation missionary James Legge, of the Anglo-Chinese College from Malacca to Hong Kong Island, one of five new treaty ports granted in 1843. In 1841 the American Nathan Dunn's "Ten Thousand Chinese Things," the first major exhibition about China, opened in London.[22] Post-1840 the study and representation of China would change significantly and attitudes would harden in the run-up to the second Opium War, and the notorious looting of the Summer Palace in 1860. Probably, the most significant event in this period occurred in 1792–94 when the British government sent its first diplomatic embassy to Qing China in an attempt to open formal relations between the two world empires, and regularize the substantially expanding trade in tea, porcelain, and other commodities. Famously, the Chinese required payment in silver bullion for their desirable teas, occasioning a substantial specie crisis for the Company. This flow of silver bullion from the West to the East was later reversed when the Company began to harvest opium in Bengal and sell this on to independent, private traders ("country traders") with China. Brief though its acquaintance with China was, the Macartney embassy generated a mass of textual commentary that signaled a definitive move away from the earlier, Jesuit-inspired writing on China to a new British or "Romantic Sinology."

Though extremely prominent in historical scholarship, Britain's problematic relationship with the China of the Qing empire in the early nineteenth century itself has received comparatively little recent attention in studies of British literature and culture, certainly in the comparison with the masses of scholarship and enquiry devoted to the cultural impact of the British in India, their participation in the transatlantic slave trade and plantation slavery, and their response to Islam at this time. The urgent issue of the expanding presence of China in the global economy now obliges contemporary enquiry to delve back into the historical, intellectual, and cultural origins of the relationship between Britain and China and to reassess the complex ways in which Britain interacted with the Qing empire.[23]

This book is a contribution to the current critical debate exploring this crucial historical moment and the literary culture of the Romantic period's engagement with China. Though there are now a series of exemplary publications by Porter, Markley, Ballaster, Yang, Hayot, Keevak, and Chang on Britain's cultural relationship with China in the longer historical view, the British Romantic period has been somewhat neglected.[24] Similarly in contrast to the substantial amount of excellent and authoritative scholarship on Jesuit sinology in the early modern period, there is still no authoritative and standard history of sinology in Britain, though several important accounts exist, notably T. H. Barrett's *Singular Listlessness: A Short History of Chinese Books and British Scholars* (1989). There are still no major studies of Britain's early sinologists, prior to Legge, and though Robert Morrison has attracted the attentions of a recent biographer, it is largely his religious and missionary activity in China which remains the focus and rationale of such study.[25]

Four recent sophisticated studies have defined the field in which *Forging Romantic China* attempts to intervene. Robert Markley's *The Far East and the English Imagination, 1600–1730* (2006); David Porter's *The Chinese Taste in Eighteenth-Century England* (2010); Chi-ming Yang's *Performing China, Virtue, Commerce, and Orientalism in Eighteenth-century England 1660–1760* (2010); and Elizabeth Hope Chang's *Britain's Chinese Eye* (2010). Markley's, Porter's, and Yang's studies are concerned primarily with the earlier eighteenth century. Markley's study considers British writing between 1600 and 1730 and places this writing in the context of a world economy dominated by China and India up until around 1800. British writing, notably Defoe's *Farther Adventures of Robinson Crusoe*, is thus engaged in a series of compensatory strategies to address European marginalization.[26] The methodological focus of *Forging Romantic China* is thus cognate with that of Markley but my study examines the crucial later period when British confidence is increasing and Qing power on the wane. Porter's study also has significant overlaps with *Forging Romantic China* in terms of his pioneering scholarship on Thomas Percy (in many ways a terminus for his study rather than the beginning of mine). His earlier *Ideographia* (2001) likewise contained a groundbreaking reading of the discourse of sovereignty and economic liberalism relating to the Macartney embassy to China in the 1790s to which all scholars remain indebted. In a major collection of essays "China and the making of Global Modernity" for *Eighteenth-Century Studies* (2010), edited by Markley, Porter further argues for the importance of "historical cosmopolitanism" in global early modernity, questioning "deep-seated assumptions of exemplarity," re-situating England "within an expansively global context," and counseling against reliance on "sterile orientalist clichés concerning the stagnant traditionalism and uniformity of societies that missed the fast train to modernity."[27]

Yang's major study of the representation of China in literature, theater, and material culture between 1660 and 1760 has contributed much to our understanding of this European construction of the ambivalent idea of China, especially as regards the spectacular performance of China. This crucial work is focused on certain key areas, notably major seventeenth- and eighteenth-century plays by Elkanah Settle and Arthur Murphy, arguing that China functions in this period as a key *exemplar* for Europeans. Yang argues convincingly that China mediated between conflicting British attitudes to virtue, commerce, and luxury. It was at the same time both a "symbol of imperial excess" and of "Confucian moderation," alternately a threat and yet also an aspiration.[28] A key text for Yang's thesis is Arthur Murphy's drama *The Orphan of China* (1756), itself a redacted adaptation of a thirteenth-century Yuan dynasty play *Zhao shi guer*, which I discuss in the final chapter of this book as a crucial intertext for the transmission of the idea of China well into the Romantic period. Murphy's *Orphan* emerges from such accounts as an important text for the study of China in world literature and one that should be taught and read.[29]

Yang's study is informed by Eric Hayot's brilliant *The Hypothetical Mandarin: Sympathy, Modernity, and Chinese Pain* (2009). Taking his cue from Adam Smith's famous use, in *Theory of Moral Sentiments* (1759), of the hypothetical example of an earthquake that destroys the empire of China to explore notions of moral distance and the limitations of the European sensibility and sympathy, Hayot demonstrates how China and Chinese people frequently function in Western discourse as philosophical or literary examples or anecdotes. Smith argued that such an event would produce little disturbance in the European sympathetic imagination, as China was geographically too distant to arouse empathy with its people's plight. China is thus at the very heart of the construction of the modern, liberal, and humane European self, as an exemplar, a limit case, or horizon of otherness against which to measure the borders of "human" sympathy. This otherness has a peculiar quality distinct from the "generic Oriental otherness under whose aegis it sometimes appears." Hayot, like Markley and Porter, convincingly links this particular Chinese otherness to the pronounced economic and technological advantages that China held over Europe well into the nineteenth century, especially in the manufacture of porcelain, production of tea, and other desirable commodities: the dismissal of Chinese legitimacy and the forgetting of its massive impact is at least partly an effect of the dramatic rise of European power after Waterloo. Crucially, he argues, the "sympathetic exchange," which can to be generated between British readers of the sufferings of the Chinese, can also be understood within the parameters of the literal exchange of goods and commodities between Britain and China; "a kind of aggressive affective response ... in which British impotence at the level of the material good was assuaged by Chinese impotence at the level of the emotional one."[30] Hayot reminds us that the exchanges between Britain and China are wide ranging and that an affective and aesthetic economy is as of fundamental an importance as the literal one of goods and commodities.

This forgetting or evasion of China is a major theme of this book. In The *Chinese Taste*, Porter, like Markley and Hayot, explores this "instrumental amnesia" that deliberately occludes "rival claimants to exemplarity" and the memory of "a more truly cosmopolitan early modern past."[31] For example, a common trope of the Romantic-period literary response to China, witnessed in Baillie, Southey, Leigh Hunt, and Lamb, is that Britons knew very little about this isolated and exclusive empire, apart from what they could glean from visual representations on teacups and porcelain ware. Yet a substantial archive about China existed, formed from two hundred years of sophisticated Jesuit scholarship in several English translations. In addition, the Macartney and Amherst embassies generated numerous new "first-hand" accounts. Missionaries and traders were now resident in China, sending back narratives of their experiences of the country and translations of its literature and philosophy. Yet some Britons persisted in reading China through an older chinoiserie-inspired aesthetic with Leigh Hunt, for example, decrying the "Chinese deformities" and monstrosities of the newly designed Grand Salon of Drury Lane Theatre as late as 1817.

China was not remote for many Romantic-period writers in the simple sense that they had family and friends closely involved in trade with the empire who visited, worked there, and came back. Canton was as much a "Romantic" as an Enlightenment city, encountered by many Britons in the service of the Navy or the East India Company. Jane Austen's brother, Frank, served in the Royal Navy and acted as an agent for the Company as captain of the *St. Albans* in 1809–10 at Canton. Charles Lamb worked, as did Thomas Love Peacock, for the Company in London for some thirty-three years, and Lamb's friend and correspondent, Thomas Manning, traveled to Canton in 1807, becoming the first Briton to visit the Tibetan capital of Lhasa in 1811. Along with Morrison and Davis, Manning accompanied Amherst's embassy to China in 1816–17. William and Dorothy Wordsworth's elder brother John traded at Canton on several voyages on the *Earl of Abergavenny* as midshipman, then captain. Thomas De Quincey's son, Horace, died aged twenty-two of a fever contracted during the Opium Wars with China in 1842. In different ways the literary activities of the Wordsworths, Lamb, and, more marginally, Jane Austen, were materially benefited by connections with the China trade.

The reasons that many such writers have a tendency to evade or forget China in their writings are extremely complex and not reducible to an easy summary. Porter's notion of "instrumental amnesia" argues that Britons effaced the rival Chinese claim to exemplarity. The construction of "Englishness" that emerges from this encounter with China "is neither pure nor hybrid in any straightforward sense, but rather is constituted paradoxically through a simultaneous appropriation of and denial of 'Chineseness' and an instrumental amnesia with respect to some of the decidedly non-English origins of British aesthetic culture."[32] Both he and Chang focus on material objects and consumer cultures, while Liu tracks this process though an extended discussion of the Chinese garden on British culture. As Markley has argued, about the earlier period, when faced with the economic power of China and the superiority of its products, Britons adopted compensatory strategies to obviate such anxieties, thus focusing on an economic analysis of Far Eastern trade and its effects on Swift, Milton, and Defoe.

By the 1820s, however, the British had substantially reversed their unfavorable trade deficit with China by the expedient of boosting the export of opium and selling it to the country traders who illegally exported it to China in return for silver. This historical process has been wonderfully evoked in Amitav Ghosh's *Ibis* trilogy of novels, set in Bengal and Canton in the lead-up to the first Opium War, which brings alive the key networks between Bengal, Canton, and Britain, and the trades in tea, opium, and Chinese plants that are a key feature of this book.[33] In many ways both our works are responding to a shared set of contemporary cultural interests and imperatives. As discussed in Chapter 5, the British could not discover any legitimate item of trade or product that was sufficiently attractive to the Chinese to exchange in large quantities for tea. Though increasingly convinced of the quality of their products and frustrated by Chinese indifference to them, it was only the expedient of enabling and prosecuting an illegal opium trade with China that allowed the British to trade on favorable terms. Ultimately, in 1839, it was military force with modern artillery and fast and mobile steam warships that opened China to European trade, not the quality or cheapness of Britain's commodities or the universality of its science. Certainly, the superiority of Chinese products, China's long-standing cultural prestige, and the dirty business of the opium trade and subsequent war must have coalesced in British minds to render China a hard topos to face directly. As the former Superintendent of Trade at Canton and a future governor of Hong Kong, Sir John Francis Davis, put it, "the *pernicious drug*, sold to the Chinese, has exceeded in market value *the wholesome leaf* that has been purchased from them; and the balance of the trade has been *paid to us in silver*" (my italics).[34] Such conflicted positions are common in Romantic Sinology. Combined with the pragmatic difficulty of mastering the Chinese language, China's complex and multiple religious systems, and the universalist claims of Confucian thinking, the ambivalent view of China encouraged a sideways approach in addressing the subject.

Forging Romantic China thus seeks to explore those evasions and forgettings in addition to the very real presence of China in the writing of this crucial period. It seeks to counter the conventional paradigm of the diffusion of European modernity from the center to the periphery across a range of discourses, including that of the scientific. As will be explained below, the conceptual model that this study engages with is that of the global flows of commodities, goods, artifacts, and texts in which postcolonial notions of a European center and Asian periphery do not operate in any meaningful way.

My study covers, in eight chapters, the subjects of British Romantic-period missionary writing, accounts of travelers and diplomats, histories and general descriptions, and the growth of British sinology, political satire, popular drama, literary representations, English-language translations of Chinese literature, and scientific knowledge and exchange. Although I attempt to discuss the major areas of cultural production, this study does not aspire to be comprehensive cultural history, and familiar areas, such as De Quincey's unrepresentative imaginative encounter with China in the *Confessions of an English Opium Eater* (1821), already heavily discussed (perhaps fetishized), is eschewed in favor of less familiar, more engaging, and more representative meetings. De Quincey's evocation of China in the opium dreams passages of his *Confessions* (1821) has been unfairly adduced as metonymic of Romantic-period attitudes to China, and his succeeding bellicose essays on China and the Opium Wars primarily relate to a later set of attitudes beyond those of Romantic Sinology.[35]

ROMANTIC SINOLOGY

My thesis accepts the conventional view that the representation of the Qing empire in the late eighteenth and early nineteenth centuries suffered a staggering reversal of fortune from admiration to degradation, largely as a result of the combined onslaught of missionary writing, economic theory, Oriental scholarship, and colonial conflict, as well as from an increasingly racialized conception of human difference.[36] I argue that in the period roughly from the 1760s to the 1830s, a distinct body or form of Oriental scholarship, differentiated from early modern Jesuit writing on China, is "manufactured" from the writings of a diverse assortment of British China experts. I provisionally describe this body of knowledge as "Romantic Sinology," a wide-ranging, often conflicting, body of writing created by a group of contemporary British commentators on China, that claims validation by a personal knowledge of China and Southeast Asia through participation in the Macartney and Amherst embassies, the British East India Company trade at Canton, and Baptist and London Missionary Society activity. I use the term "sinology" loosely to describe the work of those Britons who are considered as "China experts" by their contemporaries and who devote serious attention and time to the study of China and its culture, and who publish texts which are believed to be authoritative by some in the period, however they may be viewed later. I am not, however, using the term in its modern acceptance exclusively to designate an institutionalized body of professional academics with excellent levels of proficiency in written and spoken Chinese. Nor am I concerned with the accuracy or authenticity of these commentators on China, but more with the *kinds* of knowledge transferred to Britain and the processes of cultural transmission.

I thus argue that this British sinology originates *in the late eighteenth century* with Thomas Percy and William Jones, rather than at the more usually affirmed starting point, the establishment of James Legge as the first chair of Chinese at Oxford University in 1876. Arthur Murphy's *The*

Orphan of China also represents a key transitional text. I do wish, however, to maintain distinction between Britons who could read and translate Chinese texts with some degree of accuracy, and the "China expert," who was a commentator and critic of China rather than a "sinologist." This diverse, frequently conflicted, and ambivalent body of work is created in what is known as the "Romantic period." It is a historically based category, but also has some ideational coherence. It rejects the idealizing tendencies of its early modern Jesuit predecessor as well as the more recent work of contemporary French or French-based, "sinologues," Jean-Pierre Abel-Rémusat and Julius Klaproth, sophisticated academics who never visited China. British Romantic-period sinology is composed of an array of expertise and texts including travel accounts (the Macartney and Amherst embassies), commentaries on Chinese customs, manners and mores (including religions), and translations, literary commentaries, and a new style of visual art deriving from British artists resident in China, like William Alexander, Clarkson Stanfield, and George Chinnery, as well as Chinese export artists, such as Pu Qua and Lam Qua. Romantic Sinology leads to a new style of "Romantic chinoiserie," differing from that of the eighteenth century as discussed by Porter and exemplified in the Regent's Royal Pavilion at Brighton from 1815 or so onward. This sinology and its corresponding Chinese taste is characterized above all by its insistence that it is a new and "objective" study of China based on a first-hand encounter and conducted according to empirical and scientific assumptions. It rejects the Jesuit-inspired focus on the Chinese classics as biased and self-interested; a classicizing discourse intended to convince its audience that the Chinese really are sophisticated monotheists tractable to rapid conversion to Catholic Christianity. This sinology is also ideationally "Romantic" in that it loosely shares in certain aspects of Romantic-period aesthetics or "Romanticism," from Percy's and Jones's concern with ancient and original poetry to John Francis Davis's expansion of the purview of sinology from Confucian classic books to take into account China's *belles lettres*, especially popular novels and drama, journalism (the *Peking Gazette*), and Chinese scientific and horticultural writing. Informed by Romantic canons of taste, including Wordsworthian notions of simplicity and feeling, the translations it produced were frequently aimed, especially in its earlier manifestations, at a general and non-specialist audience.

This sinology, in its missionary version, is distinctively underpinned by an iconoclastic Protestant theology that stressed the importance of individual salvation, and rejected Chinese civilization and the Manchu imperial court of which the Catholic missionaries were so enamored. Obsessed with a personal relationship with deity, this theology equated Confucianism, Buddhism, and popular oral religion as well as Catholicism and Islam (all forms of Chinese religion) with idolatry. This Romantic Sinology was first "institutionalized" at Serampore (Srirampur) in Bengal, then at Canton and Malacca (and later Hong Kong after the first Opium War), before entering the metropolitan "center" with the establishment of the Royal Asiatic Society (1823) and then a series of university chairs, first at University College (1837), then at King's College (1845), London. The impact of Romantic Sinology on Romantic-period poets, novelists, and dramatists has still not as yet been explored in much detail. My study I thus hope is especially valuable in discussing under-researched areas such as the role of British Protestant missionary writing, Chinese science, and, especially, popular drama on the London stage.

Romantic Sinology sought to reverse the process described by Porter in which, some time around the middle of the eighteenth century, a form of chinoiserie, with its "flow of unmeaning Eastern signs," had been substituted for an earlier idea of China that was ancient, authentic, monotheistic, legitimate, and moral.[37] Romantic Sinology, paradoxically, sought to substitute this chinoiserie fantasy with another "real" China that was both knowable and substantial, but increasingly the locus of illegitimacy and stagnation, capable of being understood and controlled. In this sense the Romantic period is a moment of historical watershed or transformational change in which competing views of China begin the uneven process of hardening and homogenizing. Yet even as this process takes place, moments of genuine intercultural encounter and exchange occur and are as significant as those which anticipate the brutal militarism and economic instrumentalism deployed by the British against the Chinese in 1839.

CHINA AND GLOBAL ROMANTICISM

The major research context for this book is the vibrant field of the global long eighteenth century established by a number of scholars who have traced the connections between literary sensibility and British encounters with those persons, ideas, and territories that lay uneasily beyond the national border.[38] Such studies have developed a revisionist reading of the period of British Enlightenment and Romanticism (or long eighteenth century), an age during which Britain was most aggressively but also hesitatingly building its overseas empire. This criticism often argues that the

Romantic imaginative self is founded on a sense of difference, exoticism, or alterity created by an anxiety or fear of what is foreign. For many, otherness or xenophobia is the underpinning not only of nineteenth-century organic nationalism and imperialism but also of the Romantic subject itself. *Forging Romantic China*, while accepting that this may often be the case, seeks to problematize such readings by returning to the historical and cultural complexities of Sino-British cultural exchange.

By and large somewhat neglected by cultural studies of the Romantic period, the British encounter with the Qinq empire is usually portrayed as that of a modern, technological, and industrial power confronting an older and now stagnating polity whose glories were firmly in the past. This view of late Qing China is itself one effect of the narrativizing tendency of Romantic Sinology to represent China as oppositional to the current modernizing trends of early nineteenth-century Britain. While accepting Edward Said's equation of knowledge and power in orientalist and colonial discourse and employing many of Said's crucial critical insights, this study is cognate with those that seek to problematize any simple and straightforward binaries between colonial self and colonized others by stressing instead the complexities and *multipolarity* of exchange between Britain and China in an already globalized world.[39]

Humberto Garcia has excitingly transformed our understanding of orientalism, in his *Islam and the English Enlightenment, 1670–1840* (2012) by examining the sympathetic and, at times, enthusiastic, response of Britons to Islamic culture, stressing the importance of intercultural exchange between Islam and Britain. Similarly, Srinivas Aravamudan has brilliantly argued that "a transcultural, cosmopolitan, and Enlightenment-inflected orientalism existed at least as an alternative strain before 'Saidian' Orientalism came about." Aravamudan argues for the importance of an "Enlightenment Orientalism" that existed outside of the traditional account of the "Whiggish" rise of the novel. *Pace* Said, he claims that Enlightenment orientalism was "a Western style for translating, anatomizing, and desiring the Orient." Aravamudan shows how the translational and transcultural oriental tale was effectively written out of traditional accounts of the rise of the British novel that stressed the national and the domestic within the mode of literary realism. In part, this is the result of increasing "Romantic nationalism and xenophobia" that I discuss, especially in Chapter 7 of this study. For Aravamudan the separation of East and West occurs after the 1780s "with the institutionalization of Europe's national literatures through the steady rise of print capitalism, followed by the subsequent wave of Romanticism and the establishment of imperial bureaucracies."⁴⁰ Thus the Romantic orientalism that succeeds Oriental Enlightenment "furthered an antiquarian knowledge of Asia as Europe's demonic Other, rather than its previous status as Christendom's originary source, old rival, and living contemporary." It is clear that increasing nationalism and xenophobia do play a part in Romantic Sinology, yet there are still strong transcultural and hybrid elements in the Romantic-period understanding of China, and other cultures. While the story of the former has oft been told, the latter remains to be discussed. While De Quincey may have demonized all things Chinese and Asiatic in his *Confessions*, others, such as John Francis Davis, maintained a genuine interest in Chinese culture, even despite his participation in a growing colonial bureaucracy. Though *Forging Romantic China* might seem simply to be pushing the moment of the arrival of a more recognizable mode of Saidian orientalism further forward into the mid nineteenth century, post the first Opium War, Romantic Sinology displays many of the characteristics of Aravamudan's Enlightenment orientalism, and represents as much a continuum with it as a clear fracture.

Recent historical scholarship of the later Qing has stressed the field of global exchange in which Britain and China are, arguably, the period's two most significant multi-ethnic imperial formations. Throughout, this study emphasizes the importance of the transfer and exchange between the two world historical empires and their impact on the knowledge-making process, in an attempt to negotiate a terrain beyond established postcolonial binaries, such as "West" and "East" and "Occidentalism" and "Orientalism." Since the mid 1970s a number of developments inside and outside China studies have called into question the older, functionalist, social science models used to analyze historical and contemporary non-Western societies. Within the China field, the primary challenge to these earlier forms of analysis came from "China-centered" history. A substantial number of historical and postcolonial criticisms of the mid and late Qing have transformed our historical understandings of the empire which now emerges as a much more modern, dynamic, and expansionist polity in the eighteenth century.⁴¹ This study is also indebted to this new and invigorated historical scholarship featuring the encounter between Britain and China in the period and the crucial Southeast Asian contact zones and networks between China and Britain that generated Romantic Sinology.⁴²

This book aims to add the exchange of cultural information as part of this flow of commodities and information. The underlying model for the exchange is that of global flows of trade. That this concept of a global world economy was understood in the period itself is evidenced by the insight of the great Swedish Botanist, Linnaeus, who somewhat acerbically summed up the process. He grumbled that "some people consider us happier because we have discovered the silver treasures of Potosis [Bolivia], which we pry loose from the innards of the earth with great efforts, ship to Europe with great danger, and then, with no lesser risk, export to the barbaric countries of the distant East Indies and waste them there, bringing home in exchange dry leaves of bushes and thin threads, spun by caterpillars."[43] Many scholars have noted the role of China's demand for New World silver and Britain's prodigious thirst for tea in the emergence of the modern world economy, claimed by Lin Man-houng as the real and material cause of nineteenth-century Qing vulnerability and its subsequent inability to resist Western encroachment.[44] Such studies stress the internal, economic Chinese causes of the Qing's weakness in the nineteenth century rather than the pressures brought to bear from outside. They have altered our understanding of the global economy in the late eighteenth and early nineteenth centuries, and the relative positions of Britain, Europe, and Asia.

In particular, the work of world systems theorists André Gunder Frank and Kenneth Pomeranz postulates the existence of a global network of trade in the eighteenth century dominated by China and India in which Britain and northern Europe more widely are, until after 1800 or so, merely bit players and latecomers. Frank claimed that China and India functioned as the core of a single "global world economy with a worldwide division of labour and multilateral trade from 1500 onward." European desire for superior Asian products created an expanding world trade whose net balance was easily in China's favor.[45] Frank estimates that between 1600 and 1800, China bought as much as half of the world's total production, including vast quantities of New World silver from European colonizers. It has been calculated that China's GDP as late as 1820 was still a staggering 29 percent of global production, and much larger than that of all Europe, including industrial Britain, combined. This economic strength was fully understood by Europeans. The Jesuit Du Halde judged, in 1735, that trade within China was vastly greater than that of all Europe combined, and Adam Smith famously declared in *The Wealth of Nations* (1776) that China was "a country richer than any part of Europe."[46]

Smith's economic analysis of China and global commerce is complex and still being argued over. He certainly criticized the Qing empire for the restrictions it imposed on foreign trade, yet he also foretold the future equalization of power between Europe and Asia due to the workings of international commerce. Giovanni Arrighi, in his influential *Adam Smith in Beijing* (2008), has argued that Frank's prediction of the resurgence of Southeast Asia and the return to a sinocentric world economy was anticipated in Smith's writings. Arrighi points out that Smith knew very well that throughout the eighteenth century "the largest market was to be found not in Europe but in China." He claims that Smith's depiction of China's economy as "stationary" does not imply, as often assumed, stagnation but the achievement of an optimum size for the geographic and demographic limits of its empire. Smith, he demonstrates, distinguished between "natural" and "unnatural" paths of economic development. China had followed the internally oriented or "natural" path of market society, focusing on labor-intensive forms of development and on improving its domestic economy, whereas European nations had undertaken an "unnatural" path of intensive capital development fueled by extensive foreign trade, drawing raw materials from distant colonies and making profit by providing financial services to the larger world economy. Smith exemplifies the Chinese economy as an example of a "natural" economic development. His point is that this distinction is not simply in favor of the unnatural economies, such as Britain and Holland, as what distinguishes them is that they allow capitalists greater power to impose their individual class interest on the national interest. What defines the European developmental path as properly capitalist (as opposed to market based) is the "sequence of endless accumulation of capital and power" manifested in the creation of ever more powerful nation states that can impose their will on others through military might, be it through the Opium Wars or US military hegemony. Contrary to Frank, Arrighi argues that Eastern and Western geopolitics and statecraft did not become integrated into a single political-military interaction network until the European states surrounded and tried to penetrate China in the nineteenth century. Capital accumulation allowed Europeans to develop superior military forces and it was this military strength that enabled them to "appropriate the benefits of the greater integration of the global community at the expense of non-European nations." Arrighi concludes that Smith "upheld China rather than Europeans as a model of the kind of market-based economic development that was most advisable for governments to pursue" and argues that the contemporary failure of the US to forge a world state through coercive means has created unprecedented opportunities for the global South, led by China, to achieve social and economic empowerment.[47] However, Britons would later invoke Smith's criticisms of China's

restriction of foreign trade to portray the empire as isolationist and stagnant; he did not view eighteenth-century China in this way.

John M. Hobson concludes that China before 1839 was still powerful
enough to manage Europeans and "militarily defeat any European chal-
lengers who were not granted access."[48] Certainly China's prosperity was
legendary, leading Robert Markley to describe its enormous riches and
revenues as representing to the eighteenth-century European imagination
"a kind of socioeconomic sublime."[49] With this vast economic strength
came a cultural prestige that fueled the enormous consumer demand for
Asian products in the West. Other scholars and historians have reinforced
our understanding of a largely sinocentric world order, prior to 1800 or
so.[50] Such historical claims underpin a number of contemporary theoretical perspectives, which have questioned Eurocentric interpretive norms.
Dipresh Chakrabarty, for example, argues that the notion of Europe as
the original site of modernity is a largely mythical invention and yet it
"remains the sovereign theoretical subject of all histories," constituting the
"silent referent in historical knowledge."[51] Similarly, Bruno Latour's seminal works *Science in Action* (1987) and *We Have Never Been Modern* (1993)
make the case for the near equivalence of European and "local knowledge," pointing to the minimal differences between human "collectives"
and questioning European scientific notions of modernity and the famous
chasm of the "Great Divide" between a technological and industrial West
and a pre-modern Asia, paralleling the "great divergence" of Western and
Asian economies.[52] My study also seeks to problematize any straightforward Eurocentric understandings of a stationary China and a progressive
technological Britain in the context of knowledge and culture.

My work has benefited enormously from the critical endeavors in the
field of cultural translation and transformation that seek to utilize theoretical models based on a nuanced understanding of the many sites of
the process of knowledge formation in sinology, and to draw attention
to the collaborations which produced such knowledge. In the context of
the Indian subcontinent Kapil Raj and Rajani Sudan have stressed the
collaborative processes by which scientific knowledge of the region was
produced.[53] This recuperative strategy has already been applied to Qing
China, notably by Laura Hostetler with regard to Qing cartography and
ethnology, and by Fa-ti Fan in his crucial study of British naturalists in
China and their encounters with Chinese horticulture and horticulturalists.[54] Hostetler shows how Qing China actively participated within, and
helped to shape and determine, the new emphasis that Romantic Sinology
later exploits on empirical science and evidential research.

Whereas, writing about the period after the first Opium War, James L. Hevia has powerfully argued that before the British and other powers dismantled the Qing polity in the later nineteenth century, they had already destroyed it textually, this study generally discovers a less confident, often conflicting, and confused series of cultural strategies by which "expert" British knowledge of China was constructed, manufactured, or "forged" in the crucial transformative period of the early nineteenth century.[55] Pedagogically, the British were still *learning* from the Chinese and trade, not instruction, was what they wanted to foster in China. Mary Louise Pratt argued that some Europeans were "transculturators" who transported to Europe indigenous knowledge, thus producing a body of knowledge infiltrated by non-European presences.[56] I attempt to build on Pratt's influential understanding of "transculturation," applying it to cultural relations and understanding between Britain and China. But rather than view the site of encounter as "contact zones" where the asymmetries of power were pretty much always in favor of the British, I draw attention to the self-understood, comparative disempowerment and weakness of the missionaries, merchants, and diplomats in the period leading up to the Opium Wars. There is also a mirroring and inversion at work here in this reciprocal encounter. The fashion for "chinoiserie" in the West, for instance, had provoked its counterpart, a Chinese interest in European goods known as "Euraserie." Styles and commodities circulated and shuttled back and forth around the globe as British designs were sent to Canton to be transferred to Chinese porcelain manufactured at Jingdezhen and then exported back to Britain. This cultural exchange was obvious from the sophisticated "sing-song" trade at Canton and the British clock owned by the Qianlong emperor that chimed tunes from John Gay's *Beggars Opera* on the hour. This study thus situates within this field of enquiry cultural and literary artifacts and commodities, such as the first British translations of Confucian writings and of Chinese novels and Chinese dramas by the Romantic Sinologists, Robert Morrison, George Thomas Staunton, and John Francis Davis.

Although this book is primarily a study of anglophone writing about China, its perspective is informed by recent comparative studies of Chinese and Western writing. Notably, Zhang Longxi's seminal criticism argues that the tendency of Western writing to view China as the cultural opposite of the West in literature, art, and theory has led to a distortion of social and historical reality in China. Zhang promotes the importance of the *lived experience* in this cross-cultural encounter and argues for the importance of recognizing common ground between cultures rather than emphatically insisting on their difference and alterity: "when China and the West are set up in rigid and mutually exclusive dichotomy, it is then absolutely necessary to point out the many similarities, what is shared and common in language, literature and cultures of the East and West."[57] My study emphasizes, wherever possible, this sharing and commonality and finds it in often unexpected places. Zhang has pursued this argument in a series of publications reappraising the thematic and conceptual similarities, or "unexpected affinities," that unite literary and cultural traditions in the East and West, arguing against the trope (shared by "East" and "West") of the incommensurability of cultures.[58] Similar arguments have been made in the crucial work of Haun Saussy, who has rightly demanded a new model of comparative or world literature, one that includes China within its remit. He argues that binaries such as "China" and "the West," "us" and "them," the "subject" and the "non-subject" provide a ready-made set of definitions external to historical and social reality. Instead, he seeks to restore the interpretation of China to the complexity and impurity of the historical situations in which it was always imbricated.

Informed by such powerful critical insights, my study attempts to negotiate the highly complex terrain of the cross-cultural encounter between Qing China and Georgian Britain in a way that tries to respect the shifting allegiances of power and authority (both military, economic, and cultural) between two powerful empires in the period, and which restores a sense of the complexity of that encounter, fashioned as it was from multiple poles of engagement and recognition, and often produced from on-the-ground collaborations between Chinese, British, and other peoples in the multi-ethnic and cosmopolitan cities of Guangzhou, Calcutta, and Southeast Asia generally. British Romantic-period and mid-Qing thinkers, politicians, and writers were all bound up in the same global networks sharing common and modern thoughts, concerns, and ideas.

This study falls roughly into two parts. The first five chapters set out the process of the construction of the body of writing I provisionally describe as a "Romantic Sinology" from its antecedents in the Chinese publications and studies of two major late eighteenth-century or "pre-Romantic" British literary scholars, editors, and translators, Thomas Percy and William Jones; from the accounts of the Macartney embassy; and from the work of missionaries and Company traders in Bengal, Malacca, and Canton: Joshua Marshman, Robert Morrison, George Thomas Staunton, and John Francis Davis. In particular, Percy's remarkable edition of the early Qing novel the *Haoqiu zhuan* entitled the *Hau Kiou Choann; or the*

Pleasing History (1761), and his compendium *Miscellaneous Pieces Relating to China* (1762), are viewed as crucial to the development of British sinology. Crucially, both Percy and Jones are interested in the *belles lettres* of China, not simply its Confucian classics. The contribution of "Chinese assistants" to Jones's, Marshman's, and Morrison's sinology is highlighted in my account, especially the important presence of Jones's friend Huang Ya Dong, one of the few Chinese visitors to London. This section concludes with a chapter discussing the crucial and formative encounter between the Macartney embassy and the Qing court in 1793 and the body of work that resulted from it. The allegation that Qing China was politically and economically stagnant, ossified by an inflexible ceremonialism, especially regarding its relations with foreign powers, was apparently confirmed by the accounts of the first two embassies to China which occurred during the Romantic period. I argue that these embassies should be regarded as a crucial part of the knowledge exchange and cultural translation processes between Britain and China, and major events in the formation of Romantic Sinology. From British discussions of Chinese technology and science, this study suggests that instead of a unique Western and modern science, there were national and local knowledge traditions and dynamics and that modernity and science are not simple emanations from a preexisting European center, diffused to the East. The case of Joseph Banks and the British attempt to transplant and cultivate tea from China to Bengal (along with many other Chinese plants) in the early nineteenth century is representative of this.

Part Two of this study is more, though not exclusively, concerned with British cultural representations of China that I argue both participate in an intercultural encounter and sometimes resist it. Throughout these chapters I argue that China is an important, though often under-acknowledged, presence in British Romantic-period writing and that Chinese ideas and texts are partially constitutive of British Romanticism, though frequently through unexpected affinities and fugitive resemblances. Chapter 6 shows that the complex diplomatic encounter between Macartney and the Qianlong emperor is taken up and fetishized in the British Romantic imagination as a traumatic primal scene. In this encounter the imperial ceremony of the *kowtow* (*sangui jiukou*) functions as metonymic. The chapter discusses this topos in a series of texts relating it to the depiction of China derived from the chinoiserie depictions of porcelain. In writings by Southey, Lamb, Leigh Hunt, and others, I argue that the subject of China is evaded and displaced, despite the presence of the new knowledge produced by Romantic Sinology, and speculate on the reasons why much Romantic writing fails to address head-on contemporary China, the object of study of the new sinology. Chapter 7 addresses the primary site in eighteenth-century discourse where Chinese ideas and styles are most apparent, that of the Anglo-Chinese garden, and focuses, in particular, on the extraordinary eruption of the imperial garden of *Wanshu Yuan* (Garden of Ten Thousand Trees), visited by Macartney, into Wordsworth's *The Prelude*. I argue that, whatever the origins of the natural style in landscape gardening, Chinese influence is a very real presence in the debates, however mediated, and the global networks of trade and exchange imbricate even the Wordsworths in their compass. In particular, I exemplify the rather surprising family connections between the Wordsworth family, China, and Macartney.

The final chapter deals with the most popular cultural form of the period, the drama. Rather than evade the topos of China, the theater robustly embraced it in a variety of thematic and visual ways. Set designs were directly influenced by the new views of China deriving from William Alexander's visual representations of Macartney's embassy as well as the new-style "deformities" of royal chinoiserie on display at the Regent's Brighton Pavilion. This chapter begins with Arthur Murphy's hugely significant 1756 adaptation of the thirteenth-century Chinese drama *Zhao shi guer*, an uneasy blend of chinioserie spectacle and high tragic seriousness, and concludes with depictions of a more contemporary China in dramas such as Andrew Cherry's extremely popular *The Travellers* (1806). Oddly, perhaps, the popular theater seems to have been the cultural mode in which the fruits of Romantic Sinology were most often mediated to a substantial and socially inclusive audience. If eighteenth-century drama presents China as tragedy, Romantic-period drama tropes this encounter as comedy. Rather than being a cover for colonial aggression against Qing China, I argue that this turn to comedy represents a real sense of the possibility, even hope, of a partnership between British and Chinese, and that this was not, viewed before the Opium Wars, simply an orientalist fantasy.

The forthcoming century appears almost as a mirror image of the beginning of the nineteenth as Western global economic and cultural hegemony is challenged and declining in the face of the emerging world power of China. Chinese capital and investment is spreading across the globe, rather like that of Britain at the dawn of the nineteenth century, and Chinese culture, rightfully, begins to assume a new importance in the literature of the world. In the light of this, returning to re-examine the first major cultural encounter between the two great formations of the Qing and British empires is a project which promises to shed light on our contemporary situation and demonstrate that the culture of Britain, at least since the eighteenth century, has always been global, and that within that global consciousness Chinese styles, texts, forms, and commodities have played a crucial, though under-acknowledged, role.

CHAPTER I

Thomas Percy and the forging of Romantic China

The first two chapters of this study set out the antecedents of British Romantic Sinology in the Chinese publications and studies of highly influential late eighteenth-century or "pre-Romantic" British literary scholars, editors, and translators, Thomas Percy and William Jones. These two figures began the process of the forging of Romantic China that this book describes. The construction of this knowledge was a global affair. This chapter moves from Percy's Britain, with Jones, to Calcutta (Kolkata) in British Bengal on the Indian subcontinent to trace Jones's hesitant orientalist engagement with China, before moving a few miles north along the banks of the River Hooghly (Hughli) to Danish-controlled Serampore (Srirampur), to the Baptist mission of William Carey and his associate, Joshua Marshman, who would supervise the very first translation of a Confucian text directly into English. In the work of these three men and their collaborators the origins of Romantic Sinology can be discerned. Their works, however, were heavily dependent on the prior scholarship of Jesuit sinology, an older critical tradition and paradigmatic body of work from which they struggled to extricate themselves.[1] This chapter outlines their efforts in beginning to harness and make knowable what they viewed as the real and contemporary Qing China with which Britons were now extensively trading. This new China, of course, was just as much a construction or forgery, and no more disinterested than that of previous Catholic scholarship. This chapter begins by briefly establishing the eighteenth-century consensus of understanding about China for British readers, a version of Chinese literature and philosophy that was both classicized and "Confucianized." This was a philosophy which, as David Porter has influentially argued, was based on the problematic assumption, or wish fulfillment, of an original monotheistic theology compatible with Catholic Christian doctrine.[2] This version of Chinese culture was transmitted to the West though a series of translated Confucian texts.

For the eighteenth-century Britain of Dr. Johnson and Alexander Pope, knowledge about China was a product of largely Jesuit scholarship.

Notably in the mid eighteenth century a flurry of literary activity about China occurs, including the production of Arthur Murphy's important drama *The Orphan of China* (1759), the publications of Oliver Goldsmith's epistolary novel *The Citizen of the World* (1762), the anonymous chinoiserie novel *The Bonze* (1765), and, most importantly, Thomas Percy's Chinese writings consisting of his remarkable translation of the early Qing novel, the *Haoqiu zhuan* (1683?), as the *Hau Kiou Choann; or the Pleasing History* (1761), followed by his compendium *Miscellaneous Pieces Relating to China* (1762). Percy's text, however, is not simply an imaginative recreation of China, a work of fashionable literary chinoiserie, nor another satirical depiction of Britain employing a bemused Chinese foil, but rather a serious, if flawed, attempt to translate and understand China, the pioneering project of a nascent British Romantic Sinology. Arguably, it is the founding text on which this new sinology was to be constructed.

THE EIGHTEENTH-CENTURY SINOLOGY: MATTEO RICCI, CONFUCIUS, AND THE JESUIT SYNTHESIS

It is well known that China in the seventeenth and eighteenth century was possessed of an enormous prestige in European eyes, and this story does not need to be extensively retold here. Chinese political and military successes in the eighteenth century were spectacular. China was the most admired and envied of the empires of Southeast Asia. Chinese exports, such as tea, porcelain, and silks, were strongly desired. Chinese designs in their Europeanized form of chinoiserie were extraordinarily fashionable and popular. Famously, Voltaire claimed Chinese enlightened and secular governance as a model for Europe and Leibniz suggested that the Chinese should send missionaries to Europe to teach natural religion. In 1756, a correspondent to the periodical *The World* archly suggested that as France was losing its claim to be the "empire of taste" young Britons should be sent on their grand tour to Peking, not Paris or Rome.[3] Yet, by the end of the nineteenth century, China was derided abroad as pathetic and its government seen as woefully inadequate to the new challenges of the modern world. After a swift defeat by the British in the Opium War of 1839–42 Western nations presented more and more of a threat to the empire, imposing humiliating terms on its rulers and degrading its culture.[4]

The standard eighteenth-century European interpretation of Chinese culture which Percy and Jones inherited was that it was Confucian, or at least that its most legitimate, worthy, and essential attributes were encapsulated in the philosophical and literary edifice constructed by its "scholar-literati" (*shidafu*) class. This position, however, was an artful and sophisticated "manufacture" (in the terms of Lionel M. Jensen) of Jesuit missionaries, chiefly influenced by the work of the first Catholic missionaries to China, Michele Ruggieri and Matteo Ricci, who arrived in 1579 and 1582 respectively.[5] Ricci's powerful strategy was to stress the similarity between Confucianism and Catholic Christianity and promote a strategy of "accommodation" between the cultures of the Ming Confucian literati (*ru jiao*) and his own.[6] He confessed that he made "every effort to turn our way the ideas of the leader of the sect of literati, Confucius, by interpreting in our favor things which he left ambiguous in his writings. In this way our Fathers gain favor with the literati who do not adore the idols."[7] This also meant reducing the significance of key doctrines on the Christian side, such as original sin, and the religious significance of Confucian rites, especially those performed by the Chinese for their ancestors. According to Ricci's most recent biographer R. Po-Chia Hsia, he "was inspired to find parallels between the sayings of the ancient Confucian classics and the fundamental principles of a pared-down Christianity, stripped clean of the doctrines of original sin, the Crucifixion, and the Resurrection." He sought to establish "the existence of an omnipotent God, creator of heaven and earth, called the Lord of Heaven, *Tianzhu*, in the discourse of the Jesuits, but named God on High, *Shangdi*, or simply heaven, *Tian*, in the ancient classics."[8] He argued that classic Confucian texts demonstrated knowledge of the one true God, the Lord (or emperor) on High or *shangdi*, who was prior to the "Supreme Ultimate" (*taijii*) of the Song neo-Confucianism.[9] The Jesuits identified this deity with the Sino-Jesuit neologism for the Christian God, the Heavenly Master (*tainzhu*), claiming that Chinese antiquity was monotheistic. Ricci argued that Confucianism affirmed the notions of a transcendent creator and of the immortality of the soul, but that these doctrines had been erased from such beliefs through the influence of Buddhist teachings about non-existence.[10] His ultimate aim was to provide a groundwork by which the differences between Confucianism and Christianity could be minimized, thus facilitating the work of the conversion of the literati and those of high social and intellectual standing to Christianity, hopefully spearheading the conversion of the emperor, court, and empire. Though the focus of the Catholic missions on the Chinese elite has been over-emphasized, this remained their primary interest.[11] As Porter has argued, Ricci attempted to "distil the original essence of early Confucian belief system from the syncretic potpourri of religious practices that he encountered in the pluralistic climate of the late Ming dynasty, and on distinguishing it in particular from the confused and disorderly tangle of doctrines that characterized Chinese Buddhism in his mind."[12]

After Ricci's death in 1610, his Jesuit successors, by and large, continued to promote the Christian–Confucian synthesis with the rejection of Buddhism and Daoism that he pioneered. The most extreme and outspoken version of this doctrine was promulgated by the French Jesuit, Louis Le Comte, who made the extraordinary claim that the "people of China have preserved for nearly two thousand years a knowledge of the true God, and have honored him in a manner that might serve as an instructive example even to Christians."[13] As Zhang Longxi argues, this position had the corollary that Chinese philosophy could only be properly read within an allegorical frame that could "be truly understood by a Christian interpreter, not a native Chinese scholar."[14] The Confucian–Christian synthesis with its concomitant idealization of Chinese civilization proved very attractive to seventeenth- and eighteenth-century Europe and formed the critical paradigm against which British sinology would struggle in defining itself. The detailed story of that struggle is told in Chapters 2, 3, and 4 of this study, but my focus shifts to Britain and to the work of the person who can be claimed as the nation's first serious sinologist, Thomas Percy.

Crucially, the early sinology of Percy and Jones was still dependent on this older Jesuit tradition of Confucian sinology from which it struggled to assert its independence. It largely relied on such key works as the *Confucius Sinarum Philosophus, sive Sinensis* (Confucius, Philosopher of the Chinese; or, the Chinese Learning) (Paris, 1687) and the twenty-eight volumes of the *Recueil des lettres édifiantes & curieuses écrites des missions étrangeres par quelques missionaries de la Compagnie de Jésus* (1702–58), especially in the influential redaction of its final editor Jean-Baptiste Du Halde's *Description géographique, historique, chronologique, politique, et physique de l'empire de la Chine* of 1735. Much of the *Lettres* had been the work of the outstanding sinologist Joseph de Prémare, and his researches were filtered through various translations into the eighteenth-century British intellectual mainstream as well as through the French version and its two rival English translations: *The General History of China* (translated by Richard Brookes and published by John Watt in 1736) and *The Description of China* (translated by John Green and William Guthrie and published by Edward Cave in 1738). As well as being available in Percy's writings, compilations such as *The Chinese Traveller* of 1764 and the *Modern Universal History* also printed extensive extracts of Jesuit scholarship about China, primarily based on Du Halde. Many Britons would rely on one of the English translations of Du Halde, but many, such as Percy and Horace Walpole, also knew the French version.

EARLY BEGINNINGS: THOMAS PERCY'S *PLEASING HISTORY*

British sinologists conventionally date the institutionalized origin of their discipline to the work of the missionary Robert Morrison and the establishment of the Anglo-Chinese College at Malacca, and to that of George Thomas Staunton and the East India Company trading establishment (known as a "factory"), at Canton (Guangzhou).[15] It can be argued, however, that British sinology begins substantially earlier than this with the work of its first two serious China experts, Bishop Thomas Percy and Sir William Jones. Although neither could formally read and write Chinese, nevertheless both had a sustained and serious interest in China. Though the accuracy of some of their writings on China left much to be desired, nevertheless signs of what might be called an emerging and native British sinological awareness can be seen in their work. Both also struggled against the restraints imposed on them by their inability to read Chinese or to have access to key Chinese texts except through the heavily mediated form of Jesuit scholarship, which was then translated into English from Latin or French. Percy, for example, requested that the reader of his "Fragments on Chinese Poetry" of 1761 should be patient as the poems printed were not those which he would have selected himself had he had free access to the Chinese originals, and Jones was evangelical about the possibility of translating Chinese originals, especially the *Book of Poetry*, directly into English, thus obviating any need for intermediate Jesuit translations.

This first chapter will explore these late eighteenth-century trends, dealing with the beginnings of the British literary and cultural study of China in the lead-up to what is conventionally known as the Romantic period and the construction of what we may call a Romantic Sinology, a diverse body of writing about China from the late eighteenth and early nineteenth century, but yet which shares certain leading features. In many ways Percy's rendition of the Chinese novel *Haoqiu zhuan* as the *Hau Kiou Choann* (1761) marks the beginning of this alternative British Protestant tradition of writing on China. Like Catholic missionary scholarship, it stresses the similarity of Chinese culture and Catholicism but now in terms of their shared idolatry, and ultimately rejects both. This would become the dominant British line on China in the early nineteenth century, though the continued reliance on Jesuit translations of Confucian texts (acknowledged or otherwise) continued to hamper any radical breaking away from this established position. In succeeding chapters of this study, I argue why exactly the need to translate Confucian texts into English was crucial.

Thomas Percy's reputation as an early pioneer British sinologist is now beginning to receive the critical attention it clearly deserves.[16] A number of scholars have pointed not only to the significance of this work in terms of British understandings of China, but also to its impact on late eighteenth-century and Romantic-period writing. Certainly Percy was Britain's first serious China scholar and his work marks an appropriate place for this study to begin. James Watt, Eun Kyung Min, and David Porter have all argued that the publication of Percy's Chinese works was paradoxically a crucial element in the turn towards the medievalism of the Gothic and the emergence of a northern antiquarian ballad tradition that would come to mark the canonical Romanticism of Wordsworth and Coleridge, especially their landmark poetic manifesto, the *Lyrical Ballads* of 1798. Watt argues that Percy sought to construct a "distinctively British and protestant perspective on Chinese customs and manners." China would thus provide a model for Britain to think about its native Anglo-Saxon literary heritage and its own literary past. For Min, the Chinese books provided "an important preparative" for Percy's "theorization of a non-classical, alternative English antiquity in the *Reliques*" and for the editorial techniques he would later employ in that work.[17] Porter has argued for the crucial importance of Percy's Chinese texts to his other cognate researches and regards him as a pioneer of world literature. Porter argues that the "dizzying" ambivalence or equivocation that Percy shows towards China reflects his struggle "to redeem his emerging conception of national identity in the face of plainly superior Chinese cultural achievements." For Porter, this paradoxical indebtedness to Chinese culture combined with a need to repudiate a non-English source leads to what he convincingly terms an "instrumental amnesia with respect to China's role in the production of eighteenth-century British aesthetic culture."[18] This amnesia will persist into the Romantic literary period where it functions almost as a major structural device.

Such criticism generally argues that Percy's Chinese publications provided a kind of negative counter-example inspiring a newly confident

British literature to seek outs its own early and native Saxon traditions, antecedents wedded to constitutional notions of English freedom and liberty, and opposed to what were conventionally viewed as forms of Chinese despotism under the orientalist gaze. Thus the origins and development of British Romantic Sinology in Percy's Chinese writings is closely associated with the emergence of the literary aesthetic we know as Romanticism, conventionally regarded as deriving from Percy's championing of the ancient English ballad in his *Reliques of Ancient English Poetry*, especially as practiced by Wordsworth and Coleridge. Percy is certainly keen to differentiate his scholarship and editorial technique from that of his Jesuit predecessors. In his "Preface" to the *Miscellaneous Pieces* of 1762 he draws particular attention to Jesuit editorial practices, which he equates with their incessant political intrigues:

The various arts, intrigues, and resources of this politic society, the several turns of fortune to which they have been exposed, their first introduction, their consequent power, and present depression, are subjects that cannot fail to interest our curiosity, and afford matter for reflection to a contemplative mind … In China they were once almost sovereigns, at present they are there on a more abject footing: yet never discouraged, never subdued, this indefatigable body are still practicing every art to insinuate themselves once more into favour again, and render themselves necessary at the Chinese court.

Grudgingly admiring, Percy sets up his own, rival Chinese scholarship as one that is inevitably tainted with Jesuit artifice, and which needs the skilled intelligence of an informed and discerning reader to penetrate between the lines of the text and understand the problems inherent in translation as a form of interpretation practiced by this most sophisticated yet insidious order. He often makes the point that Jesuit writing about China is outdated and archaic. The information that is contained in their works was chiefly derived from their experience of Ming rather than Qing China and it is *modern* China that should be, and now *will be*, the focus of contemporary British interest and study.

Percy's most important Chinese study, the anonymously published translation of the early Qing Chinese novel or "scholar-beauty romance," the *Haoqiu zhuan* (1683?), combined with his collection of *Miscellaneous Piece Relating to China* (1762), represent almost a false start, or missed opportunity, for British Romanticism.[19] The date and authorship of the *Haoqiu zhuan* are unknown but it has been attributed to Mingjiao Zhongren or "Man of the Teaching of Names."[20] Percy published his translation as the *Hau Kiou Choaan; or, the Pleasing History* in 1761. These Chinese writings were very much a part of the great literary and cultural interest in China in the decade of the late 1750s and early 1760s, which gave rise to Murphy's *Orphan of China* (1759) and Oliver Goldsmith's *A Citizen of the World* (1762), the debates over the Anglo-Chinese garden, and many other similar cultural manifestations. In another manner it could also be argued that they mark a departure from the works of a rococo-inspired chinoiserie, indicating, instead, a new seriousness and a willingness to comprehend what they figured as the actual "Chinese mind" itself. Such writings could have provided models as fertile for later poetic developments as Jones's translations of Sanskrit or Percy's *Reliques of Ancient English Poetry* (1765) or Walpole's medieval Gothic novel, *The Castle of Otranto* (1764). Certainly, British Romantic writers felt unable to acknowledge their Chinese influences in the same way that they could celebrate those derived from Indian and Arabic origins, for instance in the tales of the *Arabian Nights*. That they did not is a subject intimately tied up with Britain's developing relationship with the Qing empire in the late eighteenth century and a major question for this study.

Percy's version was the first European translation in abbreviated form of any Chinese novel, and is remarkable for that fact alone.[21] According to Percy, the actual translation of the *Haoqiu zhuan* was made by James Wilkinson, an East India Company employee at Canton, as a language exercise undertaken with his Portuguese tutor around 1719. This is strong evidence that English Company men already had a serious interest in learning the Chinese language and discovering more about China's literature and culture, and that Wilkinson was not alone in studying Chinese. Wilkinson's manuscript was given to Percy some time before 1756 by Wilkinson's nephew, along with some other materials, and subsequently returned to his widow, after which unfortunately they disappear.[22] Percy tells us, and there is no very obvious reason to doubt him, that three of the volumes had been translated into English direct from a Chinese original by Wilkinson and the fourth, translated by an unknown hand but presumably Wilkinson's tutor at Macao, remained in Portuguese, a language of which Percy knew something. Percy then revised Wilkinson's English translations and translated the fourth volume into English from the Portuguese. The novel was published in four volumes with copious notes gleaned from a large body of Jesuit scholarship available from the libraries of his publisher Dodsley or his then patron, the Earl of Sussex.[23] In an age much noted for ingenious literary forgery as well as for sophisticated impostors, such as the pretended "Formosan" George Psalmanazar, the authenticity of the text would always be under question.[24] Unsurprisingly, Percy's edition of the *Haoqiu zhuan* was challenged on the grounds of its authenticity, a charge Percy found it hard to defend against, especially when he entertained his own suspicions on the subject. He included a note by his friend James Garland, who had been resident at Canton, testifying to the authenticity of the novel in the second edition of his *Reliques* of 1767, and brought forward information relating to his acquisition of the manuscript from Wilkinson in an advertisement to the second edition of the novel in 1774.[25] He even approached Macartney as late as 1800 requesting any evidence he could locate of the novel's existence in China, which the former ambassador was unable to supply.[26]

By 1810 at the latest, the novel's authenticity was assured, as British sinologists were keen to claim it as their own special preserve. George Thomas Staunton commented favorably on Percy's translation, which he judged sufficiently accurate for the editor's purposes, presenting a reasonably informed view of the legal context of Chinese marriage.[27] In 1817 Robert Morrison recommended the novel along with the now much more famous *Hong lou meng* (*Dream of the Red Mansions*) as a good starting point for those wishing to acquire the Chinese language; both novels, he claimed to be written in a colloquial style.[28] Perhaps with his suggestion in mind, his pupil, John Francis Davis, issued an enlarged and more populist translation of the novel in 1829 under the title *The Fortunate Union*. Davis was less complimentary about Percy's work. Percy's translation did not sell well yet it was extremely influential. It was translated into French in 1766 and 1828, into German in 1766 and 1869, and into Dutch in 1767. Both Goethe and Friedrich Grimm read it with great enthusiasm.[29] The novel was finally published in its original Chinese form by Frederick Baller for the American Presbyterian Press at Shanghai in 1904 and 1911, and appeared in two later twentieth-century editions.

James G. St. André has identified three periods of extensive translation activity regarding this text, the Percy-inspired phase of 1761–74; the John Francis Davis-inspired phase of 1829–42; and a later phase in 1895–1926. All three periods coincide with specific historical, political and imperialist phases in Britain and Europe's relationship with China. The differences between Percy's and Davis's versions will be explored in Chapter 4.[30] Percy's text reflects a specific moment when China was regarded as largely unknown to the British imagination and when its cultural superiority was, by and large, assured and acknowledged. Davis's later version, a product of the more developed phase of Romantic Sinology, reflected a time when China, in the eyes of its practitioners, was more familiar, capable of being known, categorized, and appropriately placed with some precision on a Eurocentric scale of civilization. Percy's *Hau Kiou Choann* is in every way a scholarly edition, with extensive footnotes; Davis's version is more of a popular romance, with comparatively few references and glosses, about a world whose language and culture is rapidly losing its mystique in response to the increasing British presence in Southeast Asia. In addition to the novel itself, Percy's volumes contained a substantial selection of "Chinese proverbs and Apothegms," "The Argument of a Chinese Play Acted at Canton, in the Year MDCCXIX," and "Fragments of Chinese Poetry: with a Dissertation." As Nick Groom has pointed out, the "Fragments of Chinese Poetry," taken from the *Shijing*, was originally a part of Percy's much wider interest in ancient poetry and was to be included in his projected *Specimens of the Ancient Poetry of Different Nations*. Percy notes in this work that the "Elegiac Verses, addressed to the Emperor *Tai-kang*," if actually composed by the Emperor's brother, would constitute "the most ancient piece of Poetry extant in the world."[31]

The novel tells of the domestic courtship of two idealized lovers, the son of an influential Beijing magistrate, Tieh-chung-u (Tie Zhongyu or "Iron-within-Jade"), and the daughter of a disgraced military commander, Shuey-ping-sin (Shui Bingxin or "Water with Heart Pure as Ice"). The novel is a type of the *caizi jiaren xioashuo* or "scholar-beauty" fiction that features romances between beautiful maidens and talented scholars, though its pronounced Confucian "Puritanism" is not typical of the genre.[32] The novel tells the story of how the two young people resist the attempts of their enemies to undermine their moral integrity and how they remain chaste and virtuous until their much-delayed marriage. Tieh-chung-u establishes a reputation for himself early in the novel for probity by exposing the machinations of corrupt officials. Following her father's exile to Tartary, Shuey-ping-sin is subject to a series of attempts by her uncle to marry her to the son of a mandarin of the Privy Council, Kwo-khe-tzu (Kuo Qizu). She is a woman of extraordinary virtue and intelligence who manages to extricate herself from these designs. In Percy's version, one of the characters in the novel describes her as possessing "a mouth, whose words are keener than the edge of a pen-knife or razor" (2.62).[33] In one case, after being villainously abducted, she is rescued by Tieh-chung-u. She helps Tieh-chung-u by subsequently saving him from the attempt of corrupt bonzes, or Buddhist priests, to poison him in retaliation for rescuing her from Kwo-khe-tzu's attempt to forcibly abduct her, and nurses him back to health in her own house despite the appearance of impropriety. After foiling a series of further attempts to force Shuey-ping-sin to marry and then to disgrace her, she and Tieh-chung-u are married with the blessing of the emperor. The novel eschews any typically Western expectations

for orientalist spectacle and resembles more closely the novel of domestic
sensibility, notably Richardson's *Pamela* (1740), with its sustained praise
of female virtue and concern with virginity under threat. As André Levy
notes, Percy's translation actually showed Britons "how much the mysterious Chinese were like the Europeans in their sentimentality."[34] Percy's
"Dedication" to the translation indicates that "the strict regard to virtue
and decorum" which is shown by Chinese writers is a useful corrective to
the "most licentious and immoral" narratives of British fiction. Of course,
late Ming and early Qing literature also included a substantial amount of
racy and erotic fiction of which Percy had no knowledge.

Unlike William Jones, who enthusiastically advocated Persian and
Arabic poetry as a new source of images and subjects for Europeans,
Percy insists that his task is not so much literary as ethnological, in that
he is attempting to provide a scholarly introduction to Chinese literature
as well as presenting "a faithful picture of Chinese manners, wherein the
domestic and political economy of that vast people is displayed" for his
readership (i.xv). As Porter argues, Percy assumes a new *faux* stance of
apparently disinterested objectivity when discussing China, at odds with
the highly polemicized discourse of the past.[35] In a letter to William
Shenstone, Percy had claimed that the edition sought not to amuse or
entertain but to "give us a history of the human mind in China," and
readers must give up every "beauty of composition for the sake of seeing
the workings [of] the human mind under all the peculiarities of a Chinese
education."[36] Percy argues that fiction may present a more accurate and
truthful account of China than the biased Jesuit eyewitness accounts. As
such, it could be argued that Percy's translation partakes of the Saidian
imperative to understand and arguably facilitate the control of Chinese
peoples through controlling the processes of textual translation.[37] This
novel, Percy argues, should "not be admired because of the beauties of its
composition" but viewed as "a curious specimen of Chinese literature."
The narrative itself he describes as "frequently dry and tedious" and deficient "in what should interest the passions or divert the imagination"
(i.xii). He argues that previous Jesuit accounts are "partial and defective,
especially insofar as they describe the religious ceremonies of the *Chinese*"
(i.xviii). Unsympathetic to the former Jesuit idealization of Chinese culture, Percy is often downbeat about the novel's achievement. He writes
that "there is a littleness and poverty of genius in all, the works of taste
of the Chinese … the abjectness of their genius may easily be accounted
for from that servile submission and dread of novelty, which enslaves the

minds of the Chinese, and while it promotes the peace and quiet of the empire, dulls their spirit and cramps their imagination." The Chinese, he writes, "do not take such bold and daring flights as some of the other Eastern nations" but "pay a greater regard to truth and nature in their fictitious narratives" containing "less of the marvelous and more of the probable," closer to the neo-classical desiderata of "an unity of design or fable, and the incidents all tend to one end, in a regular manner, with little interruption or incoherence" (I.xii–xiv).

In his extensive notes to the text, which anticipate and may have influenced those of Robert Southey's later orientalist epics, Percy mediates a substantial body of textual knowledge about China from a wide range of sources. His notes contain much information about Chinese manners, customs, governance, culture, and mores, as well as about Chinese produce. As St. André argues, the translation and its notes are "firmly embedded in a critical structure which proclaims its usefulness, amends and disciplines the original text, directs the interpretation of its readers, and claims to give them a holistic grasp of Chinese literature, society, mores, customs and racial characteristics."[38] The volumes contain, for instance, two substantial notes on tea and porcelain production that were of especial interest to Percy's industrializing commercial national audience, trading in a world market in such commodities.

Percy's attitudes to China are conflicting. As Fan Cunzhong persuasively argues, Percy is balanced or caught straddling two conflicting attitudes to China, that of the Jesuit admiration of his sources and that of British accounts by Commodore Anson, Daniel Defoe, and others which stressed the more negative aspects of Chinese culture. Percy's sinology is on the cusp of two readings: an older one, beginning to decline and a new emerging program, which will become the consensus of Romantic Sinology. Porter has convincingly described this process of Percy's "ambivalence" to China formed of admiration and anxiety about the world's oldest and most populous civilization. My own reading of Percy's Chinese writing stresses more his role as the anticipator of a new Romantic Sinology, and thus accentuates his more negative comments.[39] Yet that odd ambivalence would always remain very much a part of Romantic Sinology, though the exact measure of praise or condemnation would vary. Even at its most culturally robust, Romantic Sinology never entirely shook off this cultural ambivalence.

Throughout his notes to the novel, Percy often denigrates both China and his Jesuit sources. For instance, rather than celebrating his heroine

Shuey-ping-sin's clear ingenuity in outwitting her antagonists, Percy feels it necessary to explain her apparent display of unfeminine calculation:

The Chinese, who are the most subtle and crafty people in the world, may naturally be supposed to esteem and admire subtlety and craft ... The Chinese morals notwithstanding their boasted purity, evidently fall short of the Christian, since they know not how to inspire that open and ingenuous simplicity, void of all guile, which more elevated principles of morality propose to our esteem and imitation. (1.129)

When Shuey-ping-sin dwells on the injustices she has suffered, Percy writes "the morality of the Chinese author ... appears in a very contemptible light compared with the Christian, which strongly recommends the forgiveness of injuries, and the return of good for evil" (2.51). Percy's notes are studded with such ethnic slurs against the Chinese; for example, they are "to the highest degree greedy of gain, libidinous and vindictive" (2.197), "avaritious" (2.166), and "the most cowardly people in the world" (2.256). Rather than enhancing the longstanding Jesuit program of accommodation with China, Percy instead emphasizes the difference of the "manners and customs of the Chinese" and "their own peculiar ways of thinking, and modes of expression ... so remote from our own, that they frequently require a large detail to make them intelligible" (1.xxiv). China to Percy is often unintelligible and needs the expertise of scholars to render or translate it into terms that can be grasped by a British audience.

Percy emphasizes what he sees as the Chinese sense of cultural superiority: "they have learnt to hold all other countries in most sovereign contempt, supposing their own Empire to comprize not only the best, but the greatest part of the habitable world" (1.91). He notes that the Chinese are beginning to understand a little about Europe and have begun to add it to their world maps, "as if it were one of the *Canary* Islands, or some little barren spot" (2.92). Ominously, in the light of future events, Percy identifies as another "pleasant instance" of Chinese "national pride" their proclivity in regarding communications from other nations as "tribute and a mark of submission." Such nations as do send communications "are set down in their history among those, which are tributary to *China*" (2.92). Percy's remark is something that members of Macartney's embassy may have noted, and it may have influenced their expectations. Indeed, both Percy and Macartney were members of Dr. Johnson's Literary Club at which such discussions about the manners and mores of other peoples and nations occurred. Already the rhetoric of submission and humiliation that would frame relations between Britain and China during the nineteenth century is being developed and deployed as part of Percy's allegedly new and objective Chinese study.

Percy's notes to the *Hao Kiou Choann* present a substantial re-visioning or refocusing of the version of China manufactured by Jesuit scholarship especially regarding the religious ceremonies of the Chinese for which, he states, the Jesuits have been most criticized as "partial and defective." Percy attacks the Jesuit accommodationist synthesis of Confucianism and Christianity undertaken by Ricci. He claims that they have made "very improper concessions to their Chinese converts, and of so modeling Christianity, as to allow an occasional conformity to many pagan superstitions, under a pretence that they are only of a civil nature" and propagated an account of China that favors their own cause (1.xviii). He is ambiguous about the specifics of Chinese religious practices. Though suspicious of Jesuit accommodationism, he does allow that the Chinese may have a belief in a "Divine Providence" which is generally associated with "Heaven" (1.156, 156n). The Chinese scholar-literati class "profess no other religion than that prescribed in their ancient classical books, which is the worship of one Supreme Being, the Lord and Sovereign Principle of all things, under the name of *Shang-ti*, i.e. *Supreme Emperor*: but more frequently under that of *Tien*, or *Heaven*: which their interpreters explain to mean, *that Spirit which presides in* HEAVEN, because HEAVEN *is the most excellent work produced by this first cause*" (1.156n). Having outlined Ricci's equation of an original classical Confucianism with Christian monotheism, Percy concludes with Ricci that "the modern Literati understand the word *Tien*, &c in their ancient books in a low material sense, and are downright atheists" (1.156n). Yet he disagrees in denying that the observations paid to ancestors are civil ceremonies and claiming that they are carried "to an idolatrous excess" (1.163–64n). He notes that the Chinese have no term in their lexicon for God and have thus been regarded as atheists; nevertheless, he concurs with the Jesuits that whatever they currently believe, they originally had a "belief of a Divine Providence" (4.42).

Anticipating one of the central claims of Romantic Sinology, Percy notes the similarities between what he sees as the idolatry and monasticism of the Buddhists and Daoists, *and* Catholic practices, archly commentating that when confronted by this obvious resemblance, Prémare could only explain it by supposing "the devil had in view to counterfeit the holy rites of the Church" (2.3–4n). Percy is aware of the Jesuit's strategic denigration of Buddhism that Porter has argued was essential to authenticate the Confucian–Catholic classicist synthesis.[40] The Buddhists may be "great hypocrites" and have "little real virtue" yet they are careful enough of their public reputation to avoid the worst excesses of which the Jesuits accused them. Percy is also aware that Ricci and Ruggieri had originally assumed the guise of Buddhist monks on their first residence in China (2.13–15n). Though able to praise Confucius for recommending the returning of hatred with piety and virtue, Percy points out that Confucius does not *insist* upon this practice as a duty nor back it with any sanction: "where is this divine maxim taught with that precision; urged with that glowing benevolence; or inforced from those sublime and affecting motives, which it is in the mouth of the SAVIOUR of the world?" (2.52).

Percy reminds his readership of their own sacred texts of Luke 6.27, 28, 35, and 14.4, and Matthew 6.15 to hammer home this point – a technique which will become depressingly familiar in later British missionary translations of Confucius of the early nineteenth century. Where Voltaire and others could admire a China that achieved a high level of rational civilization without revelation, in the increasingly evangelical British climate of first decades of the nineteenth century it becomes harder to validate the system of Confucian thinking. Thus Chinese laws remain "merely political institutions, and are backed by no sanctions of future rewards and punishments." Lacking the Christian consciousness of an afterlife and a system of future rewards and punishments, Percy denies that Chinese laws can seriously influence the heart and will only create the appearance and not the reality of virtue (2.167n, 168n, 267n). Yet Percy can also hint that Confucius approaches closely to a Christian sensibility as when he prints the maxim "Let us love others, as we love ourselves" in his collection of "Chinese Proverbs" in the third volume of the *Hau Kiou Choann* (3.212). In contradiction to his views of an afterlife, Percy dismisses Buddhist and Daoist beliefs in the doctrine of a future state of rewards and punishments as ridiculous superstitions (2.267–71n). He argues that the progress of "the religion of FO" among the Chinese is only to be accounted for by its "supplying the doctrine of a future state, so agreeable to the mind of man" and lacking in Confucianism (2.291n). Despite the lack of any supernatural sanction for moral behavior, paradoxically Percy states that Chinese history demonstrates "instances of firmness and integrity in opposing oppressive measures, that would do honour to the patriots of *Greece* and *Rome*" (4.141).

Percy anticipates the tone of later Romantic Sinology by highlighting the treatment of women in the Chinese empire. Commenting on a passage in which Tieh-chung-u may appear ungallant, Percy launches into a very critical account of how Chinese women are treated in general. It is, he opines, "impossible that there should be any such thing as gallantry among a people, who admit no intercourse between the two Sexes; whose Marriages are contracted without the consent of the Parties, and even without their personal knowledge of each other." As men are allowed a "plurality of women," their Romantic attention to any one is thus lessened. Women are held in "low esteem" and no delicacy is shown to them. From this statement, Percy then goes on to equate China, "a nation in other respects civilised and refined," with "the most savage and unpolished." As Nicholas Thomas has demonstrated, the ways in which a society regarded its females became in the eighteenth century a key ethnographic marker as to the place that nation had achieved on the scale of civilization in general.[41] In this case Percy compares China unflatteringly with the Iroquois peoples of North America (2.128–29n). Discussing the military strength of the Chinese, Percy reproduces material describing the use of blood-red war paint by generals "with the politic view of frightening their enemies." He finds support for this information from Anson's damning narrative of his time at Canton, in which the commodore had described how the Chinese arranged for a soldier of unusual size to parade on the parapets of their castles, battle-ax in hand, to intimidate the British who also suspected that the armor was fashioned from "glittering paper." Again, Percy's summary of Chinese military strength and preparedness for war is ominous: "these glittering and childish expedients are sufficient to convince us of the unwarlike turn of the Chinese, and at how low an ebb is their military prowess" (4.133n). Percy had earlier remarked, somewhat gratuitously and unpleasantly, that the Chinese "are the most cowardly people in the world" and that they "are much addicted to suicide" (1.129n). Later in the century Robert Clive would suggest that China might be annexed for the British Empire and Macartney would famously sum up Chinese preparedness for war as minimal. Although, at the time, few would have seriously contemplated Clive's expedient or thought it in anyway practicable, the military and colonial imperatives that were embedded in the new post-Macartney Romantic Sinology found antecedents and precedents in Percy's work.

PERCY ON THE CHINESE LANGUAGE

Percy's subsequent publication, the *Miscellaneous Pieces Relating to China* of 1762, is a two-volume collection of articles about China dealing with Chinese drama, Chinese landscape gardening, and the history of the Christian Church in China, taken chiefly from the Jesuit compilation

the *Lettres édifiantes & curieuses* (1702–58) and its redaction in the form
of Du Halde's *General History*, but read against the grain of its pro-
China accommodationist agenda. The work was a publication of the
research Percy had already undertaken for the *Hau Kiou Choann*. The
Miscellaneous Pieces is an important volume in mediating knowledge of
China to a British audience. It contains several translations, including a
version of a drama deriving from Zang Maoxun's landmark compilation
of Yuan dynasty song-dramas, *Yuanren baizhong qu* or *One Hundred
Yuan Plays* of 1615–16. The compilation features dramas that would be
translated by British sinologists in the early nineteenth century. Its most
famous drama for Europeans, Ji Junxiang's *Zhao shi guer* (*Sole Heir of
the Zhao Clan*) (included by Percy under the title "Little Orphan of the
House of Chao"), will be discussed in Chapter 8 of this volume. Percy
claimed he returned to Prémare's original French translation printed in
the *Déscription de la Chine* (1735). His volumes also contained a translation of Jean-Denis Attiret's influential "Description of the Emperor's
Gardens and Pleasure Houses near Peking" (discussed in Chapter 8),
as well as "Rules of Conduct by a *Chinese* Author, from the *French* of
P. Parrenin, Jesuit."

To this compendium, Percy provided his own introductory essay
as well as a dissertation on the Chinese language. His "Preface" argues
that though the Chinese "judgement and fancy" may now be held in
"low esteem," yet they still deserve respect for "their taste in gardening,
and knowledge of moral truths." His "Dissertation on Language and
Characters of the Chinese" in the first volume of the *Miscellaneous Pieces*
is notable for its criticism of the once current hypothesis that the Chinese
language was closely related to the primordial language of paradise, spoken by Adam and Eve; as Porter puts it, "here was a peculiar form of
writing that seemed to transcend the fatal transience and ambiguity of
Western vernaculars to convey the timeless essence of ideas and things in
themselves."[42] Related to this fantasy was the theory that Chinese writing
might be a means of conveying ideas ideogrammatically, without regard
to speech, and thus of potentially universal intelligibility, once the appropriate key was discovered to render them accessible. John Wilkins, John
Webb, Andreas Muller, and Leibniz had all speculated on the Chinese as
a potential source for a universal and rational language, and Jesuits such
as Prémare and Le Comte argued that the language also incorporated a
knowledge of Christian revelation in its forms since lost by the Chinese
themselves. Percy debunks all these linguistic notions, arguing that the
creation of the alphabet some time after that of hieroglyphic languages

such as Chinese and Egyptian is the real key to human linguistic progress, possibly even the result of divine intervention. Unfortunately, in his "Preface" to the *Miscellaneous Pieces* Percy gives credence to the mistaken claim by the natural philosopher and antiquarian John Tuberville Needham, published in the *Critical Review* for 1756, that he had identified Chinese characters on an Egyptian bust of Isis located in Turin, thus seeming to prove "beyond a doubt that the Chinese received them from the Egyptians" ("Preface," n.p.). Percy argues that the Chinese language, rather than being an Adamic or original language, is instead derived from the Egyptian hieroglyphs, "demolishing at once all the pretences of the Chinese to that vast antiquity, which has been want to stagger weak minds" and which is "utterly incompatible with the history of the Bible" ("Preface," n.p.). For Percy, China's non-alphabetic language is actually a primitive and savage invention, "by way of picture, or hieroglyphic" akin to the picture writing of the North American Indians (1.6–7). An alphabetical language is seen as essential to create a progressive society, and China has not yet progressed to this more sophisticated linguistic stage. Percy claims that the Chinese would greatly benefit from exchanging their language for an alphabetic one, even at the cost of losing most of their historic literature and culture. Thus, as Porter points out, by the third quarter of the eighteenth century the "degradation of what had once been the prince of languages had become commonplace."[43]

In an anticipation of Romantic or Wordsworthian notions of education, Percy criticizes the rote learning of the Chinese. He argues that they spend much of the most vigorous parts of their life learning the characters of their language, thus accounting for the slow progress that the sciences have made among them, a point that John Barrow would later exploit in his account of Macartney's embassy. More troublingly, Percy also suggests that the deficiencies he identifies in the spoken language of the Chinese may be due to a perceived and characteristic "deformity" of the Chinese mouth, an early foretaste of a nascent, nineteenth-century biological racism.[44] In the slightly later researches of William Jones, Sanskrit would begin to displace Chinese as a candidate for an original language, or at least the language closest to such *ur-sprache*, and with prestige as an ancient, legitimate, rational and potentially universal language. As Min comments, "the celebration of the native pagan ancestry of Britain required a new theory of culture that privileged a non-classical, but also a non-Chinese antiquity, defined precisely in terms not of cultural achievement but of a proto-Romantic notion of simplicity" so that "Percy's Chinese books present an image of China as Gothic England's cultural foil."[45] Percy's sinology thus represents a departure from the Jesuit consensus though using texts and information based upon it. Percy's Protestant and British suspicion of the French and Catholic would be sufficient to allow him suitable latitude to re-interpret Jesuit conclusions in the light of his own national and patriotic literary sensibility about China but he was still heavily dependent on the texts that had been transmitted to him for their scholarship as well as their editorial notions of canon formation. Despite their prestigious publication, Percy's Chinese texts sold modestly. Yet they would be avidly consulted by his successors who sought to obtain valuable information about China. His Chinese project constituted a geographical turning point at which English literature failed or refused to turn to the east of China for a new source of poetic images and literary forms, but his underlying disparagement of much of Chinese thought and culture would prove influential on later British Protestant missionary and travel writing such as that by John Barrow and Robert Morrison. Percy's work thus represents the difficult birth pangs of British Romantic Sinology and he can, with much justice, be called the first British sinologist.

CHAPTER 2

"A wonderful stateliness": William Jones, Joshua Marshman, and the Bengal School of Sinology

One of the key arguments of this study is that what emerges as a Romantic Sinology is no simple and homogenous British body of knowledge about China but a diverse group of ideas and texts about China in the process of becoming codified and hardened in the public mind by around the mid nineteenth century. Hence, like most bodies of thought this understanding of China is ambivalent and ridden with contradictions. Romantic Sinology may have achieved a consensus by the third decade or so of the nineteenth century, but it was a consensus originally based on the knowledge production of certain key geographical areas. It was, of course, still partially indebted to the knowledge constructed by Jesuits scholars and mediated to London through Enlightenment cities such as Paris and institutions such as the Royal Society in London, but it was increasingly informed by research carried out first in Bengal and then at Canton within the sphere of influence of the English East India Company. British Protestant missionaries and Company merchants, as well as diplomats and servants of government, often relying extensively on local Chinese scholarship and linguistic skills, largely created this knowledge. The knowledge produced in these several centers or contact zones was heavily inflected by the assumptions of those people producing it, places where it was produced, and the experiences of cultural negotiation and compromise they encountered. This study now moves from the "armchair" and textual Anglocentric sinology of Percy and the metropolis, to that of two Bengal orientalists working from very different sets of assumptions about China: William Jones and Joshua Marshman.

After Percy, the leading British figure to take a serious interest in China is William Jones, the celebrated orientalist and, from 1783, Judge of the Supreme Court at Calcutta (Kolkata).[1] Jones, like Thomas Percy, was a member of Samuel Johnson's famous Literary Club, founded by Sir Joshua Reynolds and also including within its membership Edmund Burke, Sir Joseph Banks, Adam Smith, Oliver Goldsmith, Charles Burney, and

George, Lord Macartney. All took a keen interest in colonial and Chinese affairs. The membership of the club was regarded as an intellectual aristocracy in Georgian England devoted to the ideals of rationality, morality, and the exchange of ideas, a discourse which framed knowledge about China.[2]

It is well known that Jones founded the Bengal Asiatic Society in 1783, the predecessor of the Royal Asiatic Society founded chiefly by George Thomas Staunton in 1823, both societies encompassing, sometimes uneasily, the academic study of matters Chinese within their remit. Jones also donated many of his Chinese books to the Royal Society, thus founding its collection in this area. However, though his writings on the languages and arts of India and Persia are familiar to most scholars of Romantic-period literature, his specific forays into Chinese studies are seldom commented on and have received little critical attention. Commentators refer often to his rather downbeat overall assessment of Chinese culture and thought from 1790 as if this were his considered and sole position on China:

> their letters if we may so call them, are merely symbols of ideas; their popular religion was imported from India in an age comparatively modern; and their philosophy seems yet in so rude a state, as hardly to deserve the appellation; they have no ancient monuments, from which their origin can be traced ... their sciences are wholly exotick; and their mechanical arts have nothing in them characteristic of a particular family.[3]

Yet Jones was also capable of a much more sophisticated and deeper engagement with Chinese culture than this unrepresentative summary would suggest. Both sinologists and scholars of Jones's writings seem to have been engaged in a conspiracy to minimize the importance of his Chinese work. The leading twentieth-century British sinologist, Arthur Waley, in 1946 unfairly claimed that Jones's Chinese studies "were not in themselves of any importance," and Garland Cannon, Jones's sympathetic biographer, judged that China "was simply outside his competence."[4] Jones mastered a series of Eastern languages including Hebrew, Persian, Turkish, and, famously, Sanskrit. His Persian and Sanskrit translations, as well as his own compositions, were extremely influential on Romantic-period writers. If Percy's Chinese studies were intimately connected to a form of Romanticism associated with the northern popular ballad, Jones's Chinese interests were just as closely involved with those other orientalist writings that inspired a different form of Romanticism in the orientalist lyrics and epics of Coleridge, Landor, Southey, and Shelley.

Jones was always interested in learning Chinese but never attained a full competence in the language. In 1767, aged twenty-one, while acting as a tutor to Lord Spencer's family, he began to learn the radicals of the Chinese language and in 1769 he wrote that he had begun its study.[5] Echoing Percy's fascination with the sheer antiquity of Chinese poetry, Jones states that he has been reading a "Chinese book with the help of a Latin translation, in which several pretty verses are quoted, which are said to have been writ 777 years before our Saviour or 2546 years ago, and are consequently the oldest pieces of poetry we know, except the Prophets and Homer."[6] Like Percy, Jones was intrigued by, and drawn to, Chinese writing. By 1770 he was reading the *Confucius Sinarum Philosophus*, composed of Latin translations of the *Daxue* (Great Learning), *Lunyu* (Analects), and *Zhonyong* (Doctrine of the Mean). In a letter of July 1770 to the Polish orientalist Charles Reviczky, Jones included a Latin translation of one of the odes from the *Shijing*. He describes how he marveled at the "venerable dignity" of Confucius's thoughts while reading the *Confucius Sinarum Philosophus* and how he managed to translate, or more accurately decipher, from an original copy of the *Shijing* in the Royal Library in Paris and then compare it with the Latin translation of the Belgian Jesuit, Philippe Couplet.

I took the manuscript in hand and after lengthy study was able to compare one ode with Couplet's version and even obtain some sort of breakdown of individual words or, rather, ideograms. So I am sending you this ode, literally translated. In spite of its brevity, it has a wonderful stateliness: each line has only four words in it. It follows that the diction is very often elliptical, which gives sublimity and obscurity at the same time. I have added a poetic version in which each verse is interpreted in the Confucian style ... You must be aware that that philosopher, whom I dare call the Chinese Plato, flourished some six hundred years before Christ; and he quotes this poem, as if in his own day it was very ancient in his time.[7]

Jones's admiration for what he sees as the "wonderful stateliness" of the Ode is more pronounced than anything in Percy's writings about Chinese poetry. Notably, Jones finds in the poetry both "obscurity" and "sublimity," key late eighteenth-century European aesthetic categories, invoked by Burke's *Enquiry concerning our Ideas of the Sublime and the Beautiful* (1757). He produced two versions of the Ode, one a literal translation, and the other a poetic version, roughly the same working method that he would employ with his other translations of Eastern poetry. He published the poetic version entitled "Ode Sinicae Antiquissima" in 1774.[8] Jones's method in translating Chinese poetry marks him out as someone moving beyond the role of the compiler and editor, reprinting, as Percy largely does, the translations of others, to someone who is genuinely engaged in a process of his own literary creation fueled by Chinese originals, however mediated. His Chinese poetry comes across as one of the few serious attempts to engage with the literature of China rather than with a formulaic and now unfashionable appropriation of a Europeanized rococo chinoiserie style. This is a true, if limited and hesitant, cross-cultural encounter not easily reducible to simple orientalist dismissal, an example of an "unexpected affinity" in Zhang Longxi's resonant phraseology. Jones's translations should be viewed more as a cultural than a linguistic activity. Percy's translations tended to "foreignize" his Chinese source texts, whereas Jones's more often domesticate them, finding, or at least attempting to find, a common ground between the two traditions. While both strategies in the context of the discourse of China facilitated the processes of British colonial policy (Jones was not in Bengal on holiday), Jones's would become the more usual mode of British Romantic Sinology.

The fact that later English-language translations of Chinese texts were very much the result of a largely unacknowledged process of British and Chinese co-authorship also complicates a straightforward orientalist reading of the translation process. Jones was keen to access the expertise of Chinese scholars but never had the native scholarly resources he needed. He tutored himself in Chinese with the aid of grammars in the Bodleian Library and the Royal Library of France, most likely Fourmont's *Grammatica Sinica* (1742). At some stage in his career we know that he also acquired a manuscript "Chinese and Latin" dictionary.[9] In his "Tenth Anniversary Discourse" of 1793, Jones claimed that the difficulty of learning Chinese had been "magnified beyond the truth" and that with the aid of a Fourmont's grammar and "a copious dictionary … in Chinese and Latin" anyone would be able to compare the works of Confucius with the aid of Couplet's Latin translations.[10] Easy for Jones to say this, as a linguist of genius; nevertheless, his point is to argue that China's famous linguistic alterity and incommensurability, the utter difference of its non-alphabetic language, is actually a myth, something that would become a leading tenet of Romantic Sinology.

Jones also sought out Chinese expertise. In 1771 he requests John Wilmot of 1771 to "enquire after a native of China, who is now in London." This young Chinese, a very rare visitor, may have been the well-known artist Chitqua or, much more likely, the Canton trader Huang Ya Dong or "Whang Atong," whom Jones had previously encountered at a dinner held by Sir Joshua Reynolds.[11] Such Chinese travelers in London were scarce and it is generally estimated that there were probably no more than hundred or so Chinese in Britain up until the 1860s.[12] Michael Keevak has correctly identified Huang with the "Whang-at-tong" named by the German natural historian J. F. Blumenbach, in his treatise of human variety of 1774. Commenting on his construction of a "Mongolian" variety of humanity, Blumenbach indicated:

Their heads are usually oval, their faces flat, their eyes narrow, drawn up towards the external corners, their noses small, and all their other peculiarities of this kind are well known from the numerous pictures of them, and from their China and pottery figures. Those Chinese whom Büttner saw at London were exactly of this kind, and so also was the great botanist Whang-at-tong *(the yellow man of the East)*, whose acquaintance was made there by Lichtenberg.[13]

"China and pottery figures" are here used as serious ethnographical data to determine human variety.

It appears, in some accounts, that Huang Ya Dong had been brought from Canton to Knole House in Kent in the early 1770s to act as a companion for Giovanna Baccerelli, a mistress of the third Duke of Dorset, John Frederick Sackville. Huang accompanied John Bradby Blake, an East India Company employee and school friend of the Duke's, with whom he also dined in company with Reynolds and Jones while in London. Blake was a naturalist who had brought back plants to Britain from Canton. He possibly selected young Huang as an appropriate companion because of his knowledge of Chinese botany. In a letter of February 18, 1775, probably authored by Reynolds, it is reported that Huang heard from the Chinese artist Chitqua of his favorable reception in England and therefore "determined to make the voyage likewise, partly from curiosity, and a desire to improve himself in science, and partly with a view of procuring some advantages in trade, in which he and his elder brother are engaged."[14] Huang, according to Jones, had by this time already passed his examinations in China and had some knowledge of the propagation and medicinal use of Chinese plants. It is reported that he advised the Duchess of Portland about her strawberry begonia, a plant used for medicinal purposes in China. Huang visited the Royal Society on January 12, 1775, and also discussed the Chinese process of manufacturing porcelain with Josiah Wedgwood around this time. What secrets Huang was able to pass to Wedgwood allowing him to produce his own porcelain, we do not as yet know. In June of that year Huang rearranged "the Chinese lexicon" and books in the library of St. John's College, Oxford.[15] He also explained the purpose of acupuncture to the physician Andrew Duncan.

Figure 1. *Portrait of Huang Ya Dong (Wang-Y-Tong) after Reynolds*, 1828 © Trustees of
the British Museum.

Reynolds painted the portrait of him in 1776 that now hangs at Knole
and a drawing, also said to be of him, by the artist George Dance the
younger, survives in the British Museum (Figure 1).[16] Huang appears to
have become the object of some notoriety and appeared in a satirical piece
by the Göttingen natural philosopher Georg Christoph Lichtenberg.[17]

Jones's essay "On the Second Classical Book of the Chinese" describes
how Huang was "allured from the pursuit of learning by a prospect of success in trade."[18] His career choice is evidence that the commonly argued
Chinese dismissal of the merchant profession was in practice something
of a scholarly red herring. In 1784 Jones renewed his friendship with
Huang, via John Henry Cox at Canton, in an attempt to create his new
research network exchanging knowledge about Chinese culture between
Canton and Calcutta. Huang wrote back to Jones recalling his pleasure at

dining with him in company with Reynolds and Blake and emphasizing that he would always "remember the kindness of my friends in England." Huang enclosed original Chinese copies of the Confucian text on education, the *Daxue*, and the *Shijing* for Jones to study, and he promised to procure other works for him as requested. By 1790 Jones also possessed an original Chinese copy of the *Lunyu* as well as a verbal translation that he judged "sufficiently authentick" for his purposes.[19] The actual translator of the *Lunyu* into English is not named, but this volume may well have been the very first direct translation into English from Chinese of any Confucian text, though regrettably it was not worked up for publication and was not, as far as we know, available for Marshman to use for his 1809 Serampore translation. Jones suggested that Huang might be able to help him in his cherished ambition by providing a translation of the *Shijing*, but the busy merchant declined, in probably the first letter written and published in formal English by a Chinese, on the grounds that this was far too ambitious a project for him to reconcile with his extensive business commitments:

The Chinese book, Shi King, that contains three hundred Poems with remarks thereon, and the work of Con-fu-tsu, and his grandson the Tai Ho [*Daxue*], I beg you will accept; but to translate the work into English will require a great deal of time; perhaps three or four years; and I am so much engaged in business, that I hope you will excuse my not undertaking it.[20]

Huang, however, offered to bring over a number of Chinese artists to Bengal, presumably for commercial purposes. Jones believed that Huang might be encouraged to visit India with some of his fellow Chinese and "considerable advantage ... might be reaped from the knowledge of such emigrants."[21] The Company, however, was not willing to fund this venture. Huang, sadly, appears to have been a "silent traveller" and to have left no written account of his time in London.

John Henry Cox, who acted as a go-between for Jones and Huang, was the son and agent of James Cox, famous manufacturer of clocks, watches, mechanical toys, and automata for the lucrative Chinese market or "sing-song" trade. James Cox had, for example, manufactured an automaton of a chariot pushed by a Chinese man as a gift for the Qianlong emperor. He also had a well-known museum in London displaying his toys.[22] Automata were one of the few European manufactures that the Chinese highly prized and desired, and the trade in them was considerable. Cox, who had voyaged to Canton in 1781 allegedly for reasons of health, formed the firm of private traders Cox & Beale, a forerunner of the major opium-trading firm of Jardine and Matheson.[23] Cox's timepieces were in heavy demand at Canton, where they were sold to the Chinese and copied by local Chinese craftsmen. In February 1785 Jones wrote to Charles Grant at Bengal to inform him had that he received a letter from "Mr Cox of Canton with a present of Chinese drawings ... He ought to be a member of our society, and would be a valuable correspondent."[24] In 1787 he again wrote to Cox, thanking him for originals of a number of "Chinese edicts" and also for his efforts in attempting to locate a translation of parts of the *Shijing*. Jones speculates that, like the Hindu Brahmins, the Chinese are esoteric and "make a mystery" of their ancient literature. He then suggests to Cox the possibility that a mandarin could be found at Canton who would dictate "a literal translation of the 300 short Odes in the Shee-king to an Interpreter" and who "for a good fee, would write the version in some European language."[25] Disappointingly, Jones reported in 1790 that Cox had informed him that "none of the Chinese, to whom he has access, possess leisure and perseverance enough" for such a major translation.[26] Jones remained keen to visit China throughout his life.[27] There is thus a process of cultural transmission and encounter occurring involving the orientalist Jones, the Chinese merchant and naturalist Huang Ya Dong, and the British private trader, all bound up in a nexus involving the global flows of people, ideas, commerce, and commodities, be they "sing-songs," tea shipments, or commissioned translations.

This potential collaboration of Jones, Huang, and Cox never got off the ground. Sadly, Jones never translated, either himself or by proxy, the *Shijing* and he remained frustrated that, although geographically so close to China, he never managed to get there. What impact a poetic translation by Jones of the *Shijing* might have had on British Romantic writing remains a matter for speculation, another tantalizing "might-have-been" in the story of this cultural encounter. Possibly, Jones's lack of any native Chinese assistance was crucial to his failure to establish himself as a major sinologist. All the major British figures that were to be involved in the study of China benefited quite extensively from Chinese help and, when deprived of such assistance, tended to abandon their translation studies altogether.

Jones managed to compose two important, though brief, early works of British sinology: his "On the Second Book of the Chinese" and his "Seventh Anniversary Discourse, on the Chinese," both written in 1790, almost thirty years after Percy's texts were published. "On the Second Book of the Chinese" discusses the *Shijing*. Jones argues forcefully that the proximity of China to British territories in India must make "that most ancient and wonderful Empire" an object of urgent attention. The

Chinese language is "so ancient and so wonderfully composed," boasting an abundance of books "abounding in useful, as well as agreeable, knowledge." As with his Hindu studies, Jones is especially keen to obtain translations of Chinese "approved *law tracts*" so he can return with this knowledge to Europe, "with distinct ideas, drawn from the fountainhead, of the wisest *Asiatick* nation." Europe, however, would have to wait until George Thomas Staunton's 1810 translation of the Qing legal code for this information. Jones gives a by now familiar description of the ideogrammatic nature of the Chinese language derived from a so far unidentified Chinese, "Li Tang Pang," and the Five Classic Books, concentrating especially on the *Shijing* which

contains *three hundred* Odes, or short Poems, in praise of ancient sovereigns and legislators, or descriptive of ancient manners, and recommending an imitation of them in the discharge of all publick and domestick duties: they abound in wise maxims, and excellent precepts, their whole doctrine, according to *Cun-fu-tsu*, in the LUNYU or *Moral Discourses*, being reducible to this grand rule, that we should not even entertain a thought of any thing base or culpable.[28]

Jones imports into the *Shijing* aesthetic notions of the Miltonic sublime, claiming that some parts of the poems are highly metaphorical while "the brevity of other parts renders them obscure; though many think even this obscurity sublime and venerable, like that of ancient cloysters and temples, '*Shedding*', as MILTON expresses it, *a dim religious light*."[29] He prints his translations of three fragments of Chinese poetry. In particular, he gives a translation of Ode 55, "In Praise of Duke Wei of Wei," that Couplet had translated into Latin in his version of the *Daxue*.[30] Jones produces a copy, inaccurately, of the original Chinese from the *Shijing* sent to him by Huang along with both a literal and a poetical version of the Ode. Jones's "verbal" translation from Couplet's Latin, enhanced by his study of Chinese, runs as follows:

> Behold yon reach of *the river Ki;*
> Its green reeds how luxuriant! how luxuriant!
> Thus is our Prince adorned with virtues;
> As a carver, as a filer, of ivory,
> As a cutter, as a polisher, of gems.
> O how elate and sagacious! O how dauntless and composed!
> How worthy of fame! How worthy of reverence!
> We have a Prince adorned with virtues,
> Whom to the end of *time* we can not forget.

Jones numbers each Chinese character in superscript above the lines of poetry. Fan judges this to be a fair version of the original Chinese and a great improvement on Percy's earlier rendition. Jones then presents his "domesticating" poetical paraphrase of the ode in six stanzas, with alternate rhyming couplets in the manner of classical eighteenth-century versification.

> Behold, where yon riv'let glides
>   Along the laughing dale;
> Light reeds bedeck its verdant sides,
>   And frolick in the gale:
>
> So shines our Prince! In bright array
>   The virtues round him wait;
> And sweetly smil'd th'auspicious day,
>   That rais'd Him o'er our State.
>
> As pliant hands in shapes refin'd
>   Rich iv'ry carve and smoothe,
> His Laws thus mould each ductile mind,
>   And every passion soothe.
>
> As gems are taught by patient art
>   In sparkling ranks to beam,
> With Manners thus he forms the heart,
>   And spreads a gen'ral gleam.
>
> What soft, yet awful, dignity!
>   What meek, yet manly grace!
> What sweetness dances in his eye,
>   And blossoms in his face!
>
> So shines our Prince! A sky-born crowd
>   Of Virtues round him blaze:
> Ne'er shall Oblivion's murky cloud
>   Obscure his deathless praise.

With this bold and innovative strategy, the moral severity and gravity of the original is transformed into an eighteenth-century pastoral reflecting a familiar hero of sensibility. The diction of the poem is also conventional, the "riv'let" "glides," the dale is "laughing," and the reeds "frolick" in the gales. The central metaphors of the original survive but are applied not to the self-cultivation of the prince, which is the point of the quotation in the *Daxue*, but to the prince's cultivation of his people. Jones's Chinese prince, meek yet manly, with "sweetness" dancing in his eye and "blossoms on his face," recalls more Henry Mackenzie's sentimental hero Harley than an ancient Chinese ruler. The conventional poetic diction and labored similes here convey little of the literal translation. In the process of translation, the economy and sparsity or *kenosis* of the original is evacuated in favor of a lyrical ease, a mode that would become characteristic of Romantic Sinology and a departure from Percy's practice.

Jones includes two more examples of how he can freely versify the original Chinese. He presents a version of Ode 6 from Couplet's translation of the *Daxue*:

> The peach-tree, how fair! how graceful!
> Its leaves, how blooming! how pleasant!
> Such is a bride, when she enters her bridegroom's house,
> And pays due attention to her family.

Here the Confucian imperative to order one's household prior to ordering the state in the original is transformed by Jones as:

> Gay child of Spring, the garden's queen,
> > Yon peach-tree charms the roving sight:
> Its fragrant leaves how richly green!
> > Its blossoms how divinely bright!
>
> So softly smiles the blooming bride
> > By love and conscious Virtue led
> O'er her new mansion to preside,
> > And placid joys around her spread.[31]

Again, eighteenth-century diction and manner obscure the moral point of the ode. The softly smiling "blooming bride" led by love and conscious virtue will preside over her home, spreading the feminine virtues and joys of domestic placidity. John Barrow, writing from a later, more militant perspective, would claim that Jones's translation substantially improved the original: "the most barren subject, under his elegant pen, becomes replete with beauties."[32] Yet from such translations Jones believes that the *Shijing* could form a model for European writing, in the same way as his Persian and Sanskrit translations. Ancient Chinese poetry is, for Jones, both beautiful yet didactic and moral, capable of both agreeable praise and the sublime of condemnation. The words "Renew thyself daily" were inscribed on the washing basin of the Tang emperor, and the Qianlong emperor famously had his verses in praise of tea inscribed on a set of porcelain cups. The practice of engraving and painting moral sentences on vessels in constant use is a facet of Jones's Chinese aesthetic.

Jones concludes his brief foray into the Chinese classical canon by restating his ambition to procure a full translation of the poetry of the *Shijing*. Yet his free translations remain disappointing; they evade the economy

and power of the original poetry, present more strongly in his verbal ren-
derings, in favor of a rather conventional eighteenth-century verse that
almost seems to efface its Chinese text. It's hard to imagine that the full
translation of the *Shijing* that Jones promised would have re-energized
Romantic poetry in the same way as his translations from the Hindu and
Persian. As Fan puts it, "unlike the Persian *Song of Hafiz*, Jones's para-
phrases from the *Shijing* are singularly free from the 'Romantic' glamour,
les appels de l'Orient. And much of the finesse and unobtrusive perfection
of form are lost in a mass of conventional verbiage."[33] Arguably, the West
would have to wait for another hundred years or so until Pound's Imagist
aesthetic appeared for there to be a poetics appropriate to provide a sympathetic translation of the form of the Odes of the *Shijing* and an awareness of the poetic potential of the Chinese character itself.[34]

Jones's second significant contribution to British sinology was his
"Seventh Anniversary Discourse" on China delivered to the Asiatick
Society on February 25, 1790. The focus of this heavily speculative discussion of China was less literary and more ethnological as Jones attempted
to answer questions about who the Chinese were and where they had
originated. Cranmer-Byng claimed that this essay shows how Jones's
"muddled" knowledge of China was derived "second or third hand from
unreliable sources."[35] The key issue from the perspective of this study
remains less the accuracy or otherwise of what Jones reports but the kinds
of knowledge that are culturally transmitted to Britain and the purposes
they are put to serve. Jones describes the vastness of China, seeing in its
power and strength in the East a cross-cultural parallel to Britain in the
West, it is "a celebrated and imperial land, bearing in arts and in arms,
in advantage of situation but not felicity of government, a pre-eminence
among Eastern kingdoms *analogous to that of Britain among the nations
of the west*" (my italics). Jones demonstrates again the ambivalence that
characterizes British writing on China. The empire is enormous and varied, with a substantial array of climates, and has been subject to widely
differing estimations between those who have lauded the nation as "the
oldest and wisest, as the most learned and most ingenious, of nations,"
and others who have "condemned their government as abominable, and
arraigned their manners as inhuman, without allowing them an element
of science, or a single art, for which they have not been indebted to some
more ancient and more civilized race of men."[36]

Jones surveys the various hypotheses about the Chinese, as an original race, as a Semitic race, as a people deriving from the "Tartars," or
as descended from the Hindu people. He inclines to the view, held by

the Brahmins, that it is probable that the Chinese descended from the
"Indian race."[37] He is not so much concerned with the physical or bodily characteristics of people but more with cultural differences, such as
language and belief. His understanding of race relates primarily to lineal
descent and culture rather than to physical typology, and his observation that Chinese ancient culture and ceremonies have an "apparent affinity with some parts of the oldest *Indian* worship" is crucial. Rather than
being the oldest of Eastern civilizations, Jones claims that Chinese culture is secondary; the Chinese were originally Hindus of the "*Cshatriya*,
[Kshatriya] or military class," who moved to Bengal and afterwards to
China, forgetting "the rites and religion of their ancestors." He bases this
flimsy hypothesis on a statement made to this effect in the Hindu *Laws
of Manu* or *Manava Dharma Shastra*, which he translated into English in
1794, and its apparent confirmation by the Brahmins he knew. For Jones,
literature and religion seem to prove that "the whole nation descended
from the *Chínas* of MENU, and, mixing with the Tartars, by whom the
plains of Honan and the more southern provinces were thinly inhabited,
formed by degrees the race of men, whom we now see in possession of the
noblest empire in *Asia*." Jones here lays the foundations for a discipline
of comparative religion that, however spuriously applied in this instance,
would prove highly influential. Chinese literature and religion appear to
confirm his supposition. Jones identifies, conventionally, the Buddha of
the Hindus with the Chinese "Foe," but he also makes a serious error,
unforgivable in the eyes of later sinologists, of identifying this "Foe" with
"the great progenitor of the Chinese … FO-HI." The Chinese also have
ceremonies and rituals that have an affinity with the older parts of Indian
worship, believing in "the agency of genii or tutelary spirits, presiding
over the stars and the clouds, over lakes and rivers," which is an imperfect
echo of the religion of Manu.[38]

It is certainly possible that had Jones had the time and material
resources to develop further his Chinese studies he might have emerged
as *the* key source and champion of Confucian thinking for the Romantic
period. The polemical Protestant Christian baggage that Percy and his
successors carried with them did not so heavily weigh down Jones and the
"venerable dignity" of Confucian philosophy was attractive to his classicizing mindset. For Jones, Confucius was "the Chinese Plato."[39] He had
read the *Confucius Sinarum Philosophus* and possessed originals of several Confucian texts, including the *Shijing* and the *Lunyu*, supplied by
his friends at Canton, Huang Ya Dong and James Henry Cox.[40] Even
as a young tutor, back in 1770, Jones had been sufficiently impressed by

the educational arguments and strategy of the *Daxue* to adopt its provisions for his own emerging educational ideas as set forth in his fascinating "Tract of Education."[41] He writes:

A celebrated Eastern philosopher begins his first dissertation with the following period. The perfect education of a great man, consists in three points: in cultivating and improving his understanding; in assisting and reforming his countrymen; and in procuring to himself the chief good, or a fixed and unalterable habit of virtue.[42]

Jones more or less arrives at the gist of Confucius's thinking here, though he slightly misinterprets the first Confucian imperative that relates to self-renovation through the cultivation of virtue rather than of the understanding.[43] Jones claims that the primary purpose of education should lie in "fixing the good of ourselves and our fellow creatures," and he considers the cultivation of our understanding and the acquisition of knowledge" as secondary purposes. Before it is possible to understand the differences between right and wrong, the "mind must be enlightened by an improvement of our natural reason."[44] The presence of Confucian pedagogy in Jones's scheme is further evidence that such knowledge in the period had a global circulation and context; as Michael Franklin aptly puts it, "the wisdom of China, imported to Europe by a Belgian Jesuit, is reapplied in Calcutta by a half-Welsh orientalist for the benefit of 'Company hands'; it is within their hands to enrich the West, and indeed India, by their researches."[45]

Jones's Chinese studies mark an important stage in the processes of knowledge formation about China. It is true that his expertise penetrated only a little further than deciphering Chinese characters, but his knowledge of Confucian writing does engage with Chinese scholarship at Canton, through his contacts Huang and Cox. Had Jones established himself as an authority on China, the emerging British reading of China might well have been very different. Although sharing the marked ambivalence towards the empire and its culture of the Anglican Percy, the deistic Jones's version of China was nevertheless, in the main, an extremely positive one. His estimation of Confucian thought was high. His treatise "On the Second Classical Book of the Chinese" and his "Seventh Anniversary Discourse" were important contributions to the emerging discipline of sinology in Britain, and Jones was certainly willing to accept Confucian philosophy and Chinese literature on exactly equal terms with that of Socrates, Plato, and Aristotle. Jones's important international attempts to construct a research network between Canton and Calcutta were, however, unsuccessful. After his death, Bengal and Canton would become rival centers of knowledge construction about China, a process inflamed by the personal and interdenominational rivalry between Joshua Marshman and his "gentlemen at Serampore," and Robert Morrison and his Anglo-Chinese College.

JOSHUA MARSHMAN'S SERAMPORE SCHOOL OF SINOLOGY

British knowledge about China was certainly growing in the late eighteenth century, fueled by personal, professional, and family contacts with Company trade at Canton. Its full extent is not known but it was probably much more substantial than we have hitherto acknowledged. To take one example, the Scottish physician James Lind visited Canton in 1766 as a surgeon on an East Indiaman, and created a substantial and notable collection of Eastern curiosities that were, according to Fanny Burney, chiefly Chinese. Burney saw the collection when she visited Lind with her brother Charles, who was fascinated by Chinese music and about which he becomes a noted British expert. In a letter of December 19, 1785, Burney tells how Lind's collection contains "a book of the whole process of preparing silk, described in prints," and also "a curious book representing every part of a Chinese monastery, – building, utensils, gods, priests, and idols; it is very neatly and most elaborately executed, and the colours are uncommonly vivid."[46] Joseph Banks, probably with Lind's Chinese knowledge and experiences in mind, hoped that he would accompany the Macartney embassy to China in 1792–94, acting as its dedicated naturalist, as he himself had famously done on Cook's first voyage to the South Seas. However, Lind effectively priced himself out of the job by demanding too high a fee for his services. Lind was probably one of a substantial number of Britons who maintained a serious but amateur or dilettante interest in China, often through personal or family connections with the Company at Canton.

Jones's Bengal, however, remained the key site for the production of British knowledge about China until the second decade of the nineteenth century. At Danish-controlled Serampore, just a few miles north of Calcutta, the Baptist missionary Joshua Marshman published a Chinese grammar in 1814 and translations of two of the Confucian Four Books, the *Lunyu* and the *Daxue* (or *Lun-gnee* and *Ta Hyoh* in his romanization), in 1809 and 1814 respectively. Marshman is the first of a new breed of ethnographers and linguists in that his role was formally that of a Christian missionary. With Marshman and his colleagues this important strand, possibly the dominant one, in British sinology begins. Throughout the nineteenth century, it is fair to say, the leading British experts on China, from Morrison to Legge were, with a few exceptions, missionaries. As Lydia Liu has noted, Christian missionaries were often "the self-appointed pioneers" of the processes of "cultural translation" in which the translator "spreads the gospel" of the "universalizing tendencies of modernity," and as such this activity and its resulting scholarship demands very close scrutiny in the context of China.[47] Marshman was one of the first of that missionary group to translate this message to Southeast Asia, though I am more concerned here with his part in the exchange of ideas from China to Britain rather than his major project, the translation of the Bible into Chinese, achieved in 1822. Marshman arrived at Serampore in 1799 to support the first Baptist missionary to India, William Carey.[48] Marshman and Carey to some extent, albeit briefly, realized Jones's ambition to create a center of learning for studies of China in Bengal. In Latour's terms, Marshman established a "center of calculation" at Serampore which would become connected in a network of knowledge formation and production about China.[49]

The very first appointment of a professor of Chinese to give instruction to British students occurred neither in London nor in Canton but at the East India Company's Fort William College in Calcutta, Bengal.[50] Studies of the Chinese language began there in 1805, motivated by the enthusiasm of the missionaries who had established their presence in Bengal. The two people chiefly concerned with China were the Baptist missionary Marshman, and Claudius Buchanan, an East India Company chaplain at Fort William College. Buchanan engaged the services of Johannes Lasser, an Armenian Christian, born in Macao. Lasser, according to Buchanan, had been taught Mandarin as a child and had been employed by the Portuguese to check and correct their official correspondence with the court at Beijing. He arrived in Bengal in 1804 on an unsuccessful trading mission with his father. Lasser was willing to be employed as a Chinese teacher and translator at Fort William and, subsequently (1807 or 1808), at the Baptist Missionary establishment at Serampore.

Serampore, on the banks of the River Hooghly, had been selected as a site for the mission as it was a Danish settlement north of Calcutta, thus evading the Company's prohibition on missionary activity in its territories. Marshman had already translated the Bible into Bengali and Sanskrit by 1806 and afterwards turned his attention to Chinese. What prompted his move into Chinese studies is not known, though Elmer Cutts speculated that the study of Chinese in Bengal might have been related to the prospect of a second embassy to China after that of Macartney. Such an embassy was already being touted in 1804–5, utilizing the skills and abilities of George Thomas Staunton, recently returned to Canton, and John Barrow was keen that the next attempt to negotiate with the imperial court should not rely entirely on the linguistic skills of French and Portuguese Catholics through the medium of Latin.[51] The leader of the Baptist Mission, William Carey, was not able to undertake the study of Chinese so this task fell instead to Marshman and his sons, John Clark and Benjamin Wickes Marshman, and Carey's son, Jabez. A press was also established at Serampore that printed works in Mandarin, employing for the first time anywhere in the world the use of moveable type to print Chinese.

The Catholic missionaries had not translated the scriptures into Chinese for public dissemination, being resistant to the fundamental Protestant stress on the transmission of the word of God in the vernacular. The Protestant missionaries would repudiate the Jesuit attempt to accommodate Christianity with Confucian thinking. Marshman published at the Serampore mission press a series of works on Chinese texts and language: the *Dissertation on the Sounds of the Chinese Language* (1810), *Elements of a Chinese Grammar* (1814), *Dissertation on the Chinese Characters*, and *Clavis Sinica* (1814). A single volume of the *Elements* was published in 1814. Both Cutts and, more recently, Hillemann have pointed to the strategic and political nature of Marshman's work for the British. Marshman was exploiting the threat faced by the East India Company from Chinese forts on the Tibetan border, and certainly stressing that the study of Chinese would aid studies of Sanskrit.[52] Although the Company disliked missionary activities in Bengal, which it regarded as troublesome and potentially dangerous, Governor General Lord Minto was willing to encourage and sponsor financially Marshman and Lasser's Chinese works.

Marshman's translation of the Confucian Lunyu of 1809 adopts a suitably anti-Gallic stance, bemoaning the fact that "it is to our French neighbours, we have been hitherto indebted for almost every effort to elucidate the language and literature of China."[53] In his Letter to Minto, Marshman admitted that, as a first attempt, his work had many imperfections; nevertheless, it was very important that the effort should be made. The translation would "convey some idea of Chinese manners" but would mainly introduce readers to the Chinese language as a means for "the ultimate introduction among them of those discoveries in science which so eminently distinguish the Western world—and, above all, of the Holy Scriptures in their purity and essence" (xxxiv). John Clark Marshman later suggested that this translation of Confucius was projected simply as a means to provide funds for the main objective of the translation of the Bible into Chinese, as the Company would not support the latter but would look with favor on the former as a means of acquiring valuable knowledge about China and its language. With Minto's political backing, "the subscription list of Confucius contained the name of every gentleman of influence in Calcutta," obtaining £2300.[54] While Marshman and the Baptist missionaries were ultimately most keen to translate the scriptures into Chinese for the purposes of conversion, their works on language and grammar were clearly of significant value to the Company. Its support for Marshman's Chinese studies would be dropped when Minto left the post of Governor General in 1813. From thence onwards Morrison's and Milne's Anglo-Chinese College would establish itself at Malacca as the key British institution for Chinese studies.[55]

Marshman went on to publish his Chinese version of Matthew's Gospel in 1810 and the first full translation of the Bible into Chinese in 1822 (one year before Morrison). This Chinese Bible was the work of Marshman and his sons, Lasser, and a number of "Chinese assistants," the chief of whom has been identified by Lydia Liu as Ya Meng or Aman. Ya Meng, the son of a Chinese father and Bangladeshi mother, had been born and raised as a Christian at Serampore and would later achieve historical importance as one of the four who made up Commissioner Lin Zexu's translation team, employed to translate English works during the opium crisis at Canton.[56] Not a great deal is known about him as yet, but, like Huang and Chitqua, he was another product of the global process of diaspora and intercultural contact alternative to the processes of the organic nation state.[57] Ya Meng must have been a natural and gifted linguist capable of moving between the worlds of Bengal and Canton. How much of Ya Meng's work found its way into the Marshman team's translations is not known, though it was probably quite a considerable amount. The extent to which he was either Marshman and Lasser's co-author or simply a mere contributor remains hidden from history. Subsequently, the extent to which his experiences of working with and for Marshman and the missionaries at Serampore impacted on his work for Lin – the commissioner charged to extirpate the opium trade in 1839, triggering the first Opium War – also remains a tantalizing unknown. Nevertheless, it is clear that the processes of the cultural transmission of the Bible into Chinese and Confucius into English that Marshman oversaw were not things that can be reduced to easy orientalist binaries or translation theories of source and host texts. It was in this case, as so often, that Chinese expertise was enabling the production of the "target texts" of Romantic Sinology.

In his *Elements of Chinese Grammar* of 1814, Marshman indicated the difficulties of translating Confucius's *Analects*. He claims that, at that time, he had no Chinese dictionary or vocabulary in either Latin or English and no existing translation of Chinese into "any language." He adds that Lasser, though a fluent speaker and reader of Chinese, knew "little more of English than he himself knew of Chinese."[58] It was not until three months after the publication of the translation that Marshman admits to having encountered his first Latin–Chinese dictionary. Although he laments somewhat understatedly that this dictionary would have saved him a great deal of trouble, Marshman believes that without it he was "compelled to form his own judgment of the nature of the language" and was not led "to acquiesce implicitly in their ideas, and to tread precisely in their track" (i–ii). Subsequent to the publication of his translation of the *Lunyu*, Marshman encountered the Augustinian missionary Father Juan Antonio Rodriguez, who had worked for the East India Company from 1805 to 1810 as an interpreter and teacher at Canton. Rodriguez was an important, though seldom acknowledged, figure in the development of British sinology, enabling Chinese studies both in Serampore and in Canton. Rodriguez, hostile to the Portuguese Jesuits at Macao, allied with the British when they briefly occupied Macao in 1802. He gave their Protestant rivals his enormously valuable manuscript Latin–Chinese dictionary. In 1810 another important figure in the development of Romantic Sinology, the traveler Thomas Manning, along with his personal Chinese tutor, also visited Serapore and was able to assist Marshman.[59] Manning's encounter with China and Tibet will be discussed in Chapter 6 of this volume.

In his group's Confucius translation, Marshman claims that he was also unaware of the previous Jesuit translations that had so profoundly influenced Enlightenment thinking, only finding out about these when a copy of Du Halde's *General History* was given to him after he had begun his task (xxxvii). If this account is to be believed, Marshman was singularly ill-equipped to embark on a translation of this crucial text. However, given the bitter and acrimonious debate and allegations of mutual plagiarism which later erupted between the LMS missionaries, Morrison and Milne, and himself, Marshman's claims about his lack of scholarly tools and assistance and Lasser's poor English need to be judged with great caution, but it is clear that the work of his international team of British, Armenian, and Chinese collaborators constituted a crucially important element in the emergence of British Romantic Sinology.[60]

MARSHMAN'S PROTESTANT CONFUCIANISM

In 1809 Marshman published his *The Works of Confucius; containing the original text, with a translation.* This volume contained the first published translation into English of the *Lunyu* (though only the first ten books). This volume was described as the first of a five-volume set, although it was the only one in the projected series ever to be published. As far as is known this is only the second published direct translation of a Chinese text into English after Percy's *Hau Kiou Choann* in 1761. Marshman's later *Elements of Chinese Grammar* of 1814 also contained a complete translation of the *Daxue* or "Ta-Hyoy" into English accomplished by Marshman's son, James Clark Marshman, Lasser, Ya Meng, and other assistants; this was a truly international collaboration.

The volume runs to some 740 pages. It prints in large woodblock type the Chinese characters, followed by a literal translation below from the classical Chinese, and below that prints a more extensive prose commentary on the text that claims to be "a strict translation from the Chinese" of the influential commentary by the great thirteenth-century neo-Confucian, Zhu Xi, supplemented by that of Cheng Yi and others (xxxiii, 2).[61] This is apparent in the comment Marshman affixes to the first sentence of the *Lunyu* which is rendered as "[t]he dispositions of men are by nature virtuous; but some make a more speedy advance in virtue while others advance more slowly" (2). It is generally Zhu's commentary that is printed. Zhu had notably denied that the Confucian "Supreme Ultimate" (*tiaiji*) was a personal God and instead placed great stress on the goodness of humanity, a view that became the orthodoxy from the Song dynasty onwards. With their access to both older and more recent commentaries, Marshman's team were thus probably closer to more recent developments in Qing Confucian scholarship than those who relied solely on the older Riccian-inspired translations of Couplet and others.[62] Again, the proximity to Canton and the presence of a significant Chinese diaspora in the region significantly enabled British sinology.[63] Generally, eighteenth-century Qing Confucian scholarship had little investment in more esoteric cosmological speculations and stressed instead individual wisdom, practical politics or statecraft (*jingshi*), and substantive learning (*shixue*).[64] A fourth level of comment supplied by Marshman's team is made up by a generally technical set of remarks on the Chinese characters. By printing the Chinese characters, Marshman exposed his translation to, in the rather stern judgment of Legge's biographer, Lauren Pfister, "the criticisms it rightly deserved."[65] Marshman's translation is a crude and inaccurate one, but while that may be a reason for it to be downplayed by later sinologists, it does not detract from its importance to this study as a key cultural document and a kind of Romantic text in itself. Again, it is the process of cultural transmission and the exchange of ideas that is crucial.

Often the sense of the translated text is lost as when, for instance, Marshman translates aphorism 2.3 as "Chee says, Lead the people to virtue by right government; regulate them, even by punishment: preserve the people from shame," which appears to be a plea for firm government and popular restraint (75). The more usual sense of the sentiment, however, can be seen in D. C. Lau's modern rendition,

> The Master said, "Guide them by edicts, keep them in line with punishments, and the common people will stay out of trouble but will have no sense of shame. Guide them by virtue, keep them in line with the rites, and they will, besides having a sense of shame reform themselves.[66]

Thus it is claimed that it is the example of a benevolent government that will lead to popular reformation, rather than the more Hobbesian defense of coercive authority. Marshman's translation does not present a very clear line on Confucius. It begins with a standard and complimentary "Life of Confucius," taken from an unattributed Chinese source and presenting Confucius as an eminently virtuous, able, and diligent man with a gift for administration, as well as an account of the five Confucian classic texts and the Four Books. When summarizing the scope of the *Yijing*, Marshman describes the book's use of trigrams "or enigmatic lines of Fo-hi" and what was believed to be Confucius's commentary on them. He believes these trigrams preceded the invention of Chinese characters and are a "first attempt to express in writing ideas relative to heaven, earth, man &c." The gloss by Confucius, however, forms the largest and "most intelligible part of the work." Marshman does not here introduce us to speculative Confucian cosmology but adds his rather whimsical comment that one of his Chinese assistants understands it "but the only idea he affixes to it is, that by studying it persons may be able to detect thieves, recover stolen goods, &c. &c" (xiv–xv). Marshman's rather odd deference to his Chinese assistant, repeated elsewhere in the edition, would provoke the scorn of John Barrow in the *Quarterly Review*.

Turning to the Confucian Four Books, Marshman sums up the *Daxue* as a manual for rulers whom it instructs on how to govern others by first learning to govern themselves, "subduing their own passions and restoring reason to its pristine authority in the soul." He argues that the *Zhongyong* counsels moderation, describing the "middle way, or the due government rather than extirpation, of the passions, as the way by which a man may attain to perfection in virtue, and arrive at the summit of happiness" (xx). He describes the *Lunyu* as consisting chiefly of sayings relating to social ethics and behavior, so much so that the volume might be termed as the "life and sayings of the Chinese sage." Marshman claims that the times of Confucius constituted the most memorable age in Chinese literature after which little advancement occurred, rendering the present-day Chinese the "mere imitators of ancient models" (xxii). Though inferior to the Greek philosophers in scope and splendor, the Chinese sages are actually superior in terms of the practical and social focus of their morality. Marshman's text is oddly reticent in terms of its value judgments on Confucius. Like the Jesuits, he is keen to harmonize Chinese chronologies with that of the Bible, but probably more with a view to confirming the veracity of the scriptural account than of denying the falsity of the Chinese. He argues that if allowed the "utmost extent of antiquity which they themselves claim," the Chinese chronology "scarcely clashes at all with the Chronology of the world given in the Sacred Scriptures" (xxxiii).

Marshman's text presents his readership with a sympathetic view of Confucian thinking. He demonstrates how filial piety and the social relationships are central to this philosophy, which has as its basis the key notion of virtue or benevolence (*ren*). This occupies a key position in Confucian ethics but it is difficult to find an English word to do it justice, "goodness rectitude of mind, benevolence, seem, each of them in different places, best adapted to express its meaning; but perhaps virtue in the widest sense, comes nearest to the idea in general" (17). Marshman emphasizes that the Confucian notion of the *junzi*, which he translates as "honorable man" rather than "Gentleman," refers to "conduct rather than birth" (10). He also seems to grasp that the Confucian idea of *li*, sometimes translated as "propriety," relates to "reason, equity, to rule according to law" (51). Similarly, the doctrine of the mean is stressed in Marshman's note to Aphorism 3.16 as "exhorting men to … be careful lest their virtues should lose their nature, by being carried beyond due bounds" (177). Marshman's text thus presents us with a theistic, rationalist, and moralizing Confucius. A translation such as that of Aphorism 4.12 – "Chee says, He who is attached to his own profit, and acts on the principle, is exceedingly detested" – is actually close to scholarly modern translations and deploys Confucius as a moralist whose sentiments are in accordance with those of a practical Christianity (232).

Yet Marshman is a hesitant scholar, intimidated by the weight of Confucian commentary. His treatment of Confucius shows some signs of a shift away from Jones's classical moralism. He attempts to re-make and accommodate Confucius in his own Protestant theological identity. For instance, when discussing the issues of the relationship between Christianity and Confucianism, Marshman is keen to stress the theistic and providential aspects he sees in Confucian thinking. His edition renders the very well known fourth aphorism of Book 2, where Confucius describes his intellectual maturity as "[a]t fifty, I understood the heaven-derived rule." This compares with a modern translation by Lau of the same passage as "at fifty I understood the Decree of Heaven"[67] and of Chan as "[a]t fifty I knew the Mandate of Heaven."[68] The phrase "Mandate of Heaven" (*tianming*) is a common English translation of a key term in Confucian thought deployed strategically to indicate an ancient knowledge of the existence of a monotheistic God (for Ricci and the Jesuits), or the operation of natural law (for Zhu Xi and the neo-Confucians). Marshman prints a translated summary of Zhu Xi's gloss that "'The heaven-derived rule,' includes the common course of nature, the conduct of *Providence*, and those ideas which are implanted by nature in the minds of men for the regulation of their conduct" (my italics, 81). He does not intervene here with any fulsome correction, as his successors David Collie or Robert Morrison might, but translates the Chinese character for sky (*tian*) conventionally as "heaven" and glosses it with the meanings, "heaven, reason, intelligence, i.e. the source of intelligence; metaphorically, the Supreme Being," thus reading into Confucian thought a Christian conception of deity and heaven not present in the source text.[69] Later, Marshman's commentary glosses the phrase "heaven derived way" as "that reason which heaven has given to men; the rule by which all mankind ought to be governed" (295). In his "Life of Confucius," Marshman also presented his subject as one who reflected on "Divine Providence" (vii). It seems that Marshman, the Baptist evangelist, imputed to Confucius belief in a supreme being who worked though providential means that were almost identical to his own theology. Like the Jesuits, Marshman is more anxious to embrace Confucius for his own theology than to reject him.

Similarly, in Book 3 Marshman translates the tenth to the thirteenth aphorisms which have to do with sacrifice in the context of worship as "Worship as though the deity were (present;) worship the deity, as though He were present," to which he attaches the commentary: "[t]o worship the Supreme Being, is to worship him without, i.e. every where, not in the temple merely." This again presents Confucius as a Protestant theist, dismissive of churches and priestcraft, engaging with his God in the classic personal encounter of reformed religion (167). Lau, however, renders the sentence in the more usual way; "sacrifice as if present" is taken to mean "sacrifice as if the gods were present."[70] James Legge, for instance, later rendered this aphorism as "He sacrificed to the dead, as if the spirits were present" and the following sentence as "The Master said, 'I consider my not being present at the sacrifice, as if I did not sacrifice.'"[71] By interpreting the Chinese character as "worship" rather than as "sacrifice," and referring to deity in the singular rather than the plural, Marshman presents Confucius as a monotheist dismissive of idolatrous sacrifices or rites. One final example indicates that this is not an isolated misunderstanding on Marshman's part but a deliberate, if hesitant, strategy of Protestant accommodation. Marshman renders Aphorism 13 as:

Wong-suen-ka, enquiring, said, Devote your attention to the *ou*. Your obsequiously regarding the *chou*, what is it?
    Chee says, I do not thus. Offending against heaven, there is no supplication which (can be acceptable). (170–71)

The sense of the saying is that paying court to the kitchen stove, which provides warmth and may be associated with "Wang-sun Chia" (a minister at Wei), is more useful than preferring the southwest corner of the house, associated with a place of honor or the Duke of Wei. Marshman's version, however, reads this as Confucius's response to the jibe that he is overly attached to the people. Confucius counters that all prayer is useless if you have sinned against heaven. Again, Marshman uses the commentary of Zhu Xi to make his point: "Heaven denotes the Supreme Intelligence; than which there is nothing greater," and "acting against conscience and reason, a man sins against heaven. By worshiping the *ou* then, or the *chou*, can he obtain forgiveness?" The "*ou*" and the "*chou*" in this reading identified with the common people and the nobility respectively. Marshman's translation thus again imports Protestant Christian notions of conscience, sin, and providence into this text. Oddly, though, these crucial points are made in rather an unobtrusive way, utilizing the authority of Zhu's commentary over Marshman's Baptist inner light theology. Possibly, Marshman is just generally conflating the tradition of Zhu, who accepted the notions similar to Marshman's understanding of destiny, natural order, or providence, though not that of a personal supreme god, with some understanding of the Jesuit claim that Confucius recognized a monotheistic creator god of some kind. Clearly, he did not at this time accept the later consensus of his missionary successors at Malacca, that Confucianism was more akin to a species of materialism or atheism. Because the translation only covers the first ten books of the *Lunyu* a number of key passages remain untranslated and not glossed. In particular, the crucial aphorism 15.24, generally regarded as an anticipation of Christ's Sermon on the Mount rather than a classical ethical precedent, goes unnoticed: "Do not impose on others what you yourself do not desire."[72]

Marshman's *Confucius* was not an especially influential text but was sufficiently well thought of by Wilhelm Schott, the German orientalist and first professor of sinology in Berlin, to merit a verbatim translation into German that he passed off as his own direct translation from the Chinese.[73] The *Quarterly Review* printed a substantial and major essay by John Barrow entitled "Progress of Chinese Literature in Europe" which reviewed Marshman's edition for a readership of some 20,000 Britons. Never overly sympathetic to the activities of dissenters in the first place, Barrow was keen to brand his subject as, like all missionaries, deficient in "taste and judgment."[74] Though praising Marshman's linguistic skills, the reviewer decries his literary abilities, branding his substantial volume, the first attempted translation into English of this world-important philosopher, as simply "laborious drudgery." The review accuses Marshman, with some justice, of being blind and deaf to the literary significance of the work as well as any notions of text and transmission, simply flattening a substantial literary tradition of text and commentary, inflected and changing over time, into a crude and rather literal decipherment. In a withering passage the review comments:

The disciples of Confucius, in preserving his moral maxims, imitated his style. That a plain man like Mr. Marshman, in attempting to translate symbols of this description into the English language, without any knowledge of the peculiar tenets and habits of thinking which prevail among the Chinese, should altogether fail, and frequently write nonsense, is not in the least surprising; but we confess that we were not prepared for the extremely mean and meager dress in which he has exhibited these homely truths of the great sage: they are absolutely disgusting from their nakedness; and we will venture to say, that the manual of a village schoolmistress or parish clerk never exhibited a set of maxims more trite and puerile than those to be found in every page from the first to the last of Mr. Marshman's tremendous quarto.[75]

As well as rubbishing Marshman's efforts, the *Quarterly* sets the tone for the new century by diminishing Confucius as a teacher and philosopher. While, opines Barrow, Confucian "dogmas" remained enveloped in "mystical characters" it might be thought that they contained wisdom and truth, but Marshman's meager translation has rendered them threadbare, demystifying them in the process. It remains the "visible symbol" of the talismanic Chinese characters that gave Confucius his celebrity and authority. Deprived of this mystique in Marshman's thuddingly literal prose, the charisma of the sage is lost. Confucius is now accused of inculcating in the reader a "dull passive morality" preaching only "patience, obedience and gravity."

Marshman's translation of the *Lunyu* was never completed, although a full translation by his eldest son, John Clark Marshman, of the *Daxue* was included in his *Elements of Chinese Grammar* of 1814. This volume, while still positive about aspects of Confucian thinking, now shows a more critical line on the Chinese in keeping with a changing estimation of China generally. The *Daxue* sums up the Confucian educational, social, and moral programs in renovating the individual, loving the people, and pursuing the highest good.[76] The work was selected for translation as a language exercise useful for the learning of Chinese, "as it puts the reader in possession of a complete work, highly esteemed by the Chinese." He claims that the work contains the substance of Confucian ethics and its morality, and that it is as suitable for fitting "a person for private as public life"[77] (xv). A change, however, seems to have occurred in the Marshman group's estimation of Confucian thought since the translation of the *Lunyu*. A new note is sounded when he identifies the foundation of all Confucian ethics as slender, "as must be the case in a system which regards moral evil as so trivial a thing, and wholly excludes a Deity, both as the object of filial fear, and as enlightening the mind." Confucius is no longer the proto-Protestant dissenter but a moralist who places all his faith in human reason and who argues that alone "knowledge is sufficient to renovate the mind." For Marshman any such system "which excludes a holy and heart-searching God" must be superficial and incomplete. Marshman, who never actually visited China, adds that the "present state of morals in China" should serve as a "practical comment" on Confucian ethics (15–16).

Whereas Marshman had previously shown no little anxiety in reconciling scriptural and ancient Chinese chronologies, now he views any effort of this kind as essentially worthless; "no judicious man will credit" the Chinese chronology. If the Septuagint is used, as the Jesuits preferred, then the annals do harmonize but "the highest pretensions of their own annals leave the Chinese inhabiting the woods, and totally ignorant of agriculture, nearly five hundred years after the deluge" (xvi, 16n). Marshman's Confucian project now seems to have shrunk from the intention to translate the whole of the Confucian canon of the Four Books into

English, to one where only the linguistic is important and the *Daxue*, so esteemed by Jones, becomes simply a translation exercise accomplished by Marshman's son to be included as an appendix in his Chinese grammar. Initially intimidated when confronted by the difficulty, scope, and sophistication of Chinese culture and language, a few brief years later, after having achieved some sense of mastery over the language, Marshman seems to have recovered his patriotic nerve. He is now abler to take on Chinese civilization and its Jesuit admirers on behalf of a British Protestant tradition. In Marshman's translations we see the very process of the waning of early modern Jesuit accommodationism, and the failure of Protestant assmiliationism, followed by the waxing of the emergent British Romantic Sinology that would gather strength and authority from the Canton and Malacca missionaries, Morrison, Milne, Collie, and Medhurst.

With Percy, Jones, and Marshman, Romantic Sinology begins to emerge from the enormous shadow of Jesuit scholarship. If Percy's Chinese studies were intimately connected to a form of Romanticism associated with the northern popular ballad, Jones's Chinese interests were also closely involved with his other orientalist writings that inspired a different form of Romanticism in the orientalist lyrics and epics of Coleridge, Southey, and Shelley. The presence of China as the major and most ancient world civilization is demonstrated *at the very heart* of British Romanticism. All three writers were nevertheless heavily, and in Percy's case almost totally, reliant on the writing of their Catholic predecessors and the various translations and versions of their texts. Jones's linguistic skills were superior to Percy's and as good as any, and he is able to consult first hand a number of Chinese originals and to adapt Chinese poetry into a British idiom. Jones, in London and Calcutta, also had valuable assistance from Huang Ya Dong in the form of advice and textual and scholarly resources, and Marshman utilized the services of Ya Meng, Lasser, and others. All three struggled with the Jesuit reading of China, though Percy's more ambivalently dismissive view of Chinese civilization chimes in more harmoniously with what would become the increasingly chauvinistic and belligerent attitudes of some element of the later Romantic Sinology. It would, however, take a number of years, arguably over a hundred, before the British had authoritative Chinese texts produced by a sinologist of their own, James Legge, to rival Ricci, von Schall, and Verbiest. The next two chapters discusses how the Romantic British sinology comes of age in the works of missionaries, Company servants, and Chinese scholars, teachers, printers, and helpers. The focus of the study moves from the knowledge production sites of Percy's eighteenth-century

London metropolitan literary society and Jones's and Marshman's Bengal to take in the emerging areas of sinology, Canton, Macao, and Malacca, which produced the dominant strain of learning about China prior to the first Anglo-Chinese War. What becomes clear, even at this stage, is that any methodology which takes into account the complex exchanges of knowledge that inform this process and seeks to understand the emerging but already sophisticated networks of expertise cannot rely simply on established binaries of orientalist – self and other, or East and West – or models derived from straightforward notions of imperial center and colonial periphery.

CHAPTER 3

"They thought that Jesus and Confucius were alike": Robert Morrison, Malacca, and the missionary reading of China

British Protestant missionaries, professional diplomats, and servants of the British East India Company stationed at Canton "forged" or "manufactured" knowledge about China and the "Far East" for Britons in the early nineteenth century. Their publications, journals, and libraries became the foundation of the institutionalized study of China in Britain as well as of more popular understandings. As Wang Gungwu puts it, "the words 'convert, trade, rule or fight,' describe the core issues in the history of Chinese relations with the English-speaking peoples."[1] Yet British knowledge about China could not have been forged without the substantial help of a series of Chinese people, some sophisticated scholars, merchants, occasionally servants or simply local people, often referred to in the dismissive phrase as "Chinese assistants." Percy and Jones would have been deeply envious of the resources in terms of Chinese expertise that their successors had at their disposal.[2] One of the defining aspects of the new British Romantic Sinology, paradoxically, was that it was created largely on the spot and with the close co-operation of Chinese people.[3] More than this, one can argue that the texts of Romantic Sinology were actually the result of a form of co-authorship, though disguised at the time and later by the familiar nineteenth-century hagiographies of the heroic missionary and pioneering colonial. This and the following chapters will discuss the laying at Canton and then Malacca of the foundations of early British sinology, before discussing the work of major participants, chiefly Staunton, Morrison, and Davis, and the leading tenets of its thinking about China in the early nineteenth century. The focus of these chapters is thus on the establishment of British Romantic Sinology and the key, and critically neglected, translations that it produced, both legal and literary.

Nineteenth-century British sinology originated with scholars who had studied China, its languages, customs, politics, and literature, often in their spare time, explicitly in pursuit of clear objectives, whether to convert the Celestial Empire to Protestant Christianity or to facilitate British trade in the region.[4] This is not to say that British sinologists saw themselves as entirely interested and partisan: they did not. The writers discussed here believed that they were presenting a much more objective picture of China as established by the eighteenth-century British empirical norms of the Royal Society and practiced on James Cook's voyages of global exploration. One of their main aims was to reveal the distortions which they believed Jesuit accounts had propagated and which "tended to mislead rather than to inform," and to provide an alternative, scientific, narrative based on first-hand observation of China and its peoples, "the first correct account of a nation."[5] Though they were frequently antagonistic to what they regarded as Jesuit misrepresentation of Chinese thought and religion, British sinologists remained, to some extent, dependent on this earlier scholarship (especially Du Halde's *General History*), and silently assimilated many of the assumptions and constructed categories on which it was based.[6]

Nineteenth-century British sinology originated from the work of a handful of Protestant missionaries in South and Southeast Asia and later of a series of East India Company officials: notably, George Thomas Staunton, who had visited China as an eleven-year-old boy during the Macartney embassy; John Francis Davis, son of a Company director destined to become the second governor of the new treaty port of Hong Kong (1844–48); and P. P. (Peter Perring) Thoms, a skilled printer sent out by the Company to produce Chinese fonts. John Barrow, another China expert, served as comptroller of the Macartney embassy and later as second secretary at the Admiralty. Even the idiosyncratic independent China scholar Thomas Manning was involved with the Company in Canton and served on the Amherst embassy. With the questionable exceptions of Stephen Weston and Antonio Montucci, domestic "China experts" who had never visited China were comparatively rare in Britain, though more common on the Continent. These men in total constituted the few what we might call "serious" British sinologists of the Romantic period and it was they who developed the new British Romantic Sinology, writing their travels, histories, and commentaries about all aspects of Chinese life, producing Chinese grammars, dictionaries and vocabularies, and translating numerous key texts of Chinese philosophy and literature, texts which were substantially reviewed in periodicals like the *Quarterly Review* and the *Edinburgh Review*. The growth of a newly professionalized sinology gave rise to specialist journals such as the *Asiatic Journal and Monthly Register for British India and its Dependencies* (1816), and the *Transactions of the*

Royal Asiatic Society (1823, and *Journal* from 1834) in Britain, and *Journal Asiatique* (1822) in France.

The first British institution specifically constituted to study Chinese literature and language was the Anglo-Chinese College founded at Malacca in 1818 (until then a British-held port on the western coast of the Malaysian peninsula), by the London Missionary Society workers Robert Morrison and William Milne. The College was established to pursue the reciprocal cultivation of Chinese and European literature. It published a series of works on Chinese subjects, including an English-language periodical, the *Indo-Chinese Gleaner*, from 1817 onwards, which contained articles and essays on Chinese language, politics, and religion.[7] One of its members, Samuel Kidd, became the first British professor of Chinese at the new University of London in 1837. Kidd had held the professorship of Chinese at the Anglo-Chinese College, succeeding William Milne and David Collie. The chair he came to occupy had been established, somewhat reluctantly, by the university in exchange for the transfer of Morrison's substantial collection of Chinese books, facilitated by Staunton.[8] In 1845, also as a result of Staunton's agitation, the first professor of Chinese, Samuel Turner Fearon (an interpreter and the first Registrar General of the new treaty port of Hong Kong), was established at King's College.[9] James Summers succeeded him in 1852. Another of the Anglo-Chinese College's professors, James Legge, who later produced what was to be *the* authoritative English-language edition for the West of *The Chinese Classics* for much of the late nineteenth and twentieth centuries, was appointed the first professor of Chinese at Oxford in 1875.[10] Cambridge's first professor of Chinese, the diplomat Sir Thomas Francis Wade, was not appointed until 1888. Wade's private library, put together while he was resident in Beijing during the period of the second Opium War, formed the basis of the University's "Far Eastern" collection. Some of the works in his library may well have been looted from the emperor's Summer Palace before its appalling destruction at the hands of combined British and French forces in 1860.[11] Wade, of course, became famous for his system, enhanced by Herbert Giles, for romanizing or transliterating Chinese ideograms: the Wade-Giles system. Giles, Wade's erstwhile subordinate in China, succeeded him at Cambridge in 1897 and notably rubbished the quality of his predecessor's learning. Wade directed students who wished to learn Chinese to go and work in China rather than study at home, an attitude that, while indicating its author's formidable dislike of teaching, also reflected much British thinking about the pedagogy of studying Chinese.[12]

CANTON, TEA, OPIUM, COMMERCE, AND WAR

Although the focus of this study is biased to the literary, cultural understanding of China, we should not conclude that Romantic Sinology was
simply, to appropriate a title of Morrison's works, "a philological view
of China." It must be emphasized that Romantic Sinology was created
almost entirely within the worlds of global commerce and none of its
practitioners could (or did) claim simply to be promoting the disinterested pursuit of knowledge. Though, as we will see, the heavily lauda-
num-addicted Coleridge did flirt with the idea of residing in Canton in
1804 to improve his failing condition, no Britons resident at Canton or
Bengal were there simply for the good of their health. They were there
either to propagandize Protestant Christianity or to make money from
the China trade, chiefly tea and later opium.[13] In the eighteenth and early
nineteenth centuries, tea was not the quintessentially British commodity we regard it as today; it was a regarded as a foreign, addictive, and
exotic drink, associated with China and imbricated in extremely complex
ways with the prestige of Chinese culture. Tea became slowly naturalized
and domesticated by the British in the early nineteenth century, as the
much sought-after China teas were gradually displaced by the varieties
of tea grown in British India (chiefly in the newly acquired province of
Assam).[14] Tea shared with the general discourse of China a dizzying tendency to be viewed in terms of opposed extremes and paradoxical ambiguities, alternately considered as either a universal panacea, an exotic and
effeminizing addiction, or a botanical enigma resistant to transplantation
elsewhere.

For almost a century the merchants of the Company had regularly
traded with the Chinese at Canton in the Pearl River delta, the only part
of the empire where the Qing court permitted trade with foreigners after
1757. It was allowed under what became known as "the Canton System".[15]
This trade was important to China as its economy netted some $26 mil-
lion from it in the first decade of the nineteenth century.[16] The Chinese
imposed both duties and restrictions on trade; it could only be carried
out in the months between October and March and in the European
factories, after which traders had to leave for Macao. No wives or depend-
ents were permitted at the national trading posts or "factories," and the
merchants' personal freedoms were somewhat limited. From 1725 all commercial dealings were managed and policed through a body of Chinese
merchants, the "Cohong," and governed by a superintendent of maritime
customs appointed by the imperial household, known as the "Hoppo."

These restrictions were largely due to Qing anxiety about the activities of Christian missionaries and their potential to ferment internal dissent. Although relations between the merchants of the Cohong and the traders of the company were generally cordial, the trade was subject to rising and unstable duties and attempts to "squeeze" individual profits, especially by the local government. The Qing insistence that foreign nationals accused of crimes were tried according to Chinese law caused tensions. The British desired their own depot on the China coast to trade and store goods. They considered taking Macao over from the Portuguese as well as obtaining Xiamen (Amoy) on the Fujian coast, situated nearer to the main tea-growing areas.[17] These were issues which Macartney's and Amherst's embassies were meant to address.

Trade with China until 1833 was thus established on the basis of a mutual monopoly, with the Select Committee of the Company and the Chinese Cohong managing trade along the largely mercantilist lines of the interaction of two state-controlled monopolies. In addition to this official relationship there was a thriving independent trade by "country merchants," or independent traders licensed by the Company and impatient with its monopoly, increasingly participating in the illegal trade in opium. These included not just Britons, but also Americans and Parsees (ethnically Persian Zoroastrians resident in India), as evocatively fictionalized in Amitav Ghosh's *Rivers of Smoke* (2011), the second volume of his Ibis trilogy. The situation was complicated on the British side in that the Select Committee in Canton answered to the Court of Directors in London, who liaised with the government's Board of Trade. On the Chinese side, the Cohong and the Hoppo answered to the governor of Canton and then the viceroy of Guangdong who was responsible to the imperial government in Beijing. All forms of contact between foreign nationals and the Qing were required to be channeled through the Cohong and not addressed directly to the mandarins and governors. When the monopoly ended and the British established a national Superintendent of Trade to negotiate on behalf of their merchants, the inability to communicate directly with the governor became a major diplomatic issue for both empires.

It has been estimated that China's GDP in 1820 was about 29 percent of entire world GDP, and larger than that of all Europe's combined share. Europeans were the "new kids on the block" of global commerce, and Britons were the most obvious "Johnny Come-latelies."[18] The bedrock of the eighteenth-century Canton trade was the exchange of Chinese tea for South American silver, acquired from Europeans. As Cranmer-Byng and

Wills point out, "tea from China was one of the transoceanic consumer goods that helped to stimulate the steady growth of intercontinental maritime connections and the emergence in northwestern Europe of prosperous and dynamic bourgeois societies."[19] All the world's tea exports came from China. It was not until 1839 that the very first Indian tea was sold on the British market.[20] In the eyes of many, the China trade was rightly "the most important in the world."[21] The British desired many Chinese products, silk, porcelain, lacquerware, and other commodities in smaller volumes – wallpapers, ginger, rhubarb, alum, mercury – but most of all and most avidly, the British craved more and more of the newly fashionable beverage of tea, the consumption of which grew exponentially in the eighteenth and early nineteenth centuries. Tea, in the terminology of Sidney Mintz, was Britain's most popular "drug food." Imbibed from the 1660s onwards in the coffee houses and pleasure grounds of London, total imports of tea from China grew from 50 tons in 1700 to around 15,000 in 1800, as consumption patterns shifted away from ale. Tea was an alternative to alcohol and provided a pleasant medium by which Britons could receive their daily sugar fix. It was during this period that tea became naturalized as a quintessentially British drink. In his *Tsiology; A Discourse of Tea* (1826), William Smith, for instance, could comment on how tea had been transformed "from a fashionable and expensive luxury … into an essential comfort, if not an absolute necessary of life" that had "descended from the palace to the cottage."[22] Yet for most of the eighteenth century tea was different, other, and a signifier of luxury.[23]

    In the early nineteenth century the disruptions caused by Latin American emancipation movements drastically reduced supplies of silver and gold, causing a global depression in the world economy.[24] It was even more important to pay for Chinese imports with currencies other than the increasingly scarce metal. It is well known that the British solution to this imbalance was indirectly to export larger volumes of opium grown in at Patna in Bengal to China. As both poison and medicine, opium is paradoxical. On the one hand, in the form of laudanum, opium was commonplace in nineteenth-century Britain, a legal and highly effective analgesic, one of the few medicinal compounds that actually worked to relieve pain and treat dysentery.[25] Yet, on the other, it was addictive, destructive, and a source of great anguish. The extreme cases of the Romantic writers Coleridge and De Quincey are well known; other addicts, such as George Crabbe and William Wilberforce, less so. Their opium for domestic use was largely imported from Smyrna in Turkey, not China, as very little Indian opium found its way back to Britain and the Company had no interest in selling on the home market. In China opium had been used for many years, but in the early eighteenth century it was increasingly combined with tobacco and smoked for pleasure. The importing of opium into China was formally, though ineffectually, prohibited by imperial decree from 1729 (reaffirmed in 1796) but only something like two hundred chests per annum were exported by Europeans at this time. This steadily rose to around 1000 chests in 1760, 1300 chests in 1780, and about 3159 by 1805. Chinese smugglers and merchants paid for their Bengal opium with their European tea silver. By the 1830s the imbalance in silver bullion exports and imports between Britain and China had been drastically reversed with a surplus in the Company's favor of around £38 million and with something like 40,000 chests of opium being exported into China per annum by the country merchants at the end of the decade. It was illegal but hugely profitable, and "the world's most valuable single commodity trade of the nineteenth century."[26]

Opium was firmly enmeshed in British commercial and colonial policy: it funded the British in India.[27] In 1773 the British established a monopoly of the drug's production in Bengal (though not Benares). As the opium trade was formally prohibited, the opium harvested in Patna was auctioned to the independent country merchants and shipped first to Macao but increasingly to Lintin on the Pearl River delta, where Chinese smugglers bought the cargo paid for in silver for distribution to the mainland. Neither the Hong merchants nor the Canton Company would officially touch it. Yet that silver would be returned to the coffers of the Company in Bengal to pay for the China tea demanded by the British. The independent traders simply claimed they were only satisfying an existing demand not creating a new one and were following the dictates of commerce. The blatant conduct of this contraband trade also required Chinese corruption on a massive scale, with conniving Qing government officials, heavily bribed, looking resolutely the other way. Fortunes were to be made on both sides. By the 1830s, Chinese farmers, attracted by the substantial profits, were also farming the foreign poppy. Judgments on the trade itself, rather like on the earlier transatlantic trade in slaves, varied from those describing it as entirely honorable and legitimate to those that castigated it as simply evil and unjustifiable by any pretexts. As Julia Lovell shrewdly sums up, "although by no means a blemish-free ethical choice, the move into opium by British traders was not, as claimed by contemporary historians in the People's Republic, a deliberate conspiracy to make narcotic slaves of the Chinese empire; it was a greedy, pragmatic response to a decline in sales of other British imports (clocks, watches, furs)."[28] The scale of the trade by the 1830s was so immense and its effects so debilitating that the Qing government appointed and authorized Commissioner Lin Zexu in Canton to take extreme steps to eradicate it. Lin's seizure, confiscation, and destruction of the merchants' cargoes of opium was the spark that ignited the military conflict between Britain and China known as the first "Opium War" with which this study concludes. Whatever the complexities of the debate, however, the opium trade had devastating economic and social effects for Qing China. It was against this background that the Romantic Sinology of the Company's agents and LMS missionaries, Morrison, Staunton and Davis, was constructed. The contribution of Canton and the global networks of trade and diplomacy will be explored in this and the two following chapters.

MORRISON, MILNE, AND THE ANGLO-CHINESE
COLLEGE AT MALACCA

The first major British sinologist was also the first British missionary to enter China, Robert Morrison (known to the Chinese as *Ma Li-sun*). The participation of Protestant missionaries was as important for British sinology as that of Jesuit missionaries was for seventeenth- and eighteenth-century European sinology. Morrison's chief rival, mentor, and friend, George Thomas Staunton, wrote to him in 1821: "you are certainly the first in the field, and if ever I possessed the palm, I certainly with pleasure resign it to you."[29] T. H. Barrett claims that "the years following Morrison's arrival in Canton in 1807 can be said to mark the first true flowering of British sinology," and J. L. Cranmer-Byng credits Morrison over Staunton as "the first really professional English sinologist." Morrison's most recent biographer argues that his subject "was arguably the pre-eminent European sinologist, the author of one of the first Chinese Bibles, the creator of a fine Chinese Dictionary, the founding visionary of the Ultra-Ganges Mission and the Anglo-Chinese College at Malacca ..."[30] By the 1820s Morrison's stature had grown from that of a relatively modest missionary engaged in propagating the Christian faith to that of an internationally acknowledged expert on all matters Chinese, consulted on a regular basis by scholars. His work was accomplished at Canton, Macao, and Malacca. As Hillemann has demonstrated, these sites on the South China coast became *the* crucial centers for the production, or "forging," of British knowledge about China in the early nineteenth century, which was then transmitted to the metropolis inflected by key local concerns, radically changing "the way China was understood in the British Empire" between the 1760s and the 1840s.[31] Canton at this time was one of the largest cities in the eighteenth-century world, and one of the places where contact between Europeans and Chinese was almost entirely concentrated. It was a place of global trade, negotiation, and exchange, economically, linguistically, and culturally. It was the location of the eighteenth-century global cross-cultural encounter *par excellence*.

As Susan Reed Stifler has authoritatively demonstrated, Britons at Canton showed a strong interest in Chinese literature and culture. Not only did James Wilkinson's partial translation of the *Hau Kiou Choann* originate from there, but Company servants such as James Cunningham (Cuninghame) and James Flint made determined efforts to master the Chinese language. Cunningham, a Scottish surgeon and naturalist, visited China twice in the eighteenth century and was the first European to export Chinese plants to Britain safely.[32] A character in Ghosh's novel *River of Smoke* (2011) justifiably speculates that the genus *Camellia* should rather have been named *Cuninghamia* after the Scot.[33] In 1755 and 1759 Flint sailed to Ningpo and then Tienjin in an attempt to break the restriction of trade to Canton. He was returned to Canton though the mainland of China under imperial escort, becoming the first Briton to make this journey. Despite some initial success he was eventually banished to Macao, where he was imprisoned for three years and expelled from China and his Chinese copyist executed.[34] Flint's initiative resulted in stricter restrictions against trade and its limiting to Canton, and further prohibitions were placed upon the teaching of Chinese by which the Chinese subjects were forbidden to act as teachers or transcribers for foreigners on punishment of death.[35] Sadly, Flint published no account of his travels, and no manuscript accounts of his time in China have as yet come to light.

Linguistically, most everyday transactions between Britons and Chinese in Canton from the 1730s onwards were carried out in a hybrid language now known as South China Coast pidgin, effectively replacing Portuguese as the linguistic medium. On other very important occasions Portuguese Jesuit translators from Macao were employed, but they were suspect and unlikely to promote British commercial interests.[36] There were usually four or five licensed translators in Canton. As Paul Van Dyke demonstrates, "the emergence of pidgin English was very much created, propelled and defined by the demands of commerce."[37] Yet the importance for the British of being able to speak the language and communicate directly with the Chinese was emphasized after the experience of Macartney's embassy. Flint, then back in Britain, was expected to be the embassy's interpreter but he died before it was organized.[38] Most of its official business therefore had to be carried on via Latin, as the embassy's Chinese interpreters did not speak English, only Italian and Chinese. Macartney, reflecting somewhat ruefully on this experience, observed:

We therefore almost entirely depend on the good faith and good-nature of the few Chinese whom we employ, and by whom we can be but imperfectly understood in the broken gibberish we talk to them. I fancy than Pan-ke-qua [Pan Youdo, a leading Canton merchant] or Mahomet Soulem would attempt doing business on the Royal Exchange to very little purpose if they appeared there in long petticoat clothes, with bonnets and turbans, and could speak nothing but Chinese or Arabic.[39]

Though characteristically viewed as a "failure" in traditional historical accounts, one of the embassy's major successes was to negotiate permission for Chinese to teach their language to the Company's employees at Canton.[40]

After 1800 George Thomas Staunton, who had acted as an unofficial interpreter for Macartney as a boy, became the chief interpreter and translator for the Company at Canton. During his two-year absence between 1802 and 1804, the Company employed the services of the Augustinian missionary Juan Antonio Rodriguez.[41] It is not generally acknowledged that the Company's "factory" (their trading warehouse) had its own substantial collection or library of Chinese works. In 1813 John Francis Davis, then a junior writer, was given "two MS dictionaries, one of them in Latin and Chinese, and the other Chinese and Latin," both "compiled by Romish missionaries, and copied by a Chinese convert." The Company also owned a copy of Fourmont's *Linguae sinarum grammatica* at the factory, but this was generally found to be unhelpful. It also held fascicles of around two hundred Chinese plays by the second decade of the nineteenth century, and it is reasonable to assume it had acquired substantial numbers of novels and other Chinese texts used by Morrison to teach and research. The Canton factory was thus better equipped for the serious and scholarly study of Chinese culture than the major libraries of Enlightenment Europe and was a key site of knowledge production about China.[42]

When Staunton undertook a further two-year absence in 1808–10 Thomas Manning, an independent scholar, supplied his place. Manning had been recommended by his friend, and Company employee, the Romantic essayist Charles Lamb. Manning, thought by many to be the best Chinese scholar in Europe, never published an important work on China.[43] He left Canton in 1810 on his expedition to Bengal, where he also aided Marshman's Chinese studies, and from thence to Tibet, becoming the first Englishman to enter Lhasa. Rodriguez already having left and Staunton not yet returned, his place as translator at Canton was supplied by the presence of Morrison.[44] In 1813 Morrison advocated the setting up of a scheme whereby Company officials might become Chinese students tasked with learning the language and taught by native speakers. John Francis Davis was one of three employees to become Chinese students. Davis would become an important British expert on China and translated several works of Chinese into English. Morrison's language classes at Canton thus trained a series of young Company men in Chinese up to the dissolution of its monopoly in 1833, when the closing of its factory, "destroyed the promising future of what was in effect Britain's earliest school of Chinese studies."[45] Practically all the major British sinologists of the early nineteenth century were products of, or associated with, the Company's factory at Canton where trade and commerce with China were managed. The end of the Company's monopoly was a major blow for Romantic Sinology. The Canton Chamber of Commerce, which thenceforth represented British, American, and Parsee traders, had little interest in the promotion of Chinese learning and the understanding of Chinese culture, as the two empires drifted into conflict and then open war.

Missionaries such as Morrison, like the diplomats of the Macartney embassy, were thus able to fashion themselves as experts on China, whose authority accrued from their presence there. One of the crucial claims made for the new Romantic Sinology was that its veracity and validity over previous knowledge was forged from first-hand expertise garnered on the spot. Obviously, the construction of such expertise, when allied with the imperatives of Company policy, gave the British a form of agency that allowed them to interpret and interact with the Qing empire. As it is increasingly recognized, the work of the missionaries, Morrison, Milne, Medhurst, Collie, and Kidd, originating from first Canton and then the Anglo-Chinese College at Malacca, was crucial in forging this knowledge about China for the West and for fashioning an alternative version of Confucian thought to that of Jesuit sinology. This group of missionaries produced a series of translations of Chinese texts and literature. Like Marshman's at Serampore, Morrison's "principal object" was not to found an academic institution but to "produce a correct version of the Holy Scriptures into the Chinese language," a feat he and his team of Chinese assistants were able to accomplish by 1823, a year after Marshman.[46]

Morrison studied both written and spoken Chinese, and his publications included grammars of Mandarin and Cantonese as well as his famous Chinese dictionary (1815–23). He was an excellent and natural linguist who had been educated by his uncle in Newcastle and then by a tutor paid for from his wages before attending the dissenting Hoxton Academy in Hackney, East London. Trained by the London Missionary Society at Gosport from 1804, he began to study Chinese while still in London during 1805. His tutor was the young Chinese, Yong Sam-Tak (Rong Sande), who had come to England to study English for commercial purposes under the protection of the East India captain, Henry Wilson.[47] Wilson passed him over to the care of evangelicals, through whose auspices he became acquainted with Morrison. Yong acted as Morrison's first Chinese teacher and also became his roommate. Yong, an educated Confucian scholar, would later act as Morrison's advisor at Canton where he taught Morrison to speak Cantonese.[48] Morrison also studied in the British Museum a Chinese manuscript of a harmony of the Gospels, "Quatuor Evangelica Sinice," transcribed around 1737 from a Jesuit source, which would feature as the basis of the New Testament element of his Chinese Bible and provide the foundation for one of the many charges of plagiarism that dogged his later scholarship.[49]

Like Marshman, Morrison availed himself of the expertise of various Chinese teachers and later converts. After Yong, his first serious teachers of Mandarin were Yun Kwan-ming (Abel Yun) and Li Xiansheng (Le Sëensáng or Teacher Li), both Roman Catholic converts able to read and speak Latin. Yun had also taught Staunton. He knew Latin and Cantonese and could speak but not read Mandarin. Li and later his son, Li Shigong, taught Morrison Mandarin, Cantonese, Chinese writing, and literary Chinese. Li possessed "considerable knowledge of Chinese, writes an excellent hand," and had obtained "one degree as a man of letters." He had also been a successful Hong merchant.[50] One of Morrison's other later teachers was "Mr Gao" (Ko Sëensáng, Ge Mouhe or Ko-mow-ho), who appears to have been the son of a mandarin and a transcriber of the Board of Rites, and who was able to aid Morrison in his study of Confucian texts.[51] Again, Morrison's endeavors at Canton were very much part of a collaborative teamwork, and Li and Gao, in particular, may reasonably be regarded as paid co-authors of Morrison's texts.[52] Morrison's other helpers included Lo Xian (Low-hëen), Liang Afa (who became the first ordained native Chinese Protestant minister), and Chen Laoyi. Tellingly, one of the reasons Staunton would relinquish his serious Chinese studies on his return to Britain was that without the "assistance of native scholars" the work was too difficult and he suspected that "no important translations from the Chinese by Europeans have ever been successfully made" without their contribution: a virtual admission of a form of Chinese co-authorship.[53]

Lydia Liu, writing about what she refers to as "translingual practice," has persuasively argued that the power relationships that are embedded in such cross-cultural encounters and exchanges are never simply unilinear. Liu, in discussing the process of later Chinese translations of Western discourses, argues that the Chinese translators of such texts functioned as co-authors and equals because they engaged in "productive distortions" of the European writers. Liu suggests that both co-authorship and agency are possible, or at least thinkable, in such unequal encounters. The hegemonic relationship between the early nineteenth-century British translator and his "Chinese assistants" is also complex and less easy to ascertain. The British controlled the production and publication of the translated text as well as the public interpretation of that text, but they were still heavily reliant on native Chinese scholarship for their translations and for access to the language at all. Morrison, if anything, was negotiating from a position of weakness and vulnerability, both intellectually and politically, as a foreign missionary in Canton. Although the notion of co-authorship in such a proto-colonial context (though none at the time so understood it) might be deemed to be problematic or inappropriate, nevertheless this process of cultural transmission significantly complicates a straightforward application of orientalist binaries when reading the transmission process.[54]

Morrison was able to exploit the shared knowledge of his Chinese coworkers in translating, transcribing, and printing his works. Only a few of these assistants were educated and cultured Chinese; the majority tended to be from less educated backgrounds, and were certainly less knowledgeable than the elite scholars and thinkers who assisted Ricci and his Jesuit brethren. He published a series of works on the language and culture of China that were useful for Company officials in dealing with the Chinese. In particular, he addressed the pressing need to acquire reliable interpreters who could facilitate formal exchanges within Canton but also with the imperial court at Beijing.[55] This was especially the case, as the Qing empire forbade the teaching of Chinese to foreigners, and local Chinese people who assisted the missionaries ran substantial risks. Morrison published his *A Grammar of the Chinese Language* in 1815 and his *Dictionary of the Chinese Language* from 1815 to 1822. In addition to his linguistic work, he made a series of key translations of Chinese literature into English, including his *Horae Sinicae: Translations from the Popular Literature of the Chinese* (1812), *Translations from the original Chinese with Notes* (1815), and *A Chinese Miscellany* (1825), as well as a more general work, *A View of China, for Philological Purposes*, in 1817, originally intended as the introduction to his *Dictionary*. The *Horae Sinicae* contained the first published English translation of the *Daxue*.

However, like Marshman, Morrison did not undertake this work to learn wisdom from Chinese writers. In his *View of China* he writes, somewhat damningly that

> an European can have little motive to enter on the study of Chinese; or at least, can scarcely have motive sufficiently strong to carry him successfully through. Abstract Science, or the Fine Arts can learn nothing from China; and perhaps as much is already known, as can be known, to aid the general Philosopher in his reasonings. Her History will not bear out the fond expectations of the opposers of Christianity, in disproving the Jewish and Christian Scriptures; nor can the friend of Christianity obtain any useful addition to his Religion or Code of Morals from her Sages.[56]

To be fair, Morrison would also make numerous much more positive statements about Chinese culture, yet his criticism here was that it was not inspired by divine revelation but was comparable in stature to classical thinking: "Pagan Chinese reading is, to my taste, as offensive (but not more so) as the profligate poets, &c of Greece and Rome, and modern Europe. Horace, the most elegant, and most read, is full of abominable stuff, much worse than *mi* lord Biron." The only purpose in learning the Chinese language and reading Chinese literature is, thus, as a prelude to the conversion of the empire to Christianity rather than to study it for "the sake of the style, or any such object."[57] Morrison's great purpose in undertaking this study was to produce a Chinese translation of the Bible. Yet this aim involved him in an extensive process of cross-cultural encounter with Chinese people, their literature, and their customs.

Morrison was sent to China in 1806, to be followed soon after by his assistants William and Rachel Milne in 1813, and a further assistant, Walter Henry Medhurst, in 1817.[58] Morrison, Milne, and Medhurst would become significant sinologists. Milne's early death, aged thirty-seven, only eleven years after he arrived at Macao, meant that he never achieved the breadth and scope of Morrison's learning in Chinese literature. His major contribution to sinology was his 1817 translation of the important *Sacred Edict* of the Kangxi emperor.[59] Medhurst was a more much prolific writer in Chinese, Malay, and English than Milne and his predecessors; he prioritized preaching over literary and linguistic study and was often antipathetic to their more academic priorities.[60] He published several linguistic and grammatical works, including his *An English and Japanese and Japanese and English Vocabulary* (1830), *A Dictionary of the Hok-këèn Dialect of the Chinese Language* (1832), a *Translation of a Comparative Vocabulary of the Chinese, Corean, and Japanese Languages* (1835), and a *Chinese and English Dictionary* (1842–48), as well as a series of influential travel and other works about China, including *China: its State and Prospects* (1838) and *A Glance at the Interior of China* (1845). Medhurst's major work was focused on a new translation of the Bible into Chinese which he undertook in 1840 as one of a committee of delegates, including Karl Gützlaff, Elijah Bridgeman, and John Robert Morrison. This "Delegates' Bible" would be influential on the Taiping Rebellion. Medhurst's major translation was of the "Classic of History," the *Shijing*, as *Ancient China: The Shoo-king, or, the Historical Classic* – the first translation of that work into English, and published by the Shanghai Mission Press in 1846.

The study of China in the early nineteenth century and beyond was to be substantially informed by the writings of these three men. The Jesuit missionaries had tended to efface signs of cultural and religious difference between China's Confucian court culture and that of their own Catholicism, in a strategy of accommodation, reserving their especial disdain for the more popular Chinese religious practices of Daoism and Buddhism. Not so Morrison and Milne. From the start, the British Protestant missionaries were generally hostile to the Manchu Qing court and associated the spread of Christianity to the empire with the demise of the imperial system. Though hostile to political revolution at home, they identified their work in China as revolutionary. Morrison commented that he thought it "very likely the time is nearly arrived, when the ruling dynasty will be shaken to pieces," making "way for the Gospel to run in a free course, and be glorified." Milne praised Morrison for setting "on foot what all the emperors—and mandarins—and priests—and literati—and people of China can never destroy, nor effectually stop; what will raze their temples, destroy their idols, change their lives, and save the souls of many."[61] The freelance German missionary and opium trader Karl Gützlaff, closely identified with the British presence in China, was even more explicit about the importance of combining missionary and colonial crusading. In his *Journal of Three Voyages along the Coast of China* of 1833, he writes:

We will hope and pray, that God in his mercy may, very soon, open a wider door of access; and we will work as long as the Lord grants health, strength, and opportunity. I sincerely wish that something more efficient might be done for opening *a free intercourse with China*, and would feel myself highly favoured, if

I could be subservient, in a small degree, in hastening forward such an event. In the merciful providence of our God and Saviour, it may be confidently hoped, that the doors to China will be thrown open. By whom this will be done, or in what ways, is of very little importance.[62]

Yet, as Andrew Porter has demonstrated, there is no neat and easy correlation between missionary enterprise and the building of empire. Missionary groups such as the LMS were genuinely nervous of the combination of commercial and missionary activities, arguing that the spread of British and European influence was of providential value in the spreading of Christianity and that it would be remiss of Christians not to encourage the spread of the Gospel now such networks existed.[63]

Morrison favored Malacca as a place to found a missionary station precisely because it was *not* a commercial territory like Canton, and he affirmed his belief that commercial and missionary activity should be unrelated.[64] In his sermon "The Missionary Rehearsal," preached on April 1, 1824, while he was on a visit to London, Morrison made this providential point most forcefully to his domestic admirers: "To sit still, and do nothing, but wait till Heaven shall miraculously convert the nations ... is a course as unscriptural and irrational, as to be all bustle and activity, in the use of means, without any regard to the Supreme Agent." God will "employ human means" to effect his renovation of the world.[65] It was this strong belief in the providential aspect of his work that led Morrison to respond to the mocking jibe of the American captain whose ship conveyed him to Canton as to whether he alone would make any impact on the idolatry of the Chinese: "No Sir, ... I expect God will."[66] Morrison's personal cosmology would enable his sinology in just the same way as Confucian cosmology enabled Qing ritual diplomacy (*li*).

While the Company officially discouraged missionary activity in China, especially after the imperial edict of 1811 against the propagation of Christianity, and while its members generally disapproved of nonconformist dissent, it was willing to make full use of Morrison's skills as a linguist, and as willing to sponsor his non-religious publications. Morrison decided to propagate Christianity by the translation of the scriptures rather than by the more visible activity of preaching and proselytizing, and this made him acceptable and less troublesome.[67] His position was, however, delicate and he was obliged to travel to New York to obtain passage on an American vessel to Canton, rather than ship out directly on an East Indiaman from London. He was also obliged to reside with the smaller America factory at Canton on arrival rather than with the British.[68] The vulnerability of Morrison's position throughout his time in

Canton, Macao, and Malacca should not be underestimated. Although he would be employed by the Company and, after the loss of its monopoly, by the British government, he continually worked under enormous pressures, both physical and political. He was often entirely dependent on the paid services of his servants, or the goodwill of the servants of the Company and the various jurisdictions, Qing, Dutch, and Portuguese, that he worked within. He was employed by the Company but never fully accepted by it. His position was not one of cultural hegemony in either Britain or China, and while in later life he achieved academic and scholarly recognition, for much of his career as a sinologist he led a very lonely, precarious, and even perilous existence.

Morrison was fortunate in obtaining early the patronage of both Sir Joseph Banks in London and Staunton at Canton. Banks, the intelligence behind the Macartney embassy, supplied him with an introduction to Staunton. Staunton in turn introduced Morrison to John Roberts, the head of the British factory there. The costs of residing in Canton soon proved excessive and Morrison considered moving his mission to the British colony at Penang in Malaysia before, in 1809, accepting the post of Chinese secretary and translator for the Company at Canton with a salary of £500 per year (in 1812 this became £1000). In 1816 he would also serve as the official Chinese secretary to the embassy of Lord Amherst to the court of the Jiaqing emperor in Beijing with Staunton, Davis, and Manning. Morrison worked for the Company, despite some not inconsiderable prejudice against his nonconformity, until the end of its monopoly in 1833. Afterwards he served as the unfortunate Lord Napier's Chinese secretary and interpreter in the remaining months prior to his death in 1834.[69] Morrison's career as a missionary and sinologist was thus intimately, if uncomfortably, intertwined with British commercial and diplomatic policy in Southeast Asia.

Morrison clearly agonized about the propriety of such pragmatic engagements, but he judged that the financial support provided by his employment for the mission and the providential nature of the arrangement ultimately rendered them appropriate. Unlike Gützlaff, who distributed religious tracts via the merchant William Jardine's opium boats, Morrison privately deplored the opium trade; writing to friends in Dublin in 1828, he declared that this "poison depraves and corrupts the Heathen and yet Christians actuated by the lust of gold smuggle immense quantities of it into China from our Indian possessions." His moral outrage is partially disingenuous as he was aware that most of the opium derived from the Company's possessions in Patna and that, though the Company did not technically deal in the drug they sowed and harvested, their captains did.[70]

At the foundation ceremony of the Anglo-Chinese College at Malacca, Morrison commented in familiar terms on the strategic commercial importance of China for the British: "the proximity of British territory to that of China, and the very important commercial relations which subsist between the two countries, certainly make it a point of high political consideration to understand fully the Chinese laws, opinions, and manners, and that can only be done effectually by a knowledge of the language."[71] The Company was an enthusiastic sponsor of the publication costs of Morrison's *Chinese Dictionary*, providing £15,000 and sending out the printer Peter Perring Thoms in 1814 to supervise its publication at Malacca.[72] Yet Morrison was always ambivalent towards the Company, and in later life increasingly alienated from it.[73]

Though Morrison, the son of a Northumbrian boot-frame maker, and Milne, the son of an Aberdeenshire farmhand, were dismissive of aspects of Manchu authority, both were fully aware of the enormity of the task ahead of them. "Many among the Chinese are highly refined and well-informed," Morrison wrote; "they will not be beneath us but superior."[74] He was capable of a surprising degree of cultural relativity, as when he decried the "hideous and distorted pictures formerly drawn of the rest of the nations, either by ignorance or artifice, as well as the representations of savage innocence" as complete untruths. Human nature, he argued, "is found much the same in every land. It is depraved, and vicious, and degraded by superstition; but it is improvable by the diffusion of knowledge, by human kindness, and can be renewed by the grace of God." All humans without exception are capable of being "changed, and civilized, and sanctified, and glorified."[75] Underlying Morrison's comments is the Protestant evangelical stress on the "manifest kindred and equality amongst all mankind."[76] For Morrison and his missionary colleagues, this stress on the equality of humanity in the eyes of God is crucial. Obviously, he did not mean by this any adherence to or sympathy with democratic or reformist political ideologies, but neither did he accept any claims for the intrinsic superiority of one people over another. In his "Address to the Public" of 1823, he emphasized that "all the various tribes of men have equal rights, and every system … has a right to be heard. When this shall be the case, mighty Truth shall prevail."[77] Morrison, like other missionaries, stressed the full equality of humanity in the eyes of God, even prior to Christian conversion, and he accepted that the Chinese were in most ways more civilized, sophisticated, and refined than he and his fellow Britons.

The world of Southeast Asia the China missionaries encountered was also one of quite extraordinary diversity: cultural, linguistic, and religious. First, the Qing empire practiced three major historic forms of religion known to the West by the terms "Confucianism" (*rujiao*), "Daoism" (*daojiao*), and a form of Buddhism (*fojiao*). In addition, they encountered another form of religious belief obtained from the synthesis of the three traditions, known as the "three teachings" (*sanjiao*), as well as popular forms of religious belief (*minjian zongjiao*), which though very prevalent and vigorous were generally dismissed by Catholic missionaries and their successors largely because they were oral religions without sacred written scripts. The orthodoxy of the "three religions" of China propagated in numerous British accounts of the nineteenth century was very much a Jesuit construction, deployed for strategic purposes.[78] To further complicate matters, the religion practiced by the Manchu imperial court was a Tibetan or Lamaist form of Buddhist belief. The empire also contained a substantial Muslim population and some Jews, both of which were fully tolerated by the Qing. Islam had migrated to China during the "Tartar Peace" established by the Mongols in the thirteenth century. There were also numerous religious "sects" or teachings, proscribed by the government as "Religious banditti."[79] There was little uniformity on the Christian side either; the empire contained Roman Catholic missionaries and their extensive numbers of converts (estimated around 300,000) and a Russian orthodox enclave at Beijing, as well Portuguese and Spanish Catholics, Dutch Protestants, and East India Company men of various religious persuasions from Anglican to nonconformity. At Malacca, where Morrison and Milne founded their college, the majority religion of the people was Islam. This part of Southeast Asia in the early nineteenth century thus contained a staggering diversity and complexity of global religious belief.

MORRISON ENCOUNTERS CONFUCIUS

John Barrow's dyspeptic estimation of Confucius in his review of Marshman's edition sadly set the tone for much of the early and mid nineteenth century prior to the serious and sophisticated re-evaluation in the translations of James Legge later in the century. Legge would sympathetically reappraise and remake Confucian thinking within the framework of Max Muller's comparativist understanding of religion.[80] Up until that historic reappraisal, Confucian thinking in Britain would come to be seen as an integral and informing part of China's problem, an ossified system of established textual learning which functioned mostly as an obstacle to China's progress and a reason to explain its allegedly stationary and non-progressive status. Such a view would gain support from contemporaneous Romantic notions of spontaneity in education, as famously exemplified in the fifth book of William Wordsworth's *The Prelude*, itself influenced by Barrow's negative account of Confucian educational theories in his *Travels in China* of 1804, discussed in Chapter 8. Morrison and his fellow missionaries at Malacca were instrumental in this process. While Marshman strenuously attempted to accommodate Confucius to a Protestant theology, Morrison and his group would identify the Chinese philosopher with atheism, materialism, and idolatry. There was, however, no inevitability about this process.

The group of missionaries organized around the Anglo-Chinese College at Malacca published a series of new translations of Chinese texts and literature and, in particular, the first British translation of the *Daxue* by Morrison in 1812 and the complete Four Books, including the first direct English translation of the complete *Lunyu*, the *Zhongyong*, and the *Mengzi* by David Collie in 1828. It is clear that the missionaries gave Confucian texts their serious attention and understood their importance, but they were unsympathetic to their subject, often reducing Confucius's hugely influential works to the status of translation exercises and exemplars of the limitations of human achievements when deprived of the blessings of divine revelation. They also confronted the bare classical Chinese texts without the knowledge and understanding of the sophisticated and established tradition of Chinese commentary that left them puzzled by the reputation of Confucianism. Scandalized by the Chinese equivalence of the Four Books to their Christian New Testament, they began their program of Confucian degradation, a prelude to the political degradations of China in the Opium Wars, the first course of those nineteenth-century English lessons, described by James Hevia as part of the pedagogy of imperialism.[81] Their statements about Confucian thinking become harder and less ambivalent as the decades pass, though it seems likely that they began their study with the Jesuit accommodationist reading in mind and became progressively disillusioned by what they saw as Confucianism's refusal to engage with their cherished shibboleths of an afterlife, immortality, and human sinfulness. This process culminated in David Collie's largely philistine and unsympathetic translation of the Four Books in 1828.

Some sense of the missionary's frustration with the status of Confucianism in Chinese culture can be gleaned from Morrison's account of his conversations with his Chinese assistants about Christianity and Confucianism. His was a frustration borne from a personal encounter with Chinese people. Although Morrison had opted to translate the scriptures rather than preach the word as a more effective strategy for propagating Christianity, he was very anxious to achieve his first Chinese conversion. The single most significant obstacle to this process was the cultural prestige of Confucius. Confucianism has no conception of either the original sin or the fallen nature of humanity that were the bedrock of Protestant evangelical theology. The Chinese word *zui*, signifying a crime or transgression, is usually used in translation for sin.[82] When discussing his assistant "Kô Sëen-sáng" in 1812, Morrison commented that he "does not manifest that conviction of his own sinfulness, and necessity of the work of the Redeemer, which I wish to see manifested."[83] It is his assistants' commitment to Confucian values that frustrates Morrison most:

they thought that Jesus and Confucius were alike – the one intended for Europe, and the other for China. I urged the striking difference that appears in one atoning for the sins of men, and teaching them so largely the way of a sinner's being accepted of God, whilst the other never mentioned God's name, nor taught anything respecting him. Observing that there was blame on the part of those who were unwilling to learn the right way – here the conversation dropped.[84]

Both Morrison's Christianity and Kô's Confucianism were, and still are, belief systems that claim universal applicability: Christ will save and Confucius will civilize. Low-hëen emphasized to Morrison that without Confucius, "the Chinese must have been mere brutes, and that not to worship him would be the highest ingratitude."[85]

The messianic equivalence of Confucius and Christ and the apparently sacred nature of the Four Books and the Bible irritated Morrison. After reading the Four Books he genuinely saw much in them that was excellent, but also that "taken together they are miserably defective." Morrison decried the virtual fetishization of Confucian texts in the educational system of China, where the "exercise of the literati, at their examinations consist of a paraphrase on a word or sentence as taken from the Four Books. The excellence consists in adhering to the idea of the text, and in the goodness of the style."[86] This practice of the literati is almost a mirror image of Morrison's own fundamentalist reading of his sacred scriptures. Similarly, the mass of textual commentary and exegesis surrounding Confucian texts paralleled those surrounding the Bible. For Morrison, Confucians are "atheists in the world; which, in the eye of reason, aided by divine revelation, is quite as irrational as the superstitions of the vulgar."[87] The Chinese, Morrison finds, neglect the teachings they see as foreign and exotic; and as "the depths of knowledge contained in the Four Books have never been fathomed; and, till that be done, it is folly to attend to any other."[88] From his experience as a resident at Canton and Macao, Morrison very quickly realized that Confucian thought would prove to be the greatest obstacle to the progress of Christianity in China. Whereas the Jesuits were keen to access and exploit the prestige of Confucianism to facilitate their own project, the Protestant missionaries knew that this prestige had to be obliterated in the eyes of the Chinese as surely as British howitzers would destroy the forts of the Qing government in the forthcoming Opium War. Once Morrison had lived in China, conversed with Chinese people, and read the Four Books, he realized that Confucius had to be metaphorically murdered.

Whereas the eighteenth-century Jesuits emphasized the centrality and importance of Confucianism in Chinese religion, identifying the popular religion of Buddhism of Fo (Fuh) with Reformation sectarianism and heresy, the Protestant missionaries repaid the compliment by portraying China as an empire more completely divided between the three religious beliefs (as constructed by Ricci) of Confucian, Daoist, and Buddhist. Their comments on this subject are scattered in a series of memoirs, essays in the *Evangelical Magazine* (1825), the *Indo-Chinese Gleaner*, and their various studies of China. In his *A View of China for Philological Purposes* of 1817, Morrison, for instance, described his understanding of the three religions of China, or what he calls, with a nonconformist's nod to his audience, "the Established Religions of China." He comments that the Chinese seem to have imported "many of their divinities from India" though thankfully leaving behind "entirely the gross indecent parts of the Indian superstition." Their mythology is "quite as ridiculous as those parts of the Greek and Romans, though certainly not so offensive to good morals as some parts of those elegant systems." Morrison is still, however, ambivalent when it comes to Confucianism. He frequently remarks on the value of its moral and ethical philosophy and can invoke its teachings: "As Confucius taught, our dislike of a man's vices should never be carried to such a height, as to make us blind to what is really good about him."[89]

In his later *Chinese Miscellany* of 1825, Morrison provides one of his most extended discussions of Confucianism. Confucianism, he argues, has the appearance of the Christian religion with the Five Classics approximating to the Old Testament and the Four Books to the New. The latter represent the "sayings of a Master, compiled by Four Disciples," resembling the four Gospels. What continues to disturb Morrison about this ancient philosophy is its lack of any conception of deity. Commenting on the classical texts, he writes:

with the exception of a few passages in the most ancient part of the Woo-king which retain seemingly something of the knowledge which Noah must have communicated to his children, the rest appears a godless system of personal, domestic, and political moralities, drawn only from the pride of the human heart, or a love of fame, or present expediency. The sanctions of the Eternal and Almighty God, arrayed with every natural and moral perfection; wise and good, and just and merciful; and the fears and the hopes of immortality; and the grace of a saviour; are wholly wanting in these ancient Chinese works.[90]

Commenting on the Confucian notion of the first cause of *taiji* (supreme ultimate) or *li* (principle), Morrison denies that the belief has "anything at all resembling the natural and moral perfections of the Deity; it is not the object of esteem, of reverence, of awe, of hope, trust, or of worship." The dual system of the Chinese universe he regards as a "baseless and atheistical theory."[91] Morrison attacks the Jesuit attempt to accommodate neo-Confucian cosmology with Christianity. He criticizes Le Comte's well-known conflation of Christian and Confucian systems in which "the Chinese *Shang-Te*" is placed at the top of the system, "next their words for *God* or *Spirit*, and *Saints*; below these are placed the three Chinese Powers, Heaven, Earth, and Man: then the *Ke*, which he [Le Comte] calls the breath of the Almighty; and next the *Yin* and the *Yang*; the *Tae-keih*, the eight *Kwa*, &c." Morrison accepts that the ancient belief in a "Supreme Ruler" or "Shang-Te" may have once referred to "Almighty God" but claims that the literati of China from the Song dynasty onwards, have explained away the theism of ancient writings; and have given them "that form of materialism, which the Dual system presents, and which some French writers still call, 'Pur deisme, ou religion naturelle.'"[92]

Elsewhere Morrison interprets the neo-Confucian notion of heaven (*tian*) as a form of pantheism, "a divine energy inherent in, and inseparable from, all matter."[93] In a letter to the *Indo-Chinese Gleaner* of July 1819, he set out his summary of the cosmology of the Confucians, identifying their notion of *taiji* or *li* with the "PLASTIC NATURES of the western philosophers," presumably of the Cambridge Platonist Ralph Cudworth, the monadology of Leibniz, or even the active force of Joseph Priestley, viewed as "an independent principle" not under the control of "any Sovereign Being." The Confucian cosmology of a female Yin and male Yang producing the universe, he identifies as a sexual system which has parallels only with Egyptian Pharonic mythology, leading him to suspect that rather than being the bearers of an original divine revelation, the "Chinese derived both their written character and their philosophy from Egypt." For a dissenting minister, the notion that the universe is created from a relationship between the Yin and Yang forces resembling "that of the sexes, in the generation of men, and brute animals" is most unpalatable. In neo-Confucian cosmology the primordial mass (*hun dun*) actually divides into two spontaneously and naturally without the intervention of any creator god.[94]

Morrison countenances the possibility, though unproven, that the Chinese may indeed have in ancient times possessed some "just sentiments concerning the Divine Being"; however, rather than elevating the Chinese in his eyes, this merely damns them even further (as for other peoples) for losing this dispensation. The men who composed the Five Classics lived at a time when "traditional revelation was less obscured by idolatry and superstition" and the "original revelation" was carried to "all parts of the earth" but the "depravity of man did not suffer this revelation to continue long in its pristine purity."[95] Rather than stressing the positive of the knowledge of an original divine revelation like Ricci, Morrison stresses instead the negative of the natural depravity of humanity that allowed the Chinese to lose this precious body of knowledge. Turning to the Four Books, Morrison characterizes their philosophy as "magnificent talking, founded upon gratuitous data." Yet baseless though it may be, it still might be called an "orderly" and "beautiful" system but only if its "various fanciful unfounded theories of nature, of religion, of morals, of politics, of medicine, &c." are accepted as coherent premises. The Confucian system, however, has "nothing of a Divine sanction."[96]

He regards Confucianism as essentially a form of atheism and materialism, which prevents him from admiring those ethical aspects of its doctrines for which he seems have had genuine sympathy and understanding. Ultimately, it is Confucian cosmology that prevents Morrison from praising Confucian thinking, no matter how, as what Wilberforce would call a practical Christian, he is drawn to the ethical and quotidian aspects of this thinking. Referring to 11.12 of the *Lunyu*, Confucius, it seems, "confessed, he did not understand much respecting the gods, and therefore he preferred not speaking on the subject."[97] Morrison's influential depiction of Confucian thought becomes the orthodoxy of the Anglo-Chinese College established at Malacca. Nevertheless, like Marshman and the "gentleman of Serampore," the Malacca missionaries thought it most important that the Four Books were translated into English. However skewed the underlying assumptions and methodologies they brought to bear on this project, it nevertheless involved engagement with and the cultural transmission of knowledge between China and Britain, however troubled and tortuous that process might be.[98]

The eighteenth-century consensus was that there were, essentially, four world religions: Christianity, Islam, Judaism, and Idolatry, with all the non-Abrahamic religions included as varieties of the fourth category. This consensus was to be overturned by British missionary writing, with far-reaching consequences for the future reputation of China. These missionaries were possessed of a familiar Protestant faith that stressed the importance of the scriptures and the personal relationship between human and God. They stressed the importance of a personal conception of sin and depravity from which the individual can be redeemed through faith in Christ. Knowing "what is right and doing what is wrong," for both Chinese and Europeans, "can be accounted for only on the principle that human nature is depraved, or fallen from its original purity and rectitude."[99] They were thus dismissive of what they viewed as priestcraft, hierarchy and idolatry, all things they claimed to find in Qing China, as well as in the religion of their Catholic predecessors and contemporary rivals. Their writings are thus obsessed with the prevalence and sinfulness of idolatry that interrupts the personal relationship with God, mediated through the word, hence their fixation on the need to translate the word of their God as revealed in scripture to the Chinese masses. Of course, Chinese thought and culture simply did not recognize such Christian notions of a personal creator God, Heaven, soul, original sin, Satan, retribution, or salvation and grace. There is no equivalent word for "sin" in the Chinese language. The Chinese were possessed of their own Confucian cosmology and ethics with its own universalist aspirations.[100] British Chinese studies were thus inflected throughout by religious concerns and tensions. Their vision of China and the powerful but ethnologically cosmological assumptions that supported it would condition and shape the Romantic Sinology, especially with regard to their virtual destruction of the *apogée* and metonym of Chinese civilization and favorite of Enlightenment thought, Confucius.

CHAPTER 4

"Fruits of the highest culture may be improved and varied by foreign grafts": the Canton School of Romantic Sinology – Staunton and Davis

A crucial element of Romantic Sinology was the contribution of the East India Company school at Canton.[1] Although Morrison's role as a teacher and scholar there was vital, more characteristic of its approach was the work two of its senior officers, George Thomas Staunton and John Francis Davis. Both were serious early scholars of Chinese literature and its language. They were resident at the East India Company's factory and Davis was, by far, the most accomplished student of the school of Chinese studies set up there by Morrison. Both produced important translations of key Chinese texts. Their sinology was, however, markedly more sympathetic to Chinese culture than that of the missionaries of the Anglo-Chinese College, though their approach was just as interested in different ways; they were there to facilitate the lucrative tea trade and make money for the Company and themselves. Notably, they were free from the classicizing imperatives that had driven the Jesuits and still, to an extent, permeated the missionary sinology of Morrison and the Malacca school, obsessed as they were with the theological and spiritual nature of Chinese orthodoxy. Staunton and Davis were freer to explore the more popular and practical aspects of Chinese life and culture and to translate works about Chinese law and diplomacy, as well as popular works of fiction and drama for both a specialist and a general audience. This is especially so in the case of Davis, who substantially expanded the very meager provision of Chinese literary texts in English. Notably, Staunton translated the Qing legal code and Davis produced a vocabulary of Chinese words and terms currently used in the commercial exchanges of cosmopolitan Canton, as well as an essay on the writing of Chinese characters, all essential knowledge for the British factory at Canton. Increasingly, the literary criteria which were being brought to bear upon Chinese literature were not the neo-classical desiderata of the Jesuits and Voltaire, but those of an aesthetics informed by emerging Romantic or Wordsworthian concepts of the simple and the natural, in which the national British bard, Shakespeare, features as a comparative touchstone of artistic value and worth. Davis's interest in the drama and the novel, for example, was as a means of understanding China and the Chinese; "what we now want," he argued, "is a little *practical knowledge* of Chinese Literature, instead of speculative dissertations on the nature of the language" (my italics).[2]

CHINESE LAW: THE EAST INDIA COMPANY SINOLOGY OF GEORGE THOMAS STAUNTON

George Thomas Staunton was Robert Morrison's major rival as a sinologist for early nineteenth-century Britain. Barrow claimed that he was "unquestionably the first who opened to Europeans any of the useful treasures of Chinese literature."[3] Staunton was fully initiated from a very early age into British colonial and commercial concerns in Southeast Asia. He was to become a crucial expert on China in Britain during the period of the Anglo-Chinese wars. He was the son of George Leonard Staunton, Macartney's deputy on the British embassy of 1792–94 to China. The eleven-year-old boy, who acted as a page to the ambassador, began to learn Chinese with the two Chinese Catholic missionaries who acted as interpreters for the embassy while in London in 1792 and then on the voyage itself. He turned out to be the most accomplished student of the language among the embassy and, famously, was presented to the Qianlong emperor and conversed with him in Chinese. He also copied several letters in Chinese for Macartney when the embassy's interpreters were anxious not to be associated with their contents. The emperor was apparently delighted by these accomplishments and presented the boy with an imperial purse, a singularly favored gift (Figure 2).

Staunton's early experience of China led to his later appointment as a junior writer for the Company at Canton in 1798 and in 1804 he became a supercargo (managing the trading of the cargoes of the Company ships), finally becoming president of the Select Committee in 1816. In 1805, he translated into Chinese a tract written by Alexander Pearson, the Company's surgeon, about Edward Jenner's recently discovered process of vaccination for smallpox. In 1816, he acted as second commissioner on the Amherst embassy to China. He had hoped, unrealistically, to be its ambassador though the Chinese were unhappy about his presence and that of other commercial agents on a diplomatic mission. Staunton subsequently returned to Britain in 1817. Outbid in 1818 by Thomas Wildman for Byron's Newstead Abbey, he instead purchased the Leigh Park estate in Hampshire, where he erected a three-arched "Chinese" bridge in 1831,

Figure 2. William Alexander, *The Reception of Lord Macartney by the Qianlong Emperor at Jehol in 1793*; in the foreground is the emperor carried in his chair and to right, Lord Macartney with his entourage, including the young Staunton as page, 1796 © Trustees of the British Museum.

followed by a Chinese boathouse, summerhouse, and fort, displaying the imperial flag of China. Leigh Water was thought to resemble the imperial lake at Beijing in shape. The billiard room of Staunton's hall housed his China display.[4]

Staunton sat as MP for several constituencies in the pre- and post-reformed parliaments, at first as a Liberal Tory and then as an independent, generally siding with the Whig reforming government. In Britain he was regarded as a China expert, though his Chinese studies in effect ceased, largely because he no longer had access to Chinese expertise. He became increasingly robust about China as his Chinese experience receded in time, supporting Palmerston's bellicose war policy over the opium trade. Yet Staunton was also instrumental in the process of establishing the chairs of Chinese at University College and King's College in London, as well as in the founding of the Royal Asiatic Society in 1823, to which he offered his substantial collection of Chinese printed books and manuscript dictionaries, establishing the first significant Chinese library in Britain.[5]

Staunton published three very important works on China. He translated the Qing legal code *Ta Tsing Leu Lee* in 1810 and produced his *Narrative of the Chinese Embassy to the Khan of the Tourgouth Tartars* in 1821. His privately printed and circulated *Notes of Proceedings and Occurrences during the British Embassy to Peking* (1824) is a major account of the Amherst embassy, along with those by Ellis, Davis, and Abel. The *Ta Tsing Leu Lee* is an extremely significant translation that has received comparatively little critical attention yet is closely related in importance to William Jones's vastly more celebrated translations of the Hindu legal statutes in terms of its scholarly and cultural importance.[6] Francis Jeffrey extensively reviewed the volume in the *Edinburgh* and Barrow in the *Quarterly*. Interestingly, Robert Southey possessed a copy, though the pages remained uncut at his death.[7] Staunton's translation of the code was heavily used and survived as a document for consultation for non-Chinese-speaking researchers until as late as 1994 when it was superseded by a new translation.[8]

The *Ta Tsing Leu Lee* is a crucial document in the knowledge transfer process from China to Britain and the West. China experts regarded it as an essential tool for the rest of the century. The translation was, however, partial in featuring only the fundamental laws and not including the important supplementary legal sub-statutes or *li*. Staunton's main motivation in translating the Qing codes was to provide the Company at Canton with reliable information relating to the various legal issues with which the trade with China was inevitably embroiled.[9] The most famous examples of legal tussles related to a number of accidental homicides of Chinese subjects occasioned by British sailors. Formally, accidental homicide was punishable by execution, though the sentence could be commuted with the payment of a fine and compensation to the injured family. In 1799 William and Dorothy Wordsworth's cousin, Captain John Wordsworth, had been involved in such an incident concerning the wounding of a Chinese man by one of the crew of the British schooner *Providence*. The wounded man was taken to Captain Wordsworth's ship, the *Earl of Abergavenny*, for medical assistance, leading to a dispute with the Chinese authorities.[10] In 1807 a more notable case, involving Edward Sheen of the *Neptune*, was resolved through the payment of an indemnity.[11] The appendices to Staunton's translation provide copies of Chinese documents relating to this case. Two years later in 1809, Jane Austen's brother Frank, captain of the *St. Albans*, was similarly involved in a dispute at Canton in which it was claimed a Chinese man had been killed.[12] This was the sharp end of the Chinese and British encounter, involving interactions with ordinary Chinese and Britons, as well as their respective authorities. Throughout such cases the British continued to have grave doubts about the transparency and fairness of the Chinese justice system, and their problematic demands for extraterritorial legal jurisdiction in China over their own subjects became a crucial issue and later treaty provision. Staunton's translation thus is a direct response to British concerns about the Qing legal system and their worries about being subject to it. He claimed that his decision to translate the code resulted from his personal witnessing of "unnecessary provocations, groundless apprehensions, and embarrassing discussions" relating to a "false or imperfect" knowledge of the "spirit" of Chinese law.[13] The emphasis here, however, is clearly on the *imperfections* of British understandings, rather than any such failings with Chinese law itself.

As St. André has argued, Staunton's translation is, in the main, a response to the criticism of his former tutor John Barrow's characteristically negative account of Chinese justice and notions of legality in his *Travels in China* (1804), whereby Staunton "strives to present the Chinese legal code as something comprehensible, reasonable and just."[14] Staunton argues that the code represents a fine illustration of the "system and constitution" of the Chinese government. The translation serves as an intended correction of Jesuit bias by an "objective" British observer in the wake of the accounts of the Macartney embassy (i, iii). Notably, Staunton's translation is much more positive about China than the embassy account of Barrow, finding it difficult to arrogate "any violent degree of moral or physical superiority" to Chinese or British. Against Barrow's rather gothicized allegations of the horrors of the Chinese practice of infanticide (which he never witnessed), Staunton claimed that this rarely happened except in cases of "the hopeless anguish of poverty" or "such unhappy and defective formation, as might be conceived to render life a painful burden" (vii). Though he admits the practice exists, its prevalence has been over-emphasized and should not be used "as a proof of the cruelty or insensibility of the Chinese character" (347). Staunton also argues that the slavery which exists in Chinese society is rather a "mild form of servitude" and "not very degrading in a country, in which no condition of life appears to admit of any considerable degree of personal liberty and independence" (293). He finds many positive aspects of Chinese life and customs. In particular he pays fulsome and perhaps unexpected tribute to

the sobriety, industry, and even intelligence of the lower classes; to the almost total absence of feudal rights and privileges; to the equable distribution of landed property; to the natural incapacity and indisposition of government and people to an indulgence in ambitious projects and foreign conquests; and lastly, to a system of penal laws, if not the most just and equitable, at least the most comprehensive, uniform, and suited to the genius of the people for whom it is designed, perhaps of any that ever existed. (vii)

Staunton points out that although under Chinese law there is no presumption of innocence, as there is under English law, nevertheless there are other parts of the legal code that compensate for this. He is keen to mitigate the impression which other commentators, notably Cornelius De Pauw and Barrow, had propagated of the almost omnipresent practice of corporal punishment in the Chinese empire, which he denies is "in universal use, or administered with such undistinguishing severity, as has sometime been imagined." He points out that the use of judicial torture was subject to clear legal limitation and regulation, and the instruments permitted for this purpose were explicitly codified. Magistrates who used torture excessively or inappropriately were themselves liable to punishment (488–89).

Staunton's primary target here is George Henry Mason's sensationalist volume *The Punishments of China* (1808) with its twenty-two color illustrations of various Chinese punishments in which "the fancy of the painter has given, in some instances, a representation of cruelties, and of barbarous executions, which it would be very erroneous to suppose have a place in the ordinary course of justice" (xxvii).[15] In particular, Staunton singles out both Mason and the Abbé Grosier who claimed that the Chinese code contained a law making the wearing of pearls a "capital crime." He denies that such claims have any substance in theory or practice (186). Similarly, the spectacular Chinese punishment of the *lingchi* or "cutting into death by ten thousand pieces," generally fetishized in the West as the "death by a thousand cuts," is seldom enacted. Staunton notes that the emperor would normally commute such a sentence to beheading (269). The *lingchi*, as Brook, Bourgon, and Blue have brilliantly argued, would become "for Europeans the *supplice chinois*, the archetype of a supposed Chinese penchant for 'refined cruelty'" in which the complex history of the punishment and the discourse surrounding it, as well as the context of spectacular European punishments, were obscured.[16] Of course, in Staunton's Britain around two hundred crimes carried the sentence of death by hanging, including several for petty thefts, such as pickpocketing.

Enlightenment thinkers and Jesuit missionaries often praised Chinese theories and practices of punishment in contrast to those of European states. The Kangxi emperor, who condemned the use of torture as contrary to Confucian thought, had been hailed in this regard as an enlightened despot, in the mode of Frederick II of Prussia and Joseph II of Austria, both sinophiles who abolished torture in their dominions. However, with the general decline in estimations of China in the late eighteenth century onwards, the more pervasive view became that of an oriental despotism, governed through fear and ruled by the rod and brutal corporal punishments, as exemplified by Mason's *Punishments of China*. Such views combined with an increasingly racialized ideology that fancifully associated extreme physical and cruel punishment and torture with an allegedly Asiatic mentality and physiology that sadistically enjoyed the inflicting of pain on bodies more able to withstand it.[17] Staunton's translation is notable for its downplaying of such spectacular and somatic aspects of Chinese punishment and torment. Although these punishments are present, Staunton believes that they were exceptional in practice and frequently mitigated. Similarly, with regard to the section of the code relating to offenses committed by foreigners, he denies that such laws have been enforced "except with considerable allowances" in favor of the Europeans (36). In the case of homicide, he affirms the notion that "no allowance is ever made in cases purely accidental" is without foundation. Alluding to the case of Edward Sheen, Staunton shows that the flexibility contained within the code permitted the Company to use its provisions to allow for the victims of the homicide to be compensated (315).

Reviewing the work in the *Edinburgh*, the Benthamite Francis Jeffrey found much to praise in the Chinese code, emphasizing that it contained "nothing … of the monstrous verbiage of most other Asiatic productions" with their "miserable incoherence, the tremendous *non sequiturs* and eternal repetitions of those oracular performances." Instead, we have "a calm, concise, and distinct series of enactments savouring throughout of practical judgment and European good sense" approaching to British standards.[18] Brook, Bourgon, and Blue argue convincingly that Jeffrey's qualified praise for the Qing legal code represents a displaced Benthamite transcultural criticism of the English common law tradition with its archaic precedents and routine and brutal flogging of British sailors and soldiers.[19] It is clear that Chinese jurisprudence impacted on debates about British and European legal practice. Nevertheless, for Jeffrey, the Chinese resort to torture and flogging was an indication of the level of civilization achieved by the empire and a reflection on the nature and customs of Chinese peoples. Barrow's more substantial review of May 1810 for the *Quarterly* was also generally favorable to Staunton, but, as one might expect, returned to the more negative view of Chinese law and punishment as outlined in his earlier *Travels in China* of 1804. China is thus like "a great school" the population of which is "kept in order entirely by flogging." Barrow, however, regards the government of China as "profligate and corrupt" and it is in the execution of its laws that tyranny and corruption are present.[20]

Staunton's translation of the Qing laws is a classic product of the "Canton school" of Romantic Sinology. Born from a sustained residence in a world where British and Chinese encountered, traded, and negotiated with each other on a daily basis, the *Tsa Tsing Leu Lee* reflects a rational and, in general, humane body of law, aware of the complexities of the governance of the huge empire. The nineteenth century, however, would not follow Staunton's lead in this respect and Chinese punishments would achieve a notorious and spectacular presence in the European imaginary. The *lingchi*, unfettered from its grounding in Chinese debates about punishment, would come to typify a particularly Chinese approach to punishment and the Chinese body come to exemplify abnormally high pain thresholds. Gothicized, racialized, and aestheticized, such extreme punishments, spectacularly illustrated in the burgeoning global print media and, towards the end of the century, available through visual technologies, would increasingly serve as a justification for the European colonial presence in China.

Staunton's presence as a serious sinologist, along with his comparatively sympathetic response to Chinese culture, notably diminished when he left Canton for London in 1817. Writing to Morrison in 1813, he openly deferred to him as the leading China scholar, certainly much more advanced than "the gentlemen at Serampore" from whom he expected little in terms of new translations. Realistically, he is aware that "the true spirit and idiom of the language" is impossible to achieve without a "ready and constant access to the natives."[21] Staunton's sinology thus provided a substantial body of new knowledge about China from the perspective of an established Company official and diplomat. His emphasis was on those kinds of knowledge about China that could be construed as useful in allowing the British to understand contemporary China and the policies of its government. This often led him into sympathetic transcultural engagements with Chinese law and diplomacy. These facets were important in constructing the body of knowledge that became Romantic Sinology in the lead-up to the Opium War in 1839. Certainly, from looking at Staunton's translations with their focus on the practical business of trade and diplomacy, it could be argued that the conflict that broke out between Britain and China was by no means an inevitable or predetermined event. His writings on China often demonstrate a sympathetic engagement with the peoples (if not the government) with whom he worked on a daily basis in cosmopolitan Canton. Both Romantic Sinology as a body of knowledge and the individuals that produced it contain this shifting ambivalence towards China.

JOHN FRANCIS DAVIS'S CANTON SINOLOGY

John Francis Davis became the leading sinologist of the "Canton school" of Romantic Sinology but his interests were far more literary than those of Staunton. Davis is an important figure in British sinology and with Percy and Goethe one of the pioneers of China's presence in world literature. Despite his importance to the development of orientalism and sinology in Britain as well as his significance as an historical agent for the Company and then the British crown, very little has been written about him, in stark contrast to his voluminous works about China. A true child of the Romantic age, and born in the same year as John Keats, Davis as a young man working in the Company factory at Canton must have found Chinese fiction and drama a much easier and more congenial proposition to translate than the more austere and difficult Confucian texts and commentaries, written in classical Chinese, with which he had little sympathy. Neither was he driven by the theological and ontological concerns that tormented and perplexed his missionary contemporaries. Whatever the reason, Davis's move to study the *belle lettres* of China is a deeply significant moment for British sinology and Romantic understandings of China, as well as for the presence of Chinese literature in the world. As St. André argues, Davis's translations were marked by a new kind of professionalism linked to the growing institutionalization of British sinology.[22] He became a fellow of the Royal Society in 1821 and a key member of the Royal Asiatic Society, founded by Staunton in 1823, where his papers were read and debated. He was also a member of its Oriental Translation Committee, which funded the publication of several of his translations.

Even more than Staunton, Davis was fully integrated into the British colonial ethos. His father was a director of the Company and he was educated at its College at Hertford. It is thus unsurprising that at the age of eighteen, in 1813, he was appointed as a writer to the factory at Canton, where he encountered Staunton, Morrison, and Manning. Throughout his life, first as a Company man, and then as a servant of the British crown, Davis was a key instrument in carrying out British policy in China. He was writing during a period of increasing political instability in China, or "the late unsettled state of the empire" as he describes it.[23] Davis considered that the translation of Chinese literature was closely related to British interests in the region.[24] His scholarly study of Chinese was motivated by the "necessity" for the British to study and understand Chinese. Ominously, he writes that with the "extension of our Indian frontier to the northward and eastward" this necessity will become greater if Britain is placed in relations of a "far more weighty and important nature, than such as are simply commercial."[25]

Davis had a pronounced flair for languages and was able to master Chinese relatively quickly, becoming proficient enough to serve with Morrison, Staunton, and Manning as an interpreter on Amherst's embassy in 1816. He was promoted to be the last president of the Select Committee of the Company in 1832 and was appointed joint commissioner in China in 1834 with Napier, for whose policies he had little sympathy. Davis briefly became Chief Superintendent on Napier's death that year and pursued a policy of "absolute silence and quiescence" while awaiting new instructions from the foreign secretary, Palmerston. His ingrained Company prejudices against free trade led to conflict with the independent country traders, whom he loathed, and who accused him of acting spinelessly in his dealings with the Chinese. After three months of their hostility, he resigned from the post in 1835.[26] Returning to China in 1844, he succeeded Sir Henry Pottinger to become second governor of the newly seceded territory of Hong Kong in 1845. In April 1847 Davis resorted to force in dispatching warships to secure the Bogue (Humen) ports and troops to occupy the Canton factories to implement the British right of entry to the city under the Treaty of Nanjing, a clear act of colonial aggression.

As governor, Davis was instrumental in setting up the Hong Kong branch of the Royal Asiatic Society in 1847.[27] He subsequently established himself as *the* major British expert on China after Morrison's death and Staunton's retirement; his *The Chinese: A General Description of the Empire of China and Its Inhabitants* (1836) and *Sketches of China* (1841) became standard works on China. The former went through many editions and was substantially revised after the second Anglo-Chinese War. A synthesis of his many previous writings on China, *The Chinese*, serves as perhaps the definitive summary and statement of Romantic Sinology, and, indeed, British Sinology, prior to Legge. Davis also published a *Vocabulary, containing Chinese words and phrases peculiar to Canton and Macao* (1824) as well as several contributions to the Royal Asiatic Society, such as his "Eugraphia Sinensis, or the Art of Writing in Chinese character," which was read in 1825. He contributed numerous translations of Chinese texts to the new Romantic Sinology, including: *San-Yu-Low; or* the *Three Dedicated Rooms* (1815); *Laou-Seng-Urh or, "An Heir in His Old Age"* (1817); *Chinese Novels* (1822); *Han Koong Tsew or the Sorrows of Han* (1829); *Poeseos Sinensis commentarii: on the Poetry of the Chinese* (1829); and his masterpiece, the translation *The Fortunate Union* (1829). He returned to England in 1848 and continued to recycle and augment his writings on China late into the century, including his *Chinese Miscellanies: a Collection of Essays and Notes* (1865).

Davis presents himself as providing a more objective but also a more comprehensive sinology than that of the Jesuits. The Catholic missionaries were "led astray by their Chinese prejudices" and their respect for the Confucian classics, having ignored "the *modern* state of *general* literature" (my italics).[28] Part of Davis's importance and significance to British understandings of China lies in the fact that he sought to widen the scope of British knowledge of Chinese literature, moving beyond the Jesuit preoccupation with the Confucian Five Classics and the Four Books to encompass novels, drama, and poetry. In his *Chinese Miscellanies* of 1865, he justified this concern by his claim that "there appears no readier or more agreeable mode of becoming intimately acquainted with a people, from whom Europe can have so little to learn on the score of either moral or physical science, than by drawing largely from the inexhaustible stores of their lighter literature."[29] In this venture he was part of the general tendency of the Romantic age, evidenced variously in the works of Wordsworth and Herder, to investigate authentic national cultures more widely as a means to understand their national spirit. St. André argues that Davis, unlike Percy, adopts a "nativizing" or "domesticating" approach to Chinese literature, insisting on the many points which it has in common with European writing, using familiar British terms to translate Chinese equivalents, thus presenting novels and dramas to the British reader which look "as little foreign as possible" and which could pass for English novels. Thus two forms of translation practice become current, one that translates and domesticates Chinese texts for a general public and one that retains the foreignness of the texts and the specialist terms and language for the scholarly journals. Davis's work employs both practices, though moving from the foreignizing to the domesticating.[30]

SORROWS AND SHADOWS: DAVIS, CHINESE LITERATURE,
AND ROMANTIC POETICS

Davis is thus notable as the first commentator on Chinese culture to apply the European notion of *belles lettres* to Chinese literature, under which heading he describes "Drama, Poetry, and Romances or Novels."[31] When discussing Chinese writing, Davis demonstrates canons of taste that are unmistakably Romantic in origin.

His sinology is especially significant in its reappraisal and construction of Chinese drama, a genre generally dismissed by both Jesuit and British writers. *The Chinese* (1836) contains a substantial description of the popularity of the drama and its various forms and stagecraft. Domesticating the form, Davis emphasizes its close similarity with European opera. In his translation of the drama *Laosheng er* by Guan Hanqing, he urges that his readership should be wary of dismissing Chinese drama after reading the existing critical accounts of performances such as those by John Bell, De Guignes, Isbrant Yves, Macartney, Barrow, and Staunton. They often located lowness, vulgarity, and even obscenity in the performance, but Davis reminds his readers that English drama, even Shakespeare, contains similar scenes and situations. Davis describes how Chinese theater is a popular and vibrant part of the nation's culture, "universally performed and encouraged from the court to the cottage," and of which the "Chinese are so passionately fond." There are no public theaters as the Chinese construct them on the spot, resembling "those booths erected for similar purposes in Bartholomew Fair." Such pieces, he allows, may appear to the European viewer absurd, but without an understanding of the dialogue of the drama any reliable judgment as to its worth simply cannot be formed. Europeans have had little opportunity to make any informed judgment as "a garbled translation of a single drama by Pere Prémare, a Jesuit" is the only European translation available. Prémare's translation of the *Zhao shi guer* or *The Orphan of the House of Zhao* (discussed in Chapter 8), reprinted by Du Halde and translated in the two English editions of his *History* and Percy's *Miscellaneous Pieces*, was problematic in that it omitted the poetic parts of the play, which are the most accomplished elements and correspond to the Greek choruses and in which "sentiment, eloquence, passion, are all expressed."[32]

Significantly, Davis chose to translate from the two hundred fascicles of Chinese plays held by the Company at Canton two dramas from Zang Maoxun's collection of Yuan plays: *Laosheng er* (*An Heir in His Old Age*) and *Hangong qiu* (*The Sorrows of Han*) in 1817 and 1829 respectively.[33] These were the first nineteenth-century translations of Yuan dramas that would become well-known plays in Europe. The first of these, the relatively minor drama *An Heir in his Old Age*, Davis describes as "the simple representation of a story in the domestic life … in which Chinese manners and Chinese feelings are faithfully delineated and expressed, in a natural manner, and in an appropriate language." Davis utilizes the critical vocabulary of Wordsworthian poetics from the famous "Preface" to the *Lyrical Ballads* (1798) to describe this drama which deals with "filial piety ... the first of virtues, and the lack of it, one of the worst of crimes," as well as the moral imperative to have a son, which allows a man to take inferior wives and concubines. He brings his Chinese drama close to the subject of Wordsworth's poems and ballads such as "Michael" and "The Idiot Boy," which deal with the fundamental relationships between parents and their children, another "unexpected affinity." The drama explores the predicament of the second wife or concubine. Such wives have no rights and their children are considered as the children of the first wife.

The characters in the drama derive from "a family in the middling class of society" (xxxiv–xxxvi). It exhibits "the unity and integrity of action and design," and all the incidents of the narrative turn on the "misery arising out of the want of an heir to perform the duties which filial piety demand, both to the living and the dead." The scenes and acts are "as properly divided as those of an European drama" and the "sentiments are naturally expressed, often tender and affecting, and always friendly to virtue" (xliii–xliv). The drama concerns a rich and aging merchant who has no male heir. To rectify this he takes a second wife who becomes pregnant but his first wife and her daughter and son-in-law conspire to remove the second wife to secure the inheritance of his entire property. The merchant also has an unworldly nephew whom his daughter and her husband brutally abuse and cheat. The key act of the drama for Davis is the third, in which the nephew, though poor, conscientiously performs the rites of oblation at the tomb of his parents while the wealthy daughter and husband fail to do so for the deceased family of the merchant. This underscores for the merchant the crucial importance of having a son to perform the rites for him when he is dead. After the disowning of his son-in-law, his daughter reveals to the merchant that she has sheltered his second wife and his son, now three years old. The merchant is overjoyed to find that he has indeed an heir in his old age to perform the rites on his tomb.

Davis finds many things in common between this Wordsworthian comedy and the subjects of European and classical writing. His mode of criticism is a comparative one, in many ways a cruder version of that championed by recent critics, such as Zhang Longxi.[34] Although he admits to removing some passages in the drama that he regards as "grossly indecent," he praises its lyrical elements which he believes recall the chorus of the Greek drama and its opening introductory sections that resemble the "prologues of Greek drama, and particularly ... those of Euripides." Davis compares the drama's heightened dialogue to the recitative in the Italian opera, further domesticating the drama and stressing what it has in common with the European tradition (xlii–xliv). Unlike Prémare, he attempted to translate both the "irregular verse which is sung and chaunted" and the part of the drama in the "language of common conversation." The former is often obscure and seems to take as its main purpose "the gratification of the ear" rather than the explication of character or plot. In line with current Romantic theories of translation, Davis hopes to render both these registers into English to "best convey the spirit of the original, without departing from its literal meaning" (xlvii–viii). Whatever its merits, the Chinese drama is unquestionably authentic to China in a Herderian sense and thus to Davis represents in some loose way the culture of the Chinese *volk*. In comparing Chinese with Hindu drama, Davis also pays the former a very real and unmistakably Wordsworthian compliment: Chinese drama, he claims, "adheres strictly to nature ... describing human manners and human feelings," whereas the Indian drama soars "beyond nature, into the labyrinth of an intricate and inexplicable mythology" (xli–xlv). Dismissing the escapism of the Hindu dramatic canon, made accessible to the West in William Jones's Sanskrit translations, Davis argues for the human value of Chinese literature, a literature that speaks to the human heart, what Keats famously referred to in his letter to Benjamin Bailey of November 1817 as the "holiness of the heart's affections."[35]

Davis dispenses with the neo-classical preferences of both Jesuit scholarship and Voltaire's criticism. Voltaire famously adapted Prémare's version of the Chinese drama as *L'Orphelin de la Chine* in 1755 and maintained that the Chinese drama was superior to the "monstrous farces" of Shakespeare. Davis, writing nearly three decades after James Boydell's Shakespeare Gallery was established in London, patriotically boasts that "few Englishmen would give up the worst 'farce' of Shakespeare, for the heavy monotony and blustering declamation of the best 'tragedy' of Voltaire" (xxxii). He feels no need to undertake a cultural cringe before the sophistications of French civilization, and his cultural confidence in the British rejection of French neo-Classicism (and Frenchified rococo chinoiserie) is apparent. This validation of British cultural superiority, as demonstrated by Shakespeare's achievement, is intimately related to the nation's global presence, as Davis's career as scholar, trader, and, later, colonial administrator demonstrates.

Davis returned to Chinese drama in 1829 with his translation of the beautiful opening drama in Zang's collection, Ma Zhiyuan's *Hangong qiu* or *Autumn in the Han Palace*, which he translated as *Han Koong Tsew or the Sorrows of Han* (1829).[36] In a similar manner to the various adaptations of the *Orphan*, Davis placed the historical context of the drama's treatment of Han dynasty conflict with Northern Xiongnu barbarians into the generalized dichotomous strife between Tartar and Chinese, or when "the growing effeminacy of the court, and consequent weakness of the government, emboldened the Tartars in their aggressions" (v). The drama concerns the love of the Han emperor for a beautiful lady who becomes his princess. However, the Khan of the Tartars demands the princess as his bride as the price of his continued alliance with China. En route to his camp the princess throws herself into the River Amur to avoid the match. The treaty is thus preserved but only at the cost of her life. The emperor yearns for his lost love and dreams of her being torn from him by the Tartars. He awakens to hear the mournful cries of migrating geese, in Davis's truncated version "'Hark, the passing fowl screamed twice or thrice!—Can it know there is one so desolate as I?'" (17). In Chinese poetic symbolism, the wild goose is a messenger bird here bringing the emperor news of his beloved's death.[37] Davis is keen to establish the drama in the context of European notions of tragedy despite the fact that he admits the Chinese recognize no such formal distinctions: "love and war constitute the whole subject of the piece, of which the moral is to expose the evil consequences of luxury, effeminacy, and supineness in the sovereign." In subtitling his translation "A Chinese Tragedy" Davis is following the tradition established by Prémare, Du Halde, Murphy, Voltaire, Percy, and others of explaining Chinese dramatic practice by European notions of tragedy.[38] The debates about this subject frequently focused on the keeping of the classical unities, but Davis, with the example of Shakespeare in mind, is able to apply the genre more loosely. He argues that the drama corresponds to the European definition of tragedy as the unity of action is maintained and the unities of place and time are more present than they are in British tragedies. The "grandeur and gravity of the subject, the rank and dignity of the personages, the tragical catastrophe, and the strict award of poetical justice" should satisfy the neo-classicist critic (vi). Frequently, Davis makes comparison between the action of the drama and that of Shakespeare's tragedies. For instance, when his beloved princess appears before the Han emperor in a dream vision, he states that, "there is nothing in this more extravagant than the similar vision in the tragedy of Richard III" (15, 17). Thus does Davis incorporate Chinese drama within a familiar British paradigm. In so doing he is not estranging Chinese writing but stressing its similarities with British practice.

Davis also champions Chinese poetry. His most substantial discussion of the subject is his *Poeseos Sinensis commentarii: on the Poetry of the Chinese*, read to the Royal Asiatic Society on May 2, 1829, and published under that title later in the year. Demand for this essay was substantial enough to merit its republication in 1870. The essay has been judged as "by far the most extensive, and the best, of the few accounts of Chinese poetry available" in the early nineteenth century.[39] The essay covers the rules of Chinese versification and discussion of the "style and spirit of Chinese poetry." It presents a vigorous defense of the excellence of Chinese poetry, denying that the Chinese language is any less inimical to the art of poetry than the European. Davis spends much time refuting the view that all Chinese words are simply monosyllables and thus not conducive to poetic expression. As Chinese people find English much harder to pronounce than English find Chinese, Davis concludes that "our own language, though certainly more varied, is the harsher of the two," and that Chinese possesses the usual expedients to "give harmony and rhythmical effect to their verse" (396). Chinese poetry has its own conventions and rules but is nevertheless harmonious, melodious, and beautiful (397).

In the manner of Thomas Love Peacock's *The Four Ages of Poetry* (1820), Davis argues that as civilizations progress their poetry becomes smoother, more sophisticated, and less authentic. Conventionally, he regards the Tang dynasty as representing the true "Augustan age of Chinese poetry … in the eighth century of our era, or about 1100 years ago, when the whole of Europe was involved in barbarism and ignorance."[40] Following a hint by Morrison, Davis finds in Chinese poetry the same kinds of parallelism that Robert Lowth influentially discovered as an informing structural feature of Hebrew poetry. In Chinese poetry, this parallelism is rendered "much more striking and obvious—as it is usually *word for word*, the one written opposite to the other" (411, 418, 418n). Parallelism pervades Chinese poetry "universally" and "forms its chief characteristic feature, and is the source of its artificial beauty" (415). Thus Davis again absorbs the distinctiveness of Chinese verse into a European critical paradigm. He is generally concerned to ascertain how far Chinese literature may be arranged according to the "divisions and nomenclature of European criticism" (429). While he acknowledges that the Chinese might make no distinction between tragedy and comedy, a translator, he believes, should be free to apply those terms. He comments also on the absence of the epic in Chinese, which he ascribes to the fact that for poetry to be esteemed good "it must be so highly elaborated, that the costliness of the material may place limits to the size of the structure" (42).

Davis translates, among other verses, two of the odes from the *Shijing* and several poems from the Tang period. One of the odes from the *Shijing* depicts how a rich and powerful suitor carries off a bride engaged to a humbler rival by employing the familiar metaphor of the cuckoo. In language that anticipates the contemporary criticism of Zhang, he argues that this "antique specimen" serves to show the "similarity that pervades the tone of human sentiment in the most distant ages and countries:"

> The nest yon winged artist builds
> The robber-bird shall tear away;
> – So yields her hopes th' affianced maid
> Some wealthy lord's reluctant prey. (33)[41]

Yet, like Percy, Davis thinks that whatever its literary merits, the *Shijing* is remarkable for the fact that it was compiled "more than twenty centuries prior to our time, and some portions of it composed at a still earlier date" (35). Surveying the history and kinds of Chinese poetry, Davis particularly notices what he describes as "Descriptive" poetry, "the most agreeable of all." In Romantic vein Davis tells how the language of such poetry abounds in figurative expressions "derived from the most striking objects and circumstances in nature":

"spring dreams and autumnal clouds" mean flitting visions of happiness—unattainable good is represented by "the moon's reflection in the wave"—"floating clouds obscuring the day" express the temporary shade thrown by detraction on illustrious characters—difficulty of acting is figured by "the grass and tangle in one's path"—female beauty by the obvious and common semblance of "a fair flower"—spring is the emblem of joy, "autumn" of sorrow. (48)

Under the rubric of this descriptive class of poetry Davis includes what he claims to be a rare written example of a Chinese poem about London from 1813. The reviewer (probably Barrow) in the *Quarterly* of 1817 had briefly noticed the poem in an evaluation of Davis's translations, but here Davis prints both the whole of the original poem and his literal translation "considering that it is a native of the remotest shores of Asia who sings the glories of the British capital."[42] The poem is modeled on the traditional form of eight lines and five characters to a line. The poem is written in vernacular or plain Chinese without any literary allusions, which would be unusual for an educated Chinese person. Davis's translation is an accurate one.[43] The author of the verse is not named but Davis describes him as "in a respectable station of life, and a person of good acquirements, who accompanied home an English gentleman as his instructor in the language." Davis claims that the poem is confined "exclusively to objects as at once strike the eye" given the author's "very limited knowledge of our language, and total inability to comprehend the nature of our institutions" and the verse thus contains few flights of fancy (53).[44] It is quite possible that Davis may actually be masquerading as the poet. He prints a literal translation of extracts from the poem, just three of the stanzas I include here:

> Their theatres are closed during the long days;
> It is after dark that the painted scenes are displayed:
> The faces of the actors are handsome to behold,
> And their dresses are composed of silk and satin:
> Their songs resound in unison with stringed and wind instruments,
> And they dance to the inspiring note of drums and flutes:
> It constitutes the perfection of harmonious delight,
> Everyone retires with a laughing countenance.
>
> The two banks of the river lie to the north and south;
> Three bridges interrupt the stream, and form a communication;
> Vessels of every kind pass between the arches,
> While men and horses pace among the clouds (fogs?):
> A thousand masses of stone rise one above the other,
> And the river flows though nine channels:
> The bridge of Loyang, which out-tops all in our empire,
> Is in shape and size somewhat like these. – – –
> .   .   .   .
> The spacious streets are exceedingly smooth and level,
> Each being crossed by others at intervals:
> On either side perambulate men and women,
> In the centre career along the carriages and horses:
> The mingled sound of voices is heard in the shops at evening;
> During winter the heaped-up snows adhere to the pathway:
> Lamps are displayed at night along the street-sides,
> Whose radiance twinkles like the stars of the sky, &c. (56, 58)

The poem depicts, the Thames, the palaces, and buildings, the fashionable men and women, and the liveliness of the city. Annual excursions to the country are also described. The poet comments on the rise and fall of the price of provisions and notes that the climate of the country is "too cold for the cultivation of rice." The inhabitants of the city drink their "strong tea" mingled with cream and their "baked wheated bread" is spread with "unctuous lard" or butter (59). What the poet finds interesting about London and different from China is remarkable in this, possibly the first work of Chinese and English cross-cultural encounter, apart from brief letters, that we know. The rendition makes a very interesting companion with other descriptions by Wordsworth, Byron, Blake, De Quincey, and Mary Robinson. The questions of authenticity and authority in this poem are difficult. Davis says that his translation avoids giving "dignity in verse to matters so perfectly domestic and familiar to ourselves." Although such verse might sound well in Chinese, he omits what he regards as "all the extravagancies and hyperboles of the original." It may be that our Romantic Sinologist Davis is employing the persona of a Chinese visitor to strategically defamiliarize the city of London, thus removing the "film of familiarity" from common sights as Coleridge had famously advocated in the *Biographia Literaria* (1817) about this time.

Davis's account of Chinese poetry is remarkably sympathetic and accurate for its period. Although in accord with the drift of Company policy in the region, Davis admires Chinese verse and argues that it could well provide a source of novel and fresh imagery and new thoughts for British writing. He rejects the view that the comparatively indifferent response that Chinese literature has met with in Europe so far is in any way due to the quality of Chinese art, blaming it on "a want of choice and selection in the subjects" and an "absence of taste and judgment in the mode of treating them" (420). One presumes that he has in mind previous Jesuit translations, as well as the recent publications of the amateur British sinologist Stephen Weston in London. He argues that, although Chinese poetry may be indeed difficult, "some effectual means of increasing our acquaintance with it is perhaps one of the greatest desiderata in eastern literature" (62). Drawing upon the example of those like William Jones, Walter Savage Landor, and Robert Southey who have made use of "oriental thoughts and imagery, derived from the languages of Asia," Davis argues that Chinese poetry can and should provide a similar inspiration. Employing the suggestive metaphor of the cross-cultural transmission of ideas and plants from China, discussed in the following chapter, that had such an impact in the eighteenth century, Davis suggests that as "fruits of the highest culture may be improved and varied by foreign grafts and as our gardens have already been indebted to China for a few choice flowers," so too could British poetry profit by borrowing from the Chinese (62–63). Literature, like the highly prized Chinese chrysanthemums and camellias, was fully imbricated in the global flow of trade.

Davis substantially increased British understanding and knowledge of the Chinese novel, and fiction and the novel became a central concern of the Romantic Sinology.[45] Davis was personally responsible for the translation of four Chinese fictions: "The Shadow in the Water" (*Ho-ying lou*) (1822), "The Twin Sisters" (*Tuo-chin lou*) (1822), "Three Dedicated Rooms"

(*San-yü lou*) (twice, in 1815 and 1822), and *The Fortunate Union* (1829). The first three are the opening short stories by the major Qing writer Li Yu collected in his *Shier lou* (Twelve Towers [1658]) in which all the stories have the Chinese character *lou* (approximately translated into English as "tower") in their title and feature architectural themes.[46] This would imply that Davis may have intended to translate the entire collection but had only the leisure or inclination to complete the first three of the tales. He argues that the "chief value" of these translations resides in the incidents of behaviors that are practiced in China, such as, in "The Shadow in the Water," where the hero espouses two wives on equal terms as an expedient to overcome the hostility of the father of his childhood sweetheart.[47] In "The Twin Sisters," in which a mandarin takes upon himself to find husbands for two beautiful sisters whose parents cannot agree, it is the power possessed by officers of public justice which is relevant to the "intimate connexion with national manners and ways of thinking."[48]

In the "Three Dedicated Rooms," a man who ruins himself in building a great house is forced to sell it cheaply to avaricious neighbours but retains three rooms dedicated respectively to men, ancestors, and heaven. Despite being told some valuable treasure may be buried in one of the rooms, the man is forced to sell these also. When treasure is later discovered, the new owners are charged with harboring thieves and robbers. In what also serves as an intriguing early detective story, the mystery of the treasure is solved by an astute magistrate who deduces that it was secreted in the chamber by a generous friend of the builder as a means of supplying him with money without ruffling his pride. The property is returned to its rightful owner, the son of its builder. In such fictions Davis claims that the literature of China generally shows how the "principles of parental authority, and of filial submission" are "carried to a most extravagant length."[49] Though not as evangelical as Morrison and the missionaries, Davis identifies the lack of a revealed religion in China with its peoples' apparent susceptibility to "temporal self-interest." Davis opts to translate the first three of the stories, which would be the easiest to accommodate to British tastes, but these may also be the only ones he actually read through or had time to accomplish.[50]

DAVIS'S *FORTUNATE UNION*

Davis's most important contribution to Romantic Sinology was his new translation of the *Haoqiu zhuan* as *The Fortunate Union* (*Haoukewchuen*) in 1829. He was criticized at the time for providing another translation of a novel already translated once into English rather than translating one of the other classic Chinese novels that did not yet exist in an English version. Yet, in translating this novel, Davis is consciously re-claiming the text for a new, more professional, and populist version of British sinology, one that is based on a first-hand encounter with the country, language, and peoples all of which are capable of being understood by Britons. Unlike Percy's, this translation was accomplished "in the country which it describes" and during the times in which Davis was not busy with his Company duties. It is only because of his "long and personal acquaintance with the people" of China that he is able to accomplish the translation at all and it is this experience that validates his notes and observations on Chinese customs, "the result of careful examination and enquiry, and derived in China from native authorities."[51] The access to "native authorities" is absolutely crucial for Davis and once more indicates the collaborative nature of this new sinology. Later Davis somewhat airily affirms that the business of translating the Chinese of the novel is not troublesome if one is "daily accustomed to speak the language of the country" (xvii). Davis was aided in his translation by the resident expert help of Morrison as well as John Reeves, "a gentleman well versed in the natural history of China" (vii).[52] Davis's first-hand knowledge of China is conspicuously exploited in numerous footnotes; for instance, when glossing the description of the delivery of an imperial warrant, "reverently in both hands a yellow cover which concealed the warrant," he states that "this was precisely the way in which the Viceroy of Canton delivered to Lord Amherst the emperor's letter to the Prince Regent," an event he witnessed (1.40). In providing a note on Buddhist priests, Davis mentions that "a monastery similar to one in the text, exists at Canton, and served as a lodging for the embassy of 1816," containing "an enormous style of privileged pigs, whose lives are spared as an act of merit of this sect" (1.129n).[53]

Davis is keen to identify his work with the new Romantic Sinology of Staunton and Morrison, but to distance it from that of both his predecessors, Percy and Jones, and the European rivals of Britain, notably Abel-Rémusat and Klaproth, neither of whom went anywhere near China.[54] His translation does not contain anything like as many notes as that of Percy, and his notes are much more concise and sparing; nor does he show much reliance on older Jesuit authorities such as Du Halde. Davis refers almost exclusively to the contemporary modern British sinology of Morrison and Staunton, in addition to his personal knowledge and experience as a China hand. Of course, he did not have access to the sumptuous, well-stocked aristocratic libraries of Percy's patrons so he was reduced to using his own knowledge and what was to hand. He would make this into a cardinal virtue of his translation, arguing that any authentic translation is simply impossible without an acquaintance with "the most popular tales, traditions, or fancies of the Chinese" combined with the availability of "all the means of original information" (1.xvii). Although praising Percy's edition in the past tense as "by far the best picture of Chinese manners and society that we possessed," he continues that it is "little better than a copious abstract of our romance, and without the poetical passages" (1.viii).

Davis is keen to point out what he sees as the numerous errors, omissions and interpolations in Percy's original. Indeed, he shows that he got even the title of the novel wrong, printing a mistranslation that might be more accurately rendered as *The Fortunate Union* rather than *The Pleasing History*. He also omitted things including Shueypingsin's (Davis's romanization) important visit to the tombs and pavilions of her ancestors in chapter four (1.x, viii). Percy's *Pleasing History* makes many errors; it "speaks of a penknife among a people who have no pens—makes delicate talk of her enemies being sacrificed, and their flesh offered to appease her resentment," and so on. Percy was working from an imperfect manuscript translation that caused him unnecessary problems, while Davis had the original Chinese novel in front of him. Whereas Percy stresses the modesty of the author, Davis claims the reverse is sometimes the case and that he has been forced to suppress one of the passages in the novel that deals with some explicit lewd slanders made against the couple (1.ix). It is also possible Davis may have been uncomfortable with some of the pronounced homoeroticism of the novel, which is a feature of writing of the genre and period. Teichungyu, for instance, is described as having features resembling those of a beautiful woman, gaining for him the nickname of the "fair lady" (1.1–2). Such areas Davis avoids.

Rather than Percy, however, Davis's real targets are the French "sinologues" Abel-Rémusat and Klaproth. He criticizes the former's translation of a Chinese novel, *Iu-kiao-li or, the Two Fair Cousins* for containing many mistranslations and errors. Being unaware of even one of the "commonest stories in China," Abel-Rémusat is led into many errors, which a residence in China and a familiarity with its spoken language would have made unlikely. Davis, however, praises Abel-Rémusat's work in general as well as the respectful tone of his commentary. This Frenchman does not "decry those advantages which are inseparable from a residence in China itself," unlike the quarrelsome Klaproth, a German scholar resident in Paris. Klaproth had previously made a pretty stiff attack on the originality of Morrison's Chinese dictionary, and Davis was keen to defend

both his own scholarship and that of his tutor. The Morrison dictionary is described as "that colossal labour of *utilty*, which is an honour at
once to himself and to his country (my italics)," against Klaproth's rather
mean-spirited criticisms.[55] Klaproth may be excused as a foreigner from
not understanding English but "he should at least be able to understand
what he pretends to condemn" (1.xxii).

The Davis translation presents the reader with a more positive reading of
China and the Chinese mind, than Percy's. Davis argues that the *Haoqiu
zhuan* shows the "most singular people on earth, (self-insulated as they are
from the rest of the world), portrayed by a native hand in almost every variety and condition of human life" (1.x). The novel is characterized by strong
dialogue and characterization as well as "the *generally* excellent moral that
is conveyed throughout" (1.x). Both the hero and heroine are depicted as
Confucian moralists, "a sect which in its high tone of self-sufficiency and
pride, assimilates somewhat to the ancient Stoics" and whose tenets are
hard to surpass in terms of their "wisdom and practical excellence" (1.xi).
The novel is praised as its hero marries *one* wife. Davis is at pains to argue
that strictly the Chinese do not practice polygamy but a form of concubinage. Despite his earlier translations, which feature the double marriage
of their heroes, he maintains that those fictions are not a true "picture of
existing manners" (1.xiv). The wife is always of equal rank to the husband
while the concubine or "handmaid" is only "bought for money," much
like the case of Hagar and Sarah in the Old Testament (1.xv). The off-
spring of concubinage are also admitted to legitimate rights because of
the importance attached by the Chinese to "the securing of male descend-
ants." St. André shows in his detailed comparison of the Davis and Percy
translations that the former exhibits a persistent tendency to nativize the
Chinese novel and present it in terms familiar to a British reader, seeking
to make the text read like an English novel rather than a translated text.
Percy, in contrast, preferred to maintain the foreign nature of the text and
render it accessible through the use of extensive and detailed footnotes,
rather like Southey's orientalist epics. The strategy, however, reflects the
differing phases of British sinology and the growing experience and contact of Britons with Chinese people and culture at Canton.

DAVIS'S *THE CHINESE* (1836): OPIUM, TEA, AND WAR

The two key works of Romantic Sinology are John Barrow's *Travels in
China* (1804), which informed so much of Romantic-period attitudes to
China, especially those of Wordsworth, Southey, and their circle, and

Davis's *The Chinese* (1836). The latter, in its revised formats, became the major nineteenth-century British work on China, superseding Barrow. Published too late to be of crucial influence in the earlier period covered by this study, Davis's work was a synthesis of his earlier writings on China, packaged with additional substantial discussion of British dealings with the Qing empire on the eve of the first Opium War, and focused on trade and diplomacy, areas his translations tended to avoid. Davis's *The Chinese* draws extensively on his observations during his residence in China, especially his crucial travels and experiences in the interior of China during the Amherst embassy, recounted fully in his substantial *Sketches of China* (1841). It also benefits from the accounts of Barrow and Staunton, father and son, and both the 1793 and 1816 embassies. Davis also has access to copious materials published in the new journals, the *Chinese Repository* from 1832, instituted by the first American Protestant missionary, Elijah Bridgeman, and the *Canton Register*, founded by William Jardine and others in 1827. The 1836 two-volume edition was substantially enlarged into three volumes in 1844, preceding Davis's then authoritative account of the first Opium War, *China during the War and Since the Peace* (1852). The first of these works sum up Davis's Romantic Sinology before the first war; the latter moves beyond it to a position of full support for British colonial aggression, the legalization of the opium trade, and the opening of Chinese markets to free trade.

Davis's *The Chinese* thus aims to provide the first "general and systematic work on China." The authority of Davis's volumes rests squarely on his "residence of more than twenty years" in the country.[56] *The Chinese* seeks to replace the work of Du Halde and the Jesuits and supersede the accounts of Barrow, Morrison, and Staunton. In so doing, it attempts to give a systematic view of all aspects of Chinese life and culture, with especial stress on the commercial and economic intercourse between China and Britain, for the "general reader" (1.1). Up until its appearance, Davis's publications were generally more concerned with literature, culture, and philology. His *The Chinese*, however, begins with four substantial chapters on European relations with China, three of them focused on Britain. Davis's views of China reflect his pragmatic ideas in general, built on his extended work in the country. He is fully aware that British trade with China has come to exceed that with all other nations and he praises the Macartney embassy for directing the public attention to the language, literature, and customs of this "vast and singular empire" (1.55). He claims that for many years subsequent to the 1793 embassy, there was progress in commercial affairs. Nevertheless, after 1814 the "jealousy and

suspicious nature of the Chinese government" reasserted itself a series of
ways, troubling commerce (1.57, 70–74). Davis approves of the conduct of
Lord Amherst in 1816 in refusing to perform the kowtow except on terms
of mutuality and reciprocation (1.74–81). As with the Macartney embassy,
Davis quarrels with the notion that the Amherst mission was "unsuccessful," as it actually inaugurated a "longer interval of tranquility and
freedom from Chinese annoyance" than previously experienced, with no
major stoppages in trade between 1816 and 1829 (1.81). He is generally critical of the local Chinese government at Canton, as well as the Manchu
court with their "jealous and watchful Tartar dominion," that have created unnecessary obstacles to trading with the British (1.11, 35). Though
he frequently praises both the Kangxi and the Qianlong emperors, he
is highly critical of the empire's treatment of foreigners and traders. He
claims that they are subject to "rapacity and faithlessness" and deprived of
all the benefits of Chinese law, especially with regard to cases of accidental homicide (1.36, 49, 52–53).

Davis was well aware of the business of the tea and opium trade, yet
he is somewhat disingenuous about it. He knew of the importance of the
trade to the Company, but seeks to blame the "universal corruption of the
government officers at Canton" for not suppressing the trade (1836, 2.130).
The local government having placed itself in a "false position" by "its long
course of secret and prohibitive practices in relation to the prohibited
drug" was after the end of the Company monopoly unable to counteract
its growth (1.96–97). Despite the fact that his employer harvested and sold
the opium in Patna for Chinese consumption, Davis regards the drug as
a "pernicious narcotic" used by "all ranks and degrees in China." Yet in
the next few sentences he can state that the value of the commodity has
"exceeded the aggregate value of *every other English import*" (my italics)
and stresses its crucial importance to the "revenues of British India." He
calculates that in 1833 opium accounts for a full half of the value of British
imports at Canton and Lintin, and exports of tea somewhat less. Some
23,670 chests of Bengal opium were imported at this time into China,
increasing fivefold over the decade. The value of this trade is something
like three to four millions of pounds sterling annually. Yet he also emphasizes that this "contraband trade" has "always been prohibited as hurtful
to the morals of the people." Translating a Chinese state paper on the
subject, Davis is fully cognizant of the debilitating effects of the drug,
the full scale of its misuse, and of genuine Chinese alarm at its spread.
He concludes, "the *pernicious drug*, sold to the Chinese, has exceeded in
market value *the wholesome leaf* that has been purchased from them; and

the balance of the trade has been *paid to us in silver*" (my italics: 1836, 2.432–36). Clearly conflicted, Davis offers no justification of the trade, except to blame the Chinese authorities for corruption.

The trauma of the ending of the Company's monopoly in 1833 Davis regards as a "most important national experiment" in answering the "grand question" of "the expediency of free trade against the *Chinese monopoly*" in which it remains to be seen how individual free traders would succeed against "the union of mandarins and mandarin merchants" (1.100). He clearly has little sympathy with the coming wave of free traders to Canton, emphasizing the view that the end of the monopoly would result in an increase in smuggling and of "all those circumstances which were calculated to embroil the English with the government of China," leading to conflict and war. Davis, always the Company man, out of sympathy with the Whig reforming administration, argued that the government should remain the conduit for both parties. This sudden "revolution" in trading terms caught both the Canton government and English traders by surprise and led to the debacle of Napier's period in the new role of Superintendent of Trade.

Davis remains sympathetic to the Chinese stance that Napier's position should have been announced from Beijing by the Chinese government and not *de facto* by Napier himself. After Napier's death, Davis briefly took over his role, repeating his advice that there should be an "appeal to Peking." He emphasizes that it was the "subversion of the long-established system" of the Company's monopoly that led to this new friction with the Chinese government, as it was not the existence of the opium trade *per se* but the new "barefaced mode of carrying it on" that exasperated Beijing, leading to the appointment of Commissioner Lin Zexu to extirpate the trade (1.114–15). Davis's narrative concludes with the outbreak of war, "the most important and momentous enterprise, next to the conquest of India, itself in which the British arms have ever been engaged to the eastward of the Cape of Good Hope" (2.133). The apparent hardening of Davis's attitudes to "the Indo-Chinese nations" is made clear in his *China during the War* (1852) where he predicts that China and Japan will not be "allowed much longer to remain in state of hostility to the rest of the world" (1.viii). In this work he justifies the British expedition against China in the light of Lin's "opium seizure, and other outrages at Canton." The British are justified and no "moderate proposals" would have had any chance of success against a Chinese government "bent on their annihilation." His attitude to the opium trade changes, and he argues that it was undeserving of the "infamy" heaped upon it and, bizarrely, that it only supplied "the poison which the Chinese were not obliged to take." Davis persists in his view that the piracy the trade engendered was the main cause of hostilities, not "the honest trade." The full legalization of the trade he now judges to be a "wide and salutary measure" for both empires. This history of the war, with its attacks on Commissioner Lin and the "old literati of china," who instead of enlightening their country keep it in a "Cimmerian darkness, in which the dim and dubious glimmering of the lamp of Confucius is deemed more than sufficient for all purposes," rewrites much of Davis's earlier more positive estimations of China's peoples and its it cultures. Now "no country in the world presents such formidable obstacles to innovation as antiquated China, where the mind and body are enslaved by old custom." This history marks the demise of the more open attitudes of Romantic Sinology and the beginnings of that pedagogy of imperialism described by Hevia as "English lessons."[57]

With the end of the monopoly, the arrival of free trade, and the outbreak of hostilities, the study of China that I have described as Romantic Sinology comes effectively to a close. After the Treaty of Nanjing in 1842, cultural relations between Britain and China inevitably assumed a new character, between those of a victorious and a beaten empire. But just a few years earlier figures like Davis and Morrison did not see this conflict or state of affairs as inevitable, nor would they have assumed such easy victories. Yet the war changed many things. It ushered in the start of the "Century of National Humiliation" for the Chinese, and for the British tarnished the notion of the great prestige of Chinese civilization and diminished their often ambivalent admiration for Chinese thought and culture. Romantic Sinology thus comes of age in Davis' synthesis of the combined body of work created by Barrow, the Stauntons, Morrison, and their many colleagues and assistants, just as its view of China becomes outdated.

Romantic Sinology was supported through the increasingly institutionalized collections and libraries of Chinese books and texts and the inauguration of dedicated scholarly institutions. It was reflected in the creation of a series of chairs at British universities and elsewhere for the study of China and its languages and literature. This sinology was one that originated in what has been unsatisfactorily known as the colonial periphery, first in Bengal, with Jones and Marshman, and then at Canton, Macao, and Malacca, with Staunton, Morrison, Milne, and Davis. In fact, these were not peripheries at all, but central and important areas producing serious, though inflected, knowledge about China and Southeast Asia through extensive cross-cultural collaboration. It was a body of work which stressed the crucial importance of an empirical encounter with China through first-hand observation and experience, as a means of evaluating China's true place on the Enlightenment scale of civilization. It was a sinology that stressed the study of contemporary China, that of the reigning Jiaqing and Daoguang emperors. It advocated the vital importance of practical and useful knowledge of China that could be put to use by Britons in their increasing involvement with the empire. It privileged the study of Chinese literature in all its forms, but *especially* in both its popular and its literary manifestations of romance and drama. It was a body of work that aspired to overturn and replace almost two hundred years of previous, mainly Jesuit-inspired writing about China.

CHAPTER 5

Establishing the "Great Divide": scientific exchange, trade, and the Macartney embassy

This chapter focuses on the role of science in Romantic Sinology and places the exchange of cultural artifacts in the context of the flows of trade that constituted the eighteenth-century world economy, especially commodities such as silver, tea, plants, and opium. Although the main focus of this study is on the processes of cultural exchange, Romantic Sinology was not simply concerned with texts and ideas but also with commerce, economics, and material objects. A major argument of this study is that things as well as texts constituted British knowledge of China, and the exchange of goods and commodities between the two empires was crucial to this process. With the rise to prominence of China in the twenty-first-century global economy, the first British embassy to arrive in China in 1793 thus claims a place of new importance in studies of the literature and culture of the Romantic period. Science, or "natural philosophy" as it was mainly known in the period, played a substantial part in Romantic Sinology. British understandings of Chinese scientific and technological proficiency were vital to their overall estimation of the Qing empire. At a time when sinologists did not restrict themselves to simply textual matters, first-hand knowledge of China, through the researches of the Canton factory, undertaken by company amateur naturalists and company gardeners, was crucial in the formation of the new body of knowledge about China. Of central importance were the two embassies to China of 1792–94 and 1816–17, both of which were supplied with personnel and instructions by the then president of the Royal Society, Sir Joseph Banks, a key figure in this chapter and the dominant scientific administrator of the period. The substantial contribution to this body of knowledge by Chinese gardeners and Hong merchant gardeners and traders is also vital. The British were highly desirous of obtaining Chinese knowledge and expertise (*techne*) in horticulture and husbandry. Both as residents in China and as temporary visitors, they maximized whatever opportunities they were presented with to access the enormous riches of China's natural resources, in the same

126

way that textual scholars attempted to harvest the treasures of Chinese culture. Collecting and researching Chinese natural history were important elements of Romantic Sinology.

The first British embassy of George, Viscount Macartney, to China might from the perspective of the early twenty-first century be regarded as of equal and crucial significance to those events that Romanticists have conventionally viewed as essential to the formation of the Romantic self. In September 1793, when Macartney presented a letter from his sovereign George III to the Qianlong emperor at the imperial gardens of *Wanshu Yuan*, few, if any, Britons regarded China as a polity in decline, or seriously contemplated any form of colonial, military, or naval activity against it. Rather, the official discourse of the embassy was that of recognition of the status of "brother monarchs" and equal partners. Yet by the end of the third decade of the nineteenth century, Britain and China were at war for the first time in their histories. The events of the Macartney embassy are well known but its meaning and significance in Sino-British relations are still being argued about.[1] Certainly the Qing court attempted to articulate the embassy within their established rituals compiled in the *Comprehensive Rites of the Great Qing* (*Da Qing tongli*) whereas Macartney sought to present the embassy in the narrative of the established European Westphalian system of international diplomacy and sovereignty.

The relevant details and events of the embassy in brief are as follows. It sailed from Portsmouth for China on September 26, 1792, on HMS *Lion*, the *East Indiaman*, and the *Hindostan* with the brig *Jackall*. After stopping at Canton it proceeded to the gulf of Zhili in July 1793, where at Tianjin (Tientsin) it disembarked and journeyed to Beijing. Macartney and a part of the embassy were then transported to the imperial palace at Bishu Shanzhuang (Mountain Retreat for Avoiding the Heat) at modern-day Chengde (then known as Jehol or Rehe), north of the Great Wall. There on September 15, 1793, in the park of Wanshu Yuan (Garden of Ten Thousand Trees) Macartney was presented to the Qianlong emperor. Rather than performing the traditional ceremony of the full imperial kowtow of three full kneelings accompanied by three knockings of the head on the floor (nine times in all), Macartney famously knelt on one knee and bowed his head as he would to his sovereign.[2] Macartney's entourage took part in the elaborate ceremonies to make the emperor's birthday on September 17. The embassy presented the emperor with gifts including an orrery, a planetarium, a large lens, a diving bell, an aerial ballon, a coach, ornate clocks, and numerous examples of British manufacturing.

The emperor and his court seemed to express a studied indifference, indicating that they had already seen such wonders. Returning to Beijing, the embassy's formal requests were rejected and its personnel requested to leave the capital. The party journeyed overland via the Grand Canal system back down to Canton, from whence it departed in December 1793.

What is notable in the accounts of the Macartney embassy, however, is a strange ambivalence between a recognition of the superiority of Chinese civilization combined with a real sense of disappointment about China – what Barrow refers to as "a woeful change of sentiment" produced by the "more intimate acquaintance" with Chinese "manners and habits."[3] This Romantic disappointment is a variation on the "temporalization trope" that Nigel Leask identified as a frequent figure in Romantic-period travel accounts of "antique" lands where former glories are contrasted with a degraded present.[4] Although ostensibly about trading and diplomatic issues, the Macartney embassy was an attempt to present and impress the older, sophisticated Qing culture with the brave new world of British science and the progressive modern entity of the organic nation state. Confronted by the magnificence of British manufactures and scientific progress, it was thought that the Chinese could not help but be impressed. As Martin Adas has shown, it was at about this time that "European observers came to view science and especially technology as the most objective and unassailable measure of their own civilization's past achievement and present worth ... few disputed that machines were the most reliable measures of humankind."[5] This chapter returns to London, Canton, and Beijing with Macartney and his entourage to discuss the contribution to British understanding of China occasioned by this first-hand but extremely limited encounter with Chinese peoples and their cultures in the two British embassies to the empire in the Romantic period, though my main focus will be, in this present enquiry, on the first of those embassies.[6] It reinforces the argument that Britain and Qing China were "co-constituted" in the eighteenth and nineteenth centuries and that China was not simply the passive recipient of new European concepts of scientific and commercial modernity.

The allegation that Qing China was politically and economically static and ossified by an inflexible ceremonialism with little impetus to change, especially regarding its relations with foreign powers, largely originates with the accounts of the first two British embassies and the alleged rebuff of the British attempts at developing closer ties. Behind this lay a selective reading of Adam Smith's criticism of the Qing's restrictions on foreign trade and his depiction of the empire as wealthy but "stationary."

Influential nineteenth-century thinkers, notably Mill, Hegel, and Marx, as well as twentieth-century sociologists, most influentially Max Weber, adopted this skewed reading of Qing China. Mature British and American sinology of the 1950s followed this reading, viewing China largely from the vantage point of its troubled entry into the "modern" world system and its "response to the west."[7] The Macartney embassy was thus crucial in the production of the new knowledge about China, not just textually, but also visually through the many illustrations of the embassy's resident artist, William Alexander. The chapter argues that the embassy should be regarded as a crucial part of the processes of knowledge exchange and cultural translation between Britain and China and a major event in the formation of Romantic Sinology.

Recent studies of the Macartney embassy have tended to focus on the construction of British and European discourses of sovereignty and commercial exchange in their relations with the Qing imperium, uncovering regional and national assumptions underpinning their universalistic pretensions.[8] In such readings, the embassy was neither a success nor a failure but a key transformational event, at least in the minds of Britons like Macartney, Staunton, and Barrow, forging their nation and those of others. In 1822, for example, John Francis Davis could argue that the Macartney embassy "had its full effect in clearing away much of the *obscurity* which involved *the subject*, not only immediately, through the *personal observations* of those who composed it, but also by its more remote tendency to *awaken a general curiosity*, and a desire to *know something* concerning so singular a people" (my italics).[9] In 1827 Barrow in the *Quarterly Review* judged the embassy to be as significant as the extraordinary achievement of Champollion in the translation of Egyptian hieroglyphics. In particular, the embassies of 1793 and 1816 confirmed the China credentials of five Britons: Robert Morrison, George Thomas Staunton (who took part in both), John Barrow, Thomas Manning, and John Francis Davis.[10]

Alain Peyrefitte influentially argued that "the mission and its failure represent a microcosm of the confrontation that marked the two centuries to come: the cultural collision of the West and the Far East; the clash of the industrialized countries and the Third World."[11] Macartney's and Amherst's apparent refusals to perform the kowtow became the key symbol of relationships between the two empires, and representative of this apparent "collision of two civilizations." My study rejects such beguiling, but highly suspect, grand narratives of the tragic emplotment of history with its "fatal impacts," "clashes of civilizations," and "incommensurability of cultures." Its reading of the cultural significance of the event is informed by James L. Hevia's revisionist account of the embassy and Qing guest ritual in which we "cease interpreting the Macartney embassy as an encounter between civilizations and cultures, but as one between two imperial formations, each with universalistic pretensions and complex metaphysical systems to buttress such claims … commonalities between the Qing and British imperial formations have been ignored or denied, while their differences have been distorted." In Hevia's account both Georgian Britain and Qing China were more similar polities than we tend to recognize; certainly "neither was egalitarian or democratic" and both were striving to "consolidate an imperial formation that placed users of the discourse at the pinnacle of sets of complex hierarchical relationships." Both sides were aware of what was at stake and were competing to impose their "incompatible views of the meaning of sovereignty on the other; neither was (at the time) successful." Hevia argues that China annoyed the British because it existed outside of a Eurocentric conception of the world, resisting the "British penetration of China on British terms." In fact, the embassy might rather be considered as a Qing "success."[12] Surprisingly, this was very much the view of Horace Walpole who wrote in August 1794, on the embassy's return, that he was not surprised at Macartney's "miscarriage about the failure of the first official diplomatic effort to open up more trade with China," and he rather admired the "prudence of the Chinese … they would be distracted to connect with Europeans, and cannot be ignorant of our usurpations in India, though they may be ignorant of Peruvian and Mexican histories and the no less shocking transactions in France."[13] Contemporary historians are now willing to grant China a much greater degree of understanding and sophistication about international affairs than was hitherto admitted, and they certainly knew enough about troublesome Europeans and their potentially subversive religions to be wisely cautious. Such an attitude was not the result of an anti-commercial or inflexibly ritualistic outlook, but simply prudent statecraft.

CHINA, SCIENCE, AND MODERNITY

In many ways this book describes the cultural manifestations of a global encounter, sometimes but not always conflictual, between universalizing ideologies possessing a history, symbolism, or mythology which to those who accepted their claims were natural, rational, and self-evident, but to those who did not were irrational, wrong-headed, and false. Protestant Christianity and Confucianism thus locked horns across the globe, each with its claims to universal applicability. Similarly, European Enlightenment science emerged in the period as a universally applicable ideology that critiqued and dismissed those beliefs that did not share its rationalist underpinnings. Increasingly, scientific progress becomes the chief defining character of European modernity and hegemony.[14] Conventionally, modern science has been viewed as a largely European phenomenon, originating from the "scientific revolution" of the sixteenth and seventeenth centuries.[15] One of the issues that this line of thinking raises concerns why modern science thus only emerged in the West rather than in other parts of the globe, in effect the "Great Question" posed by Joseph Needham.

Contemporary historical scholarship has stressed that "the Qing Empire in the mid-eighteenth century was an enormously energetic society with considerable social and cultural diversity … [its] rulers were capable of complex and stable differentiations among aspects of complex situation."[16] Yet it was increasingly subject to those stresses and strains, which were a product of its geographical and demographic expansion.[17] We should be wary of reading nineteenth-century British imperial supremacy and its concomitant confidence back into the earlier, less assured and more vulnerable history of eighteenth-century history. The British encounter with the Qinq empire has often been portrayed as that of a modern, technological, and industrial power confronting an older, stagnating polity whose glories were firmly in the past. This view of late Qing China became an effect of the narrativizing tendency of Romantic Sinology to represent China as oppositional to the current modernizing trends of early nineteenth-century Britain. Yet the Macartney embassy was conceptualized and organized by Joseph Banks and others with a very different and rather less assured set of assumptions and expectations about Britain and China.

The standard historiographical line on science and China is still dominated by the monumental scholarship of Joseph Needham. Convinced of the universal nature of modern science as a human project and possessed of the notion of a teleological path of human development, Needham postulated his famous "Great Question." Given that China demonstrated an apparent technological superiority over Europe at least until the seventeenth century, why then did it fail "to give rise to distinctively modern science"? Needham defined science as the combination of the mathematization of nature, associated with the work of Galileo, Kepler, and Newton, with the experimental method of Baconian empiricism.[18] He argued that the answer to this puzzle largely lay with the formidable

resilience of China's agrarian bureaucratic culture that denied any public, neutral space relatively free from the interference of political censors
for modern science to develop in.[19] Needham differentiated between science as a body of theory and technology, and the application of science,
arguing that the Chinese superiority in the latter was assured. Chinese
"science," like that of Islamic countries, was based upon local knowledge
which allowed the transmission of technical innovations, but inhibited the
development of the theoretical mathematical reasoning that, allegedly, is
the prerequisite for modern scientific rationalism, producing an "ecumen-
ical" science universally applicable for all peoples. According to George
Basalla, Western science was then transmitted to non-European societies
through processes of colonialism, which absorbed this new learning and
developed their own national, independent scientific traditions and institutions, grounded on European norms.[20] Modern science thus becomes
the driver of human progress and the key marker of human civilization.
Studies of Chinese science have largely worked within the parameters of
Needham's historiography, accepting China's lack of modern scientific
advancement after 1700 or so, and refining the reasons for this.[21] The failure of the Chinese to engage in a legal and social revolution that happened in twelfth- and thirteenth-century Europe, by which cities and
towns were able to make their own laws and processes of self-jurisdiction,
combined with the failure of the ideographic nature of the Chinese language to express ideas with clarity, making it inappropriate for commu-
nicating scientific ideas that inhibited the rise of modern science, have
variously been identified as crucial issues.[22]

In many ways such accounts further elaborate and substantiate the
narratives about China and Europe that were developed by the accounts
of the Macartney and Amherst embassies and the Romantic Sinology
to which they contributed; narratives based on Western assumptions
relating to modernity and science. Other critics not directly inspired by
the Needham tradition have queried the assumptions upon which this
narrative tendency rests. In a parallel movement, following the familiar critiques of Enlightenment rationality of Adorno and Horkheimer,
and Foucault, modern European science has also increasingly been subject to a sociological analysis which attempts to understand the norma-
tive assumptions on which science rests and demonstrate the processes
or networks by which it functions.[23] Exemplary is the critique of the
French sociologist of science Bruno Latour. Latour argued that rationalist
Enlightenment thought produced a series of disciplines that empowered
those who mastered them to reduce the world to order. He argues that

moving from a weak rhetoric to a strong one created scientific knowledge. Scientists thus created the famous "Great Divide," an apparent asymmetry between the knowledge of the "centre" and that of the "periphery," such as that which would be applied to China in the nineteenth century. Latour further maintained that our conception of modernity is premised on a division between politics and science and technology, a division that initiated and fueled the formidable expansion of European empires.[24] He argues that we have never been "modern" and that only relatively very minor differences separate societies. The "Great Divide" describes only how "Westerners" established "their relations with others as long as they felt modern."[25] Cognizant of Latour's crucial problematization of modernity and the concept of the "Great Divide," my study departs from his analysis in its swerving away from the model of center and periphery to embrace an eighteenth-century shared world order in which Qing China was an active participant.

The contribution of the "East" to world history and the history of science has been emphasized by a substantial number of historians and critical theorists.[26] Notably, Kapil Raj has proposed an alternative model whereby the "unity of modern knowledge practices across European space" or "science" is illusory, questioning the accepted diffusionist model of this science along with the values of modernity for the rest of the world. Modernity and its institutions are thus not emanations from a pre-existing center but the result of a complex historical process of collisions, negotiations, and compromises. In this understanding of things, Britain and its colonial possessions undergo a process of "co-constitution." Scientific knowledge is "local everywhere" and disseminated neither through its innate universality nor by forcible imposition, but "through a complex process of accommodation and negotiation."[27] In such accounts, science is defined more widely than Needham's stress on mathematical reasoning and the empirical method, to include the production of instruments, services, and techniques used in the production of knowledge without any distinction between theory and technology. Such "open-air" pursuits as cartography, botany, and horticulture are as significant as Needham's paradigmatic mathematical rationalism. Taking the example of the "applied" science of cartography, for instance, Laura Hostetler has shown how sophisticated Qing techniques were. It chose to engage with new "cutting-edge" technologies for state-building purposes, in the same ways that European early modern states adopted the same technologies, to position itself as a major world power.[28] Similarly, Benjamin A. Elman authoritatively demonstrates how in the seventeenth and eighteenth centuries Europeans were desirous of obtaining Chinese secrets of producing silk, fine textiles, and porcelain, as well as large-scale tea cultivation. In turn the Chinese literati borrowed new algebraic notations of Hindu-Arabic origin, Tychonic cosmology, Euclidian geometry, and various computational advances. Under the influence of both Jesuit and Protestant missionaries, Elman claims that the Chinese effectively produced a modern science but one on their own terms.[29]

In 1708 and 1718 the Kangxi emperor commissioned a team of European Jesuit missionaries to survey and map the extent of the Qing empire in an analogous way to that of British hydrography and cartography, preceding and during the Cook voyages. William T. Rowe and Joanna Waley-Cohen have stressed the similarities between the scientific approach of the "evidential research" movement (*kaozheng*) of Qing scientists, such as Mei Wending, and that of the experimental method championed by the British Royal Society. The Qianlong emperor's famous dismissal of British inventions and manufactures in his edict to George III, delivered into Macartney's hands, was thus highly disingenuous.[30] As Waley-Cohen argues, when, for political reasons, the Qing denied their very real interest in European science, Europeans naively took this "as evidence of an entire mental attitude: ingrained xenophobia and a concomitant resistance to progress."[31]

Far from being on the periphery of developments of the early modern period, then, Qing China both participated in and helped shape the new emphasis on empirical scientific knowledge that was simultaneously transforming Europe and its colonial possessions. By looking at certain discrete British discussions of Chinese technology and science, the thesis that instead of a unique Western and modern science there were national and local knowledge traditions and dynamics, and that modernity and science are not simple emanations from a pre-existing European center, gains support. In particular, the open-air science of botany and horticulture and the case of the British attempt to transplant tea from China and to cultivate it in Bengal in the early nineteenth century provide evidence in support of this.

BANKS, GLOBAL BOTANY, TEA, AND
THE MACARTNEY EMBASSY

Plant collecting, nurturing, and distribution became a patriotic activity, and botany a colonial science. It was also a profitable, if minor, export business, as exotic Chinese flowing plants, such as azaleas, camellias, roses, peonies, and chrysanthemums, fetched high prices from British market gardeners and horticultural societies, transforming the concept of the Chinese garden in the nineteenth century. As Fa-ti Fan succinctly puts it, "horticulture and natural history formed part of the circulation of aesthetics, information, wealth, goods, and other material and cultural productions in global maritime trade."[32] Modern science was not simply a metropolitan activity undertaken around the globe. Once again, both Bengal and Canton emerge as important areas for researching and producing knowledge about China. Fan has demonstrated in fascinating detail how Canton served as a key site for researching Chinese natural history. The port served as a meeting place for British company naturalists and gardeners, British trader-naturalists and collectors, and Chinese gardeners and specialists, as well as a place where Chinese plants of all kinds were exchanged, bought, and sold. Here the British had direct access to Chinese horticultural knowledge and skill. As Fan writes, "with minimal effort, British naturalists effectively reconfigured the entrepôt of Canton, turning it into a site of knowledge production."[33]

One of the main authors of the Macartney embassy was a leading British botanist, the natural philosopher and, since 1772, President of the Royal Society, Sir Joseph Banks. Banks had, as David Miller argues, established in the years after 1780 a network of scientific and global enquiry which centered upon his house at 32 Soho Square, London. Miller and Gascoigne have identified Banks's house as functioning as what Latour describes as "a centre of calculation" in a network of scientific exchange.[34] Indeed, Banks's project was to ascertain technological and scientific knowledge about other parts of the globe and transfer that knowledge within the boundaries of the British Empire. As Gascoigne comments, for Banks "the advancement of science and the advancement of Britain's imperial interests formed a natural partnership."[35] Like the translated texts of Romantic Sinology, what was of use was to be preferred and acquired. With the Royal Botanic Gardens at Kew at its hub, Banks created an institute for botanical exchange that helped to stimulate the creation of a network of colonial botanic gardens transferring and cultivating specimens ultimately for the benefit of the British Empire. Canton and Bengal were a part of this network.

Banks, as is well known, was responsible for the *Bounty* expedition to Tahiti under Lt. William Bligh. Charged by the Board of Trade and Plantations, he advised on the scheme to collect and transport the breadfruit plant from Tahiti to the West Indies to serve as a cheap food for slaves. However, he was also responsible for initiating and advising on numerous other similar schemes and expeditions. The then prevailing mercantilist economic imperative, to which he subscribed, was to promote self-sufficiency within the empire for the benefit of the home nation. Bengal played a crucial role in this ideology and in the new Romantic Sinology of plants and animals. In 1786, with Banks's encouragement, Lt. Robert Kyd founded the Calcutta Botanic Garden. Kyd wrote to Cornwallis in August of that year promising that in a few years the garden would enable the Company "not only to afford all the articles now required from India, China and Arabia but to effect plantations of them to the aggrandizement of the power and commerce of Great Britain."[36] Kyd had argued that the botanic gardens would allow Britain to "outstrip its competitors in every valuable production which nature has confined to this part of the globe."[37] For this purpose, he had been privately growing his own tea plants since 1780.

Banks's ideas were informed by an eighteenth-century Enlightenment comparativist ideology. As his wide-ranging interests in non-European cultures demonstrated, he believed that Europeans could learn much about themselves by studying other societies. China and India were special cases of highly sophisticated and ancient societies and his views on China were informed by the sinophilia of Enlightenment philosophes. Very quickly he spotted the enormous potential of the Calcutta Botanic Garden for the China trade. Writing in 1787 to Sir George Yonge, a few months after the garden was founded, he speculated that the articles desired by the Chinese might be produced at the garden and pondered whether the British might not "be able to undersell the Chinese at their own market, and diminish at least, if not annihilate *the immense debt of silver* which we are obliged to furnish from Europe?" (my italics).[38] The silver problem loomed large in his thoughts and the botanic garden might supply the answer. It would produce many things, including hemp, coffee, tobacco, medicines, sugarcane, sago, teak, dates, pepper, cinnamon, and indigo. These plants would be sent to all parts of the empire for transplanting; but most of all Banks was focused on the transplanting and growing of the Chinese tea plant in British Bengal. In February 1790, the garden took in 272 tea plants sent from Canton though the Governor General ruled the plan as impracticable.[39] It was also about this time that Company captains and officials introduced the spectacular Chinese chrysanthemum into English gardens. Banks used his connections to place his protégés, such as William Kerr, and John and Alexander Duncan, at Canton to supply him with plants and information in return for his patronage. According to Bretschneider, Banks is credited with introducing twenty-nine Chinese plants to Kew Gardens.[40] While the popularity of an artificial chinoiserie visual style may have flagged from the mid century, actual Chinese plants became highly prized and priced acquisitions that contributed to the idea of China. For example, the first Chinese double azalea exported to Britain fetched the sum of £100 in 1833, and the Horticultural Society offered as much as £250 for such a specimen.[41] This horticultural quest for the rare and beautiful flora of China is one of the key narratives in Ghosh's novel of Bengal and Canton, *River of Smoke* (2011), in which Fitcher Penrose and Paulette Lambert search for the fabled Golden Camellia (*Camellia sasanqua*).

For Banks, the embassy might unlock access to China's vast treasures of flora and its secret and highly esteemed knowledge of plant cultivation of which Jesuit accounts had hardly skimmed the surface. Writing to Macartney in January 1792, on the eve of the embassy, Banks expressed his enthusiasm, confessing that he felt "much interest in the Success of an undertaking from whence the usefull as well as the ornamental branches of Science are likely to derive infinite advantage." Banks viewed China not as a stagnant and unprogressive polity in need of Western civilization but as one from which the British had much to learn and to steal. He advised Macartney that the Chinese possessed

the Ruin of a State of Civilization in which when in Perfection the human mind had carried all kinds of Knowledge to a much higher Pitch than the Europeans have hitherto done.

What is there of the great inventions as we call them that are not known to these people Gunpowder Printing the Arabic notion of figures as we call it Paper making with infinite others upon which the very state of Science & Civilisation absolutely depends were only reinvented if not perhaps Stolen from that Country.[42]

Banks here pinpoints what Hobson refers to as the "resource portfolio" of the Chinese: gunpowder, printing, and paper making, which were crucial in enabling European modernity. In particular, he mentions two Chinese achievements as central to his bio-colonialist agenda: "there Porcelane is a chef d oeuvre of Chemistry" and their "very Tea depends upon a Chemical Process were are unable to imitate which takes from the Leaves of the Plant not only an unpleasant taste … but a deletrious Quality & substitutes in its room a flavor agreeable to all Palates leaving just enough of the Poison to afford possibly the most Exhilirating medicine we possess." Tea, like China, is figured here as an ambivalent balance of restorative medicine and debilitating toxins. For Banks, chief among the objectives of the embassy was to engage in a form of technology transfer, or bio-piracy: to obtain and unlock the secrets of the manufacture of Chinese porcelain and of the cultivation of Chinese tea, among other skills and knowledge. He argues that that "to learn these arts alone would be to grant to Europe an invaluable blessing and a few Lernd men admitted among their workmen might in a few weeks acquire Knowledge for which the Whole Revenue of the immense Empire would not be thought a sufficient Equivalent." With his letter Banks included seventy-eight volumes of a "Chinese Encyclopedia" from the illustrations of which Macartney might be "able to understand the Point at which their Science is now Fixd nearly as well as if you was acquainted with the Chinese Language."[43] As Latour might argue, Banks's European knowledge is here weak in comparison to that of the Chinese. It would take the extension of his scientific network, via Calcutta and Canton, to convert this into a position of strength, thus would be established the mythical "Great Divide" and the triumph of nineteenth-century British modernity.

It is seldom even acknowledged in the standard accounts of the embassy how extremely active Banks was in both advising the embassy and recruiting its key personnel.[44] He wrote extensively to Macartney and Staunton, and to other members of the embassy, including Dr. Hugh Gillan, both before and throughout the progress of the embassy, soliciting information and supplying advice. For example, he wrote to many leading manufacturers and potters, notably Josiah Wedgwood, for recommendations for an industrial spy, "well Skilld in all the mystery of Pottery who may ... acquaint himself with any mode of manufacture used by the Chinese" and who might be smuggled in "under the appearance of a servant." He wrote to the leading Manchester medical practitioner Thomas Percival (who later attended the childhood death of Elizabeth, Thomas De Quincey's sister), suggesting that a master of the Manchester Board of Dyers should attend the embassy.[45] He was insistent that the embassy should include a professional naturalist and botanist, serving a similar role to that which both he and then Georg and Johann Reinhold Forster had undertaken on Cook's first two voyages. Unfortunately, he was not able to persuade the government to appoint a professional naturalist after James Lind withdrew because he was not to be paid sufficiently. Nevertheless, he chose the embassy's two botanical gardeners, David Stronach and John Haxton. Stronach was a paid member of the embassy and Haxton was funded by George Leonard Staunton, Macartney's deputy and an enthusiastic amateur naturalist and member of the Royal Society.[46]

Keen to encourage the promotion of agriculture and horticulture, Banks composed a lengthy paper, "Hints on the subject of Gardening suggested to the Gentlemen who attend the embassy to China."

Providing a list of Chinese plants, taken from Jesuit accounts, that he was keen to source, he urged the embassy to take special notice of techniques, such as for "accelerating the blossoming of Plants" which would be "very desirable to our Gardiners here." He was especially interested in the Chinese art of dwarfing trees that Wordsworth would find so objectionable, as discussed in Chapter 7. Banks counseled the embassy to return as many plants as possible and to pay special attention "to the more Obscure & minute there that have the least pretention to Elegance & beauty" as these "are the less likely to have been before taken notice of."[47] He ranked the desirability of plants he wished to acquire and gave instructions to the embassy along with a book of plant drawings by Chinese artists. He also later supplied William Kerr, whom he sent to Canton in 1803, with the same guidance. Restricted as he was at Canton, Kerr was nevertheless able to obtain and introduce plants such as the double yellow Banksian rose and the Tiger Lily to Britain.[48]

Following Banks's advice, hundreds of plant specimens were collected by George Leonard Staunton and the embassy gardeners and listed in the official *Account* of the embassy.[49] Writing to Staunton in 1796, Banks, in one of his more Pollyanna-ish moods, was able to imagine an idyllic scene in which the brother monarchs George III and the Qianlong emperor enjoy a mutual respite from their imperial responsibilities:

> many of our Common flowering shrubs as Lilac Althea Frutex &c are in the Collection /sent with this/ Whether they were gatherd from the hedges or Collected in the Imperial Gardens at Jehol we do not know if the Latter is the Case it would be pleasant to a Reader to Learn that our King at Kew & the Emperor of China at Jehol Solace themselves under the Shade of /many of/ the Same Trees & admire the Elegance of many of the same flowers in their respective gardens.[50]

Kew Gardens, landscaped by the sinophile architect William Chambers with its ten-story pagoda and transplanted Chinese horticultural specimens, and the Qing emperors' *Wanshu Yuan* are joined in the Tory royalist Banks's whimsical and sympathetic imagination of civility, global exchange, and reciprocity (Figure 3). Their love of flowers and trees, and the universal language of botany, unite these brother monarchs in their enjoyment of their mirrored royal gardens. The apparent sympathies between Hanoverian and Qing monarchs would be used to very different effects, however, by Whig satirists, such as William Mason and Peter Pindar, and Kew and *Wanshu Yuan* would be identified more problematically in the larger political consciousness of the late eighteenth century, as will be discussed in Chapter 7.

Figure 3. Chambers' Kew Gardens *c.* 1763. *A View of the Wilderness with the Alhambra, the Pagoda and the Mosque* © Trustees of the British Museum.

In addition to capturing the most prized specimens of Chinese flora, from the 1780s onwards Banks was intrigued by the "very serviceable object" of growing tea in some part of the British possessions in the East or West Indies. In a paper of 1788 addressed to Sir Francis Baring at the Company, Banks suggested that Kyd's botanic garden in Calcutta might be the most appropriate place for cultivating the plants. He also identified suitable areas, such as Bengal and Assam, for their transplantation. In this memorial Banks judged, correctly, that Chinese tea grew best between the 26th and 30th degrees of latitude. He cited James Cunningham to the effect that "all the sorts of Tea imported into Europe are gathered from the same species of shrub, and … the differences between them arise from the soil in which the shrub is Planted & the Season in which the Leaves are gatherd."[51] Banks proposed that Chinese workers might be tempted to Calcutta with their tools and their tea shrubs. The garden "could not Fail to suit, in every particular this infant adventure." He claims that Bengal, "Blessd with advantages of soil climate & Population," would yield a "Tribute" that "binds itself to the mother Country by the strongest & most indissoluble of Human ties that of common interest & mutual advantage."[52] Notably adopting the rhetoric of China's tributary system, Banks applies this to the colonial relationship of Bengal to Britain. Ironically, Banks was unaware that in Assam an indigenous variety of *Camellia sinensis* was already growing, a fact accidentally hit upon in 1823 by Robert Bruce.[53] In Banks's eyes, a major, but unstated, aim of the embassy, was to get hold of *Camellia sinensis* and, by transplanting it in the soils of Bengal, solving at one stroke the problem of Britain's trade deficit with China.

Banks desired that tea should be cultivated for the British within their colonial possession and the plant must be obtained by fair means or foul. The Macartney embassy, despite its idealized formal diplomatic aims to establish mutual recognition between the two empires, was simply another and more golden opportunity for obtaining young specimens of the tea plant for transplanting to India where they would mature and establish a native tea industry. On August 10, 1792, Baring wrote to Macartney that Banks had collected "memorandums about the [tea] trade with a view to its culture in Bengal which he will communicate to your Lordship."[54] Inspired by this imperative to discover ways in which both tea and silk production might be initiated in Bengal, Macartney's team avidly sought opportunities to filch mulberry trees, silkworms, and tea plants.

Although some silkworms were indeed sent to India, they had little success. Tea fared somewhat better. The embassy noted frequently how the Chinese were devoted to the beverage. Macartney, when quitting the mountains beyond Hangzhou on the overland journey to Beijing, gave directions to have "some of the young tea plants taken up with an intention of sending them to Bengal" for Kyd to transplant in the hope that "one day or other they may be reckoned among the commercial resources of our own country." Macartney also adds that he intended to obtain the eggs of the silkworm but the Chinese, "whether from jealousy or superstition or both could scarcely be persuaded to part with them." In February 1794, he wrote to Cornwallis of the progress of his mission to procure "some shoots of the best tea plants." Courtesy of the "benevolence of the new Viceroy of Canton," he was "able to observe and take samples of the highest quality." These samples were then entrusted to James Dinwiddie to take to Kyd's garden to propagate.[55] Here the plantations were developed as planned.[56] The Calcutta Botanic Garden nurtured and cultivated the plants (as well as groves of varnish and tallow trees) and sent shoots to nurseries around India. The extent to which the plants were successfully propagated and what actual part they may have played later in the development of the Indian tea industry in either in their own right or as hybrids is not clearly known.[57]

It was Banks's sustained and relentless pressure for the embassy to include artists, gardeners, botanists, and naturalists that transformed what might have been a narrower diplomatic mission into a voyage of Enlightenment comparative anthropology, probably the last such diplomatic expedition of its kind. The British returned with masses of ethnographical information and hundreds of extraordinarily influential and beautiful illustrations of Chinese peoples, society, customs, and costumes, by the embassy's draftsman, William Alexander. Sadly, for Banks at least, botany fared less well.[58] He lamented the failure of the gardeners, Stronach and Haxton, to provide detailed notes on the plants in their growing habitat, which he believed "rendered the dried specimens virtually useless."[59] Staunton admitted, somewhat defensively, in 1796 that if another embassy were to be planned then "it is to be hoped that more careful and able persons may be found for the Department of natural History, as well as that better opportunities and more leisure will be allowed in the Country for finding out and preserving every object worthy of attention."[60] In 1816, Banks was able to place Clarke Abel on the staff of Amherst's embassy as its chief medical officer and naturalist. Unfortunately, all of Abel's specimens of Chinese plants were lost in the wreck of the embassy's ship the *Alceste* on the homeward voyage in 1817.[61]

Banks's espionage was somewhat in vain. What actually happened to Macartney's tea plants remains uncertain. The plants cultivated in Calcutta, rather like Bligh's breadfruit, could not be turned to profitable account. After Macartney, when exporting opium to China emerged as an effective way of returning the vast amounts of silver bullion that had been spent in purchasing its tea, the Company had no longer an urgent incentive to develop an alternative Indian source of tea while its monopoly of the China trade lasted. It showed little interest in Bruce's "discovery" of the tea plant (*Camellia sinesis* – var. *assamica*) growing wild in Assam. Yet in 1834, amid growing tensions with China and less than five months after the Bill to abolish its trading monopoly in China, a government committee was hurriedly set up to investigate the cultivation of tea in Assam, annexed by the British in 1826. The tea that was to form the basis of the nineteenth-century British tea trade was found growing wild there from trees in the Muttuck region on the Brahmaputra River.[62] Yet, mindful of the enormous prestige of Chinese civilization, received scientific wisdom, following Banks, preferred the apparently more refined and prestigious China tea variety to the wilder and more robust native Assam variant. Professional advice also favored the utilization of expert Chinese planters, such as A-mong, Lumqua, and E-kan, over Indian laborers to supervise the cultivation of the tea plant.[63] Further numerous attempts were made to introduce Chinese tea plants to Assam and other temperate mountain regions, by C. J. Gordon, Robert Fortune, and others, as well as to hybridize the two variants. Yet, in the end, the robust and native Indian plant won out, as the prestige of Chinese civilization declined after the two Opium Wars. By the 1860s, when Anglo-French forces sacked the Summer Palace and Banks had been dead some forty years, native Indian tea cultivation had triumphed over its more effete Chinese cousin. In 1888 the production of tea from India outstripped that from China. Britain had come a very long way from the times when Enlightenment anthropologists, such as Banks, possessed of a genuine admiration for the achievements of China, informed the colonial policies of the government.[64]

SCIENCE AND MODERNITY: BRITONS BEARING GIFTS

As Marcel Mauss and many others have argued, the exchange of gifts is a complex and sophisticated process. Mauss maintained that in pre-commercial societies the gift is a "total social phenomenon" that serves to organize religious, ethical, legal, and economic relationships and institutions, at the same time investing them with symbolic importance. In the context of the long eighteenth century, Cynthia Klekar and Linda Zionkowski have also demonstrated how the gift "produced and responded to changes in traditional concepts of class, gender, national and personal identity, social authority, and property."[65] The role of civility and the function of the gift exchange and similar ceremonial events in constituting the semiotics of international trade and exchange is an area beginning to receive significant critical attention.[66] Klekar has persuasively argued that the language of gift exchange, reciprocity, and obligation feature heavily in Macartney's understanding of his embassy to China. Although the emperor returned his kindness for the British presents, what the embassy hoped to gain "in exchange for their innovative and scientifically advanced gifts" was "a diplomatic trading treaty, commercial ports of trade, and compensation for the English merchants." Here the notion of the gift as "an equal exchange between reciprocally respectful nations—becomes problematic: what the English viewed as civility the Chinese interpreted as a ritual of subjection." British Eurocentric notions of a mutually beneficial trade were thus promoted by a "fantasy of equal exchange that sutured over relations of subjection and domination."[67] What the British also hoped to gain was some form of recognition of their perceived scientific superiority over the Chinese.

Robert Markley has similarly argued, in the context of Anson's account of his 1743 arrival at Canton with his captured Spanish prize ship, how such ceremonies were crucial in establishing extremely complex relationships of obligation, deference, and duty. Drawing upon Žižek's and Derrida's writings, Markley shows how the economic self-interest between Qing merchants and officials and Company traders at Canton was masked by the complex symbolic significance of the gift exchange with its fantasy of mutual obligation and reciprocal friendship. It was Qing policy to locate trading and customs relations within the context of gift and obligation: "the shipboard ceremonies of gift exchange and measurement encoded the always imperfect ideal of reciprocal exchange" invoked to "reassure each of participants that all parties are acting in measured self-interest to maximize profits but not succumbing to greed or fraud." Anson thus blunders into this network with his concerns to establish a hypermasculinized form of British identity exempt from participation in "the semiotics of the always self-interested, even cynical, economy of exchange and deference that enables teas and silks to be packed for consumers in England." In this account the customs officials, Hong merchants, and Company traders function as sympathetic figures embodying "the transcultural values of civility that make palatable the cynical manoeuvrings and asymmetries of economic exchange." Yet such ceremonies of gift exchange are always liable to be misinterpreted or misappropriated.[68] Informed by the crucial insights of Markley, Klekar, Hevia, and others, this section attempts to demonstrate that the gift transaction, involving competing notions of reciprocity, mutual obligation, and deference (both Chinese and British), was at the heart of the Macartney embassy and cultural relations between China and Britain in the late eighteenth century.

The British version of the gift exchange with its rhetoric of civility and the equality of brother monarchs, planned to mask the objective of securing national advantages in the marketplace, but also the more cynical objective of locating and taking away the technology of Chinese applied science, while impressing the imperial court with the presumed excellence (indeed superiority) of British manufactures and science.[69] In contrast, the gift exchange for the Qing was a means of symbolically regulating its complex relations with its Asian tributary states. Although a symbolic exchange of gifts would occur, the British were acutely aware of both the use and the monetary value of the items they presented to the emperor on his birthday, as well as the cultural capital they had accumulated. Involved in this encounter, from the British perspective, was an assessment of the relative strengths of both empires. Macartney cheerfully allowed the

Chinese to excel in "many braches of the arts," especially the manufacture of silk, cotton, and porcelain, but he claimed that in modern science they were far behind. Their knowledge of mathematics, astronomy, and experimental science he thought limited, as was their knowledge of "medicine, surgery and chemistry."[70] The embassy thus hoped to make a favorable impression with its prestigious scientific gifts for the emperor's eightieth birthday; encoded in this affective gift exchange was an attempt to establish a form of scientific hegemony which, it was assumed, the Qing court would instantly recognize and appreciate.[71]

In Hevia's account of the Chinese tributary system, such gifts (*gong*) to the emperor were meant to embody the specific kingship of the tributary sub-lord, symbolizing a relationship of deference and obligation, which masked the political realties and complexities of the Qing's substantial inner Asian empire. As the then Chinese understanding of European or "Western Ocean" nations was still vague, they would be puzzled or even feel cheated if the new British tribute resembled articles that they had previously received from other European nations. In the "Catalogue of Presents" the British carefully described their understanding of the nature of their gifts. They were to be presents which "should be worthy the acceptance of a wise and discerning Monarch." Their number and cost should not be of any consideration to a wealthy monarch rich in treasures, nor should they be "trifles of momentary curiosity but little use." The British had been "careful to select only such articles as may denote the progress of Science and the Arts in Europe and which may convey some kind of information … as may be practically useful."[72] Use value is again privileged over symbolic value in this British philosophy of exchange, and giving is designed to establish in Chinese minds the assumed scientific hegemony of Britain. Crucially, the British presents also had to be distinguished from the many expensive, "ingenious and complicated mechanisms … toys of this kind, or sing-songs … gaudy trifles" that were familiar in Canton and which the court already had in abundance. The British presents, according to Staunton, were to illustrate science and promote the arts. Macartney was genuinely worried that the gifts "would suffer by being confounded with mere curiosities, which however expensive or even ingenious were more glittering than useful."[73] As it was known that the imperial court highly valued astronomy, the "latest and most improved instruments for assisting its operation" were to be sent. In addition, "specimens of the best British manufactures" were also included with a view to "exciting a more general demand for the purchase of similar articles."[74] Noting this, Maxine Berg has persuasively argued that though the embassy perceived itself as "an industrial and scientific exhibition, a showcase of Europe's and especially Britain's 'industrial enlightenment,'" it ended up depicting very "confused issues of empire, tribute, commerce and science."[75]

In this process of gift exchange, the Qianlong emperor reciprocated by presenting the embassy with various examples of traditional Chinese arts and crafts, including jade sculptures, silk purses, and vases. In Qing guest ritual, argues Hevia, the gift must be explicitly linked to the "lesser lord's domain" and must consist in "things that are differentiable from other things of other domains."[76] Commenting on the emperor's gift to him of a scepter (*ruyi*), symbolizing peace and prosperity, Macartney noted that it was "a whitish, agate-looking stone about a foot and a half long, curiously carved and highly prized by the Chinese" but not appearing "in itself to be of any great value." Macartney's understanding of the economic value of the gift "in itself" shears off the highly symbolic cultural capital invested by the Chinese in the artifact. What is at stake here are differing and conflicting notions of value, a symbolic versus a utilitarian exchange, metonymic of the larger cultural encounter in which Macartney's embassy engaged, rather like that of Commodore Anson in Markley's account. In return for the scepter, Macartney presented the emperor with "a pair of beautiful enamelled watches set with diamonds" which he recently and extemporaneously purchased from a naval captain.[77] The actual status of these presents was also in contestation. Were the materials either gifts (*li*) or tribute (*gong*)? When queried, the mandarins explained that all gifts for the emperor were always referred to as *gong*.[78]

In some recent criticism, however, there has been a tendency to conflate the differences in the categories of the presents themselves. The embassy brought to the Chinese court both examples of British manufactures and scientific instruments designed to impress, as well as some more ceremonial objects. The embassy was not short of scientific and technological expertise. Staunton was a fellow of the Royal Society and a gifted amateur naturalist. Among the embassy's personnel were the natural philosopher and mathematician Dr. James Dinwiddie, and a surgeon, Dr. Hugh Gillan. Dinwiddie, a graduate of Edinburgh University, was a noted public lecturer on scientific subjects in Scotland and Dublin. His lectures featured entertaining displays of scientific equipment. He pioneered the new and exciting science of ballooning and experimented with diving bells. Dinwiddie was entrusted with the task of erecting and displaying the various complex scientific instruments to the Chinese. After the conclusion of the embassy, he sailed to Bengal where he delivered Macartney's tea, silk, and other specimens to William Roxburgh at the Calcutta Botanic Garden. He continued thereafter to lecture on scientific subjects in Calcutta and Madras, and was appointed professor of mathematics, natural history, and chemistry at the new Fort William College.[79] He was an important, though under-acknowledged, figure in the intercultural exchange of scientific ideas. Gillan had studied medicine at Edinburgh and acted as physician to the embassy. He also treated Heshen, the powerful Grand Councillor and imperial favorite responsible for hosting the embassy, for a hernia and rheumatism. His notes on Chinese medicine, surgery, and chemistry compiled for Macartney were added to the ambassador's journal and constitute a crucial statement of British understandings of Chinese medicine.[80]

The British were well aware of the Qianlong emperor's great love of clockwork automata and timepieces, and they sought to impress the court with the ingenuity of similar British artifacts. Their presents were also selected with the explicit intention of reversing the substantial flow of both commercial prestige and commodities from East to West. One commentator enviously looked "beyond Canton, just out of reach" where "lay the great internal market of China: 400 million people ... the manufacturers of Manchester told each other – an extra inch of cloth on every Chinaman's shirt-tail, and our mills will be kept busy for decades."[81] Barrow later dreamed of "the day on which a single penknife or pair of scissors, the manufactures of England, could be introduced into every family of China ... a *White Day* in the calendar of Sheffield or Birmingham."[82] Celebrated manufacturers such as Josiah Wedgwood, Matthew Boulton, and Thomas Gill were invited to submit examples of their products.[83] Indeed, Wedgwood had long been bullish about the potential of his new porcelain in China reversing the flow of missionary activity, asking in 1767, "Don't you think we shall have some Chinese Missionaries come here soon to learn the art of making Creamcolour?"[84] The embassy took with it a vast array of pottery, textiles, prints, carriages, muskets, pistols, swords, cannon, and other items. When the crunch came, however, Macartney failed to present the manufactures and the less glamorous technical scientific presents, such as the airpump, pulleys, and chronometer, relying instead on the time-honored Jesuit policy of grandstanding astronomical instruments and clocks. It was probably a mistake. Many of the more technical instruments were given instead to Dinwiddie on the embassy's conclusion to use in his scientific demonstrations in Bengal. Macartney speculated that had he remained at Canton, Dinwiddie might "soon have realized a considerable sum of money from his Chinese pupils alone."[85] According to Berg, it was Macartney's theatrical fetishization of scientific objects, "enlightened objects of consumption," that effectively displaced those trade manufactures associated with the middling and lower classes.[86] With the notable exception of Berg, criticism of the embassy has largely appropriated Macartney's fetishism, concentrating on the reception of expensive scientific instruments. It was this scientific display that would apparently impress the Chinese, and lead to the establishment of Latour's chimera of the "Great Divide."

Aware of the high prestige of astronomy among the Chinese and the access it had granted Jesuit missionaries into the Chinese court, the British focused on this area in the choice of their presents. Staunton confidently, but wrongly, second-guessed that "the latest and most improved instruments for assisting its operations … could scarcely fail of being acceptable."[87] Similarly, knowing of the Qing's fascination with cartography and the determination of borders, various measuring devices were also included in the lists of presents. Simon Schaffer has discussed the embodied symbolism of these apparently utilitarian scientific instruments, arguing that they had to be both "distinctively British yet universally meaningful and had to be seductively and theatrically impressive while displaying the principles of civil rationality and utilitarian commerce."[88] The presents included a Herschel reflector telescope and a famous lens made by Parker. Smaller reflecting telescopes, manufactured by Dollond, were also included. Numerous scientific measuring instruments were added, including thermometers, barometers, batteries, magnets, chronometers, an air pump, electrical machines, model steam engines, and so on. The major scientific presents, however, were the celestial and terrestrial globes made by Adams of London and an orrery designed by William Fraser, featuring Herschel's recent, spectacular discovery of an entirely new planet *Georgium Sidius* (Uranus), the great achievement of Georgian astronomy, surely guaranteed to impress the Chinese.[89]

Chief of all the gifts, however, was the complex and substantial planetarium known as the *Weltmaschine*, manufactured by the German Philipp Matthäus Hahn. The *Weltmaschine* was the *piece de resistance* of the gifts. It was described by the embassy as

the utmost effort of Astronomical Science and mechanical art combined together, that was ever made in Europe. It shews … with mathematical exactness the several motions of the Earth according to the Systems of European Astronomers … It is calculated for more than a thousand years; and as simple in its construction as it is complicated and wonderful in its effects. So exquisite a machine does not remain behind in Europe.

The *Weltmaschine* had recently been acquired at auction by the Company for £600 after Hahn's death and heavily embellished at more than its original cost with oriental decorations by the London-based Swiss watchmaker Justin Vulliamy.[90] The embassy seems to have believed that the strong medicine of British science had to be coated by a sugary chinoiserie pill to make it palatable for a scientifically infantilized Chinese audience. British assumptions about the Chinese or oriental mind are thus displayed in these decorative preferences.[91]

The *Weltmaschine* was the centerpiece of the Macartney gifts. Schaffer has shown how it was designed to embody both Copernican astronomy and pietistic millenarian eschatology. The device thus represented a European cosmology equally imaginary as that of neo-Confucian China. One of the machine's clocks was set to count the seconds until the end of the world (originally 1776, then deferred to 1836). Schaffer brilliantly argues that in this most "complex cross-cultural encounter with multiple audiences," the "displacement between the enlightened optimism of Macartney and Dinwiddie, the aesthetics of the sing-song trade, and the terrible timetables of German pietism" were enacted.[92] Far too delicate to travel overland to Jehol, this gift, with Vulliamy's clocks, Wedgwood's porcelain, and other scientific instruments, were to provide the focus of the British presentation for the emperor at *Yuanming Yuan* in Beijing. Macartney proudly described this German arrangement as "an assemblage of such ingenuity, utility and beauty as is not to be seen collected together in any other apartment, I believe, of the whole world besides."[93]

The Chinese response to the British presents was, as is well known, disappointing, and would become a primal scene of cross-cultural encounter serving as an index of Qing China's lack of progress in British eyes. Yet China's response was as ambiguous as that of the British, hungry for the Chinese secrets of tea, porcelain, and silk. The model of the British man-of-war HMS *Lion* fascinated the emperor, and Macartney noted that his grandsons showed interest in the clocks and the Derbyshire porcelain. Macartney and Barrow both reported Chinese admiration for "the presents and specimens of different manufacture," being particularly struck with Thomas Gill's "flexible sword-blades."[94] Yet the Chinese could not understand why all the presents should not be given to the emperor at Jehol as required by their ritual. They believed that the British were simply boasting about the complexity of the instruments and they were justifiably suspicious that the gifts were not as unique as they claimed. Macartney notes how the Legate, Zhengrui, supervising the presents in Beijing expressed surprise that it would take several weeks to assemble the *Weltmaschine*, "imagining that labour, not skill, was the only thing necessary, and that putting together so complex a system of the universe was an operation almost as easy and simple as winding up a jack."[95] While visiting *Wanshu Yuan* in Jehol, however, he later made a revealing comment indicating how the Chinese might have viewed his embassy's gifts. Reviewing the fabulous pavilions of the garden and their contents, Macartney noted that their rich furnishings also included, "every kind of European toys and sing-songs; with spheres, orreries, clocks, and musical automatons of such exquisite workmanship, and in such profusion, that our presents must shrink from the comparison and hide their diminished heads." The European-style building at *Yuanming Yuan*, Macartney was told, held other such items that "far exceeded those." The diplomatic point of this Chinese display, according to Hevia, was to communicate to Macartney that the British really had nothing to boast about after all.[96]

Dinwiddie and Barrow were the two members of the embassy most concerned with the displaying of the presents, and the personnel who experienced most annoyance from their Chinese courtiers. In his career as a scientific lecturer, Dinwiddie always took care to "draw the attention to the useful and practical applications of science."[97] He lectured on natural history, chemistry, and the arts, and on such subjects as fortification, gunnery, and the diving bell. From the outset, Dinwiddie stressed that that mandarins were curious but unacquainted with science. For instance, they showed suspicion that China had been deliberately reduced in size by the English on Fraser's globes. While an unreasonable view for the British, a modern-day audience, familiar with the distortions of cartographic projections, might well sympathize with the Chinese response. Describing the assembly of the planetarium, Dinwiddie complained about the incessant interference of "impertinent eunuchs." Worried that, by being examined in a state of disassembly, the planetarium might lose its spectacular effect, he argued that "an ignorant people should always be taken by surprise." Allowing the Chinese to view the machine in the process of assembly had "much lowered" their estimation of the machine. Dinwiddie judged that the Chinese acted "very much like children" being "easily pleased and as soon tired." This charge of adult infantilization was one to be repeated against the British by the Chinese: Dinwiddie reported that after cursorily surveying the presents, including the lens and air pump, the emperor commented that "[t]hese things are good enough to amuse children."[98]

It was at this point that the Qianlong emperor's famous letter of September 23 to George III was presented to the embassy. In words that

have often been too easily interpreted as a classic statement of Qing isola-
tionism and hostility to trade, the emperor delivered his considered evaluation of the British embassy's gifts, and not commerce in general:

We have never placed great value on unusual and rare things. You have sent gifts
from a long distance and offered them with profound sincerity: therefore, I spe-
cially ordered my officials to accept them. In fact, because Our fame is known
throughout the world, many other kingdoms ... have sent valuable gifts to us.
We already have a sufficient number of similar things. Your ambassador saw
them personally. But since we do not overvalue such things, we are not eager to
have you send any more that are made in your own country.[99]

The emperor accepts that the British gifts were indeed "rare and unusual,"
but it is only because of his belief in the sincerity of the givers that he
is willing to accept them; similar gifts have already been received, so
their status as appropriate gifts is denied. The emperor restores the gift
exchange, emphasizing the sincerity of the giver and the reciprocal return
of his personal kindness to them in accordance with Qing guest ritual.
The emperor was rejecting not commerce and trade, which provided valuable finance for his government, but the British claims that their gifts
were *unique* and extraordinary, thus restoring Qing cultural hegemony
over the tributary nation. In an act of childish petulance belying his status as a dispassionate scientist, Dinwiddie mischievously removed key
parts from the *Weltmaschine* before departing so that it would never conclude its remorseless countdown to Hahn's apocalypse and the end of the
world. Barrow recorded in 1804 that the Dutch embassy of van Braam
Houckgeest came across their gifts, carelessly stowed in one of the buildings at *Yuanming Yuan*, two years later. Finding the new trope of infantilization irresistible, he responds that "capricious as children," the Chinese
have thrown aside "the toy once played with ... for something new." An
outraged Barrow rewrites the gift exchange as one between tolerant parents and spoiled children. For future embassies he recommended as gifts
"articles of gold, silver, and steel, children's toys and trinkets, and perhaps
a few specimens of Derbyshire spar," as the Chinese are not able to appreciate "anything great or excellent in the arts and Sciences."[100] Yet, despite
Barrow, the experience of the embassy's gifts was much better understood
in later years by John Francis Davis, who commented, correctly, that the
emperor was more likely to be impressed by "strange fowls and beasts"
native to Britain and that it would be better to offer modest symbolic
gifts rather than "confining the selection of presents entirely to works of
art, as they were in our past embassies ... unintelligible and useless to the
emperor and his court."[101]

The legacy of the Macartney embassy to the study of China is problematic and ambivalent. With its overdetermined scenes of kowtowing and gift exchange, which entered the British imaginary as speedily as an opiate, the embassy functions as a key watershed in British understandings of China. From its narratives, the notion of China as a stationary, non-progressive polity, devoid of historical change and that rejects European science and technology, is established. Yet read against the grain of the story of the "Great Divide" as the writings of Latour, Hostetler, Waley-Cohen, Raj, Klekar, and Markley and others would encourage us, it can be seen that this was an extraordinarily complex inter-cultural encounter in which both parties showed a very real interest in each other, irreducible to any simplistic readings of failure and the incommensurability of cultures. Neither British nor Chinese correctly read the symbolism of each other's rituals. Nevertheless the secrets of Chinese tea production would benefit the British, and the Chinese were clearly interested in British military and naval technology. Banks and the originators of the embassy worked from the premise of establishing a rhetoric of civility and rationality, involving the mutual equality and reciprocity between Britain and China according to their naturalized, Eurocentric concepts of international diplomacy, national sovereignty, and commerce. This exchange masked their very real interest in China as a potentially enormous market for British manufactures and trade. Anything but empirical and objective, Romantic Sinology thus further established its idea of China on the basis of a brief sojourn of a few months in a few places in a massive empire, of the language of which it was almost entirely ignorant. The following chapters will explore the some of the ways in which these narratives and this knowledge was culturally manifest in Georgian Britain.

CHAPTER 6

"You will be taking a trip into China, I suppose": kowtows, teacups, and the evasions of British Romantic writing on China

The apparent refusal of Macartney and Amherst to perform the full ritual ceremonial of the imperial kowtow is taken up in this chapter, focusing on the literary and cultural manifestations of, or resistance to, Romantic Sinology. This chapter is concerned with the textual and the visual, discussing satires of the ambassadorial reception and the treatment of the kowtow or rituals of prostration in Romantic-period writing, before turning to manifestations of Chinese taste, or chinoiserie. Following the discussion of the Macartney embassy, the chapter will focus on what becomes the traumatic "primal scene" for the British in their encounter with China: the ambassadorial reception. It is concerned with the surprising forgettings, avoidances, and evasions of Romantic-period writing when related to Chinese subjects. It argues that China was a very real, though frequently suppressed and evaded, presence in the literature of the period, and that leading writers failed to engage directly with the *topos* as they did with British India.

Elizabeth Hope Chang has written persuasively of the ways in which China, with its "willow trees, porcelain pagodas, and countless other designs," occupied "a familiar yet exotic place in the British visual and literary universe even as its governing empire became increasingly entangled with British political and commercial concerns." Chang's stress is on the visual, which conveys a particular form of knowledge about China that is at once ubiquitous (the blue-and-white porcelain) but, at the same time, heavily mediated, ironized, and, I argue, indirect.[1] This "indirection" is what makes the presence of China in Romantic-period culture qualitatively different from that of, say, India or the "Near East," hybridized as it was. This "indirection" is akin to what David Porter, referring to earlier times, tellingly describes as an "instrumental amnesia," or what might be called a knowledge to presence ratio by which the more Britons know about contemporary China (and they knew a great deal), the less they often admit to knowing.[2] Southey makes this point when, despite his familiarity with the Romantic Sinology of Percy, Barrow, and others, he playfully makes the case that what we truly know of China originates from blue-and-white plates, teacups, and saucers: material objects and commodities in a global trade. This chapter explores the fugitive presence of China in Romantic-period writing and argues that, while there is no substantial canonical or "high Romantic" work with an obviously Chinese subject or theme (with the problematic exception of Coleridge's "Kubla Khan"), the presence of China appears in a number of genres in often fleeting ways. It suggests that the reason why China was not addressed directly, as had been earlier by Percy, Goldsmith, Murphy, and others, was because of a complex anxiety when faced with China's established cultural and global hegemony and Britain's problematic rivalry.

CHINESE KOWTOWS

The controversy over the kowtow entered British culture in the early nineteenth century in various forms, some open and some disguised. It seeped into the nation's wider understanding of ceremonial prostrations before despotic Asiatic courts. Clearly early nineteenth-century Britons objected strenuously to the idea of ritual prostration, and the kowtow became *the* symbol of that abhorrent behavior to be used in various oriental and domestic contexts. The kowtow controversy, with its refusals, negotiations, and compromises, merged seamlessly into that long-standing, oppositional Enlightenment tradition running from Montesquieu to Volney and beyond that typified China as a despotism, and was frequently played out in more generalized oriental settings – Ottoman, Persian, Moghul, and Javan.[3]

John Quincy Adams stated that the cause of the Anglo-Chinese War of 1839–42 was not opium, but the kowtow, "the arrogant and insupportable pretensions of China that she will hold commercial intercourse with the rest of mankind not upon terms of equal reciprocity, but upon the insulting and degrading forms of the relations between lord and vassal."[4] In response to such statements, Hevia has convincingly claimed that the Qing demand that foreign ambassadors to the imperial court perform the full imperial kowtow of the three kneelings and the nine knockings of the forehead came to be seen as metonymic of European relations with China in the nineteenth century and quite out of step with accepted norms of the sovereignty and equality of nations, derived from the Westphalian system, established in 1634 as a consequence of the bloody Thirty Years War between emerging European nation states.[5] For Hevia, Britain went to war with China over diplomatic and commercial issues and the kowtow became "a kind of fetishistic object around which the great divide between China and the West, between archaic and modern civilizations, came to be represented."[6] Lydia Liu has similarly argued that later in the century "the overwhelming rhetoric for waging war against China invariably invoked the perceived need to redeem the honor and cultural superiority of the British, which had been compromised in the earlier encounter between Lord Macartney and the Qianlong Emperor."[7]

Macartney was aware of and, to an extent, sensitive to the issue of the kowtow, and the imperial court were understanding, to an extent, of British sensibilities. The full kowtow was dispensed with, after a period of prolonged negotiation, for the Macartney audience with the emperor at Jehol of September 1793. Macartney formally negotiated a compromise by which he knelt on one knee before the emperor as he would before his sovereign George III, and bowed his head, delivering the letter from his king directly into the emperor's hands. Significantly, Macartney *never rejected* the ceremony out of hand, but willingly agreed to perform the full public kowtow if a Chinese official of equivalent rank agreed to perform the ceremony before a portrait of the British king, or if the emperor undertook to promise in writing that on a future occasion a Chinese official of equivalent rank, if presented to the king, would also perform the full ceremony. Rather than the Qing court insisting on an inflexible ceremony, it was willing, albeit reluctantly, to allow an altered version of the ceremony to take place both to accommodate British concerns and to successfully (in Chinese terms) complete the visit. This was because it understood that the visit of a British embassy was unprecedented and needed bespoke handling.[8] In this reading, Macartney's resistance to undertaking the full imperial kowtow, then, had little to do with the apparent "failure" that the embassy was later charged with.

It was from the fifteen or so accounts of the Macartney embassy and the somewhat fewer, but important, accounts of the Amherst embassy that the British discourse of the kowtow and resistance to it emerged into British culture. In his Journal of the embassy, published by John Barrow in 1807, Macartney presents his refusal to kowtow as a successful instance of the benefits of masculine British firmness and rectitude. He provides a detailed account of how the subject of the kowtow was carefully broached, promoted, and, finally, tailored for the British. Macartney informed the Chinese that "whatever ceremonies were usual for the Chinese to perform, the Emperor would prefer my paying him the same obeisance which I did to my own Sovereign." He stressed his "first duty" was to "do what might be agreeable to my own King" whose " dignity" was "the measure of my conduct."[9] On September 10, 1793, Macartney recorded that the Chinese agreed to "adopt the English ceremony," being willing to "kneel upon one knee only on those occasions when it was usual for the Chinese to prostrate themselves."[10] Macartney is anxious to differentiate between kneeling on one knee and bowing, which he perceives to be a manly form of ceremonial, and kneeling on two knees and bowing which he describes as a foreign act of "prostration," unacceptable to a subject of His Britannic Majesty.

In the public account of the embassy, officially authored by his deputy, Staunton (actually by Hüttner), we can see the emergence of the kowtow into a more redolent symbol of China's despotism. Here it is "difficult to imagine an exterior mark of more profound humility and submission, or which implies a more intimate consciousness of the omnipotence of that being towards whom it is made." The *Account* details Macartney's negotiations, imputing to him an awareness "of the tenaciousness of the Chinese court in exacting ceremonies, in which the humiliation on the one part, contributed, perhaps to render the embassies so grateful to the other."[11] The *Account* argues that, as the Chinese did not know the English yet, any "sacrifice of dignity" would fail to impress them with their true character. Hence Macartney determines on his "well-judged, courteous, but not abject, conduct" with which to impress the Chinese in the face of the "unconditional compliance demanded by the Legate."[12] By 1804, in Barrow's *Travels in China*, the kowtow has become transformed into a true test of the British character. In this account the Qing court is presented as proud, haughty, and insolent, jealous of its rigid "long established customs" until confronted by a determined British resolution. The lesson learned by the embassy is clear: "a tone of submission, and a tame and passive obedience to the degrading demands of this haughty court, serve only to feed its pride, and add to the absurd notions of its own vast importance."[13]

Yet during the 1816 Amherst embassy, there is evidence that the Jiaqing emperor was willing to adapt the ceremony of the kowtow in an analogous manner to that practiced by Macartney.[14] Amherst's instructions likewise directed him to conform "to all the ceremonies of that court" which did not lessen his dignity or "commit the honour of your Sovereign."[15] Henry Ellis, while admitting the ceremony to be repugnant, believed that it was no more than a point of "etiquette" that might have been complied with rather than sacrifice the entire objects of the embassy.[16] Amherst also proposed to repeat his kneeling and bowing nine times as an extension of the Macartney compromise.[17] Thomas Manning, who accompanied the embassy as interpreter, actually rather enjoyed kowtowing. While even his Chinese servant by this time understood the British aversion to "bending," Manning was "always asking when I could *ketese* or kneel," and if offered "an option between one and three kneelings" he would always chose the full ceremony. A disappointed Manning never got to kowtow to the Jiaqing emperor, but he was the first Briton to kowtow to the seven-year-old Dalai Lama at Lhasa in 1811.[18] Writing in 1818 in the *Edinburgh Review*, John Crawfurd, friend of Raffles and advisor to the Company, argued that the ceremony did not appear "much more humiliating than other court ceremonies" and the negotiations to avoid it were "absurd."[19] British attitudes to kowtowing were thus not by any means homogenous and it could be regarded simply as a necessary evil, a point of etiquette, or even a pleasurable experience. There was still substantial flexibility on both Chinese and British sides with regard to the performance of the ceremonial.

This chapter argues that in many ways this ambassadorial reception functioned for the British as a primal scene of trauma in the collective national unconscious that became grafted onto a domestic discourse of manliness and humiliation. The "bowing back" of the ambassadors and the rejection of the gifts combined with the suspicion that some great miscalculation had been made was evocatively summed up by James Gillray's epiphanic satire, *The Reception of the Diplomatique & his Suite at the court of Pekin* of 1792 (Figure 4). Macartney's encounter with the Chinese is shown as one of submission before a heavily orientalized and unpleasantly racialized depiction of the imperial court. The ambassador kneels on one knee, but the remainder of the embassy prostrate themselves absurdly in front of an unrecognizable version of the Qianlong emperor. The emperor is portrayed as a stereotypical oriental despot dressed in Mongol attire, smoking and holding out his hand to receive a bribe. A recognizably handsome Macartney, wearing the insignia of the Bath, kneels before him. Behind Macartney are Staunton, Hüttner (with a magpie), and Barrow (with a rocking horse). The presents that the embassy brings are reduced to the status of toys, including the balloon, coach, and rocking horse. These are included with other toys such as the rat-trap, bat, dice-box, battledore and shuttlecock, a toy windmill, magic lantern, and man-of-war. A volume of Boydell's Shakespeare, mercilessly satirized in Gillray's earlier "Shakespeare Sacrificed; or the Offering to Avarice" (1789), is also present. The weathervane that the embassy carries has inaccurate directions, indicating, perhaps that the embassy has lost its

Figure 4. James Gillray, *The Reception of the Diplomatique & his Suite at the court of Pekin*, 1792 © Trustees of the British Museum.

geographical and moral compass.[20] Gillray's depiction was described by James Northcote to Hazlitt as "the Emperor of China a complete Eastern voluptuary … and Lord Macartney is an elegant youth, a real *Apollo*; then, indeed, come Punch and the puppet show after him, to throw the whole into ridicule."[21] Presciently, Gillray has focused on the two major issues raised by the embassy in the contemporary mind; the kowtow and the gifts. Macartney's refusal to kowtow indicates his unwillingness to participate in this ceremonial: a potent and prophetic iconography of the new British imaginings of the Asian ritual. Gillray's satire of the British embassy presents no new meaningful knowledge about China but rather propagates an established oriental stereotyping far removed from the visual style of the embassy illustrations with their aspirations to a new form of ethnographical precision.

In 1795, the young Unitarian dissenter in religion and politics S. T. Coleridge criticized the repressive measures of the Tory government of William Pitt by analogy, recalling how "in some eastern courts the

Ambassadors from Europe have their arms pinioned while they speak to the Despot." George III's ministers, "faithful to despotism, intend to improve on the hint."²² In his "Religious Musings" of 1794–96 he employed the image of the blasting desert wind, the "Simoon," famously described in James Bruce's *Travels to Discover the Source of the Nile* (1790), as "emblematical of the pomp & powers of despotism." Coleridge claims that present-day Europe is "Fitliest depictur'd by some sun-scorcht waste," where "The SIMOON sails, before whose purple pomp / Who falls not prostrate dies!²³ Coleridge was not specifically writing about China in either piece, but he may well have had the full imperial kowtow of Macartney's recent embassy in his mind.

Similarly, in key works by both Shelley and Byron some form of bodily or psychological prostration before an imagined tyrant frequently becomes symbolic of a peculiarly British reading of freedom and liberty. An avidly hellenistic Percy Shelley described the "stagnant and miserable state of social institution" of nineteenth-century China and Japan in the "Preface" to *Hellas*.²⁴ In his *The Mask of Anarchy* (1820), ritual prostration is clearly identified with submission. Faced with Anarchy and his troop, the lawyers and priests "To the earth their pale brows bowed ... Whispering— 'Thou art Law and God.'"²⁵ Anarchy is presented as an oriental despot before whom his followers prostrate themselves. While resistance to both metaphorical and bodily abasement and humiliation is thus an informing context for Shelley's politics, other key elements of the discourse of the kowtow, such as the Macartney negotiation and compromise, are not present in this scene of ritual prostration. Byron, however, presents a much more detailed examination of the ceremony and the discourse of humiliation in at least two important moments of his substantial oeuvre. His tragedy *Manfred*, composed in 1816 and published the following year, was written too early to be directly influenced by the published accounts of the Amherst embassy but its composition during the time of the embassy itself argues that Byron might well have had China in mind when writing.

The second Act of the drama presents an apocalyptic confrontation with the European counter-revolution as "mortals dared to ponder for themselves ... and to speak of freedom, the forbidden fruit."²⁶ Byron chooses to stage this crucial dramatic confrontation between Manfred and the Zoroastrian deity, Arimanes, as an encounter between a free-spirited European and an Asiatic despot over the issue of ritual prostration. This encounter can be viewed as a displaced version of the Sino-British kowtow controversy. Arimanes, a personification of the Manichean principle of evil, is described in a parody of the kinds of language used to describe the Son of Heaven in British discourse about China. The Second Destiny acts like a Chinese mandarin, stating that "we who bow / The necks of men, bow down before his throne" (II.iv.20–21; 4, p. 81). Immediately Manfred approaches the fiery throne of Arimanes he is repeatedly commanded by the spirits to "Bow down and worship!" in the same way that the Chinese mandarins were described as exhorting Macartney in 1793 and Amherst in 1816 to perform the full imperial kowtow. Manfred refuses to kneel and prostrate himself before the demon, a process he associates with a form of humiliation that is acceptable only within a personal context of guilt and remorse: "I have known / The fullness of humiliation" (II.iv.38–41; 4, p. 82). Humiliation is not, necessarily, a bad thing; it is just the context in which it occurs.

Manfred's crucial response to Arimanes' court is similar to that of the British brought up with a horror of idolatry:

> Bid *him* bow down to that which is above him,
> The overruling Infinite, the Maker
> Who made him not for worship; let him kneel,
> And we will kneel together.
>
> (II.iv.46–49; 4, p. 82)

What is seldom pointed out is that Manfred's response to Arimanes' ministers and courtiers is not to reject the required prostration out of hand, but rather, like Macartney and Amherst, to agree to carry out the ceremony but only on certain conditions of equality and reciprocity. Macartney and Amherst would kowtow provided a Chinese official of equal rank would kowtow to a portrait of George III, or in response to an imperial edict to the effect that future Chinese ambassadors would carry out the full ceremony at the British court. Manfred's offered compromise with power is one that stresses equality and reciprocity, but one that Arimanes cannot make. Instead, impressed by the manly and exceptional conduct of Manfred, he backs down. In the Macartney fantasy of power, a firm and steadfast refusal to indulge in the degrading and humiliating Asian ceremonial results in an increase in respect and agency. Arimanes' powers are thus, like the Qing emperor's, circumscribed. Whether intended or otherwise, Manfred's confrontation with Arimanes is strongly reminiscent of the British accounts of their disputes with the Qing court over the issue of the kowtow in terms of its staging and symbolism (II.iv.80–81, 115–16, 119; 4, p. 86).

This action of prostration and resistance also recurs in the harem sections of the fifth canto of Byron's *Don Juan*. In this canto the eunuch,

Baba, buys Juan in a slave market for the pleasure of the Sultana Gulbeyaz. He then insists that Juan dress as a woman, threatening him with castration if he fails to comply. On being presented to the Sultana, Gulbayez is commanded to kiss her foot:

> A second time desired him to kneel down,
> And kiss the Lady's foot; which maxim when
> He heard repeated, Juan with a frown
> Drew himself up to his full height again;
> And said, "It grieved him, but he could not stoop
> To any Shoe, unless it shod the Pope."
> (V. 809–16; 5, p. 273)

In this scene where Juan, a man dressed as a woman, is requested to prostrate himself before a woman acting as a man by a eunuch who threatens to castrate him, very complex issues are raised about gender, nation, religion, and identity. In the face of such pressure Juan finally re-asserts his masculinity, drawing himself up "to his full height again," refusing to stoop to kiss any shoe, unless it be that of the Pope. Juan thus is technically willing to perform the ceremony, but only on the condition that the honored party be the spiritual leader of his own religion. Despite Baba's threats to bowstring him (a Chinese as well as an Ottoman mode of execution), Juan "would not bend" but maintains a straight back and resolved mind. Faced with this firm resolution, Baba backs down and proposes instead the now familiar Macartney compromise of an alternative version of the ceremony, here kissing the hand rather than the foot. For Juan, this "was an honourable compromise, / A halfway house of diplomatic rest" where they meet "in much more peaceful guise (V.833–36; 5, p. 245). Juan's firm resistance to the prostration and foot-kissing leads to a renegotiation of the form of the ceremony to one that is acceptable and which conforms to the customs of his nation. The ceremony is thus accomplished after negotiation and "compromise" leading to "*diplomatic rest*" has occurred, as it was at Jehol in September 1793.

Said notably situated Jane Austen's *Mansfield Park* (1814) in the context of the debates about Transatlantic slavery featuring Sir Thomas's involvement with his estates in Antigua.[27] One could argue, however, that the informing colonial and commercial contexts of *Mansfield Park* are as much China, opium, and tea, as the Caribbean, sugar, and slavery. Jane Austen's brother, Frank, served with the Royal Navy at Canton in 1809–10, employed in charting the South China coast. Frank also visited the British factory. Staunton was in Britain during the period of Frank's visits, but he would probably have met Morrison and Manning. Frank became embroiled in a local disturbance that allegedly ended with the British killing of a Chinese man.[28] He was initially favorably disposed to the Chinese but became disaffected by the conduct of the Viceroy of Canton, who kept him waiting. In a letter to Admiral Drury, Frank wrote angrily about what he viewed as the Chinese management of the incident: "A mandarin is not a reasoning animal, nor ought to be treated as a rational animal," he spluttered.[29] The £1500 Frank made from his private trading relieved his financial anxieties considerably.[30] Austen wrote letters, one of which has survived, from the Chawton cottage to China.[31]

Peter Knox-Shaw, Maaja A. Stewart, and Joseph Lew have all located the novel in the context of the embassy and the kowtow controversy.[32] Knox-Shaw first argued that Fanny Price's refusal to accept the domestic despotism of her Aunt Norris or, in milder form, Sir Thomas Bertram, is reminiscent of the kowtow controversy. Lew further argued that "Macartney teaches Fanny to recognize that a usually kind and indulgent despot, is still a despot."[33] Significantly, Fanny is interrupted in the "East Room," during her reading of what is usually identified as Macartney's "Journal of the Embassy," published in the second volume of John Barrow's *Some Account of the Public Life of the Earl of Macartney* (1807). It is argued that this book is a "great" or large folio volume. Edmund identifies the volume as dealing with Macartney's embassy, and the supposition is that the ambassador's name must therefore appear on the title page of the volume, as Edmund is not really interested in what Fanny is reading but, as always, has Mary Crawford uppermost in his thoughts. The interruption is occasioned when Edmund informs Fanny that Mary has now persuaded him to take part in the amateur dramatics:

"... *You*, in the meanwhile, will be taking a trip into China, I suppose. How does Lord Macartney go on?"—opening a volume on the table and then taking up some others ... He went; but there was no reading, no China, no composure for Fanny. He had told her the most extraordinary, the most inconceivable, the most unwelcome news; and she could think of nothing else. To be acting! After all his objections—objections so just and so public! After all that she had heard him say, and seen him look, and known him to be feeling. Could it be possible? Edmund so inconsistent. Was he not deceiving himself? Was he not wrong? Alas! it was all Miss Crawford's doing.[34]

Knox-Shaw argues suggestively that the narrative of Macartney's resistance to the kowtow is an informing context of the novel in which the politics of resistance and inducement are central. This theme is also represented in Fanny's resistance to the blandishments of Sir Thomas to accept the marriage proposal from Henry Crawford. Fanny refuses, symbolically at least, to kowtow before her Aunt Norris or Sir Thomas Bertram. Edmund's submission to the Crawfords' plan is highlighted in Mary's comment that she never "knew such exquisite happiness" until she witnesses his "sturdy spirit bend as it did!" Mary, like the Sultana Gulbayez, delights in exerting a masculine and orientalized authority over her chosen subject or slave, and witnessing him "bend" before her; the moment is "sweet beyond words" to her.[35] Fanny is also obliged to participate in the drama *Lover's Vows* despite her sensitivities to the decorum of the action. All these examples of British resistance to orientalized pressures to perform a type of ritual prostration, real or imagined, it can be argued take as their informing context the contemporary discourse of the kowtow, even if China is not an obvious referent in the symbolic exchange. Thus China enters the Romantic imagination through a process of displacement in which the most obvious and most important practical example of the role of the ceremonial in diplomatic exchange in not discussed in its own terms but, by and large, used as a metaphor for domestic political (Byron and Shelley) or political domestic (Austen) situations.

ROBERT SOUTHEY'S CHINESE FAILURES

In his seminal oriental poem of 1801, *Thalaba the Destroyer*, Robert Southey teasingly alludes to the topos of China. In Book 6, Southey describes how Thalaba sleeps after journeying at night to a dark valley. On waking, he is confronted with "a scene of wonders" as a thousand streams wander across the plain into the "blue ethereal ocean," creating isles of colorful mosses and lichens and spectacular gushing fountains:

> This was a wild and wondrous scene,
>   Strange and beautiful, as where
> By Oton-tala, like a sea of stars,
> The hundred sources of Hoangho burst.[36]

Southey here refers to *Huang He*, or the Yellow River. He directs the reader to two sources. The first, "A Description of Tibet," collected in the fourth volume of Astley's *New General Collection of Voyages and Travels* (1745–47), indicates that "in the place where the Whang ho rises, there are more than an hundred springs which sparkle like stars, whence it is called Hotun Nor, the Sea of Stars." This remark is attributed to the Jesuit Antoine Gaubil. The second source is Percy's *Hau Kiou Choann*. Percy supplies a note describing how the "Whang ho, or as the Portughese call it Hoam-Ho, i.e. the yellow River rises not far from the source of the

Ganges in the Tartarian mountains west of China." He points out that the river receives its name from the "yellow" mud which stains the waters and composes a third part of its volume: "the Chinese say its waters cannot become clear in a thousand years; whence it is a common proverb among them for any thing which is never likely to happen," a proverb used in the novel.[37]

Southey's tentative engagement with the literature of China, through Percy's edition of the *Hau Kiou Choann*, might be regarded as metonymic of the canonical or "high Romantic" response to the Qing empire of the late eighteenth and early nineteenth centuries. He was clearly fascinated by the Chinese empire and he absorbed much of Percy's translation, yet his interest in, and knowledge of, China was not itself translated into a major work of the Romantic imagination. In a letter to John Rickman of October 1808 Southey remembered the novel well enough to use it in a discussion of one of his *bêtes noires*, the practice of polygamy by non-European peoples. Southey argues that the moral fault of polygamy was in some way responsible for the perceived stagnation of eighteenth-century China. Contra Southey, Rickman argued that it was the "want of an alphabet" that really accounted for what he conventionally describes as "the frozen limits of Chinese science." Southey ascribed China's successes to the "unique circumstance of its having a literary aristocracy." The "demoralizing effects" of polygamy are the same there as elsewhere, as "Shuey-ping-sin exemplifies."[38] The *Hao Kiou Choann*, however, centers on the issue of an arranged marriage rather than polygamy, which is not heavily featured though it is briefly mentioned in Percy's notes.[39]

Southey read a great deal more about China than Percy. While still at Westminster school, he encountered the seven-volume English translation (1733–39) of Jean Frédéric Bernard's syncretist *Cérémonies et coutumes religieuses de tous les peuples du monde* (1723–43), lavishly illustrated by the engraver Bernard Picart. These volumes included substantial material on the religions of China, especially what was then known of Chinese Buddhism, or the religion of Fo. It was this volume that inspired Southey's project to write a series of heroic poems "exhibiting all the more prominent and poetical forms of mythology which have at any time obtained among mankind."[40] It is somewhat odd, then, that in his well-known letter to Anna Seward, Southey mentions a series of religions, including that of Japan but not that of China. His design was write a poem using "every poetic faith that has ever been established, and gone on after the Mahommedan in *Thalaba*, and the Hindoo in this present poem, with the Persian, the Runic, the Keltic, the Greek, the Jewish, the

Roman Catholick and the Japanese."[41] The sale catalogue of Southey's library of 1844 lists several prominent Jesuit accounts of China, as well as more recent accounts by the naturalist Clarke Abel who served on the Amherst embassy to China of 1816–17, and Staunton's translation of the Qing penal code, the *Ta Tsing Leu Lee* of 1810.[42]

Southey encountered China in Barrow's *Travels in China* (1804), which he reviewed for the *Annual Review*. He swallowed Barrow's account more or less whole, and likely promoted its understanding of China to the Wordsworths and Coleridge. Southey claimed that Barrow showed "the Chinese as they really are," and laid before the reader facts "to settle in his own mind the point of rank which China may be considered to hold in the scale of civilised nations." He presented a "new" account of China, its peoples and customs, including such issues as religion, Confucianism, foot-binding, infanticide, politics, landscape gardening, drama and education. Southey's review approved of this compendiousness: Barrow had, he declared, "communicated more information concerning this extraordinary empire and its inhabitants, than could be collected from all our former travellers." Southey admitted that China had achieved a much higher state of civilization than Europe in the past, but declared, after Barrow, that he judged modernity had bypassed the empire: while "Europe has been progressive in all the arts of life ... China has stood still." Crucially, Southey spotted that the Chinese were no longer a naval power; their ships were "round and clumsy" and lacked keels. The Chinese may have discovered the compass but their main use for it was to keep their ships as near to port as possible. Similarly, he remarked, they had "no reckoning" for latitude and "no idea of drawing charts." All this went to show that in China civilization was regressing rather than improving and that the state of China was "materially different now from what it was some centuries ago."[43]

Most interestingly, Southey seems to possess a decent knowledge of the religious beliefs of Qing China, perhaps unsurprisingly for a poet who was fascinated by Islam and Hinduism. The review presents Barrow's synthesis of Chinese religions as composed of Confucianism, Daoism, and a form of Buddhism. For Southey, Confucianism was a form of pantheism. The other belief systems, however, are "more adapted to human folly." The Daoists should be classed with sectarians such as mesmerists. Like Catholics, they "devote themselves to a state of celibacy, and associate in convents," and their temples are "crowded with images." Sadly, Southey writes little about Buddhism, which would have made an excellent subject for one of his religious epics. Archly, he comments on how the two sects often took up arms against each other, burning their monasteries and kill-ing their priests, but as the people were not involved such wars were more useful to the state, which has reconciled them "by the sure method of neglecting both."[44] The outcome was the adherence of the present dynasty to a hybrid religion – that of the Lama, or Tibetan Buddhism. It is tempt-ing to think that Southey might have found in this synthetic religion material for a Chinese Madoc or Thalaba – an Asiatic, proto-Protestant, reforming iconoclast, smashing the idols of Daoist or Buddhist supersti-tion. And yet, despite, his interest and knowledge, he never did write a Chinese epic – an evasion that is symptomatic of the Romantic writing.

SOUTHEY, BAILLIE, AND PORCELAIN

"China" has always retained its double identity of geographic nation and commercial commodity.[45] As Porter has argued, Chinese imported objects "were never simply passive objects of consumption, evaluation, and symbolic appropriation" but were also "active catalysts for the trans-formation of sensibilities and identities."[46] China as porcelain, of course, is a complex signifier, which does not point to a simple referent. Chinese export porcelain consisted variously of Ming and Qing pieces which bore no trace of any foreign influence, pieces made in European designs, pieces decorated in China with European designs, and white porcelain exported to Europe and painted by European artists. Towards the end of the eight-eenth century china was increasingly manufactured in British potteries for middle-class consumers. The famous blue-and-white willow pattern was a design produced by British engravers from about 1790 onwards, inspired by Chinese export models. Thus, with some comparatively rare exceptions, porcelain in Chinese designs and with Chinese scenes was an extremely sophisticated hybrid consumer product purveying multiple meanings and associations.[47] China signifies the foreign and exotic, but also hybrid exported porcelain, as well as domestically produced earth-enware, some of which displays an orientalized, chinoiserie design. The extent to which these discriminations were popularly understood in the period further complicates interpretation.

As Chang has argued, China in the nineteenth century is increasingly perceived through a visual hermeneutics of Chinese and European per-spectives and this process is central to the constitution of the British sub-ject. The related and recurrent trope of reading the imperium of China through the porcelain commodity of china is commonplace. In her *Fugitive Verses* of 1790, Joanna Baillie included her remarkable "Lines to a Teapot" in which a Ming export porcelain teapot serves analogously to the Grecian urn of Keats's 1819 ode. In Baillie's poem, written at a time when tea was not identified as a natural British drink, the domestic, yet exotic, teapot serves not as a "sylvan historian," but rather as a silent chinoiserie sinologist, informing us indirectly of the topography and customs of China. The "vivid dye" of the pot's sides invites the viewer's eye to take in a "distant nation's manners" expressed "whimsically" to the "quick fancy."

> The small-eyed beauty with her Mandarin,
> Who o'er the rail of garden arbour lean,
> In listless ease; and rocks of arid brown,
> On whose sharp crags, in gay profusion blown,
> The ample loose-leaved rose appears to grace
> The skilful culture of the wondrous place;
> The little verdant plat, where with his mate
> The golden pheasant holds his gorgeous state,
>
> .   .   .   .
>
> The smooth-streaked water of a paly gray,
> O'er which the checkered bridge lends ready way,
> While, by its margin moored, the little boat
> Doth with its oars and netted awning float:
> A scene in short all soft delights to take in,
> A paradise for grave Grandee of Pekin.

Like the Grecian urn, intact and unravished by time, the teapot "standest complete … a goodly vessel of the olden times." The scene on the antique teapot is a chinoiserie scene yet one created by Chinese potters as the object evokes in the poet, not a Keatsian meditation on the relationship between art, life, and history, but an imaginative recreation of the teapot's creation by the "magic skill" of the Chinese potter. Baillie then describes how the artifact is "packed in a chest with others," and shipped across the ocean to "Britain's polished land." Bought at auction, the teapot becomes the cherished possession of "dames of pride." The item is the center of the evening's social activities. Baillie uses the history of the teapot to chart the social history by which the "watery drug" of tea grows in popularity, and now comes to be served in a domestic British "pot of vulgar ware," while the imported exotic vessel languishes on the "shelf / Of China closet" in "most ignoble uselessness."[48]

Baillie's trope of viewing the manners of "a distant nation" on the commodity of the teapot is one that recurs throughout the nineteenth century. While this idea, of course, is willfully naïve, it is combined with a more knowing understanding of the process of manufacture and transmission of the object. Though not depicting the quasi-industrial production process of the Jingdezhen potteries and Canton craft shops, nevertheless Baillie is aware that this is an orientalized work created to satisfy a specific British demand. Baillie's poem also reflects the increasing popularity of British home-produced Staffordshire and Worcester earthenware, especially after 1790 when import duties raised the price of the foreign product, as well as the increasing popularity of tea-drinking. Yet this sound understanding of economic and cultural trends is crucially not reflected back in problematizing the teapot's depiction of the manners and topography of the "distant nation."

Similarly, despite the knowledge he had accrued from Percy and Barrow, Southey has the narrator of his *Letters from England* (1807), the Spanish Catholic Don Manuel Alvarez Espirella, discuss China via the topos of the blue and white as if it tells the viewer something meaningful about China. Espirella describes the manufacturing city of Worcester and, briefly but notably, its famous porcelain. Espirella depicts domestic British copies of Chinese designs by Worcester or Staffordshire. This encounter is thus distanced, as what we see are British copies of Chinese scenes which themselves were exaggerations designed by Chinese artists for export, appealing to a European market obsessed by the fashion for chinoiserie and orientalism. Espirella praises the "semi pellucid and pearly delicacy" of Chinese porcelain as much superior to that produced by the English ware in quality but not in taste. Nevertheless, Britons prefer such "grotesque and tasteless patterns of the real china." This leads to the English copying the "hair-lined eyebrows of the Chinese, their unnatural trees and distorted scenery," as if Britons were equally "ignorant of perspective," instead of producing their own landscapes and aristocratic emblazonings. The apparent Chinese ignorance of perspective is used here as an indicator of their lack of modernity, another example of the "Great Divide."

Southey's *Letters* pre-empt the essays of Lamb and Hunt by claiming that Europeans know about China from the stylized designs of the blue-and-white porcelain, even though the author, if not the narrator, is highly knowledgeable about the subject:

plates and tea-saucers have made us better acquainted with the Chinese than we are with any other distant people. If we had no other documents concerning this extraordinary nation, a series of engravings from these their own pictures, would be considered as highly curious, and such a work, if skilfully conducted and annotated, might still elucidate the writings of travellers, and not improbably furnish information which it would be in vain to seek in Europe from other sources.[49]

This passage sums up the Romantic paradox of China. The British are, in one sense better acquainted with the Chinese than with *any other* people, through the domestic omnipresence of the Chinese designs – what Chang refers to as the "familiar exotic" that can serve as both "a comforting icon of British domesticity" and "a dangerous token of visual difference."[30] But, Espirella, like Baillie's narrator, gives the game away by fully admitting to much more knowledge than this. There are, in fact, many "other documents" (many held in Southey's compendious library) that present a very different China from that of the blue-and-white plates and tea-saucers, and these documents contradict the chinoiserie historians of the teapots, cups, and saucers. The series of engravings taken from the porcelain would also need, like Southey's own literary and historical writings, to be extensively "annotated" to "elucidate" and "not improbably furnish information." Espirella presents a metaphor for the refusal of his creator to undertake a substantial work about China that, in many ways, would be among the most important and urgent things he could do. In a sense Romantic Sinology is present in these representations of China, but its new realization of Chinese customs, manners, culture, and art is effaced in preference for an older artistic style of China, now mediated through British-designed and -produced wares. It is relegated, literally marginalized, to the position of providing annotation to an elaborate, hybridized form of commercial foreign and domestic design.

CHARLES LAMB'S CHINESE EVASIONS

If China appears only briefly and surreptitiously in Southey's work, it features more strongly, if equally problematically, in the writings Charles Lamb, albeit through the mediated medium of chinoiserie. Lamb worked at India House for the Company in London for some thirty years, his employment intimately bound up with the tea and opium trades. His friend Thomas Manning was the "friend M" from whom "Elia" professed to have obtained the translation of a Chinese manuscript that furnished the essay "Dissertation upon Roast Pig" published in the *London Magazine* in 1822. This essay returns its readership to an ancient China out of the *Arabian Nights* in which Bo-bo the swine-herd's son accidentally sets fire to his father's cottage, inadvertently roasting a pig, and accidentally discovering the delights of roast pork. The essay reverts to the orientalized version of China deployed through a stylized narrative in the manner of the contemporary tales and pantomimes of *Aladdin* discussed in Chapter 9.

Mankind, says a Chinese manuscript, which my friend M. was obliging enough to read and explain to me, for the first seventy thousand ages ate their meat raw, clawing or biting it from the living animal, just as they do in Abyssinia to this day. The period is not obscurely hinted at by their great Confucius in the second chapter of his Mundane Mutations, where he designates a kind of golden age by the term Cho-fang, literally the Cooks' holiday.[51]

Lamb, servant of the Company and friend and correspondent of possibly one of the greatest China scholars of the age, eschews the realities of contemporary China and the tea trade for a fairy-tale ("antediluvian") ancient China that also contains commercial firms selling domestic insurance against household accident. Lamb's essay is comic, and it burlesques Manning's curious obsession with China and its language and culture. Alluding to James Bruce's notorious claim that he witnessed the Abyssinians dining on living cattle, Lamb spins his tale whereby the Chinese become addicted to roast pork after Bo-bo's accidental discovery. As Felicity James argues, Lamb's target is as much the traveler's tall tale as Manning's China fixation. The reliability of such tales, as Nigel Leask and Jonathan Lamb have argued, was a crucial issue in the period.[52] Discovering the joys of roast pork, the Chinese continue to replicate the practice of "accidentally" firing their houses to cook the pigs until "the insurance offices one and all shut up shop."[53] Comically, they make the secondary discovery that it is not necessary to fire the house to cook the pork. China and Manning thus become an excuse for Lamb to indulge in a manic disquisition about the delights of eating roast pork, an entrée to his comic main course.

Recent Lamb criticism has rightly shifted the focus of enquiry from the biographical and metropolitan to the global networks of the periodical culture in which Lamb's work is situated. Notably, Karen Fang ingeniously relates "Roast Pig" to an emerging British consumer society and the imperial periodical culture in which Lamb moved. The Chinese and British addiction to roast pork once tasted may reflect the growing craving for opium in China that Lamb knew very well both as a Company employee and as a friend of Coleridge. Lamb anticipates such conflict through his representation of "addled Chinese consumers and the social degradation their consumption depicts."[54] James argues that British cruelty (whipping the piglet to death) and gluttony in pursuit of pleasure are identified with the practice of cannibalism ("the child pig") of savage races, cleverly reversing stereotypes of Western superiority. Yet again, contemporary China as a topos and location of knowledge is absent from the piece, despite Lamb's personal and professional connections.[55]

The nexus of China, consumption, commerce, and global expansion is clearly present in Lamb's writings. A more evocative idea of China is contained in Lamb's plangent essay "Old China," published in the *London* for 1823, which describes his "almost feminine partiality" for Chinese porcelain; in particular, the blue and white. Porter has drawn our attention to the "pronounced clustering" of Chinese ceramics around "ideas of the feminine."[56] It is not clear whether Lamb's cup is actually Chinese export porcelain like Baillie's teapot, or one of the British imitations by Worcester or Staffordshire. If the former then its pattern has traveled from Britain to Canton, where it was painted or printed by Chinese hands, and returned to London as ballast for the tea purchased by the Company for sale in Britain. Like the texts of Chinese translations, the cup is thus a product of global exchange and commerce. Lamb identifies the cup as a whimsical chinoiserie object with its "merry little Chinese waiter holding an umbrella, big enough for a bed-tester, over the head of that pretty insipid half-Madonna-ish chit of a lady in that very blue summer house" (p. 252).

Lamb's use of the porcelain teacup to evoke memories of things long past, recalls both Keats's philhellenic use of the Grecian urn and Coleridge's fluttering blue flame in "Frost at Midnight", both poems exploiting the high Romantic concern with temporal and spatial imagination. Fang's suggestive reading of the essay argues that the teacup is actually an inverted domestic and quotidian version of the oriental pleasure dome of Coleridge's "Kubla Khan," and that his essay "figures porcelain" instead of opium "as a stimulus to 'imagination,' and thereby conflates commodity culture with aesthetic inspiration to suggest an inclusive, consumer version of the Romantic tradition." Fang argues that Lamb does not deploy an idea of China independent of the teacup.[57] However, like "Roast Pig," the essay evokes China in an indirect, allusive, ironic, and evasive manner, belying Lamb's substantial knowledge of commercial relations with China including the complex exchanges of tea, silver, and opium, present obliquely in the essays by allusions to addiction and inspiration.[58] Nostalgically, Lamb describes how he never had any "repugnance" to

those little lawless, azure-tinctured grotesques, that under the notion of men and women, float about, uncircumscribed by any element, in that world before perspective—a china tea cup ... Here is a young and courtly Mandarin, handing tea to a lady from a salver—two miles off. See how distance seems to set off respect! And here the same lady, or another—for likeness is identity on teacups—is stepping into a little fairy boat, moored on the hither side of this calm garden river, with a dainty mincing foot, which in a right angle of incidence (as angles go in our world) must infallibly land her in the midst of a flowery mead—a furlong off to the other side of the same strange stream! (p. 281)

Lamb's recollection of his delight in this chinoiserie pattern presents us with another antediluvian fantasy China, timeless and defying the laws of Western physics and rules of perspective, and becomes the occasion for nostalgic recollection of former, less prosperous, though happier times. For Porter, the essay works through the structural ambivalence of the cup's "aesthetic monstrosity" with the visual space it conjures up for Elia, the narrator.[59] For Fang, the porcelain serves as prelude to a serious discussion between Elia and Bridget (Charles and Mary) about their former financial situation and their present affluence, situating their class mobility within the overlapping frames of commercial (India House/South Sea Office) and professional literary (*London Magazine*) cultures. For Chang, Elia's focus on the Chinese absence of an interest in linear perspective signifies their indifference to the systems of perception that formed Western subjectivity at a crucial point in its construction. Here the teacup depicts a chinoiserie version of China before the *felix culpae* of Western subjectivity, traditionally associated with a Romantic construction of childhood innocence in works such Blake's *Songs of Innocence* (1793) and Wordsworth's *The Prelude* (1805). Elia remarks how his acquaintance with china predates his adult subjectivity being "not conscious of a time when china jars and saucers were introduced into my imagination." Elia's cup performs exactly the same function as nature in the first two books of the 1805 *The Prelude* in this alternative commodity version of Wordsworth's "spots of time" where memory and imagination coalesce to create the unified Romantic subject. For Lamb, China/china is at the very heart of this construction of selfhood.

In Lamb's account Chinese art is depicted as "decorous" and "lawless," outside the laws of perspective and physics. The scene is miniaturized and aestheticized, arguing that the Chinese are imprisoned in an unprogressive and non-technological pastoral. The Chinese are "womanish," "courtly," "grotesques," and virtually identical to one another. While, as Porter, Fang, and Chang have shown, such imaginings are heavily imbricated in the contexts of visuality and commerce, additionally the use of the china trope severs Lamb's essay from the extensive scholarship of the Romantic Sinology and the material processes of the China trade about which he knew so much from Manning and India House. In its pleasant, whimsical, and dream-like irrationality, the scene also vaguely and fitfully suggests an opium vision, conflating once again the Eastern drugs of tea and opium, but only obliquely. Again, as with Southey, Lamb is developing a series of strange evasions here, a wish to concentrate on the commodity of china (likely in its British manifestation) to the profound exclusion of the polity of China, while at the same time acknowledging the centrality of China/china to the construction of his adult self, child and man.

This tendency is also displayed in the many letters Lamb wrote to Manning which are remarkable for the infrequency and indirection of their addressing China. In August 1801, Lamb quizzed Manning on his motivation to visit China, responding to a spurious rumor that Manning had been commissioned by the Wedgwoods to "collect hints for their pottery, and to teach the Chinese *perspective*": twin concerns of his two China essays. Responding to Manning's suggestion that he intends to enter China via "Independent Tartary" and can think of nothing else, Lamb negotiates the subject via more Romantic notions of Tartary. He jokes that his "good friend Tibet Kulm" has translated an important dissertation on English politics, which may be of use to the "Emperor of Usbeck Tartary." Tibet Kulm is an emissary to the English with a "civil invitation from the Cham … to go over to the worship of the Lama."[60] The contemporary processes of British missionary activity and the institutionalizing of Romantic Sinology are thus doubly displaced or deflected onto a process of reverse conversion originating not from China, but from Tartary.

Throughout these letters, Lamb's register and tone remain at the level of gossip, whimsy, and often melancholy. In May 1806, he requests presents as tokens of memory, a shawl for Mary and "a sprightly little Mandarin for our mantle-piece, as a companion to the Child I am going to purchase at the Museum." Yet he also encourages Manning to seek out Samuel Ball, an inspector of teas at Canton, and school friend of Lamb, thinking it will be good to be the subject of a conversation in that part of the world (2.225–26). Just a few months later in December he can exclaim "China—Canton—bless us—how it strains the imagination and makes it ache!" despite having an old friend residing there, working in an office with frequent official contact, and already imagining Ball and Manning casually chatting about him in the factory. This odd double register is also apparent when Lamb questions the existence of China's Great Wall: "I shall cease to talk to you, and you may rave to the Great Wall of China. N.B. Is there such a wall! Is it as big as Old London Wall by Bedlam?" (2.244, 247). Similarly, in December 1815 Lamb comically chastises his friend for his time-consuming efforts in learning the Chinese language while the familiar world of London and his friendships slowly but inevitably decay: "St. Paul's Church is a heap of ruins; the Monument isn't half so high as you knew it, divers parts being successively taken down which the ravages of time had rendered dangerous; the horse at Charing Cross is gone, no one knows whither,—and all this has taken place while you have been settling whether Ho-hing-tong should be spelt with a —— or a —." (3.205). Lamb, as an employee of the Company, knew how very serious the attainment of the Chinese language was to British understandings of China and its crucial purpose in commerce. As Chang argues, Lamb uses his possessions to capture "a sense of distant aesthetics without directly engaging with the contemporary crisis that enforced that distance."[61]

THOMAS MANNING'S CHINESE ABSENCES

Thomas Manning returns us to the very center of Romantic Sinology at Canton as well as Serampore and Lhasa in Tibet. He was a crucial figure in its development. The role he played in aiding Marshman and the Company, Staunton and the Amherst embassy, and the Royal Asiatic Society has already been touched upon.[62] Regarded by many as the preeminent expert on China in the Romantic period, his presence in the field remained largely a personal one. Unlike Marshman, Morrison, Staunton, or Davis, Manning contributed no really significant work to Romantic Sinology. His chief fame, ironically, rests on his being the first Englishman to enter Lhasa and receive an audience with the ninth Dalai Lama in 1811, an event that took place only because Manning had chosen the Tibetan route in another failed attempt to visit China as an independent scholar. The substance of Manning's published sinology is slight, with only one essay on the more idiosyncratic subject of "Chinese Jests" appearing in the *New Monthly Magazine* in 1826, and an unpublished Chinese dictionary. The journal of his visit to Lhasa remained unknown until Clements Markham edited a version of it in 1886, and his many letters to Charles Lamb, some of which touch on China, were not published in full until 1925.

Manning became interested in the Chinese language while at Cambridge where he studied mathematics. Son of a liberal-minded Norwich clergyman, Manning moved in dissenting Unitarian and Quaker circles. At Cambridge he developed an obsession to visit China and study its language and customs. He studied Mandarin in Paris for three years in 1802 under Jean Hagar, before returning to London where a native Chinese, most likely Yong Sam-Tak, Morrison's tutor, taught him.[63] He then undertook six months training at Westminster Hospital to acquire sufficient medical skill to persuade the Company at Canton to employ his services as a doctor. Obtaining Joseph Banks's recommendation to Court of Directors, he voyaged to Canton in 1806 where he repeatedly and unsuccessfully petitioned the Chinese authorities for permission to travel to Beijing as an astronomer and physician. Manning wrote to Banks in 1807 to say that he had "made very little progress in the language … the difficulties are extraordinary, but so much more absolute & invincible is my determination to learn it." He also sent Banks a full account of the "accidental homicide" committed by "the hack-culprit, Edward Sheen" as well as the current state of his beard, a subject of great moment for him.[64] By January 1808, he reports to Banks that though he goes "very slowly with the Chinese language, but I hope soon to be able to give some account of the tones (as they are called)."[65] In March 1808 he claimed in a letter to Lamb that he was able "to talk a little *China*" and in August that the "the veil'd Mysteries of the Chinese language gradually" were opening to his view.[66]

In 1810 Manning moved to Calcutta where he provided valuable assistance to Marshman, and where he sought assistance from the Company for his plan to enter China via Tibet. Manning informed Banks in August 1811 of his frustrations and the lack of support from Company officials in Calcutta. He was keen to distance himself from both Company and government. Although not "in the Company's service," he claims to know its affairs better than any other Englishman. Desirous of accompanying any new projected embassy, Manning declares that his "Quaker principles" meant that he would not wish for any place or appointment. Yet he argued that if an embassy were not sent it would not have "so clever a man again in the situation I am actually in!"[67] In a letter to George III, enclosed in a letter of September 1811 to Banks, Manning, untroubled by self-doubt, advised sending an embassy to capitalize on his talents:

The Englishman who has the high Honour of submitting this notice to Your Majesty, has, with great labor, acquired such a critical knowledge of the Chinese Idioms, both oral & written, as, he believes, no European before ever reached to.[68]

Manning claimed precedence here not only over Morrison but also over Ricci! In his journal Manning would comment more freely that the Company were "fools, fools, fools" to neglect an opportunity they would never have again.[69]

In 1811 Manning set off with the assistance of a single Chinese servant, whom he refers to by the Urdu and Persian term as his *munshi*, for Lhasa, where he resided for several months. Failing to obtain permission to enter China, he went no further and returned to Canton. Finally, in 1816, he traveled into China as a junior secretary and interpreter accompanying Morrison, Staunton, and Davis on Amherst's embassy. Manning's eccentric behavior, his wish to dress as a Chinese (which he gave up), and his insistence on sporting his full beard (which he maintained) profoundly irritated Amherst, though Staunton was strongly in support of his inclusion.[70] As Davis later remarked, Manning was simply odd; he "was seldom serious, and did not argue any matter gravely, but in a tone of banter in which he maintained the most monstrous paradoxes, his illustration being often highly laughable … he did everything in his odd and eccentric way."[71] Subsequently Manning became the honorary Chinese librarian at the Royal Asiatic Society. His substantial collection of Chinese books was bequeathed to the library on his death in 1840.[72] His reluctance to publish should not minimize his significance as a Romantic Sinologist. He gave his expert advice and assistance at Canton, Serampore, and London to Marshman, Staunton, Davis, Banks, and many others. On his death Staunton recalled the "delight with which the learned Chinese heard him quote Confucius, and other ancient sages, in argument with them."[73]

Perhaps fittingly, then, the career of the man who might have been the Romantic period's most accomplished sinologist is marked by a profound absence of published writing. Although associated with the various wings of the British political, scientific, and commercial establishment, Manning's motives seem to be entirely personal and disinterested. China was for him a psychological obsession, rather than a field of learning to be mapped. His greatest contribution to scholarship of the East is his journal composed of rough notes of his travels to Lhasa, not Beijing, and, fascinating as it is as a travel log, it lacks any sustained and serious account of the languages and customs of China or Tibet. Manning describes the object of his sinology in familiar terms as

> a moral view of China; its manners; the actual degree of happiness the people enjoy; their sentiments and opinions, so far as they influence life; their literature; the causes of their stability and vast population; their minor arts and contrivances; what there might be worthy to serve as a model for imitation, and what to serve as a beacon to avoid.[74]

Yet the notes that Markham edited and published focus more on the difficulties and trials of the journey than any serious ethnographical enquiry. Much of the journal is concerned with Manning's fractious and, frequently, comic relationship with his Chinese *munshi*, of whom he comments, "a spaniel would be better company" (p. 216).

Manning encounters many Chinese in Tibet as well as native Tibetans and interacts with them in ordinary ways. He laughs and jokes with Chinese soldiers and negotiates with numerous mandarins on the way (241). He notes the preponderance of Chinese in the region, and is increasingly critical of their rule. Equating the Qing with the British as comparable imperial formations, he comments that "the Chinese lord it here like the English in India" and that their "politeness, even in common soldiers, forms a great contrast with the barbarians of this place" (217, 227). In Tibet, they are the "master nation," and Manning believes that the Tibetans would "view the Chinese influence in Tibet overthrown without many emotions of regret" (273). The most unpleasant person encountered in the travels is a "Tatar" mandarin at Lhasa who, having been banished there from Canton, "hated the English and all that were in any way connected with them." Concerned that he may be in danger of being executed by this mandarin, Manning confesses that the "sight of their despotic pomp of mandarins at canton … has almost turned me sick," and what he reads of "their absolute power, not only in China, but in various Asiatic countries, has always appalled me" (278). Generally, however, he is more respectful of the Chinese who "are really civilized, and do not live like cattle" and where you are "sure of urbanity and cleanliness at least." (242).

Manning's only serious published work of Romantic Sinology, if it could be called that, was an essay on "Chinese Jests" published in the *New Monthly Magazine and Literary Journal* in 1826. In it he argues, rather like Percy on Chinese proverbs (or indeed Freud in a different context), that surveying "lighter productions" can most accurately assess the real opinions and manners of a country. For a joke to work and gain currency it must address shared concerns and issues, whereas a novel, drama, or satire may only reflect an individual or a sectional interest. For example, Manning gives the situation of the "too particular attentions of the master of the house to his daughter-in-law while his son is abroad" as a particular "irregularity of morals" that often takes place in China.[75] The subject of examinations and bonzes also frequently recurs in Chinese jest books. Paradoxically, Manning maintains that it is from those jokes that seem least funny that we can gain some serious information about the cultural differences between Britain and China.

Both Laurie McMillin and Felicity James have persuasively argued that Manning's writings cannot easily be reconciled with stereotypical orientalist and colonialist attitudes, and that he remains an idiosyncratic and eccentric figure capable of cross-cultural understandings and sympathy, devoid of any obvious racial stereotyping. Of course, such sympathetic identifications were common among orientalists. Manning's willingness to cross-dress and immerse himself in the culture of China and then Tibet marks him out as a comparatively unusual figure in the period. Aware of the imperial pretensions of Britain in India and China in Tibet, and dismissive of all forms of colonial bureaucracy, Chinese or British, Manning remains a fascinating figure. His contribution to Romantic Sinology remains hard to assess, existing, as it does, at the personal and institutional level in the tuition and advice he gave to others and the important establishment of his collection of Chinese books. His inspiring Lamb to write the essays "Dissertation on Roast Pig" and, possibly, "Old China," however, cannot be reckoned as either increasing the flow of knowledge or enhancing the process of cross-cultural encounter. In many ways, he remains an absence, the great might-have-been of Romantic Sinology.

LEIGH HUNT'S CHINESE LIBELS

The strategic evasion of the subject of Romantic Sinology can also be seen in the writing of Leigh Hunt. In 1817 he wrote a review of the new interior decorations of Drury Lane Theatre for the *Examiner*. He complains that the interior of the theater's Grand Saloon has been filled with "Chinese pagodas and lanthorns ... adorned with monsters and mandarins, and shedding a ghastly twilight!" Written just after the debacle of the recurring primal scene of the reception of the Amherst embassy, when the Chinese "hustled us out of doors," Leigh Hunt views these new decorations as "puerile and tasteless." Once again, like Lamb and Southey, he reads back into this manifestation of late chinoiserie design an idea of China and the Chinese.

> what mummeries and monstrosities! On one lanthorn, a man like a watchman; on another, a dragon or some unintelligible compound of limbs; on another, some Chinese pothooks and hangers! Then the pagodas rise one over the other, like the card-houses of little boys; and as if there were not monsters enough on the lanthorns, a set of huge tiger busts, or some such substitutes for Grecian sculpture, gape down upon you from the sides of the ceiling, and only want some puppet-shew men to ventriloquize for them and make them growl, to render this exquisite attraction complete.[76]

Reminiscent of the eighteenth-century neo-classical attacks on chinoiserie as illegitimate, hybrid, luxurious, and monstrous discussed extensively by Porter, Hunt's attack on these "seductive horrors" that have usurped the rightful place of hellenistic neo-classical "Grecian sculpture" is surely a coded attack on the Regency style of the Prince of Wales, in the manner of Cruikshank's cartoon, discussed in the final chapter of this book. Hunt, who had been imprisoned for two years for a seditious libel against the Regent in 1813, implies that these new decorations in the Grand Saloon are "a complimentary imitation of the prince Regent" who has rooms "full of such lumber." These "Chinese deformities," he argues, are simply "humiliating to the national taste." Here, Hunt identifies the chinoiserie style with the Regent's passion for expensive Chinese artifacts that leads to an enfeebling of British masculinity and a form of aesthetic humiliation before a foreign style. It is as if a personification of British taste has abandoned its masculine, martial neo-classical perfections to perform a kowtow to an oriental fashion just at the very moment that the Chinese have expelled Amherst for his refusal to perform the degrading ceremony at Beijing. Chinoiserie, the Regent, and the embassy are all linked in Hunt's diatribe, but China is largely absent.

Hunt's temptation to prefer stereotype over contemporary sinology is evident in an 1828 essay in which he actually reviews the contents of the new English-language newspaper, the *Canton Register*. He surveys the first three numbers of what he describes somewhat sniffily as a "curiosity." He indicates that the paper gives "us as much information as possible relative to the manners and proceedings of that very populous, cunning, twinkle-eyed, tea-drinking, petti-toed, and out-of-the way country; which has so long contrived to keep its monotony to itself."[77] Hunt rehashes older, chinoiserie-inspired racist stereotypes of the Chinese completely at odds with the accounts of contemporary China in the *Register*. He is well aware, however, of the substantial body of writing about China. Jesuit accounts have "besides the history of their own praises and progress, furnished us with some Chinese *dramas* and novels, which turned out to be genuine." He quotes from one of the most important works of contemporary Romantic Sinology, Staunton's translation of the Qing legal code. From these old and new accounts, with their substantial body of knowledge Hunt, concludes absurdly that the Chinese are:

A people naturally intelligent, humane, and fanciful, who, by reason of an excess of veneration paid to their fathers and forefathers, have been kept for an extraordinary period of time in a state of profound submission to their "paternal government": ... that their gentleness has been converted into effeminacy, their intelligence into cunning and trickery, and the whole popular mind rendered stationary for centuries. (214)

Hunt's summary of China is determined to deny the impact of any serious account by sliding once again into the register of chinoiserie and remorselessly miniaturizing, feminizing, and patronizing the Chinese: "it is impossible," he remarks, "not to be sensible of the miniature scale upon which everything proceeds in their novels. They take little sups of wine, little cups of tea; have little feet and eyes; write little poems, and get on in the world by dint of very little tricks." With the *Canton Register's* account of daily events in China in front of him, including an account of a case of accidental matricide, Hunt reverts again to his chinoiserie stereotypes. The unwillingness to transfer his reading of the paper to his larger understanding of China here borders on the pathological.[78]

Hunt's later essay "The Subject of Breakfast Continued – Tea-drinking" (1834) demonstrates that the increasing portfolio of knowledge about China has had little effect in penetrating his armadillo refusal to engage head-on with Romantic Sinology in favor of another disquisition on Chinese taste. Again, this essay approaches the matter of China via the topos of china porcelain. Like Baillie, Lamb, and Southey, Hunt returns to the familiar worn-out stereotypes, drawing a picture of China from the blue-and-white willow pattern, and then extrapolating this to a general idea of China:

that extraordinary people, of whom Europeans know little or nothing, except that they sell us this preparation, bow back again our ambassadors, have a language of only a few hundred words, gave us China-ware and the strange pictures on our tea-cups, made a certain progress in civilization long before we did, mysteriously stopped at it and would go no further, and if numbers, and the customs of the "venerable ancestors" are to carry the day, are at once the most populous and most respectable nation on the face of the earth.

Hunt is entirely disingenuous here in that a great deal more was known about China by 1834 than he admits, and his essay persists in viewing the country through the prism of a heavily aestheticized chinoiserie. The "bowing back" of Britain's ambassadors in 1793 and 1816 still rankles and is the occasion for a virtual stream of chinoiserie consciousness, one long quasi-Joycean sentence, bordering upon racial hatred:

as individuals, their ceremonies, their trifling edicts, their jealousy of foreigners, and their tea-cup representations of themselves (which are the only ones popularly known) impress us irresistibly with a fancy that they are a people all toddling, little-eyed, little-footed, little bearded, little-minded, quaint, overweening, pigtailed, bald-headed, cone-capped or pagoda-hatted, having childish houses and temples with bells at every corner and story, and shuffling about in blue landscapes, over "nine-inch bridges," with little mysteries of bellhung whips in their hands.[79]

Hunt, however, fleetingly refers to the translations of Romantic Sinology. He admits that from reading the translations of their novels it is possible to "acquire a notion that there is a great deal more sense and even good poetry among them" than can be obtained from the "accounts of embassies" or the "auto-biographical paintings on the China-ware." Here Hunt hints that these porcelain Chinese autobiographies may be as much items of self-fashioning as the embassy accounts of Macartney, Staunton, and Barrow. While all knowledge is thus problematized and rendered a matter of artifice, even the apparently solid first-hand accounts of Romantic Sinology, Hunt does not countenance the possibilities here that the autobiography is in fact constructed for Western eyes, or maybe has even been written by British hands.

Whether we describe this strange evasion of China in Romantic-period writing as an "instrumental amnesia" (Porter) or something more, it is clear that something unusual is occurring here. Southey, Lamb, Hunt all had good first-hand understandings of China. Southey, in particular, had an enormous grasp of contemporary and older geographical exploration. In their writings, they allude to the substantial archive about China enhanced by new works of Romantic Sinology. Yet they persist in the chinoiserie trope of the reading of China through export porcelain and its British imitators. Underlying this refusal to engage with contemporary China, one suspects, is a simple anxiety about how to deal with the subject whose presence is everywhere, in theater designs, in landscape gardens, and on the very porcelain from which they drink their tea. Behind such writings, and often within them, is the primal scene of the 1793 reception of Macartney at Jehol in which the British came to believe, whatever the reality, that they had in some way been snubbed and humiliated: their presents cast aside. This primal scene recurred in the Amherst encounter, but in a more brutal, less forgivable way. Contemporary China, the world's most populous and richest empire commanding around a full third of world GDP, now being poisoned by British Bengal opium, was perhaps too big a subject to be tackled explicitly, unlike Romantic India, now securely administered by Company personnel.

CHAPTER 7

Chinese Gardens, Confucius, and The Prelude

In 1948 Arthur Lovejoy's seminal essay "The Chinese Origins of a Romanticism" argued that the notion of "horticultural naturalism," introduced in eighteenth-century England as a reaction to neo-classical desiderata of regularity and formality, led to a new appreciation of nature and privileging of the natural, culminating in a form of Romanticism.[1] Others, including Leask, Liu, Porter, and Chang, have located aspects of Romantic-period writing about nature within the long-established discourse of the Anglo-Chinese Garden, newly invigorated and politicized by the Macartney embassy's accounts of the Gardens of *Yuanming Yuan* (Garden of Perfect Splendour) at Beijing and of *Bishu Shanzhuang* (Mountain Retreat for Avoiding the Heat) at modern-day Chengde (then known as Jehol or Rehe), north of the Great Wall. This chapter explores the intercultural encounter between Chinese ideas and Romantic-period writing as mediated through the newly produced knowledge of Romantic Sinology.[2]

The gist of Lovejoy's argument is that a preference for a form of "horticultural naturalism" or wildness entered the aesthetics of English gardening in the seventeenth century through the writings of Sir William Temple and was instrumental in the sweeping movement away from the geometrical formalism of neo-classical practice. Temple's "Essay Upon the Gardens of Epicurus" (1692) introduced the influential term of *sharawadgi*, possibly derived from the Chinese *sa luo we qi*, or "careless grace." He used the phrase to express his notion of "beauty without order," and this term was used by others, notably Horace Walpole and Joseph Addison, more widely to express a preference for the natural, variety, asymmetry, and irregularity. As Porter and Watt have pointed out, Walpole's early enthusiasm for chinoiserie gave way to later dislike and a strong preference for a nativist Gothic tradition, so much so that he claimed that the beauties of chinoiserie were in fact English rather than Chinese.[3] He stated in 1784 that the French had adopted the English style in gardening, but preferring to be "obliged to more remote rivals" ascribed the "discovery to the Chinese ... by calling our taste in gardening Le Gout Anglo-Chinois."[4] A year later, however, the Frenchman Georges Louis Le Rouge included the Qianlong emperor's forty woodcuts of *Yuanming Yuan* in a collection of views of the *Jardins anglo-chinois a la mode* (1775–89), commenting: "everyone knows that English Gardens are nothing but an imitation of those in China."[5]

Walpole's claim for the native origins of the Anglo-Chinese garden was largely accepted until recent criticism, sensitized by current notions of global cultural encounters, championed the significance of Chinese influences permeated through Jesuit accounts, textual and visual, of the major Chinese landscape gardens of *Yuanming Yuan* and *Wanshu Yuan*, both crucial locations in the progress of Macartney's embassy.[6] For Chang, the Chinese garden became "the first way that British literature came to conceive of China as space of visual difference in the post-chinoiserie century."[7] In this argument genuine Chinese influence is nativized or erased in an attempt to efface indebtedness to the most powerful empire of the East. Others have argued that English antecedents of the style existed before Temple's introduction of the *sharawadgi* concept, and still others have argued for the genuine influence of an English misreading of Chinese theory and practice. Certainly, the preference for a natural and relaxed asymmetry that Temple and Addison associated with Chinese gardens was available to English practitioners before Temple, and such practitioners neglected to employ other stylistic features associated with Chinese practice in their work. The example of Milton's Eden in Book 4 of *Paradise Lost* (1667), depicting an ideal, natural, and informal garden, was hailed by Walpole as prophetic of the modern style of English gardening. Milton's commonwealth politics and his opposition to royalist absolutism substantially enhanced his appeal to Walpole and others.[8]

Issues of priority in such complicated discursive fields are notoriously difficult to establish and demonstrate conclusively; however, such issues are not central to my argument. At some level the example, however mediated, of the great gardens built by the Kangxi and later Qianlong emperors was communicated to English minds, such as Temple, via the well-known account of the Jesuit, Jean-Denis Attiret, who worked extensively at *Yuanming Yuan*. Visual representations of *Yuanming Yuan* also circulated. The Qianlong emperor had forty views of the garden published in a woodcut edition of 1744 that Attiret and others had sent to Paris by the 1760s.[9] An earlier series of thirty-six engravings by Matteo Ripa of the *Bishu Sanhzhuan* also circulated in Britain. As Greg Thomas has persuasively argued, "to Attiret, Yuanming Yuan was no simple, debased exotic Other but a real, living model of an alternative imperial culture, one logically ordered yet distinct from Europe's, occupying a kind of parallel aesthetic universe."[10] *Yuanming Yuan* was the Versailles of China and vice versa. Just as, at Versaille and elsewhere, Louis XIV constructed Chinese features and buildings, the Qianlong emperor in 1747 commanded his Jesuit servants Attiret, Castiglione, and Benoît to design and construct Western-style buildings containing European artifacts for *Yuanming Yuan* (named the Hall of Western Ocean Pleasure).[11] This exchange occurred between Chinese and European royal or aristocratic cultures on a basis of equality. Chinoiserie in Europe was met with "Euraserie" or "Européenism."[12] Srinivas Aravamudan has strongly argued for the wider transcultural perspective of the oriental tale within his construct of "Enlightenment Orientalism," which he regards as producing substantial cross-cultural encounter. Aravamudan, however, also sees this as a period of open Enlightenment Orientalism that is succeeded by an orientalism informed by increasing "Romantic nationalism and xenophopbia." For Aravamudan, the separation of East and West occurs after the 1780s with the institutionalization of European national literature through the steady rise of print capitalism.[13] Aravamudan's focus is on the oriental tale, effaced by the critical tradition rise of the national, domestic, and realist novel. My study complicates this argument by featuring sinology rather than a broad orientalist canvas, and highlighting the persistence of transcultural exchange within the parameters of an over-emphasized critical concern with xenophobia and nationalism. It is certainly clear that the debates about Chinese gardening and architectural styles were conducted within the parameters of Britain's cultural relationship with Chinese aesthetics as then understood, or misunderstood.[14]

WILLIAM CHAMBERS, GEORGE III, AND THE ROMANTIC CHINESE GARDEN

For the purposes of this study of Romantic-period ideas of China, the obvious starting point is the mid eighteenth century and the key publications of Sir William Chambers on Chinese designs that re-ignited older debates about the relationship of Chinese ideas to English gardening practice and appreciation. Chambers was George III's Surveyor General and Comptroller of the Works since 1787 and the neo-classical designer of Somerset House and Kew Gardens, with its famous ten-story pagoda and House of Confucius. He had visited Canton twice as a young man, in 1744 and 1748, with the Swedish East India Company and made many sketches and notes. This experience led him to advocate a more authentic account of Chinese designs in his influential *Designs of Chinese Buildings* (1757) than those of the then fashionable chinoiserie. He followed this up with his polemical attack on current gardening theory under the guise of an advocacy of Chinese gardens in his more extravagant *A Dissertation on Oriental Gardening* (1772), much of which he invented. Like Percy's Chinese publications and Murphy's *Orphan of China*, Chambers' publications are the unacknowledged progenitor texts of Romantic Sinology in that they claim, at some level, an authentic understanding of China formulated within the new context of an emerging British subjectivity. Chambers' work constituted his attempt to correct the current inauthenticity of fashionable chinoiserie inventions with an account containing his own observations and inventions based on a personal, if circumscribed, knowledge of Chinese styles, the hallmark of Romantic Sinology.[15] Yet Chambers' work imbricated such debates in a supplementary British hermeneutics whereby the semiotics of the landscape park was read politically, according to an established eighteenth-century code of viewing and taste. As Stephen Bending has demonstrated, "the English landscape garden was a contentious site for competing concerns, acting as a locus for discourses ... ranging from connoisseurship to radical politics and agricultural improvement."[16] Later travelers to China would refer back to Chambers' accounts as the *locus classicus* of their, usually contradictory or disappointed, understanding of Chinese gardens. Certainly, the members of Macartney's embassy were generally disenchanted with Chambers' wilder descriptions of *Yuanming Yuan* and *Wanshu Yuan* when they visited. In 1836, J. F. Davis's *The Chinese* would authoritatively proclaim that Chambers' description of Chinese gardening was "a mere prose work of imagination, without a shadow of foundation in reality."[17] Chambers thus served as a convenient summary of what had gone before and a point of reference for later commentaries.

Chambers' understanding of Chinese styles was perforce limited and subject to his idiosyncratic interpretations and personal innovations. His publications on Chinese gardens criticized both the overly formal and excessively geometric European landscape garden of the "antient style," as well as what he regarded as the insipid and bland naturalism of William Kent and Lancelot "Capability" Brown, whose gardens, he claimed, "differ very little from common fields, so closely is vulgar nature copied in most of them." Chambers praised the Chinese art of gardening for its use of the European aesthetic categories of imagination, variety, novelty, and surprise. He claimed that the Chinese "take nature for their pattern, their aim is to imitate all her beautiful irregularities." Yet he also argued against a bland naturalism, claiming that gardens should be "natural, without resemblance to vulgar nature," and that it was the role of the landscape gardener to stimulate the vision and imagination of the visitor. He claimed that the "scenery of a garden should differ as much from common nature as an heroic poem doth from prose relations and Gardeners, like poets should … even fly the bounds of truth, whenever it is necessary."[18] As such, Chambers' espousal of the artifice and tact of the sophisticated and philosophical Chinese gardener in improving vulgar nature ran directly counter to the central premise of Wordsworthian Romantic thought as expressed in the "Preface" to *Lyrical Ballads* (1798), and Wordsworth would take his revenge in *The Prelude*. Chambers divided Chinese garden scenery into three kinds, each associated with an emotion: the "pleasing," the "terrible" or "horrid," and the "enchanted" or "surprising." Yet Chambers' advocacy of Chinese styles is also marked by a pronounced equivocation and even a denial that such styles were Chinese at all, so much so that several critics have taken him at his word and denied the relevance of China to his work.[19]

Most sensationally, when describing *Yuanming Yuan*, Chambers claimed that there were "temples dedicated to the king of vengeance, deep caverns, and descents to subterraneous habitations, overgrown with brushwood and brambles." Scenes of the supernatural also abound; according to Chambers, "flutes, and soft harmonious organs, impelled by subterraneous waters, interrupt, at stated intervals, the silence of the place, and fill the air with solemn melody." There are "colossal figures of dragons, infernal fiends, and other horrid forms, which hold in their monstrous talons, mysterious, cabalistic sentences, inscribed on tables of brass. The ears of men are struck with different sounds, some resembling cries of men in torment, the raging of the sea, the explosion of cannon, the sound of trumpets and all the noise of war." Chambers' use of the Chinese taste in landscape gardening for the future George III at Kew was read in the period as an appropriation for the Tory establishment of this visual style (Figure 3). In attempting this, Chambers reversed the political polarities that had previously governed chinoiserie; rather than being understood as an illegitimate, monstrous, disruptive, hybrid, and proto-Jacobinical aesthetic in the tirades of eighteenth-century neo-classicist writings, *Yuanming Yuan*, as fancifully described by Chambers, with its sublime of the terrible, where "half famished animals wander upon the plains" and "gibbets, crosses, wheels, and the whole apparatus of torture, are seen from the roads" would now serve to terrify and intimidate subjects into rightful obedience.[20] As Leask has demonstrated, the designer of Kew Gardens left himself wide open to charges that he was attempting to impose an imperial chinoiserie style to validate Hanoverian absolutist pretentions.[21] Certainly in the 1790s and through to the Regent's Royal Pavilion at Brighton, this chinoiserie style would become associated with Georgian extravagance and its alleged propensities to despotism, luxury, and corruption.

Walpole wrote to his close friend, fellow Whig, and gardening aficionado William Mason in 1772 that he found Chambers' *Dissertation* "more extravagant that the worst Chinese [wall] paper."[22] He encouraged Mason, to compose a satirical response, *An Heroic Epistle to Sir William Chambers* of 1773. Mason's satire is a Whig attack on Chambers, laying bare the political principles he understood as underlying his Tory motives in appropriating the Chinese aesthetic in landscape gardening.[23] In a note to the satire Walpole recorded that the "English taste in gardening" was the "growth of the English Constitution and must perish with it."[24] Chambers would recreate both the garden and the conditions of Asiatic despotism in Britain, prolonging the Asiatic dream of George III. Walpole's rejection of chinoiserie relates to his growing awareness of it as an imported foreign style that had been overlaid onto native English models and, more troublingly, which had become associated with Tory politics. In his authoritative discussion of Kew and the debates between Mason/Walpole and Chambers, Bending shows that "Mason's landscape garden is an image of Whig oligarchy" and Chambers' that of "Tory monarchism," an imperial mansion that "looks from the center out" seeing "mere pleasure palaces ... that gain their significance only as they relate to that single central eminence."[25]

S. T. Coleridge, who flirted with the idea of residing in Canton for health reasons in 1804, writes almost nothing about China, though he produces one of the most celebrated poems in the English language about a thirteenth-century Mongol emperor of China, "Kubla Khan," and his Chinese garden or "pleasure ground." Coleridge's poem was probably composed around 1797–98, the year when the official account of the Macartney embassy to China appeared, and was formally published in 1816, the same year as the Amherst embassy. Such coincidences should further sensitize us to the extraordinary patterns of global economic and cultural exchange in what we call the Romantic period. Coleridge's early response to China was, by and large, governed by the political discourse of China and Eastern despotism to which he then subscribed. Leask has persuasively situated the poem in this context, arguing that, read against the long-standing debates surrounding the Anglo-Chinese garden, and the recent accounts of the imperial gardens in China and Mason's satire, the poem is a Unitarian dissenting work attacking the orientalized British despotism of the Tory monarch. Locating the topography of "Kubla Khan" with its pleasure domes, caverns, savage chasms, and wailing woman in the accounts of the Chinese gardens visited by the embassy (as well as James Bruce's Abyssinia), Leask claimed that Coleridge is, like Mason though less directly, presenting a coded satire on George III's government for emulating the Chinese emperors in constructing a sublime of terror to enforce political obedience as outlined in Mason's satire on Chambers. Elsewhere I have also argued that "Kubla Khan" is a very Chinese poem, indebted to Chambers, enacting a racialized discourse of China and Tartary, associating the Qianlong emperor with Kublai Khan as "Tartars" via the Macartney embassy accounts.[26] Although the kowtow does not figure in the poem, the emperor Kubla's unanswerable decreeing of the pleasure dome implies, perhaps, a corresponding kowtow from the many invisible agents in the poem who construct the dome. That "holy dread" that the inspired poet/prophet awakens in his implied audience, though conventionally sourced to Plato's *Ion*, might just as easily be associated with the frame of mind expected from those participating in the quasi-mystical guest ritual of the kowtow.[27] "Kubla Khan" may be for many modern readers the most quintessentially Romantic poem, yet in Coleridge's lifetime it was regarded as something of a curiosity and a poem about which he says very little beyond the famously ambiguous "Preface." After a long period of manuscript circulation, he published the poem in 1816 – the same year as the second major British embassy to China – at the behest of Byron, as a "psychological curiosity." Read against the backdrop of the Jiaqing emperor's abrupt dismissal of the embassy, and the popular critique of the new and lavish chinoiserie style of the Regent's Royal Pavilion, the poem takes on different, less idealized meanings.

THE WORDSWORTHS' CHINESE MONEY

Coleridge was a very intimate part of the Wordsworth circle and that circle had a strong family interest in China, or at least the China trade, and an odd unexpected connection with Macartney that occasioned Wordsworth's notable, though seldom discussed, entry into the discourse of the Chinese garden in Book 8 of *The Prelude* of 1805. William and Dorothy's brother, John, the "never-resting pilgrim of the sea," like many of the personalities discussed in this book, visited Canton on several occasions.[28] He served as a midshipman, then captain, with the East India Company in the China trade. Officers such as John were allowed two tons of their own goods to sell at a profit in China, and opium was one of the most profitable of the trades then flourishing. A profit of between £4000 and £12,000 could be made by East India Company officers on the round trip to China, and sometimes as much as £30,000.[29] The official Company trade in Chinese tea, and its unofficial trade in the Bengal opium, are important, if under-explored, material contexts of exchange impacting on the literature and culture of the Romantic period. China, tea, and opium are very real presences that erupt into the work of the poet in fugitive and unexpected ways.

John entered in the Company in 1788 intending make a fortune for both himself and the Wordsworth family, and then to retire to Westmoreland. He was a rising star in the Company and destined for great things. The Wordsworths' older cousin, Captain John Wordsworth, had retired after a very lucrative career at sea and was a promising role model for John. The younger John wrote in late 1800 that it was his "object ... to get as much money as possible." He was aware that his cousin had "made a very handsome fortune" and that in eight or so years he himself would be "a very rich man."[30] John was appointed a midshipman, by his cousin's influence, on the *Earl of Abergavenny*, which took him to China for the first time in 1790.[31] He rose quickly through the merchant ranks, becoming fifth then second mate. From 1801 onwards John sailed to the East twice as captain of a newly refurbished *Earl of Abergavenny*, a 1200-ton East Indiaman bound for China with a complement of some four hundred people on board. Captaincy of the *Abergavenny* was a major and much envied posting. Notably, among John Wordsworth's cosmopolitan crew and passengers in 1805 were thirty-two Chinese sailors, returning home.[32] In addition to undertaking Company business, senior employees such as John were able to engage in a lucrative private trade. He hoped to profit from trading opium and use the proceeds to support his talented sibling. The material processes of commerce and empire are thus deeply imbricated at one level at least in the northern British Romantic art that both Wordsworths produced.

The issue of the opium trade is historically and ethically complex and the Wordsworths could not have fully known of the pernicious nature of the drug and its historical part in the growing conflict with China. By 1804 they may have understood something of its addictive and debilitating properties through their experience of Coleridge's suspected growing dependency on laudanum. Indeed, in the spring of that year, crippled by his addiction, Coleridge had set sail for Malta in the hope that the Mediterranean climate would prove restorative to health. Previously, he had suggested to John the possibility of sailing to China on his second voyage as captain in 1803–4 for the same reason.[33] John argued that Italy would be a better destination for the ailing Coleridge, but he informed Dorothy that "if he *really* wishes to go & I can take him (for the Comp orders are agai[n]st it) I shall with great pleasure."[34] Exponents of counter-factual literary history might be entranced by the prospect of Coleridge in China, encountering Confucianism, speculating on what paths British Romanticism might have taken had he settled on Canton as a place to recuperate rather than Malta. Those more Romantically inclined might find the prospect of Coleridge destined for the ancestral home of Kublai Khan a source of fabulous conjecture. The development of British Romantic Sinology might have taken a very different course if Coleridge, a linguist of genius, had made the journey.

Opium meant private profit that would allow John to retire from the Company service and support his brother's poetic career for life. Returning from a two-year voyage in 1797, John had made a £100 profit on a single chest of opium that he brought back from Canton for sale in England.[35] We know that Dorothy and William invested the sum of £350 in John's first voyage as captain to China in 1802 in return for which John had promised to reimburse Dorothy with a contribution of £20 per annum for the Dove Cottage finances; cousin John Wordsworth invested £1650, and brother Richard, £1014.[36] Altogether John raised something like £9000–10,000 for his first voyage and gloated that he would "soon be as rich *as a Jew*—" hoping to make in the region of £6000 profit.[37] Although John had assured his brothers and sister of the substantial profits to be made in private trading of this kind, when he returned he had to inform them that due to fluctuations in the market he had made substantial losses. Rather than prospering, John's first voyage left him several thousand pounds in debt.[38]

In 1803 Richard Wordsworth succeeded in negotiating an advance of £3000 of the Lonsdale money, the unpaid debt owed to the Wordsworths' father (also John), by James Lowther, the first Earl of Lonsdale. This money had been spent in paying the election expenses of Lowther and his brother-in-law in 1768, the latter of whom would later develop important connections with China as we will see. Brother John requested that this money should be made over to him to invest in his second voyage of 1803–4. The total family investment in that voyage was some £7827. John returned disappointed once more to London in 1804. He wrote to his cousin that he "neither did well or ill" with the outward part of the voyage, and that the success of the whole voyage would depend on how his teas sold in London. He added: "Opium and Quicksilver were the only things in the China market that sold to any profit."[39] Almost immediately he set about campaigning for the more lucrative route to China, stopping off in Bombay or Bengal, and raising yet more money for investing in his third and fatal voyage of 1805, optimistic of "a very good ... if not a *very great* one."[40]

John's previous two voyages had been made direct from Britain to Canton; however, for his third voyage he finally acquired (through the patronage of powerful family connections, William Wilberforce and Charles Grant) the coveted and much more lucrative route which stopped over in Bengal to take on cotton and, privately, opium, allowing for greatly enhanced personal profiteering. As Kenneth Johnston argues, "John needed the opium trade not only to recoup his recent losses, but to realize the great profit that had always fired his schemes for making a 'quick fortune at sea,' which were motivated in turn by his desire to give his brother the independence 'to do something in the world.'"[41] If the *Abergavenny* was the first ship to get the Bengal opium to China that season then John could sell his private cargo at the very top of the market, netting huge profits. He expected to profit most of all by trading Bengal rice and opium at Canton.[42]

The value of the *Abergavenny*'s cargo was estimated at the princely sum of £200,000, including goods for the British community in Bengal as well as £70,000 in silver bullion to pay for China's tea, silk, and porcelain exports at Canton.[43] John clearly expected this voyage would reverse the losses of his previous voyages and finally establish his fortune, enabling him to support his brother's poetic career. As William wrote, "He encouraged me to persist in the plan of life which I had adopted; I will work for you, and you shall attempt to do something for the world. Could I but see you with a green field of your own and a Cow and two or three other little comforts, I shall be happy."[44] John viewed it as a "most melancholy thing" that William should suffer anxiety over money and that Coleridge should be forced to "write for Newspapers."[45] Again there is thus an intimate connection between the trade with China and the artistic and intellectual aspirations of British Romanticism. It is estimated that John and his investors raised the huge sum of £20,000 for this voyage.[46] As is well known, on February 5, the *Earl of Abergavenny* struck the Shambles of Portland Bill and John and 250 or so went down with the ship. The

Wordsworths' enormous grief at the loss of their brother would have been mixed with alarm and anxiety at their huge financial exposure, only subsequently and uncertainly met by insurance. John's letters to his brother and sister say little about his time at Canton, what he saw and did. Yet the presence of China must surely have impinged substantially and evocatively on their northern English life at Dove Cottage. China was a real presence in their lives and would feature in Wordsworth's writing in very unexpected ways.

CONFUCIUS, BARROW, AND WORDSWORTHIAN
THEORIES OF EDUCATION

Having established the links between the Wordsworth family and the China trade, I would like to suggest two ways in which we can read Wordsworth's spiritual autobiography in the light of this context. Firstly, I would like to approach this subject via the theories of education outlined in Book Five of that poem, before turning again to the central topos of this chapter, the Chinese garden in Book Eight. This returns us to a central concern of this book, the interpretation and status of Confucian thinking in the Romantic period. In a conversation with John Cam Hobhouse in May 1819, George Thomas Staunton expressed his view that "Confucius had been formerly too much cried up, and now too much cried down."[47] Staunton was summing up what he regarded as the Jesuit and Enlightenment idealization of Confucian thinking and the opposite tendency in Romantic Sinology. As such, Staunton may well have been reflecting on the earlier reviews of Marshman's edition in the *Quarterly Review* by his friend, Barrow.

In reviewing Marshman's translation of the *Lunyu* in his substantial essay on the "Progress of Chinese Literature in Europe" for the *Quarterly Review* in 1814, Barrow attempted to demolish the prestige and importance of Confucian thinking that he argued had resulted from a conspiracy between Catholic missionaries and deistic *philosophes*. Denouncing the "extravagant misrepresentations" of the "Catholic missionaries" and the comparisons made between Confucius and classical philosophers and "even the Saviour of the world," Barrow is puzzled to understand the nature of the benefits Confucius "conferred to his grateful countrymen, and which through so many ages have procured for his memory little short of divine honors, and enriched his posterity with the more substantial advantages of wealth, honour, and distinction."[48] Barrow's militantly anti-Confucian posture was developed as a result of his formative, though ambivalent and brief, encounter with China as the comptroller of the Macartney embassy. He was by upbringing and temperament hostile to the Confucian scholar-literati in a way that sophisticated scholars such as Ricci were not. He was a fairly classic example of the phenomenon of the nineteenth-century self-made man, keen to play up his importance in government affairs. Brought up in a modest Lancashire household, Barrow was obliged to quit schooling at the age of fourteen to go to work as a clerk in a Liverpool iron foundry. Largely self-taught, he progressed from the role of clerk to become the overseer of the foundry, and after studying mathematics in his own time, he secured the position of teacher at a boy's school in Greenwich as well as serving as tutor for the son of Sir George Leonard Staunton, George Thomas. Barrow, who would become the Second Secretary of the Admiralty in 1804, could regard himself with some justice as a person who had by his own efforts risen to some degree of eminence in the world. His rise had been facilitated by his knowledge of applied sciences at the foundry and his mathematical and astronomical pursuits.[49]

Barrow's account of his experiences, his *Travels in China* (1804), is an influential text in its depiction of contemporary China as a stationary, stagnant and regressive despotism. Like many commentators of the Romantic period, Barrow ascribes a substantial importance to education and locates China's problems in what he sees as its stultifying educational system. According to Benjamin A. Elman, the Chinese educational system was indeed formidable, with Chinese children having to memorize some 2000 Chinese characters by the age of eight, before reading and memorizing over 500,000 characters of the Four and Five Books for the next seven or so years.[50] Barrow describes how Chinese youth begin to study the language around the age of six. They memorize characters without at this stage understanding their meaning, thus not "adding to the mind one single idea, for five or six years, except that of labour and difficulty." Then "a regular scholar" is "required to get by heart a very large volume of the works of Confucius so perfectly, that he may be able to turn to any page or sentence from hearing the sound of the characters only, without his having one single idea of their signification." The student then spends the next four years of his life tracing characters and learning to write them. By the time he is sixteen, a young man is able to write a great many characters yet "he can affix no distinct idea to any one of them." Significantly, Barrow compares the Chinese mode of learning language with that of the learning of Latin in the public grammar schools of Britain, which he implies is also a waste of time for young minds.

Yet the youth of Britain, despite being made to learn Latin, is acquiring new ideas from their knowledge of other languages as well as "entertainment and instruction" from the books they read in English. Barrow, the self-made man, gives as an example of "the best book … that can be put into a boy's hand" Defoe's *Robinson Crusoe*. This is both a useful and an entertaining book in showing the boy the "numberless difficulties to which he is liable in the world, when the anxious cares of his parents have ceased to watch over him." Chinese youth, however, have no antidotes from the "dry study of acquiring the names and representations of things that … as yet have no meaning." The education of a Chinese is completed, according to Barrow, with a study of the works of Confucius. This will prepare him for the taking of his first degree in his twentieth year. A further ten years of study will be required of those who wish to be qualified for higher employment. For Barrow, such a mode of education is a barrier to progress in the sciences. Chinese examinations are "principally confined to knowledge of the language."[51] In his review of John Francis Davis's *Laou-Seng-Urh* for the *Quarterly* of 1817, Barrow sneered that Chinese education did not consist in that "vulgar wisdom which implies a knowledge of men and things, or of the pursuits of physical or abstract science, or even of the history of the great events" but rather in "knowing what *Yao* said, and what *Chun* did, on any particular occasion, four thousand years ago; and in applying the maxims of the one and the practice of the other to the events of the present time." This system simply produces "automatons" devoid of individual will and agency, submerged in "gross ignorance."[52]

Barrow denounces the Chinese educational system for its reliance on the rote learning of characters, its dependence on classical Confucian texts, its lack of imaginative relief, and its failure to engage with contemporary scientific and technological advance. Under such a system and with such a language, he argues, China's people remain dull, unimaginative, and passive and the nation stagnant and non-progressive. This form of education could be contrasted with that of Morrison and Milne's Anglo-Chinese College at Malacca from 1818 onwards. Here both Chinese and European students studied not only the Bible and the Chinese classics, but also English language, history, geography, moral philosophy, and logic. They were also taught medicine, pharmacology, and botany. The chief of the Company factory at Canton, Charles Marjoribanks, wrote in praise of the College's modern curriculum, claiming that "the son of a Malacca peasant derive[s] an enlightened education, denied to the son of the Emperor."[53] From the outset the College curriculum was devoted to both literature and science, and Morrison found himself increasingly consulted by British horticulturalists intrigued by the study of Chinese botany. Barrow would have approved.[54]

Barrow's attack on the Chinese educational system struck a vibrant chord in Romantic Britain. Robert Southey, reviewing Barrow's *Travels* for the *Annual Review* in 1805, focused a major part of his adulatory review on this subject. At the outset Southey claims that the Chinese "system of education is slow and laborious, and destructive of anything like genius." It is thus no wonder that the Chinese appear to know as little of "earth as of the heaven."[55] The novelist Fanny Burney was filled with "wonder at the preposterous pedantry that could contrive to make the whole life of man too short for learning to read and write."[56] William and Dorothy knew Barrow's *Travels*, extracts from which they copied into their commonplace book probably during the spring and summer months of 1805, very soon after John's drowning in February of that year. The trauma of John's death spurred William to renewed creativity and the completion of the 1805 version of *The Prelude*.[57] Wordsworth seems to have acquired a copy of Barrow's book very soon after its publication in July and certainly by October 1804. It is also possible that the book he used was Southey's review copy, in which case there must have been some conversations between the two about the work and China. Possibly John's increasing participation in the China trade motivated Wordsworth to discover more about China, via Barrow.[58]

In his *The Prelude* of 1805, William Wordsworth provided an extended critique of those systems that deny the merits of a natural and imaginative education for children. He celebrates the importance of a number of books which "lay / Their sure foundations in the heart of man," from Homer and the Bible, to the works of epic poets and humble ballad makers, "low and wren-like warblings, made / For cottagers and spinners at the wheel."[59] In contrast to the natural education informed by a love of books and literature, Wordsworth strategically deploys the case of the Infant Prodigy, "a Child, no Child, / But a dwarf man."

> ... the moral part
> Is perfect, and in learning and in books
> He is a prodigy. His discourse moves slow,
> Massy and ponderous as a Prison door,
> Tremendously embossed with terms of art;
> Rank growth of propositions overruns
> The Stripling's brain: the path in which he treads
> Is chok'd with grammars.
>
> (5.294–8; 318–25)

The child's arguments, imaged in the metaphor of the prison door slowly closing, is reminiscent of accounts like that of Barrow of Confucian-inspired educational theories with their stress on the learning of choking grammars. In the 1805 and 1850 versions of *The Prelude* Wordsworth does not mention China; however, in the 1818–20 "C-Stage" version of Book Five, he explicitly locates the Infant Prodigy in the discourse of China. He compares the child to the bonsai or miniaturized tree that he situates in an oriental context. The child is

> Monst'rous as China's vegetable Dwarfs
> Where nature is subjected to such freaks
> Of human care industriously perverse
> Here to advance the work and there retard
> That the proportions of the full-grown oak,
> Its roots, its trunk, its boughs, and foliage, all
> Appear in living miniature expressed,
> The Oak beneath whose umbrage, freely spread
> Within its native fields, whole herds repose.[60]

The Chinese in this account are "industriously perverse" in, for no apparent reason, miniaturizing the oak tree with its strong patriotic English associations, and converting a magnificent natural organism, famously identified by Edmund Burke with the British constitution, which serves to provide shelter for herds of animals into a toy. Possibly, Wordsworth identifies Confucian education with radical or Godwinian ideas, subverting the Burkean Oak of British conservatism, miniaturizing and trivializing its symbolic power, *à la chinoise*. Yet again this remains implied and is not developed. Wordsworth thus aligns what he defines as Chinese technique with a form of willful artistic deformity that distorts the naturally magnificent and *useful* oak. Chinese human care is thus misapplied in Wordsworth's natural, moral, aesthetic, and political register to produce only monsters, dwarfs, and freaks.

Wordsworth's linkage of the Infant Prodigy with China via the dwarfed tree remains deeply enigmatic and suggestive. It provides confirmation that at some level, he associated contemporary problematic theories of education with the accounts he read of Chinese practices and that China became in his thought a symbolic Eastern other to the organic philosophy of nature he was then constructing with the philosophical aid of Coleridge. For some reason he decided to add this trace of China in 1818–20 to the 1805 draft version of the poem, before removing it altogether from the final version of *The Prelude* published after his death in 1850. Why he chose to add then remove this simile, despite the resonances his discourse shares with Barrow's account of Chinese education and Southey's review, remains a matter of speculation but it does indicate at some level a psychological attraction to and reaction from the topos of China which we see elsewhere in *The Prelude*. Against the monstrosity of the Infant Prodigy crammed with knowledge and the dwarf oak, Wordsworth pleads for the importance of imagination in the life of the child: "the Wishing-Cap / Of Fortunatus, and the invisible Coat / Of Jack the Giant-Killer ..."(5.365–70).

For Wordsworth, the activity of reading is a major part of the child's education that must be a part of an all-round education. He later writes of how "the golden store of books" of his father's house is read while fishing and enjoying the hot summer weather (5.504). The key text which Wordsworth instances as an antidote to stultifying systems of education is not Defoe's British novel *Robinson Crusoe* – for Barrow the best book to place in a boy's hands – but an oriental text, the *Thousand and One Nights*, or the *Arabian Nights*. This volume of tales was massively influential for Romantic writers such as Wordsworth, De Quincey, and Coleridge. In particular Coleridge claimed that the volume was responsible for inculcating within him a love of wonder and mystery: "from my early reading of Faery Tales, and Genii &c &c—my mind has been habituated *to the Vast*—and I never regarded *my senses* in any way as the criteria of my belief."[61] Again, such passages destabilize Saidian orientalist boundaries, as here China represents a third term somewhere between both orientalist fantasy and British sensibility. Arguably China, the most prominent orientalist other for Britain in this period, is effaced by a different orientalist alterity, the *Arabian Nights*. For Wordsworth, here as elsewhere, China is the other that dare not speak its name.

Espousals of the importance of wonder and creative reading are not hard to find in the Romantic period; one also thinks also of the poems relating to education in William Blake's *Songs of Innocence and of Experience*.[62] The Chinese educational system, as described in Barrow's influential text, represents yet another type of the latter, associating Confucianism with all those aspects of pedagogy that were becoming increasingly criticized in the educational theory of the times. Confucianism thus, if it were to be associated with anything in the minds of Wordsworth, Coleridge, and others, would be linked with those practices that suppressed intellectual and emotional development in children, rather than with a more attractive cosmology that might have appealed to the Romantic sense of natural unity. Yet this is not the whole story. Though often contained within a framing context of dismissive and degrading remarks, notes, and introductions, the substance of the new British translations shows that engagement with Confucian ideas was still happening in one form or another. Emerson's introduction to Confucianism in America, for example, would come though a reading of Joshua Marshman's edition. He also owned a copy of David Collie's translation of the Four Books (1828).[63] The extent to which such ideas are present and understood in Romantic thinking itself remains an open question. Like so many other elements of Britain's engagement with China, however, it does represent another missed opportunity and another instance of the paradox of the relationship between the two multi-ethnic imperial formations explored in this volume as a whole.

WORDSWORTH'S CHINESE RE-ORIENTALIZATIONS:
BOOK EIGHT OF *THE PRELUDE*

China and the Macartney embassy notably erupt into that most canonically Romantic poem about the formation of the Romantic self, the 1805 *The Prelude*, but in rather odd ways. I have already just argued that Book Five contains a displacement of British Protestant attitudes to Confucian education systems. Many critics and commentators, such as Jonathan Bate, have written engagingly about how Book 8 of *The Prelude* turns on the opposition between the pandemonium of the metropolis of Book 7, "Residence in London," and the organic communal wholeness of the Grasmere Fair held in early September each year.[64] This communal life is privileged over the commercial and tawdry business of the city. Yet this familiar Romantic binary opposition between country and city, and nature and the artificial, is strangely complicated by a third term of difference and opposition, the Chinese Garden of *Wanshu Yuan* (Garden of Ten Thousand Trees) contained in the imperial estate of *Bishu Shanzhuang* (Mountain Resort for Escaping the Heat) at Chengde (Jehol), the primal scene of the imperial reception of Macartney, where he came to pay formal tribute to the Qianlong emperor, and where he performed his altered version of the full ceremony of the imperial kowtow.[65] Until quite recently, *Bishu Shanzhuang* was mainly discussed within the context of garden history, but new historical research has demonstrated its political and imperial significance. This was a place where the Qing emperors regularly received embassies, such as the British, and, as such, was a crucial geopolitical space emphasizing the Qing hegemony of Central Asia.[66] The resort contained simulacra of famous Chinese places and numerous Buddhist and Daoist temples, most notably an exact copy of the Potala at

Lhasa where Thomas Manning would kowtow so enthusiastically to the ninth Dalai Lama in 1811. In the park of *Wanshu Yuan* foreign envoys, like Macartney, were received in a large tent or yurt, recalling the practice of the Mongol Khans whose overlordship of Central and Eastern Asia the Qing claimed against competing interests. As Hevia and Forêt have argued, the codified spatial dimensions of *Bishu Shanzhuang* signified Qing aspirations to command the loyalties of both Tibetan and Mongol peoples, as well as Han Chinese, and establish a cosmic and moral order. Since 1995 when UNESCO placed the site on its World Heritage List, *Bishu Shanzhuang* is once again acknowledged as a place of global cultural significance.[67]

Neither Macartney's embassy, nor Wordsworth, was able to decipher the complex imperial semiotics of the landscape of *Bishu Shanzhuang*, but they were able to read it as a landscape of power from their own understanding of European practices. They were certainly aware of the ways in which Versailles and French royal gardens were to be understood.[68] The English picturesque landscape park, according to Walpole and his followers, codified a certain, limited Whig constitutional freedom, to be carefully managed by a largely hereditary Georgian elite of landowners, educated according to standards of taste. This was an elite which Macartney, an Ulster Scots commoner, tenaciously aspired to join. It was not an elite to which either the Wordsworths or Coleridge belonged; only Byron among the Romantic poets could and did claim that privilege. For Macartney, Barrow, and the Staunton family, China was a sure means of economic and social advancement.

Wordsworth locates his understanding of a natural, free, and unalienated landscape in the rural community of Grasmere that demonstrates the symbiosis of man and nature outwith the aristocratic landscape park. This countryside is explicitly contrasted with the artificially created *Wanshu Yuan*:

> Beauteous the domain
> Where to the sense of beauty first my heart
> Was open'd, tract more exquisitely fair
> Than is that Paradise of ten Thousand trees,
> Or Gehol's famous Gardens, in a Clime
> Chosen from the widest Empire, for delight
> Of the Tartarian Dynasty composed
> (Beyond that mighty Wall, not fabulous
> China's stupendous mound!) by patient skill
> Of myriads, and boon Nature's lavish help ...
> (8.119–28)

The natural paradise of Wordsworth's childhood in the English lakes, celebrated in the first two books of the 1805 *The Prelude*, is contrasted with the imperial park of *Wanshu Yuan*, made newly famous by Barrow's *Travels*. Chang has argued that "the idea of the Chinese garden space conveyed crucial meanings to British viewers about a kind of geography encoded as despotic, excessive, fantastic, incoherent, illogical and exotic."[69] While my reading of this encounter is indebted to Chang's insights, I nevertheless wish to stress less the issues of visual and aesthetic difference, apparent though they are, and more the ways in which this encounter between Wordsworth and an apparently oriental other is actually firmly embedded within his conscious domestic and family circumstances, themselves imbricated in the larger global flows of commodities, texts and ideas. While also indebted to the larger political readings of Wordsworth's nature poetry by Jerome McGann, Marjorie Levinson, Alan Liu, and David Simpson, in my reading China does not serve as the subject for a new historicist dark or negative allegory of evasion, displacement, or absence, but, instead, a struggle, largely conscious, which places the presence of China *at the very heart* of Wordsworth's creative endeavor, as it was in his family affairs until 1805, and at the heart of the Wordsworthian and Coleridgean Romantic project itself.[70]

For Wordsworth, the famous pleasure garden ostensibly represents an orientalist false paradise of artifice and excess, a surfeit of pleasure and luxury antithetical to the natural beauty of the peopled communities of the Westmoreland landscape. Wordsworth reads into the Manchu landscape the orientalized forms of despotism he sees as the origins of its existence, as opposed to the English landscape grounded in an idea of British liberty, though threatened at home as well as abroad. Like Walpole and Mason, Wordsworth in 1804–05 views the potential extension of the Chinese garden via the activities of local despots as being potentially as corrupting as the Regent's chinoiserie experiments at Holland House and then the Royal Pavilion, discussed in the next chapter.

Wordsworth's information on the imperial gardens is derived mainly from Barrow's *Travels in China* which he was reading during the spring and summer months of 1805, shortly after John's drowning in February. The trauma of John's death spurred Wordsworth to complete the 1805 version of *The Prelude*.[71] The Chinese imperial residence was constructed in the mountains of Jehol by the Qianlong and Kangxi emperors with the assistance of European Jesuit missionary artists and architects between 1703 and 1780. It was here on September 14, 1793, that Macartney knelt on one knee and bowed thrice, presenting in a jewel-encrusted casket the

Figure 5.   William Alexander, *View of the Eastern Side of the Imperial Park at Gehol.*
From John Barrow, *Travels in China* (London: Cadell and Davies, 1804). Reproduced by
permission of the Trustees of the National Library of Scotland.

letter from his sovereign George III to the emperor in the primal scene
of encounter. The event was notably depicted in a series of views by the
embassy's draftsman/artist William Alexander (not himself present), from
descriptions provided for him by other members of the embassy (Figure 5).
Wordsworth's vision of *Wanshu Yuan* constructs this Chinese imperial
garden as antithetical to the landscape of the English Lake District. In so
doing he goes far beyond the Macartney accounts to *re-orientalize Wanshu
Yuan* as an Eastern pleasure garden reminiscent of those contained in the
Arabian Nights tales. This process of *re-orientalizing* is cognate with, but
not the same as, Said's more general discourse of orientalism.

Wordsworth re-orientalizes the park by substituting the word "paradise" for "garden," and pinpointing the motive for its existence as the
personal "delight" of the "Tartarian dynasty." This is reminiscent of the
false terrestrial paradises of Book Four of Milton's *Paradise Lost* (1667),
Coleridge's "Kubla Khan" (1797?), and Southey's *Thalaba the Destroyer*
(1801), all of which Wordsworth's lines recall.[72] This Tartar false paradise was constructed not by individual rural laborers but by "the patient

skill of myriads" and "boon Nature's lavish help." The odd phrase "boon Nature" perhaps alludes to Milton's description of the natural garden of Eden, championed by Walpole as the origin of the English garden, where "Nature boon," and "not nice art" with its "Beds and curious Knots," has arranged the flowers on "Hill and Dale and Plaine" (4.240–43). The park is described in most sumptuous detail:

> Scene link'd to scene, an ever-growing change,
> Soft, grand, or gay! with Palaces and Domes
> Of Pleasure spangled over, shady Dells
> For Eastern Monasteries, sunny Mounds
> With Temples Crested, Bridges, Gondolas,
> Rocks, Dens, and Groves of foliage taught to melt
> Into each other their obsequious hues
> Going and gone again, in subtile chase,
> Too fine to be pursued; or standing forth
> In no discordant opposition, strong
> And gorgeous as the colours side by side
> Bedded among the plumes of Tropic Birds;
> And mountains over all embracing all,
> And all the landscape endlessly enrich'd
> With waters running, falling, or asleep.
>
> (8.129–43)

Wordsworth does not deny the attractions or temptations of the garden; rather the contrary. The elements of the scene are combined in "no discordant hue" and enriched by falling or running of waters. Yet the scene is one of "ever-growing" change and almost feverish variety as the "obsequious hues" of the component elements disappear in a subtle chase, ending with the waters falling into sleep, becoming stagnant. Sleeping or stagnant waters can represent the human mind under despotism, a frequent symbol in republican and dissenting discourse. In the 1850 *The Prelude* the poet adds the question, "could enchantment have done more?" emphasizing that this is a real Chinese location. In presenting the garden in this way, Wordsworth is obviously alluding to the long literary tradition of anti-paradises, from Circe's island of Aeaea to Acrasia's Bower of Bliss, as well as Milton's several false terrestrial paradises. The true and actual "paradise" in which Wordsworth was raised, however, is "lovelier by far," arranged or favored not by subtle and sophisticated artifice, but by "Nature's primitive gifts" (as opposed to "boon nature's lavish help" or gracious favor in Tartary). In lines that recall the prelapserian toil and bliss of Milton's Adam and Eve in Eden, Wordsworth writes:

> But lovelier far than this the Paradise
> Where I was rear'd; in Nature's primitive gifts
> Favour'd no less, and more to every sense
> Delicious, seeing that the sun and sky,
> The elements, and seasons in their change
> Do find their dearest Fellow-labourer there,
> The heart of Man; a district on all sides
> The fragrance breathing of humanity,
> Man free, man working for himself, with choice
> Of time, and place, and object; by his wants,
> His comforts, native occupations, cares,
> Conducted on to individual ends
> Or social, and still unfollow'd by a train
> Unwoo'd, unthought-of even, simplicity
> And beauty, and inevitable grace.
>
> (8.144–58)

Wordsworth presents the English lakes as a paradise arranged by nature ("unthought-of even") in which the changing seasons, the elements, sun, and sky are all combined in harmony with their "Fellow-labourer," the "heart of Man." This is a paradise of unalienated labor, where free individuals and not "the patient skill of myriads" responding to the emperor's despotic edict or decree, in the manner of Kubla Khan, build the gardens. They are free, working for themselves, choosing the time and place when and where they work, and selecting the objects of their work which are conducted for both individual as well as social and communal objectives and benefits. Wordsworth does not deny the power of these "resplendent gardens, with their frame / Imperial, and elaborate ornaments," but he locates their power, oddly, in their ability to inspire a childhood trauma. The gardens would "to a Child be transport over great":

> When but a half-hour's roam through such a place
> Would leave behind a dance of images
> That shall break in upon his sleep for weeks;
> Even then the common haunts of the green earth
> With the ordinary human interests
> Which they embosom, all without regard
> As both may seem are fastening on the heart
> Insensibly, each with the other's help,
> So that we feel, not knowing that we love,
> And feel, not knowing whence our feeling comes.
>
> (8.159–72)

Wordsworth rejects the imperial gardens with their potent but superficial "dance of images" for the "common haunts of the green earth," and for our "ordinary human interests," or the human and the natural. This Wordsworthian program of human development is well known from many works, including the *Lyrical Ballads*, where sickly and stupid German tragedies and Gothic novels are arraigned for stimulating a morbid craving for sensation and effect. The imperial garden at Jehol, with its "dance of images" breaking the child's sleep, is similarly unhealthy and unnatural, obscuring the "grandeur of the beatings of the heart." This is the kind of language Wordsworth reserves in *The Prelude* for the most serious traumas in his life, the afterlife of the mountains during the "boat stealing" episode, the death of his father, and the gibbet memory. Possibly, brother John's recent drowning retained its associations with China. The gardens are another form of idolatry, of "the dead letter, not the spirit of things, / Whose truth is not a motion or a shape / Instinct with vital functions, but a Block / Or waxen Image" made by humans to adore (8.431–6). Wordsworth here takes on the exact register used by contemporary Protestant missionaries to China, like Morrison.

This sudden eruption of the false paradise of the imperial Chinese garden into this poem about the English lakes perhaps may strike us as somewhat unusual. It certainly shows that China and the Macartney embassy had been absorbed into Wordsworth's consciousness and that they were able to be called up by his poetic imagination. The extent to which this particular effusion relates to the family's involvement in the China trade, through John, must remain speculative. Yet surely the specious and spectacular attractions of Jehol, the commercial activity of John and his family in the China trade, and the recent death of John must have, at some level, coalesced in Wordsworth's mind. Personal, domestic, and global issues thus heavily overdetermine Wordsworth's depiction of Jehol in Book Eight of *The Prelude*.

MACARTNEY'S CHINESE PICTURESQUE

Wordsworth's depiction of the imperial garden of *Wanshu Yuan* is significant in bringing to mind the key place in 1793 where the culminating formal reception of Macartney's embassy took place and the site where he did not perform the full imperial kowtow, what I refer to as the primal scene of the encounter with China in the British imagination. As Chang argues, the contemporary version of the Chinese garden became a synecdoche for political and imperial power, and the crucial site of difference between the British and the Chinese, where, the narrative runs, Macartney's masculine, Protestant, constitutional whiggism was proved and tested against an effeminate, despotic polity which had been glorified for some two hundred years by Jesuit sophistry.[73] For the purposes of this discussion, I will focus only on the account by Macartney of the second imperial garden, *Wanshu Yuan*, as mediated to Wordsworth, Southey, and others by Barrow's *Travels in China* of 1804.

Whereas the landscape of the English lakes was arranged by nature, the imperial gardens are constructed by the imperial edicts of the Kangxi and the Qianlong emperors, for the pleasure of the Tartar dynasty and the personal pleasure of its emperors. The semiotics of the garden are thus the glorification of the emperor, in the same way as the formal gardens of Versailles seek to glorify the personal rule of the Sun King, Louis XIV, or Sansouci at Potsdam, with its Chinese teahouse, that of the Prussian enlightened despot Frederick the Great. Macartney and Staunton, and to a lesser extent Barrow, were highly erudite readers and sophisticated decoders of the visual hermeneutics of the aristocratic English landscaped park, which they applied to their viewing of the Chinese imperial gardens. Staunton, for instance, commenting on the life-size simulacra of the imperial city contained within the garden of *Yuanming Yuan* made famous by Attiret and Chambers, writes: "Mountains and vallies, lakes and rivers, rude precipices and gentler slopes, have been produced where nature did not intend them ... This world, in miniature, has been created at the command and for the pleasure of one man, but by the hard labour of many thousands" – a point Wordsworth had emphasized.[74] Again, as Chang elegantly comments, "in the Chinese landscape, power rewrites nature; in the British landscape nature affirms political right."[75]

Neither Barrow nor William Alexander, who executed the illustrations for the *Travels*, were allowed to accompany Macartney to Jehol.[76] Barrow's account of the park thus defers to Macartney's more expert description and reading of *Wanshu Yuan*. Macartney was an assiduous and enthusiastic landscape gardener who designed and created the picturesque estate of Lissanoure Castle in Ulster, acquired by his grandfather in 1733.[77] A sophisticate in both contemporary landscape theory and viewing, Macartney interpreted the Chinese imperial garden through the lens of the Georgian landed elite he desperately wished to join: Barrow fawned that his Lordship's "taste and skill in landscape gardening are so well known."[78] Macartney thus reads the Chinese landscape in terms of its English analogies of the aristocratic estates and their owners that he knew personally: "we rode about three miles through a very beautiful park kept in the highest order and much resembling the approach to Luton in Bedfordshire." Macartney refers to the estate of Luton Hoo, purchased by his patron and father-in-law, John Stuart, the third Earl of Bute, in 1762. Bute had been George III's extremely unpopular Tory prime minister from 1762–63, the year following the construction of Chambers' chinoiserie pagoda at Kew. The neo-classical architect Robert Adams designed Bute's house, and "Capability" Brown enlarged and redesigned his 1200-acre park. Praised by Samuel Johnson and others, Luton Hoo was a showcase picturesque estate.[79] Describing the "wonders" of the extensive Lake at *Wanshu Yuan* with its magnificent yacht, illustrated by William Alexander, Macartney writes:

There is no beauty of distribution, no feature of amenity, no reach of fancy which embellishes our pleasure grounds in England, that is not to be found here … for in a course of a few hours I have enjoyed such vicissitudes of rural delight, as I did not conceive could be felt outside of England, being at different moments enchanted by scenes perfectly familiar to those I had known there, to the magnificence of Stowe, the softer beauties of Woburn, and the fairy-land of Paine's Hill. (130)

Macartney finds the imperial park "charming", enchanting, and delightful. His points of reference are to the key picturesque landscaped country parks of England – Viscount Cobham's Stowe (another "Capability" Brown commission), Woburn (designed by William Kent), and Charles Hamilton's Painshill – rather than to Chambers' *Dissertation* that he finds has little relevance to what he views. Macartney almost seems at home here, but not quite. The imperial park thus presents the eighteenth-century aristocrat with pleasures – in most un-Wordsworthian language, "such vicissitudes of rural delight." Macartney admits that the landscape is a little too effusive and inauthentic for his taste, as "artificial rocks and ponds with gold and silver fish" and "monstrous porcelain figures of lions and tigers, usually placed before the pavilions are displeasing to an European eye." But these he regards as mere trifles.

The following day Macartney visited the Western side of the garden. If the eastern part of the garden represented for him the European categories of the "beautiful" and the "picturesque," on the western side:

In many places immense woods, chiefly oaks, pines, and chestnuts, grow upon almost perpendicular steeps, and force their sturdy roots through every resistance of surface and of soil, where vegetation would seem almost impossible. These woods often clamber over the loftiest pinnacles of the stony hills, or gathering on the skirts of them, descend with a rapid sweep, and bury themselves in the deepest vallies … adapted to the situation and peculiar circumstances of the place, sometimes with a rivulet on one hand, gently stealing through the glade, at other with a cataract tumbling from above, raging with foam, and rebounding with a thousand echoes from below, or silently engulphed in a gloomy pool, or yawning chasm ... certainly so rich, so various, so beautiful, so sublime a prospect before my eyes had never beheld. I saw everything before me as on an illuminated map, palaces, pagodas, towns, villages, farm-houses, plains, and vallies, watered by innumerable streams, hills waving with woods, and meadows covered with cattle of the most beautiful marks and colours. All seemed to be nearly at my feet, and that a step would convey me within reach of them. (131–33)

Macartney, contra Wordsworth, is massively impressed by the sublimity and beauty of the park with its rock, woods, pagodas, and palaces; sights unparalleled in his life. Clearly, it is a sumptuous and extraordinary scene, but, ultimately, it is a prospect constructed and designed to impress only one man, the emperor, in whose place Macartney is now standing but whom he is not: "all *seemed* to be at nearly at *my feet.*"

Macartney discourses on the aesthetic informing Chinese gardening. He swiftly exorcizes the specters of the "fanciful descriptions" which Attiret and Chambers "have intruded upon us as realities" (133). The "Chinese gardener," he opines, "is the painter of nature, and though totally ignorant of perspective, produces the happiest effects by the management" of nature, rather like the picturesque theorists. As to the question of whether or not the horticultural naturalism of the English garden was "really copied from the Chinese, or originated with ourselves," that had so vexed Horace Walpole in later life, he leaves for "vanity to assert and idleness to discuss" (134–36). An agent of global diplomacy, Macartney is increasingly aware of the folly of constructing national traditions of design in such matters. He sees the difference between the English and the Chinese as, paradoxically, that "our excellence seems to be rather in improving nature, theirs to conquer her, and yet produce the same effect." In fact, this is a difference of method rather of objective, indicating that the Qing imperium is a conquering polity, while the British Empire is one of improvement and, thus, modernity, education, and consent. Macartney once again reads Chinese despotism into Qing horticultural practice.

Wordsworth, himself an enthusiastic gardener and notable designer of the Beaumonts' picturesque English winter garden at Coleorton, was rather less sympathetic to formal aristocratic country parks.[80] He filtered out Macartney's attempt to read *Wanshu Yuan* as English picturesque and found, like Walpole, much that is less winning in the managed landscapes of the Chinese garden. But oddly, Macartney drew one further comparison between *Wanshu Yuan* and a garden that he knew very well. Keen to embed the imperial garden in the semiotics of the English county estate,

Macartney makes a highly unexpected comparison between Chinese and English places.

If any place in England can be said in any respect to have similar features to the western park, which I have seen this day, it is Lowther Hall in Westmoreland, which (when I knew it many years ago) from the extent of prospect, the grand surrounding objects, the noble situation, the diversity of surface, the extensive woods, and command of water, I thought it might be rendered by a man of sense, spirit, and taste, the finest scene in the British dominions. (134)

In 1768 that upwardly mobile and assiduous befriender of the powerful, George Macartney, had married Jane Stuart, the daughter of Lord Bute, whose estate at Luton Hoo he compared to *Wanshu Yuan* in 1793. Bute's other son-in-law was Sir James Lowther, first Earl of Lonsdale and owner of the substantial Lowther estate. Macartney, the brother-in-law of the owner of Lowther Hall, was for nine months in 1768 one of two MPs returned for Cockermouth, whose election was personally managed by Lowther's agent, John Wordsworth, the father of the poet. The money that Lowther owed his agent, and then refused to pay back, had been advanced by Wordsworth senior to cover his and Macartney's election expenses and bribes.[81]

The prospect from Lowther Hall that Macartney viewed with such effusive pleasure while a guest of its owner was thus rather well known to the Wordsworth family as the home of their father's employer. Macartney's host, Sir James, though lacking the refinement, intelligence, and sophistication of an eighteenth-century Qing emperor, possessed a suitably despotic and unpleasant personality. Known variously as "Wicked Jimmy" and "Jemmy Grasp-all, Earl of Toadstool," he aspired to the full political control of the north-west of England, and has been described as "tyrannical, ruthless, without tact."[82] He controlled the votes of 800 freeholders and nine seats in the House of Commons. Sir James never fully paid the elder Wordsworth for his services, the debt remaining unsettled until 1802 when his successor agreed the reimbursement that had helped to fund brother John Wordsworth's private trading. John Wordsworth's children were notoriously bitter about Lowther's refusal to pay their father what he was owed. This was partially responsible for John's need to establish his fortune in the China trade, with such tragic consequences. Macartney's reference to the need for a "man of sense, spirit, and taste" to transform the prospect into the finest in the British dominions, surely, is his implied criticism of his brother-in-law, whom he must have found difficult. Capability Brown had visited Lowther in 1763 and produced a plan for altering the estate but nothing was ever done.[83]

China, via Macartney's account, thus once more erupts into the domestic and pastoral life of the Wordsworth family. Macartney's equation of the Chinese emperor's imperial prospect and that of Sir James's domestic prospect must have struck a deep chord with the Wordsworths. In *The Prelude*, Wordsworth severs Macartney's link between both Lowther's Old Westmoreland Hall and the Qianlong emperor's Jehol, and locates his "paradise lovelier by far" some way outside the grounds of both Westmoreland Hall and *Wanshu Yuan*, rendering the English lakes as the antithesis of the oriental pleasure ground and Lowther's estate. It clearly was a global village charged by unexpected affinities and organized by tight networks in which the Wordsworths lived and wrote.

CHAPTER 8

"Not a bit like the Chinese figures that adorn our chimney-pieces": orphans and travellers – China on the stage

This final chapter concerns China and the theater, by far the most popular form of cultural production in the period. Said notably argued for the importance of drama and spectacle in the processes of orientalism, employing the theater as metaphor in which "the orient is the stage on which the whole East is confined."[1] Both British identity and the idea of China were also forged on the stage. The theater is especially important in the performance of the orient as the drama uses scenery, costume, music, and dance in addition to character and plot. Felicity Nussbaum, Daniel O'Quinn, and David Worrall have discussed the ways in which the drama of the long eighteenth century performed, regulated, or problematized national, racial, and gender difference on the stage.[2] Primarily such exemplary criticism has been directed towards performing British, African, and West and East Indian identities, and Chinese subjects have not been discussed at length.[3] This chapter extends this critical purview to take into account Qing China and focuses on this comparatively under-researched area. Stage performances are especially crucial for an understanding of Romantic-period attitudes to China as they had the potential to reach out and touch an enormous audience.

The capacity of the Theatre Royal at Covent Garden in the period was just under 3000 people. Given that dramas had multiple performances, an audience of many thousands of people saw these plays in the metropolis alone. Worrall, for instance, estimates that George Colman the younger's popular anti-slavery melodrama, *Inkle and Yarico*, of 1787 reached an audience of around a million in the decade following its first production.[4] Literacy was also not a requirement for the theatre audience and, as Chi-ming Yang points out, the popular appeal of China as spectacle was exploited in British theater from the time of the Restoration.[5] Although heavily regulated, the commercial stage was still a place in which very complex cultural negotiations about nation, race, empire, class, and gender were played out and consumed by a diverse audience. The presence of

China on the European stage was not an inconsiderable one. Adrienne Ward has identified some sixty-eight eighteenth-century European dramas (mainly Italian and French operas) about China for which records exist. Of these, eleven were by British playwrights and there were probably somewhere between thirty and forty British dramas involving China in the first three decades of the nineteenth century.[6] Not only was the theater the most popular art form of the period, but such events also combined visual and textual performances of China.

O'Quinn argues that the popular theater was crucial in creating a sense of the British nation. He claims that the heavily legislated theaters disciplined and regulated their audience and that their dramas "orchestrated national reactions to the recalibration of imperial sovereignty" in the wake of the loss of the American colonies and the acquisition of a new empire in India. The British Empire in Asia thus emerges as a "compensatory imperial fantasy" for the loss of those colonies. For O'Quinn theatrical imperialism laid the foundations of the British imperial subject.[7] Yet distinctions between nation, race, and class were in this period porous and shifting. More specifically, Chi-ming Yang argues that China functions in the period as an exemplar for European society. In particular, China was used to mediate discourses of virtue and of commerce and luxury. This process involved an ambivalent location of China in ancient Confucian traditions of virtue as well as contemporary flows of commercial artifacts and fashionable chinoiserie ornamentation: "China's linguistic double register—empire/commodity, subject to falling and yet ultimately resilient—thus yokes together contiguous yet distinct orders of meaning and value: political, material, and moral." China was both a "symbol of imperial excess" and of "Confucian moderation," alternately a threat and an aspiration.[8] In the period covered by this chapter, however, China becomes an even more various and contested symbol, largely because of the increased knowledge transmitted to Britain about contemporary Qing China. Yet older conceptions of China as undifferentiated oriental fantasyland still coalesced with more informed representations.

Audience reaction to any drama could be multiple, and sympathetic identifications with characters intended to be perceived negatively could easily occur. Likewise, the charisma of the actors involved could also impact on the ways in which the drama was understood, as did contemporary theatrical conventions and practices. Melodrama, for instance, frequently utilized spectacular settings, and was premised on a clear distinction between good and evil characters that could intensify negative or idealized portrayals of other peoples.[9] Whereas it is clear that the stage was increasingly used to foster hegemonic notions of nation and empire and that theatrical performance functioned, at one level, as a discourse of power, such categories still involved complex cultural negotiations and appropriations. The other and the exotic were performed in various and contested ways, and national identities – Irish, Scots, Welsh – as well as regional and class identities were simultaneously performed. Nussbaum, writing of the representations of black males on the eighteenth-century stage, reminds us that "that racial markers are less an indicator of racial authenticity ... than a flexible masquerade that calls attention to itself according to the demands of context." Rather than expressing a mono-lithic discourse of power, such racial maskings and unmaskings paral-lel and substitute for the contemporary "confusion between geographical identities and hues."[10] As J. S. Bratton argues, such theatrical "cultural negotiation" was "determined by the need to reconcile many transactions simultaneously performed."[11]

This chapter begins with an examination of the most significant drama concerning China performed throughout the period, the Irish drama-tist Arthur Murphy's *The Orphan of China* of 1759 (performed in Britain and North America and printed in the 1790s and beyond). It returns this study to the concern of its opening chapters with the cultural transmis-sion of authentic Chinese texts to a European audience. Murphy's play represents a late, but not the final, stage in a highly complex process of cultural transmission from the Ming anthology of Yuan dynasty song-dramas of Zang Maoxun, via the Jesuit historiography of Prémare and Du Halde, and the emergent British sinology of Thomas Percy. It argues that Murphy's *Orphan*, like Percy's *Hau Kiou Choann*, which it precedes by only three years, is a founding text for Romantic Sinology, as well as a terminus for older interpretations of China that stressed China's ancient Confucian moralism, displayed in a visual rococo chinoiserie style. Janus-faced, the drama looks back to the great period of Jesuit sinology and forward to the on-coming revisions of Romantic Sinology. This chapter contrasts Murphy's *Orphan* with the new Romantic-period drama about China. In the case of *Harlequin and Quixote; or, the Magic Arm* (1797), for instance, a China of substantial commercial possibilities is depicted and the piece concludes with a celebratory (compensatory) rewriting of the primal scene of encounter in the reception of a new, post-Macartney British embassy to China. That scene of encounter also features in George Colman's *The Law of Java* (1822) but displaced onto Java rather than China. The most popular Romantic-period drama about China, Andrew Cherry's *The Travellers; or, Music's Fascination* (1806), intriguingly depicts the voyage of a virtuous Confucian Chinese prince to study the culture and society of Britain in an imagined anticipation of the later nineteenth-century Chinese "self-strengthening" movement. Unsurprisingly, a hardening of attitudes can be discerned later in the century after the first Anglo-Chinese War, with the popular patriotic fare of J. M. Morton's *News from China* (1844), C. A. Somerset's *Wars in China or the Battles of Chinghae and Amoy* (1844), and *Shadows on the Water or the Cleverest Lad in China* (1845) with which this chapter concludes. If eighteenth-century drama presents China as tragedy, Romantic-period drama rewrites this encounter as comedy. Rather than being a cover for colonial aggression against Qing China, I argue that this turn to comedy represented a real sense of the possibility of partnership between the British and Chinese and that this was not, viewed before the Opium Wars, simply an orientalist fantasy.

ADAPTING *THE ZHAO SHI GUER*

The claim that the theater was a highly politicized cultural space in which xenophobia and national identity were inextricably linked needs little justification. Just three years prior to the publication of Percy's landmark text in the history of Romantic Sinology, the *Haiu Kiou Choaan*, a version of a thirteenth-century Chinese drama was performed on the London stage. This authentic Chinese drama, now frequently referred to as "the Chinese *Hamlet*," was translated into French, adapted into an heroic drama by Voltaire, then translated into English and adapted for the English stage by the Irish dramatist Arthur Murphy as part of the general craze for things Chinese of the 1750s and 1760s. The *Orphan* was a crucial text, half immersed in the Frenchified rococo chinoiserie style that it originated from, yet still transmitting some more serious understanding of and engagement with Chinese thought.

Rather than the fantasy world of decorative rococo whimsy of its most obvious progenitor, the French ballet of Jean-Georges Noverre, *Les Fêtes Chinois*, or of the magic, supernaturalism, and irrationality of the literary orientalism of the *Arabian Nights*, the *Orphan* is a serious meditation on Confucian notions of family piety and dynastic loyalty. Its model, the Chinese drama, *Zhao shi guer* or *The Orphan of the House of Zhao*, is a minor operetta or song-drama of the Yuan dynasty written around 1330 by Ji Junxiang. The text of the drama derives from Zang Maoxun's landmark compilation of Yuan dynasty song-dramas (*zaju*), *Yuanren baizhong qu*, or *One Hundred Yuan Plays* of 1615–16.[12] Such song-dramas were performed in different settings, including courts and temples as well as urban locations. They were composed of both dialogue and songs, the latter being set to four different kinds of musical modes or registers with the singing role characteristically the same as that of the lead protagonist. Subsequent to 1300 these dramas were collected and textualized in a number of editions of which Zang Maoxun's, "carefully orchestrated and sumptuously illustrated," is the most compendious and famous.[13] In a Ming and Qing context, these dramas were already, rather like Percy's *Reliques*, ancient forms with strong historical traditions. Among the other plays in Zang's collection is *Lao sheng er* and Ma Zhiyuan's *Hangong qiu*, both to be translated by John Francis Davis in 1817 and 1829, and Li Xingfu's *Hui-law ji*, which inspired Brecht's *The Caucasian Chalk Circle*.[14] Plays from the collection thus intrigued writers, scholars, and thinkers from Voltaire and Davis to Brecht and beyond.

The Chinese text that Prémare translated was already a hybrid and substantially rewritten text, moving from the urban commercial theater of the Yuan to the courtly stage culture of the Ming dynasty and undergoing enormous change. In the early seventeenth century, Zang transformed such scripts into literary texts aimed at a sophisticated and educated élite. This process of textual transmission problematizes any notions that we may have of returning to the authenticity of any Chinese "original" or "source text" obscured by European appropriation. Adapted by European orientalists, Zang's *Zhao shi guer* is thus a signal text in the global flow of culture. It was first translated into French by de Prémare as *The Little Orphan of the House of Chao: a Chinese Tragedy* and included in Du Halde's *Description de l'empire de la Chine* (1735). Prémare categorized the drama as "tragédie chinoise," though the Aristotleian categories of drama were not used in China.[15] Subsequent translations and adaptations of the *Zhao shi guer* all accepted Prémare's categorization of the drama as tragedy. Prémare translated only the dialogue of the drama, removing the songs or arias. Subsequent versions, until Stanislas Julien's translation of the complete play in 1834, were derived from Prémare's text.[16] The decision not to translate the arias was an omission that signified a major cultural misunderstanding of the nature of Chinese drama, where the songs represent "a spontaneous outburst of emotion that heightens the dramatic tempo and gives a lyric quality to the play." To omit the songs in Chinese drama is equivalent to removing the choruses from Greek drama.[17]

Prémare sent his translation to Étienne Fourmont, hoping to interest the French sinologue in his *Notitiae Linguae Sinica*.[18] Instead, it was delivered to Du Halde who published the translation against Prémare's wishes as a "Chinese tragedy," a corrective to what the Jesuits viewed as morally dubious contemporary European novels and plays.[19] This song-drama attracted their attention because it was composed of five rather than the more usual four acts, and had an obviously tragic story and setting, involving dynastic loyalty, treachery, and revenge. The drama stressed the filial piety of Confucian rationalism, which the Jesuits associated with the literati and which they were keen to absorb into their conception of a cultured China. *Zhao shi guer* then became available in two English translations from Du Halde/Prémare's French, as well as in Thomas Percy's *Miscellaneous Pieces Relating to the Chinese* of 1762.[20]

The British and European (as well as Japanese interest) in this particular play and Zang's compilation more widely would later inform late nineteenth- and early twentieth-century Chinese intellectuals' understanding of what constituted culture and literature, and how European understandings of *belles lettres* informed an idea of the nation during the collapse of the Qing and later Republican periods. Again, the dramas are involved in a highly complex process of transcultural transmission and re-transmission. Patricia Sieber has shown how "the most nationalist and anti-imperialist Chinese mobilization of Yuan drama in the twentieth century was enabled by the very terms that eighteenth- and nineteenth-century European versions of Chinese drama had invented."[21] Prémare had pointed out that the drama had been written under the conquering Mongol Yuan dynasty, thus encouraging readers to associate the Mongols with the current Manchu dynasty, both of which were commonly and unhelpfully described as "Tartars" in the European racial imaginary.[22]

Du Halde included the drama not to give an example of Chinese literary excellence but more to show the nature of the Chinese taste. It is based on historical events in the state of Chin in sixth century BCE, and espouses anachronistic Confucian ideals of dynastic and familial piety. It tells the story of the saving of the life of the orphan and male heir of the house of Zhao after a villainous military leader has eliminated all three hundred members of this rival clan. To preserve the life of the child, heir to the house, a physician allows the substitution of his own child for that of the orphan. The general subsequently stabs this child to death in front of his father. Twenty years later the physician informs the true orphan of his origins, via the device of an elaborate painted scroll; the orphan then takes his revenge on the general by exposing his crimes to the emperor. The drama contains strong scenes of torture, suicide, and murder. The idea of sacrificing one's son in the name of a higher loyalty (family, state, nation) obviously fascinated Europeans, as did the twenty-year vengeance theme. The play was highly thought of, praised as equal to classical tragedy by Richard Hurd, and adapted many times by European dramatists.

In Britain, Prémare's translation of the play was adapted by William Hatchett in 1741 as an anti-Walpole polemic, though probably not performed. Hatchett made an explicit and prophetic comparison between the established flow of Chinese products and an anticipated new trade in Chinese literature, which his adaptation exploited: "China has furnish'd us long with her Manufactures ... the Importation of her Poetry will serve to regale in its Turn."[23] In 1752 Pietro Metastasio adapted it as *L'Ero cinese*, a three-act dramatic poem for the Habsburg empress Maria Theresa.[24] The drama was then more explicitly cast into the oppositional conflict between Chinese and Tartars. Voltaire, in France, used the story, altering it significantly along the way in his *L'Orphelin de la Chine* acted at the *Comédie Française* in August 1755. Voltaire classicized the piece, imposing the three unities, and changed its historical setting to that of the Mongolian invasion of China by Genghis Khan and his followers.[25] In Voltaire's play the orphan of Zhao became the Song heir to the throne of China, exchanged at birth by a mandarin, Zamti, for his own son, and subsequently hidden in the ancestral tombs of China's kings. As a deist and an opponent of the Catholic Church, Voltaire held that China was a great example of a state that had strong moral and ethical codes, which were not derived from revealed religion. The drama is his rebuttal of Rousseau's famous privileging of the noble savage, in this case the Tartar Gengis-Kan. Rousseau had argued that the Chinese had become corrupted and enfeebled by their sophisticated living, hence their conquest by the noble savagery of the Tartars. For Voltaire, the eventual triumph of civilized values, science and art, as typified by the Ming and Qing dynasties, was assured in the long run in the standard cliché of the conquered conquering the conquerors through assimilation and sinicization.[26] Voltaire's drama was published in its original French and an anonymous English translation in 1755 and was well received.[27]

GARRICK, MURPHY, AND *THE ORPHAN OF CHINA* (1756)

It was known that David Garrick commissioned John Hawkesworth to adapt the drama for the stage, yet it was not until April 21, 1759, that the Irish dramatist Arthur Murphy (probably also the English translator of Voltaire's drama) had his adaptation of Voltaire's tragedy performed at Drury Lane Theatre, with a reluctant David Garrick in the role of the mandarin, Zamti.[28] The great innovation of Voltaire's drama had been that it was performed in what was then regarded as authentic Chinese costume. In imitation, Garrick had hired Henry Woodward to produce the pantomime *Proteus; or, Harlequin in China* in 1755 and then brought a spectacular entertainment, *Les Fêtes Chinoises* (*The Chinese Festival*), from Paris to London in 1755 in an attempt to exploit the current fashion for chinoiserie.[29] *Les Fêtes* was an eighteenth-century ballet by Jean-Georges Noverre, probably created in 1751 for Marseilles where he was ballet master and staged in Paris on July 1, 1754, at the *Opéra-Comique*, with decors after François Boucher, famous for his stylized rococo chinoiserie works of art.[30] Louis René Boquet designed Chinese costumes specifically for the production.

The idea of China on display was that of the whimsical chinoiserie version of rococo art, that Porter has argued largely evacuated the referent "China" of all meaning, with mandarins and slaves, and dances and china porcelain vases. Garrick's London version of the ballet seems to have followed this template.[31] The London ballet, however, led to very serious disturbances in which the expensive sets and costumes were destroyed, and the theater damaged by furious rioters opposed to the presence of French dancers on the London stage on the eve of the Seven Years War. The crowd's hostility was largely politically motivated but xenophobia and nationalism also played their part, as well as class division and cultural politics, with the well-off in the boxes supporting the *Festival* and the pit and the gallery opposed.[32] The crowd's hostility was manifested against what they believed to be French dancers and a French production rather than China or chinoiserie, yet a Frenchified version of a chinoiserie style was overlaid on this national rivalry.[33]

It is likely that some of Boquet's chinoiserie costumes were used in the production of Murphy's new tragedy, which boasted "a magnificent set of Chinese scenes." One critic commented on the "glitt'ring palace" of Timurkan and described "many pleasant novelties." He claimed "an eastern traveller would imagine himself at Pekin and a Cockney in a new world."[34] Murphy recalled that Garrick had "prepared a magnificent set of Chinese scenes, and the most becoming dresses."[35] In his review of the production Goldsmith commented on the "glowing imagery" and "well-conducted scenery." Yet he also noted the stark contrast or ambivalence between the staging and costumes and the somber action and subject of the piece.[36] This contrast between the high moral seriousness of the piece and its spectacular showcasing of chinoiserie effect has led Yang to argue that it epitomizes the two different ways of thinking about China in the eighteenth century as demonstrating both "a desire for moral reform at a time of rampant materialism" and, paradoxically, "an appetite for the commodities of the East evoked by the sheer vision of luxury on stage."[37] Certainly this crucial dialectic between Confucian virtue and commercial luxury informs the staging and the play.

Murphy had read the Prémare translation of the *Zhao shi guer* and meditated his own adaptation before reading Voltaire's adaptation. His adaptation was completed in 1756 and then underwent a protracted process of negotiation and amendment. William Whitehead, the Laureate, and Horace Walpole substantially altered the drama and urged Garrick to perform it.[38] Murphy's version borrows much of Voltaire's, keeping the drama's setting of the Tartar invasion of China, now led by "Timurkan," but brought forward to the Manchu conquest of China of the early seventeenth century. Murphy, however, abandoned the romance between Gengis and Idame and concluded his drama with the expulsion of the Tartars, not their reconciliation with the Chinese. He altered Voltaire's drama by presenting the orphan and the mandarin's son as young men, and setting the drama twenty years after the initial switching of the infants, so as to interest the audience in their actions and situation, and bring his play closer to the Chinese original. Zamti brings up the heir to the throne of China as his own son, while the true heir is sent in safety to Korea. When his true son is captured and about to be impaled, Zamti will not endanger Zaphimri, the orphan, to save him. Murphy's drama thus restores the conflict of the Chinese original. At the play's close, Timurkan is not converted to Chinese manners, but killed in a swordfight by Zaphimri. The play contains more of the cruelty and brutality of the Chinese original; Zamti is tortured on the wheel offstage, and his wife, Mandane, is threatened with torture. Mandane commits suicide before the stricken Zamti dies from his torture in a well-constructed and emotionally powerful scene reminiscent of the death of Lear.

Murphy's drama is a fascinating cross-cultural hybrid; he claims to have tracked Voltaire "in the *snow of Shakespeare*," and the play contains allusions to Shakespeare's drama, especially *Richard III* and *King Lear*, as well as to Handel's opera, *Giulio Cesare* (1724).[39] Voltaire had famously criticized Shakespeare as inferior to neo-classical drama, and Murphy's play defends the national genius and example of Shakespeare in its practice and preface. The play's apologetic Prologue, penned by Whitehead, distances the drama from Voltaire's neo-classical practice: "Enough of Greece and Rome. The exhausted store / Of either nation now can charm no more," claiming that China will provide "fresh virtues to the source of light" and will "bring / Confucius' morals to Britannia's ears." Like

Hatchett's, Murphy's Prologue figures Chinese culture as a commodity to be acquired, an "imported boon." If Zamti's willingness to have his own son killed to save the heir to the throne shows "a patriot" too "zealous in a monarch's cause," the fault must be located specifically in imported "China's tenets," as Hanoverian "Britain knows no Right Divine in Kings" (i). Gone is Voltaire's French adulation of the despot enlightened by science and art. Murphy's Timurkan is simply "a tyrant train'd to lust and murder, A lawless ravager from savage wilds," antithetical to the "inventive race" of Chinese whose arts have humanized the world. At the end of the play the adult orphan unceremoniously dispatches the tyrant, and Chinese values are restored as Voltaire's narrative of the Tartar conqueror conquered by Chinese civilization is dropped.

Unlike *Les Fêtes*, Murphy's play was very popular at the time of the Seven Years War because it was seen to promote the values of British patriotism and liberty, through Chinese values, with the French now doubling for the ruthless despotic Khan. Here Chinese civic values are closer (though not identical) to those of Britain than those of France. From the outset of the drama, the strict Confucian piety of Zamti, with its public, masculine, and imperial virtues, is opposed to feminine, private and familial virtues, the "domestic pang," represented by Zamti's wife, Mandane. This is the focus of the tragic conflict in the drama. Whitehead's prologue leads the audience to read Zamti as "a dubious character … A patriot zealous in a monarch's cause," whose zeal extends "too far" (i). He denies that for his own son, "an unimportant boy" and a "vulgar life"; he

> Will marr the vast design: No; let him bleed,
> Let my boy bleed: in such a cause as this
> I can resign my son – with tears of joy
> Resign him, – and one complicated pang
> Shall wrench him from my heart. (20–21)

An agonizingly conflicted Zamti describes this sacrifice as "that sublime of virtue" which "ever on the rack … it feels the good, / Which in a single hour it works for millions" (34). "China's tenets" are thus to blame for the strict but sublime moralism that allows him to sacrifice his son. Such "virtue," however, must be moderated by Mandane's natural feelings. Sublime Chinese virtue is thus humanized by domestic British sensibility. Here, as Yang argues, though in a different context, "female suffering works to undo the binary between the individual and the common good."[40] The true tragic conflict in the drama is Mandane's terrible choice between saving her son or losing the orphan that she has brought up as if he were her own son for twenty years. Zamti's attempt to "conquer nature, while the heart-strings break" (19) is shown to be an unnatural and unsustainable project. Confucius's "radiant stores of moral truth" are here "unlocked in vain," as pure Confucian virtue is no substitute for Christian love (6).

Murphy's play remained the most influential version of the "idea of China" well beyond the date of its initial composition. One reviewer commented on its pervasive impact: "every one has, by this time, seen or read, and must have applauded it."[41] From 1759 to 1769 it was acted almost yearly at Drury Lane and presented for the first time at Covent Garden in 1777. In 1761 it was performed in Dublin simultaneously at the Smock Alley and Crow Street theaters. It is not clear how the Irish Murphy's drama of a conquered nation throwing off its oppressor was understood in the complex context of eighteenth-century Irish politics, but a reading of the play in which the true kings of the nation have been deposed and an alien monarchy installed in its place by force of arms was available and may well account for the play's popularity there.

The drama was also performed at the Southwark Theatre in Philadelphia in 1767 and, the following year, by the John Street Theater in New York (up to 1842). It was performed in Jamaica, and in many provincial British theaters. A French version was performed as late as 1807.[42] In all, many hundreds of thousands of people globally must have seen one of the many versions of Murphy's *Orphan*. It was surely the most popular and well-known British reading of China of the entire century.[43] The drama remained, at one level, a spectacular, glittering chinoiserie object to be viewed and consumed, and this may explain its popularity. Yet in combining this chinoiserie style with the severely tragic, the drama is a founding text for British sinology, establishing an idea of China as both chinoiserie spectacle to be enjoyed, and moral exemplar to be critically admired.

After the *Orphan*, Europe would have to wait until 1817 for the next translation of a Chinese drama, John Francis Davis's unperformed *Lao sheng erh; or, An Heir in His Old Age* discussed in Chapter 4 of this study. Murphy's *Orphan*, however, continued its extraordinary global journey from London to the Unites States and finally back to China. In 1964, the Hong Kong dramatist Li Jueben, who admits to reading Murphy's *Orphan*, produced his own version of the Yuan drama for a Chinese audience.[44] This Western interest in the *Orphan* drama led the celebrated Chinese director Chen Kaige to film the story in 2010 as *Sacrifice*. This film achieved number one status at the Chinese box office for sixteen days, grossing an estimated $27.7 million. Its popularity may be due to revived contemporary Chinese concerns with the PRC's one child policy, and the anxiety of losing a son or daughter.

So what of China survives in these adaptations of the fourteenth-century Chinese drama? Chinoiserie takes the topos of China but spins it out into whimsy, illegibility, and illegitimacy; the adaptations of the *Orphan* take a true and very serious literary source, but adapt it to their own contemporary concerns in the competing discourses about China and British debates about nation, empire, virtue, commerce, and luxury. All these manifestations are eurocentric certainly and are redacted and transmitted in a complicated manner. Nevertheless, the flow of ideas, information, goods and commodities, both economic and cultural, is evidenced by fashion and translation. Rather than see China's *Zhao shi guer* simply as a text that is adapted into something entirely different, we should view it as the problematic but very real presence of an alternative cultural tradition and cross-cultural encounter that both creates and co-constitutes a developing process of dialogue and exchange between two multi-ethnic imperial formations. Ji Junxiang's *Zhao shi guer* and Arthur Murphy's *Orphan* should now take their rightful places as a key texts in the study of world literature.

PANTOMIME AND THE NEW ROMANTIC CHINOISERIE

Murphy's *Orphan of China* remains the most serious drama about China well into the nineteenth century. There is no comparable performed Chinese play of its stature arguably until Brecht's *Caucasian Chalk Circle* of 1944, also adapted from a drama in Zang Maoxun's edition of Yuan *zaju* dramas. The new British understanding of China via the work of Romantic Sinology and the experience of the Macartney and Amherst embassies, however, impacted on a new generation of dramatists in both subject matter and style. The more realistic and ethnographically specific representations of China as developed by William Alexander clearly influenced the ways in which the new "Romantic" idea of China was portrayed though costume and set design, and some of the dramas engaged directly with specific political issues, reflecting the more intense relationship that was developing through trade and commerce. None of the dramas of the period are high moral tragedies in the mode of Murphy's *Orphan* and most continue to use China as spectacle.

The orient was a regular backdrop for the popular pantomime, the dominant theatrical form of Georgian Britain, and China became one of its frequent subjects. In Foucauldian readings, pantomime assumes more importance than elite and more polite forms of cultural production as it was a legally regulated form of artistic performance viewed by many thousands of people. Since the patent theaters of Drury Lane, Covent Garden, and the Haymarket alone were licensed to produce spoken drama, pantomime and burletta were enacted on other, illegitimate, stages as well as in the patent theaters. Rather than being simply escapist, pantomimes contained allusions to contemporary politics and events. They also reflected Britain's colonial and maritime expansion by utilizing settings derived from the exotic and oriental. Chinese scenes and settings became increasingly popular from the 1780s onwards, and especially between 1812 and 1823. David Mayer estimates that between 1806 and 1836 more than thirty pantomimes with Chinese characters and/or settings were produced.

Chinese set designs in British pantomime were strongly influenced by the visual style of Chambers' *Designs of Chinese Buildings* (1757), which claimed first-hand knowledge of Chinese designs, and subsequently by the second vogue for chinoiserie inspired by the Regent's controversial interior décor at the Royal Pavilion, Brighton. In 1797 the publication of William Alexander's illustration of China in the third volume of Staunton's account of the embassy presented a new visual style for China. In 1800 George Henry Mason's *The Costume of China* appeared with illustrations based on watercolors by the Cantonese artist Pu Qua and, in 1805, Alexander published his own volume, *The Costume of China*. These works emerged from the new Romantic Sinology and began to have a noticeable impact on Chinese theatrical settings, moving visually away from the earlier rococo-inspired chinoiserie of Garrick and Noverre's *Chinese Festival* to something claiming to be an authentic and verifiable version of China.[45] Of course, in the case of Chinese export painting, as Craig Clunas demonstrates, the consumer was not purchasing anything that was authentically Chinese but rather "he was receiving his own preconceptions … reflected back at him by an artist whose sole concern was to please."[46] Nevertheless, this new visual style reflected an intercultural encounter of great complexity and constituted a new grammar in the visual understanding of China.

The influx of Chinese export art, displayed at the Pavilion and elsewhere, contributed substantially to this process, leading to a new style of Chinese taste, or a "Romantic chinoiserie" less dependent on the whimsicalities and illegibility of its eighteenth-century predecessor. Pantomimes and dramas borrowed from Alexander's illustrations and the designs for the Pavilion for their backdrops and costumes, or utilized the talents as

Figure 6. *The Chinese Bridge & Pagoda, St. James's Park, Erected in Commemoration of the Peace of 1814* (London, R. Lambe, 1814) © Trustees of the British Museum.

set painters of various artists, such as Clarkson Stanfield who worked as an artist in Canton in 1815. Thus popular forms were markedly influenced, at some level, by Romantic Sinology's new depictions of China. This new vogue for a kind of chinoiserie appearing in the early nineteenth century was more associated with urban spaces than with country parks or domestic interior design. Rather than a pervasive middle-class consumer phenomenon of the earlier style, this revival of the Chinese taste was a fashion inspired by the royal family and was more common in a public manifestation.[47] The Regent had a long-standing taste for chinoiserie, having installed a William Chambers-style Chinese Drawing Room in his Carlton House residence back in 1790. In 1814 he sponsored a lavish Chinese pageant in St. James's Park to celebrate the recent victory over Napoleon. A Chinese bridge and a seven-story pagoda were erected (Figure 6), situating China at the very heart of an event crucial in the formation of British national identity, perhaps attempting to claim the chinoiserie style from the defeated French. Unfortunately, the bridge

Figure 7. The Banqueting Room designed by Robert Jones, from John Nash's *Views of the Royal Pavilion, Brighton* (1826). © Trustees of the British Museum.

and pagoda were destroyed by fireworks on the night. Most famously, Frederick and John Crace's and Robert Jones's extensive chinoiserie designs for the interiors of the Pavilion at Brighton left a strong impression on understanding of the Chinese taste (Figure 7).

In his invaluable discussion of eighteenth-century rococo chinoiserie, Porter argued that chinoiserie enacted "a delicious surrender to the unremitting exoticism of total illegibility," luxuriating "in a flow of unmeaning Eastern designs," and basking "in the glow of one's projected fantasies." Chinoiserie was "an aesthetic of the ineluctably foreign, a glamorization of the unknown and unknowable for its own sake."[48] Yet while Regency chinoiserie did not present in any way an accurate representation of Chinese fashions, neither was it the total evacuation of any Chinese referent of which Porter accuses its rococo predecessor. This new, royal style of chinoiserie was influenced by Alexander's views of China sketched or painted in China and themselves influenced by the hybridized visual style of Chinese artists producing a westernized style of "export" painting for the European market. Such painting assimilated "European conventions of pictorial representation," such as the picturesque, with "conventions of Chinese picture-making."[49] These new visual exchanges represent not simply a beguiling binary orientalism of East and West, but a complex example of cultural transmission. While at Canton, for instance, Alexander's manuscript journal describes how he met the notable local Chinese artists Pu Qua and Chamfou, who were engaged in copying prints by Henry Bunbury and Angelica Kauffman. Pu Qua set up the first workshop at Canton to cater specifically for Western customers. As well as influencing Alexander, Pu Qua's workshop produced large sets of watercolors, many of which depicted the occupations and trades of Canton, used by Mason's *Costume of China* (1800), itself influential on new Chinese styles.[50] Alexander also visited a Chinese face sculptor who claimed to "'sa-vy Mis-sa Banks velley well.'"[51] Presumably, this was Chitqua who is reported to have died three years later in 1796. Back in London, the Court of Directors of the Company exported around 350 of these Chinese "export" paintings from Canton.[52] Alexander's characteristic picturesque visual style thus merged with Chinese export by artists such as Pu Qua to produce a hybridized depiction of a contemporary and quotidian Qing China. While this visual style was generated by European demands and occupied, as Clunas puts it, "a space which is neither wholly Chinese nor wholly European," it aspired to gratify a new British taste for an actual and quotidian China.[53] This became the dominant visual style of Romantic Sinology (Figure 8).

Alexander's sketches and Chinese export paintings were used by the Crace and Jones firms to transcend the rococo chinoiserie of Boucher, Watteau, and Pillement (which they also incorporated) to create a new Chinese style, one that reflected developments in Romantic Sinology more generally. Patrick Conner describes how they "moved away from purely abstract themes and introduced a new repertoire of subjects, including mythical creatures and exotic figures from Chinese theatre and legend." Conner shows how the Pavilion, finally completed in 1822, represented a new version of chinoiserie, a "Romantic chinoiserie," in which not just one or two rooms were decorated in the Chinese taste but the whole interior was designed in one style, an organic unity of a kind: "the sheer scale, the richness of the colour, and the drama of plunging chandeliers and rearing dragons, evoke a 'China' of imperial extravagance and self-indulgence—something quite different from the gently whimsical realm of mid-Georgian rococo."[54] This Romantic chinoiserie style incorporated Western orientalist ideas of China, modified by the new knowledge of China, but also the styles of Chinese artists as well as Chinese wallpapers, porcelain, hanging lanterns, and Chinese export paintings. The Regent was willing to have the Hoppos at Canton bribed to acquire "pictures

Figure 8. William Alexander, "View at Yang-Tcheou," from *The Costumes of China* (1805). Alexander's illustrations of a quotidian and contemporary China heavily influenced Romantic Sinology and new chinoiserie styles. Copy in author's possession.

of their customs and particularly the Emperor's court – Armour of all kinds – Mandarine Dresses – flags ... Lanterns, etc. etc."[55] The many authentic Chinese artifacts prominently displayed in the Pavilion were almost exclusively from the contemporary Jiaqing period (1796–1820), rather than older Ming or early Qing.

This new Romantic chinoiserie style, like that of Chambers' Chinese gardens, also had its political coding viscerally revealed in George Cruikshank's "The court at Brighton a la Chinese!!" Recalling the iconography of Gillray's version of Macartney's ambassadorial reception over twenty years earlier, the print satirizes the oriental tastes of the Prince Regent in 1816 on the very eve of the second British embassy to China (Figure 9). Amherst, about to leave for his reception at the Jiaqing emperor's court, receives his instructions from the Regent at Brighton. The ambassador, however, does not have to go to China to witness oriental decadence. A grotesquely obese Regent sits on a divan smoking a

Figure 9. George Cruikshank, *The Court at Brighton a la Chinese!!* (1816) © Trustees of the British Museum.

pipe in the manner of Gillray's Chinese emperor. He holds his instruction to Amherst "to get fresh Patterns of Chinese deformities to finish the decorations of ye Pavillion," which Amherst bows to receive. The court wear Chinese costumes and a chinoiserie dragon pendant hangs from the ceiling. The Regent's court is depicted as both financially and morally corrupt. Queen Charlotte pours coins from a bag shaped like a cornucopia, inscribed "Pin Money & Royal Savings," into the Privy Purse. In this case the new presents for the emperor are not children's toys but adult items signifying vanity, greed, and lust. In an open chest labeled "Presents for the Emperor of China" can be seen two portraits of the Regent described as "Front & back view of myself." Next to these are large volumes inscribed "Fanny Hill" and "Pretty books." Curiously, behind the Prince are two statues, one an unpleasantly racialized depiction of a near naked "Hottentot Venus," Sara Baartjeman, and the other a heavily corseted and tightly clothed "British Adonis," the Regent himself. The two figures resemble each other in form, thus equating the "civilized" decadence of the court with the apparent primitivism of Africa, accusing the court of both Asian despotism and luxury and African savagery.[56]

Cruikshank's orientalized imagery is deployed to indicate that Chinese manners have infected the British royal establishment. The point had been made in a speech of March 12, 1816, opposing the government's income tax proposals in which Lord Stanley had expressed the hope for "no more of that squanderous and lavish profusion which … resembled more the pomp of a Persian satrap, seated in the splendour of oriental state, than the sober dignity of a British prince, seated in the bosom of his subjects."[57] Princess Lieven, friend and guest of the Regent, writing about the interiors of the Pavilion, similarly commented that it recalled the "days of Heliogabalus," and that there was "something effeminate about it which is disgusting."[58] By giving way to a luxurious and effeminizing taste for oriental designs the Regent has become himself orientalized and has corrupted the center of the British establishment.

This new Romantic Chinese style was increasingly employed in contemporary dramas. It was a recurrent element of pantomime and harlequinade, diffusing the new visual ideas of China to an extremely wide and popular audience. In 1783, *The Temple of Confucius; or, Harlequin the Phantom of the Day* by Thomas John Dibdin was performed at the Royal Circus in London, and it is known that a pantomime by Rayner Taylor, *The Mandarin; or, Harlequin Widower*, was performed at Sadler's Wells in London during the 1788–89 season. We know that the popular impact of Romantic Sinology begins to be felt at least as early as 1797, when *Harlequin and Quixotte; or, the Magic Arm* was performed at Covent Garden, possibly to capitalize on the increased interest in China stimulated by the publication of the official account of the Macartney embassy to China, including Alexander's new illustrations of China. T. J. Dibdin's *Harlequin in his Element* at Covent Garden in 1807 boasted a landscape with "a Pavilion and Chinese bridge," but it was Charles Isaac Dibdin Jr's *Whang-Fong; or, the Clown of China* of 1812, starring the famous clown Joseph Grimaldi, at Sadler's Wells that proved most popular. Dibdin boasted of the accuracy of his representation of China, informing his audience that his "Chinese scenes are copied from Alexander's Views in China." The opening scenes of Dibdin's pantomime included "A Chinese Summer Apartment," a "View of the Chinese City Yank Tctheou," and a "Chinese Mart," all taken from Alexander's recent embassy illustrations.[59] The following year T. J. Dibdin's *Harlequin Harmonist; or, A Trip to Japan* (1813) was performed, using similar chinoiserie scenes. Scene four of the pantomime is set in a "Japanese Temple" with "Idols—heads of Dogs, Griffins, Birds &c." Here Harlequin and Columbine escape on the back of dragons and are chased by idols.[60] In 1815 Charles Farley produced *Harlequin and Fortunio; or, Shing-Moo and Thun-Ton*, again starring

Grimaldi, at Covent Garden, complete with six detailed Chinese scenes. After the mandatory transformation of the leads, the chase moves from a "Chinese Port" to Brighton Pavilion. Mayer has shown that the five surviving scenes of the pantomime clearly demonstrate the hybridized influence of Chambers' engravings of Chinese interiors, Alexander's costume illustrations, and Crace and Sons' interiors for the Pavilion.[61]

Chinese characters appeared in numerous pantomimes not set in China or obviously advertising a Chinese theme. For example, William Bates's anti-slavery pantomime *Harlequin Mungo; or, A Peep into the Tower*, performed at the Royalty Theatre in Tower Hamlets in 1787–88, features a wealthy "Chinese Gentleman" with a Chinese servant intending to marry Columbine, the plantation owner's daughter, who is in love with the slave Mungo/Harlequin.[62] Chinese visitors to London were rare, and those encountered in the metropolis were usually highly educated. This pantomime performs a complex and transgressive version of national and racial identity; when Columbine is about to sign a marriage contract with her Chinese suitor, the wizard instructs Harlequin, formerly the African slave Mungo, to "transform himself" to the Chinese "likeness," from which point Columbine and Harlequin are united.[63]

A number of "Aladdin" pantomimes involving China began to be performed in the period. Derived from Antoine Galland's translations of the one of the *Thousand and One Nights* of 1712 onwards, the original story of Aladdin has an ostensible Chinese setting. Though its relevance to China can be disputed, subsumed under the larger context of orientalist drama, the story makes allusions to China. John O'Keefe's version of *Aladdin* was staged at Covent Garden in 1788 and contains a significant popular protest against the importation of Chinese porcelain now that British wares are high-quality products, anticipating the similar claims of Macartney's embassy:

> And why abroad our money fling
> To please the fickle Fair?
> No more China, China bring,
> Here's English China-ware.[64]

A later production of the pantomime staged at Norwich in 1810 and Covent Garden in Easter 1813 is set in a land called "Grand Tartary" but has little specific reference to China.[65]

The tendency to use China simply as spectacle persists in the early nineteenth century. T. J. Dibdin's "spectacular," *The Chinese Sorceror; or, the Emperor and His Three Sons* (*Whang Fong*) of 1823, for instance, presents the story of Whang Fong, a Chinese magician, who uses his magical powers to protect the wife and sons of Kien Long, the Sultan of a division of Chinese Tartary. The drama is set in a familiar orientalist world, relying on stereotypes of comic Chinese and ferocious Tartars. At one point the Sultan's son, Pekin, confronts three hostile Tartars who attempt to abduct his love, Briti, with the boast: "Give me but a sabre, & by the great Joss of the temple of Bob job, if I may not live with the girl I love, I'll show you how a true Chinese can die in her defence." Joss and his temple might here be a knowing in-joke alluding to the Regent and his Pavilion, by way of contemporary caricatures. In this case Chinese characters show little alterity or difference from those of the British apart from their use of a comic approximation of South China Coast pidgin, the lingua franca of Canton:

> A mandarine had a daughter fair
> And her name was O-Fi-te-cum-quam, co
> Her teeth were black, she'd pea green hair
> And her eyes half clos'd with modest blink, O
> She'd have stepp'd with grace, but her feet so small
> Wouldn't let the Lady walk at all,
> So she sat & sung,
> As her Bells she rung
> Ting a ring – ching a ring
> Ching, chang, chink O.[66]

The drama presents plenty of opportunity for spectacle with its scenery of "Pagodas, Bridges, Pleasure Grounds and Mountains." Similarly, *The Witch of the Desert; or, the Chinese Pedlar Boy*, "a New Grand Melo-Dramatic and Operatic Chinese Tale of Enchantment," performed at the Theatre Royal, Covent Garden, in 1832, exploits the stereotype of Tartar savagery, pitting the evil of Maga, the vengeful Tartar witch, against the masculine heroism of the Chinese pedlar boy, Zamti, actually a good spirit in disguise. The drama is set against wild mountain passes and forests, the "Ruined Temple of Fum-hoo," the "Cham's Pleasure Grounds, by the river See-Poe," and other exotic oriental locales.[67] Again the opposition is between civilized Chinese and savage Tartars, with its Chinese characters very close to British sensibilities.[68]

"A MODERN MODEL OF HIS COUNTRY'S PORCELAIN, USEFUL
AS WELL AS ORNAMENTAL": ANDREW CHERRY'S *THE
TRAVELLERS; OR, MUSIC'S FASCINATION*

Although there is no new play about China as serious and influential as Murphy's *Orphan* (still being performed in the period), there are a number of relatively substantial spoken dramas or farces where China is introduced to present exotic spectacle. Andrew Cherry's musical drama or "opera" *The Travellers; or, Music's Fascination* (1806) is one of the more unusual of the pieces in that it presents a reverse cross-cultural encounter as the emperor of China sends his son and heir to travel to Britain, via Turkey and Italy, to find out information of benefit to China, anticipating the later Chinese "self-strengthening" movement. Such pieces write the cross-cultural encounter with China as comedy, rather than tragedy. The piece was performed on January 22, 1806, at Drury Lane and ran for at least twenty-three nights.[69] Allowing for houses two-thirds full on average, that would make a minimum audience of around 45,000 people who saw the opera in London, and probably many more. It was judged to be a commercial, if not critical, success and broke box office records at the time. The musical was also performed at the Theatre Royal, Manchester, as well as in York, Birmingham, and Dublin.[70] It was the period's most successful drama about China after Murphy's *Orphan*, though it has received virtually no critical discussion. William Appleton judges that it transformed China from "an exotic land of wonder to a provincial empire eager to clasp the British constitution to its breast."[71]

The noted Italian composer Domenico Corri supplied the music for the opera, imitating the style of each country it featured. Corri's idea was to have an opera "wherein the national melody of various kingdoms might be effectually introduced, and the progress of music traced, commencing in China, and terminating in England." The production boasted "exquisite scenery."[72] The leading characters of the drama are Chinese, and China is depicted as a sophisticated civilization in comparison to that of Islamic Turkey and Catholic Italy. The production was an all-star performance. Robert William Elliston, the theater's leading man, played the role of the prince Zaphimiri. Elliston was much admired by Byron and a favorite of Jane Austen. She had seen him perform at the Orchard Street Theatre Royal in Bath, where he was known as "best Elliston" or the "fortnightly actor" due to his being loaned out once a fortnight to the London playhouses. One of his noted roles was Frederick in Kotzebue's *Lover's Vows*, the play that Mary Crawford persuades Edmund Bertram to perform in *Mansfield Park*. Austen saw him perform at Drury Lane in another oriental piece, the melodrama *Nourjahad*, in March 1814, though there is no evidence that she saw him in *The Travellers*.[73] The performance also boasted two famous singers. Koyan, Zaphimiri's friend, was played by John Braham, well known for his strong Jewish identity off and on stage, and the marchioness by his partner, the celebrated Italian opera soprano,

Anna Selina Storace, who had previously worked with both Salieri and Mozart in Venice.[74] The British comic actor Charles Matthews performed the part of the old Chinese gardener, Delvo. The drama features the familiar lower-class characters: the comic stage Irishman, O' Gallagher; and the British Tar, Ben Bunting.[75] These national stereotypes serve to forge the identity of the British.

In particular, the trusty Irish servant O' Gallagher is used to voice strong British sentiments and yet act as the butt of comedy. A subject of "England's eldest daughter," O'Gallagher was played by John Henry (Jack) Johnstone, the most popular contemporary performer of Irish roles, O'Gallagher is defined by his plangent homesickness for his romanticized native soil:

Let me but once more get into the land of nature—full grown shoes, and slender noses—and if ever I languish for little feet—pencilled eyebrows, and snouts of putty, may I be married to a Nankeen Beaker, and never taste the comforts of an Irish wedding.[76]

Proud of his birthright of "freedom" yet now within the fold of the political Union with England and Scotland, O'Gallagher is portrayed as profoundly loyal. In his office of translator he makes mistranslations for comic effect, but also, in doing so, punctuates the pomposity of the Turkish court.[77] Naturally bellicose, O'Gallagher informs the Turk that English valor is "employed to thrash the common enemy of mankind, and drub usurping tyrants, wherever they find them, all the world over— from Constantinople to Carrickamoss!" (26). O'Gallagher presumably refers to Carrickfergus, County Antrim, where the leader of the United Irishmen, Henry Joy McCracken, was captured. Yet this threat is never deployed against China, which seeks to learn from and not confront the British. O' Gallagher's Irishness is shown to belong to what Bratton describes as "the larger imperial identity instead of standing in opposition to it."[78] Certainly the cast of this play, written by an Irish writer with music by an Italian composer, contained a cosmopolitan group of actors, yet its purpose was to reinforce a notion of Britishness.

Adopting themes of virtue and commerce, as explored in Murphy's *Orphan*, yet in a lighter Romantic context, Cherry's drama reverses the flow of travel and commerce, as the Chinese now come to Britain to import British notions of morality and freedom into China, rather than Britons importing Confucian morality. China and Britain are the twin loci of virtue and probity in a world otherwise meshed in luxury, sexual desire, and political corruption. The drama presents no stark orientalist binaries but a range of characters encompassing the Chinese court, the court of Turkey, Italian aristocrats, the Royal Navy, and a stage Irishman. British and Chinese are presented as virtuous and sympathetic in contrast to the political and cruel despotism of Turkey (and its harem), and the sexual jealousy and violence of the Italians. Koran, the companion of the Prince of China, and his sister, Celinda, who is in love with the prince, are the twin children of Mindora and a shipwrecked British seaman, later revealed to be Admiral Lord Hawser. In both Turkey and Italy, the Prince is the object of intense female desire from a Christian slave, Safie, and an Italian marchioness.

Zaphimiri, named after Murphy's orphan, is a virtuous man who has "learnt to view the world as my country, mankind my brothers; and no proud distinction know, but what proceeds from vice and virtue" (3). His companion Koyan describes him as "young, – susceptible" with "a yielding heart, – condescending and humble as the shepherd boy that feeds his flock upon the mountain side" (8). Koyan has been elevated to the court from his obscure birth by a benevolent emperor who "rates not the merit of his subjects by their birth; but with a father's tender care, extends his fostering hand to modest worth and unassuming genius" (7). The emperor is presented not as an oriental despot, susceptible to a British thrashing, but as a truly enlightened ruler who has carried out his duty and fulfilled his "sacred trust" to make his subjects happy. He seeks to prepare his heir to rule with "mild sway," hence his wish to send Zaphimiri to England to "scan those laws which wondering nations silently admire, and envy what they cannot emulate" (8). Zaphimiri is to be a reformer, gleaning from other states what "might give strength and vigour" to the Chinese constitution, and empowered to "prune the excrescent branches of our legislature" (15). Portrayed more like a constitutional monarch than an oriental ruler, the emperor seeks to learn from British modernity. Unlike Turkey, China has no harem, and is presented as a virtuous and highly civilized nation. There Zaphimiri is imprisoned by the vizier for attempting to free a beautiful Christian female slave. In Italy the Duke seeks to assassinate him out of sexual jealousy when he becomes the object of the marchioness's desire (herself the object of Koyan's desire). She describes him as "not a bit like the Chinese figures that adorn our chimney-pieces ... more like a modern model of his country's porcelain, useful as well as ornamental" (33). The marchioness's conflation of commerce and desire signals a move away from the eighteenth-century chinoiserie ornamentalism towards the Romantic Sinology conception of China, stressing its modernity and its "uses," be they erotic or financial. Zaphimiri's availability, both sexual and economic, is premised on his physical presence in Europe.

The drama concludes with the restoration of Mindora to Admiral Hawser, the Chinese mother and British father of Koyan and Celinda, and the betrothal of Celinda to Zaphimiri. The "feeling heart" of British sentimentalism has humanized the stoic Chinese virtue of Zaphimiri, as he discovers in the British constitution the golden mean of his philosophy:

The study of your laws, your policy in peace, wisdom in war, your skill in arts and arms, shall be the subjects of my strong inquiry; and, if my native land hereafter should attain pre-eminence amongst the nations of the east, let it be recorded in its future annals, she owes her boasted glory to a firm endeavour to emulate that envied code of golden ethics, which form the basis of a British constitution. (58)

Cherry's optimistic drama, the most popular version of China in the period, stresses friendship, collaboration, and co-operation, a far cry from the idiosyncratic paranoid visions of De Quincey's *Confessions*.

CONTEMPORARY QING CHINA AND ROMANTIC DRAMA

While China remained the subject of escapist spectacles throughout the century, there was also a countervailing tendency in which popular drama responded more intimately to the new currents in British understandings of China as political and commercial forces brought the two empires closer in the popular mind. Some dramas share with the works of Romantic Sinology a curiosity about contemporary Qing China, rather than with the ancient classicized world of Confucian ethics presented in Murphy's *Orphan*. The popular impact of Romantic Sinology begins to appear as early as 1797 when *Harlequin and Quixotte; or, the Magic Arm* was performed at Covent Garden. This pantomime begins in a Peruvian temple and features the attempts of an injured Inca magician to obtain the hand in marriage of the daughter of his Spanish oppressor for his son, who is transformed into Harlequin and guarded by a "Magic Arm." After a series of colorful adventures involving a visit to England, a contemporary warehouse of the East India Company is transformed into a "picturesque Chinese apartment," thus making the crucial geographic and spatial link between commerce and China. Harlequin and his Columbine are now reunited, visit the Great Wall of China, and view the reception of "a British Embassy to China," which consists in a "Chinese and European Procession; with the Exchange of Presents in the Grand hall of Audience," once again the primal scene of British and Chinese encounter, but now rewritten as comedy, not tragedy, in which the Chinese kiss the presents of the British rather than criticize them. In the joyous choric song of the Lascar sailor:

> Legates, Mandarines, great party,
> Give de Englis welcome hearty;
> Kiss de presents dat dem bring:
> Roguish eyes so gay be glancing,
> Features smiles and hearts be dancing,

After an encounter with a Chinese magician, the comic finale looks forward optimistically to a brave new world of co-operation between China and Britain, "The sons of Britain your attention claim In Chinese hearts they 'grave their Country's fame."[79] In this pantomime, China and Britain, commerce and diplomacy, are clearly linked. In 1797, on the stage of the Theatre Royal, Covent Garden, in this replaying of the famous reception scene, the future of Chinese and British relations appeared to be rosy and no kowtows are demanded nor performed.

Edward Topham's comedy, *Bonds without Judgment; or, The Loves of Bengal* of 1787 features two Chinese characters, named Japan and Nankeen, who have a dominant role in a very topical drama about single English ladies traveling to Bengal in search of wealthy husbands in post-Hastings India. These two characters, in effect, manage the business of the Company, and easily manipulate their British masters, as Nankeen claims ironically: "An't I the Company's Officer at Calcutta here?"[80] Japan is the servant of Colonel Fury, whom he effortlessly outwits. Presenting petitions to the Colonel, the Machiavellian Japan makes the all the important decisions for the Company in Bengal. In Chapter 2 the presence of Chinese people in Bengal and their crucial but unacknowledged contribution to the development of Romantic Sinology was discussed. Topham's play indicates that this was at some level understood in the metropolis. The young British woman, Sophy, newly arrived at Bengal, exclaims to the Chinese Nankeen:

SOPHY: But Sir, why so expeditious! Besides, with Submission to the Sun here, I
    am not overfond of the Complexions of this Country: black & yellow are
    the reigning Colors I see, Mr Nankeen.
NANK: Psha! black or white makes no difference. (12)

Sophy here, as Worrall points out, "strikingly fails to register a European presence on the Calcutta quayside," and Nankeen dismisses both black and white as irrelevant.[81] Unusually, for this period, Sophy describes Chinese skin color as "yellow."[82] *Bonds without Judgment* thus presents the emerging alternative to the exotic chinoiserie spectacle of China, in which Chinese people are presented as intelligent, practical, shrewd, and, if anything, superior in intelligence and policy to British and native subjects. Allied with the classical comic tradition of the dominant servant or slave, here Japan and Nankeen, the presence of China in the eighteenth-century world economy is tellingly re-enacted at the micro-level of Topham's farce.

In 1822 two dramatic pieces were performed which demonstrate a more detailed awareness of Britain's political and economic relationship with Asia. In July 1822 the Coburg Theatre in Lambeth produced *Disputes in China; or, Harlequin and the Hong Merchants*. The artist Clarkson Stanfield, who had visited Canton in 1815, was employed to paint the scenes for the pantomime. Although the libretto for the piece is lost, it is recorded that the scenery, "painted from views of China by Stanfield," included a view of the Whampoa river and that Grimaldi "affected to astonish John China-man with his song of 'Hot Codlins.'"[83] From the title of this pantomime we can conclude that China no longer simply signified a chinoiserie oriental fantasy, but a land of commercial significance and opportunity where disputes over trade between British and Chinese merchants were taking place, and that this meant something to a popular audience: a land where "Hot Codlins" is now sung.

The dynamics of colonialism are explored more seriously in George Colman's substantial musical melodrama *The Law of Java*, first performed on May 11 at the Theatre Royal Covent Garden, also in 1822. Although ostensibly set in Java, it clearly alludes to the kowtow controversy of the Macartney and Amherst embassies and the politics of the English East India Company.[84] It features the legendary poisonous upas tree and is set against the backdrop of early eighteenth-century Java involving characters of the royal court of Mataram, a father and son from Makassar, Dutch East India Company officers (VOC), and soldiers and a would-be travel writer from Oxford, Mr Anarcharsis Pengoose. In its time the play was highly influential, and was responsible for the popularization of the myth of the upas tree which poisons all around it for miles. In the drama, the emperor of Java has kidnapped the young and beautiful Zaide for his harem. Her husband, Parbaya, is caught attempting to rescue her and sentenced to death by the emperor. Under an ancient "law of Java," his only chance of reprieve is to attempt a visit the upas tree and return with its poison. This is virtually a death sentence, as the tree's deadly fumes famously will kill any living thing approaching it. Parbaya, however, agrees to undertake the quest, but before he nears the tree another returning convict already bearing the poison drops down dead in front of him. He is thus able to take this poison and return to the imperial court, where his death sentence is suspended at the insistence of the high priest, and is finally reunited with Zaide. Frequently, colonial melodramas, as Heidi J. Holder has argued, turn on the application or misapplication of the law of "the uncivilized heathen" with the concomitant assertion (actual or imagined) of a constitutional British law.[85]

The play depicts the VOC as completely unscrupulous and rapacious, insinuating itself into power by unmanly fawning and flattery of the despotic Javan emperor. The young Dutch ingénue Hans Gayvelt refuses to participate in the game of his uncle, the Dutch commander Major Van Glozen, "to embroil a parcel of poor half-savages, in return for their hospitality,—to crawl at their feet, while I am fettering their hands."[86] It is clear that Colman's depiction of the strategies of the Dutch to establish themselves at Java, then to set the various kingdoms against each other to achieve its own rule, is a satire on the tactics of the British Company in Bengal, disguised to avoid the censure of the current examiner of plays, a role that Colman would succeed to in 1824.

Colman's version of the primal scene of encounter of European prostration before the oriental despot leads not to slavery, but power over him and his people. Van Glozen thus presents himself at court, enthusiastically performing a full prostration, much to the embarrassment of Hans:

> VAN GLOZ: Hail mighty Emperor!
>   Sapient as powerful, and good as great,
>   I kiss your garment's hem? (*prostrates himself.*)
> HANS: (*aside.*) Oh, curse his cringing!
> EMPEROR: Once, and again, I greet you; for your sword
>   Defend me, while I profit by your counsel;
>   And double service claims a double welcome.
> HANS: (*aside.*) Yes, – Nunk's a double dealer, that is certain.
>   … And he'll run
>   Your ship aground, to cheat you of the cargo.
>
>   (p. 19)

The kowtow becomes a means of entangling the Javan emperor in Dutch colonial intrigues and disempowering the native. Hans, however, refuses to undertake the full prostration, but performs the action in "his own manner" by going down on one knee only, in the manner of Macartney. His behavior shocks both his uncle and the emperor. After all, the audience knows that the Dutch in the person of Ambassador van Braam

Houckgeest had no problem with performing the full kowtow before the Qing emperor in 1795, humiliating themselves and becoming a laughing stock into the bargain:

> HANS: I shall do it in my own way. (*apart.*)
> *A little dumb show here, between the Uncle & Nephew.*
> *HANS kneels on one knee to the Emperor.*
> VAN GLOZ: (*While Hans is kneeling.*)
> My nephew, Sir, is raw,
> Unused to forms at Court; and somewhat daunted
> In so august a presence.
> EMPEROR: Rise, young man (*HANS rises.*)
> Your Uncle's credit with me, is your passport
> To my protection; – and we must advance you.
> VAN GLOZ: (*apart.*)
> Bow – bow again: – Confound him, he's as stiff
> As a Dutch kitchen-poker!
> EMPEROR: In due time
> Your judgement will be ripen'd;—Say, – if, then,
> I should require your counsel, would you give it
> With a true heart?
> HANS: That duty I should owe
> To my own honor, Sir:
>
> (pp. 20–21)

In Colman's Java, the dynamics of the kowtow are played out once more. The register of Hans's manliness and honesty is his refusal to prostrate himself and to bend before an eastern potentate. Like Byron's Manfred and Don Juan, he remains "as stiff as a Dutch kitchen-poker" in front of Eastern tyranny. The emperor is presented as a stereotypically cruel and corrupt Asian despot who keeps his harem jealously and engages in slavery. A sympathetic Van Glozen refuses to intervene to aid Parbaya at his nephew's request, pleading in justification the inadvisability of so doing: "How am I to persuade a barbarian out of his revenge for an amorous disappointment? I might as well invite a Hyaena to drink tea" (p. 36). Only the manly British drink tea (from China) and forgo revenge. In the courts and swamps of Java the now familiar story of the Macartney kowtow and its refusal is enacted once again in Colman's popular melodrama. The east is a place of despotism and tyranny, a place of extremes of human behavior. As Van Glozen comically puts it, "everything is in the extreme of the luxurious and the horrible; – all sunshine and earthquakes, – wealth and volcanoes: – pine-apples in the hedge, and serpents under 'em; – sultans, slavery, groves, tigers, beauties, and bow strings!—Oh, Fortune! send me home, to Holland, with riches, and let me enjoy them in elegance, by the side of a ditch, with the tranquillity of a Dutchman!" (85).

From the 1820s onward, then, it is notable that popular drama is more willing to engage with the contemporary picture of China and specific historical details, delivered by the Romantic Sinology. In December 1832 the Coburg's *Harlequin and the Royal Ram; or, The Brazen Dragon* presented a diorama with three Chinese scenes, "a pictorial tour of the Canton River Town and Port of Macao," "Kian Ho, Sung Si, and Wampu, with the effect of moon light on the mountains," and the city of Canton in which "is portrayed the terrific and alarming occurrence, the destruction of the European factories during the Great Fire at Canton."[87] Such dramas about China become more usual after the first Anglo-Chinese War, when a harder line on China replaces the ambiguities and ambivalences of Romantic Sinology. China remains a frequently used as a backdrop for Romantic comedy, as in the gentle farce *The Chinese Exhibition or the Feast of Lanterns* at the Strand Theatre in December 1844. Yet jingoistic dramas about China were on the increase, such as C. A. Somerset's *Wars in China or the Battles of Chighae and Amoy*, performed at the Astley Theatre in 1844. Yet even here, the melodramatic villain's part is accorded, not to a Chinese, but to a treacherous and lustful Malay. Somerset's Chinese drama is unusual in making an attempt to represent recent history including versions of the British commander, Sir Henry Pottinger, and his Chinese counterpart, Commissioner Lin Zexu, who "by command of his celestial majesty" has "come to exterminate both root & branch, the barbarian tribe, who from a distant land have braved the Ocean for no purpose than to insult and trample on our own laws."[88] Of course, Lin was commissioned by the Daoguang emperor in 1830 to suppress the illegal opium trade and promote legal commerce rather than to exterminate Europeans and is considered by many contemporary Chinese as a role for moral governance.[89]

In the latter half of the century such dramas were increasingly used to educate a British public "in the business of Empire."[90] Yet the leading idea of China on the stage in the Romantic period is one of two world empires, both civilized, ruled by brother monarchs and engaged in an exchange of goods and ideas, not so far away, in fact, from the rhetoric of rational civility featured in Macartney's embassy. With the turn from tragedy to comedy on the Romantic stage, China, in such dramas as *The Traveller* and pantomimes as *The Magic Arm*, is figured as a place of opportunity and collaboration as the empire comes closer to Britain as a major trading partner. Romantic Sinology, born from mutual encounter and negoti-ation, is deployed in its more positive aspects. Certainly, from the drama of the period, we do not see anticipations of the conflicts of the late 1830s. There was nothing inevitable about those later conflicts, and co-operation and negotiation between the two empires seemed viable options through-out the period in the minds of most Britons.

Notes

INTRODUCTION

1 Hayot, *Hypothetical Mandarin*; Porter, *Chinese Taste*; Yang, *Performing China*.
2 Lovejoy, "The Chinese Origin," pp. 99–135.
3 Ballaster, *Fabulous Orients*; Markley, *Far East and the English Imagination*.
4 Porter, *Chinese Taste*, p. 3 and "Sinicizing Early Modernity," 304.
5 The literature on this subject is substantial; for an introduction see Hayot, *Hypothetical Mandarin*, pp. 172–206, 183n.
6 Jacques, *When China Rules the World*; Callahan, *China the Pessoptimist Nation*.
7 Cohen, *Discovering History in China*.
8 Colley, *Britons: Forging the Nation* and *Captives*; Jensen, *Manufacturing Confucius*.
9 Raj, *Relocating Modern Science*.
10 Pratt, *Imperial Eyes*, pp. 1–14, 135.
11 See Casanova, *The World Republic in Letters*; Damrosch, *What is World Literature?*; Morretti, *Graphs, Maps, Trees*; Zhou and Tong, "Comparative Literature in China," in Chan, pp. 341–57.
12 Giradot, *The Victorian Translation*; Pfister, *Striving For "the Whole Duty Of Man"*.
13 Liu (ed.), "Introduction," *Tokens of Exchange*, p. 2.
14 Hayot, Saussy, and Yao (eds.), *Sinographies*, p. vii.
15 Saussy, *The Problem of a Chinese Aesthetic* and *Great Walls of Discourse*. The issues of modernism is discussed by Hayot, *Hypothetical Mandarin*, pp. 172–206. For an excellent discussion of the eighteenth-century European understanding of the Chinese language, see Porter, *Ideographa*, pp. 78–132.
16 Chan, "Translation, Transmission, and Travel," in *One into Many*, pp. 321–39. See also Liu, *Translingual Practice*, pp. 1–42.
17 See Niranjana, *Siting Translation*, and St. André, "Modern Translation Theory and Past Translation Practice," in Chan (ed.), *One into Many*, pp. 39–66.

18　Venuti, *The Translator's Invisibility*, pp. 99–186; St. André, "The Development of British Sinology and Changes in Translation Practice," 3–42.

19　Wang, *Globalization and Cultural Translation*, p. 23; see also Wang, "Orientalism versus Occidentalism?", pp. 57–67, and the essays collected in Wang and Yifeng (eds.), *Translation, Globalisation and Localisation*.

20　Chen, *Occidentalism*.

21　Wang, *Anglo-Chinese Encounters Since 1800*, pp. 43–74, 107–36.

22　Chang, *Britain's Chinese Eye*, pp. 116–18; Bickers, *The Scramble for China*, p. 88.

23　Lovell, *The Opium War*; Bickers, *Scramble for China*, p. 88.

24　Older general studies include: Appleton, *A Cycle of Cathay*; Dawson, *The Chinese Chameleon*; Mackerras, *Western Images of China*; Spence, *The Chan's Great Continent*.

25　Hancock, *Robert Morrison*.

26　Liu, "Robinson Crusoe's Earthenware Pot," 728–57; Porter, "Sinicizing Early Modernity," 304.

27　Markley (ed.), "China and the Making of Global Modernity." See also Markley (ed.), "Europe and East Asia in the Eighteenth Century."

28　Yang, *Performing China*, pp. 4–5, 10, 184–92.

29　Markley (ed.), "China and the Making of Global Modernity"; Tao, *Drawing the Dragon*.

30　Hayot, *Hypothetical Mandarin*, pp. 8–10, 95.

31　Porter, "Sinicizing Early Modernity," 305.

32　*Ibid.*, p. 10.

33　The first two novels in Ghosh's trilogy, *Sea of Poppies* (2008) and *River of Smoke* (2011), have so far been published.

34　Davis, *The Chinese* (1836), 2.432–36

35　Barrell, *The Infection of Thomas De Quincey*; Leask, *British Romantic*; Sudan, *Fair Exotics*.

36　Kitson, *Romantic Literature, Race and Colonial Encounter*; Keevak, *Becoming Yellow*.

37　Porter, *Ideographia Chinese Taste*, pp. 134–35.

38　Leask, *British Romantic Writers* and *Curiosity and the Aesthetics of Travel Writing*; Nussbaum (ed.), *The Global Eighteenth Century* and *Torrid Zones: Maternity, Sexuality, and Empire in Eighteenth-Century English Narratives*; Aravamudan, *Tropicopolitans* and *Enlightenment Orientalism*; Makdisi, *Romantic Imperialism*; Kaul, *Poems of Nation* and *Eighteenth-Century Literature and Postcolonial Studies*; Wahrman, *The Making of the Modern Self*; Carey and L. Festa (eds.), *The Postcolonial Enlightenment*; Wilson (ed.), *A New Imperial History* and *This Island Race*.

39　Said, *Orientalism*.

40　Aravamudan, *Enlightenment Orientalism*, pp. 3, 5, 8, 74, 202; see Dirlik, "Chinese History and the Question of Orientalism," 96–118; and Fung, "Orientalist Knowledge."

41　Hevia, *Cherishing Men From Afar* and *English Lessons*; Perdue, *China Marches West*; Elliot, *The Manchu Way*; Hostetler, *Qing Colonial Enterprise*; Rowe, *China's Last Empire*.

42 Hillemann, *Asian Empire*; Wills Jr. (ed.), *China and Maritime Europe 1500–1800*; Van Dyke, *Canton Trade*.

43 Koerner, *Linnaeus*, p. 136.

44 Lin, *China Upside Down*.

45 Frank, *ReOrient* p. 52; Pomeranz, *The Great Divergence*.

46 Smith, *Wealth of Nations*, ed. R. H. Campbell and A. S. Skinner, 2.202.

47 Arrighi, *Adam Smith in Beijing*, pp. 321, 92–93, 68, 1–99, 309–50.

48 Hobson, *Eastern Origins*, p. 73.

49 Markley, *Far East*, pp. 75, 110.

50 Timothy Brook located Ming and Qing China at the centre of this global economy, and R. Bin Wong claimed that late Qing imperial China outperformed the "modern" European economies in certain areas. Brook, *Confusions of Pleasure*; Wong, *China Transformed*.

51 Chakrabarty, *Provincializing Europe*, pp. 27–28.

52 Latour, *Science In Action* and *We Have Never Been Modern*.

53 Raj, *Relocating Modern Science*; Sudan, "Mud, Mortar."

54 Hostetler, *Qing Colonial Enterprise*; Fan, *British Naturalists in Qing China*.

55 Hevia, *English Lessons*; Liu, *Clash of Civilizations*.

56 Pratt, *Imperial Eyes*, p. 135.

57 Zhang, *Unexpected Affinities*, p. 19.

58 *Ibid.*

1 THOMAS PERCY AND THE FORGING OF ROMANTIC CHINA

1 See Minimika, *The Chinese Rites Controversy*, and Mungello (ed.), *The Chinese Rites Controversy*. For an excellent and authoritative recent history, see Brockey, *Journey to the East*. For accounts of the Rites controversy, see Witek, "Catholic Missions and the Expansion of Christianity, 1644–c.1800," in *China and Maritime Europe 1500–1800: Trade, Settlement, Diplomacy and Missions*, ed. John E. Wills Jr., pp. 135–82; Mungello, *Curious Land*, pp. 77–105; Porter, *Ideographia*, pp. 108–32; Rowbotham, *Missionary and Mandarin*.

2 Porter, *Ideographia*, especially chapter 2.

3 *The World*, 205 (1756), 255–61.

4 Standard accounts of this history include: Appleton, *A Cycle of Cathay*; Dawson, *The Chinese Chameleon*; Cameron, *Barbarians & Mandarins*; Ch'en, *China and the West*; Marshall and Williams, *The Great Map of Mankind*; Mackerras, *Western Images of China*; Ching and Oxtoby (eds.), *Discovering China*; Spence, *The Chan's Great Continent*; and Gelber, *The Dragon and the Foreign Devils*.

5 Jensen, *Manufacturing Confucius*. For European sinology, see Needham and Harbsmeier, *Science and Civilisation in China*, pp. 8–25 and Zurndorfer, *China Bibliography*, pp. 4–45; For accounts of the history of Jesuit and European sinology see Mungello, *Curious Land*, and Lundbaek, *T.S. Bayer*; *Joseph de Prémare*; and "The Establishment of European Sinology 1801–1815," in *The Chinese Rites Controversy*, ed. Mungello, pp. 129–45; Standaert,

Handbook of Christianity in China. See also Wilson and Cayley (eds.), *Europe Studies China*. For Ricci, see Young, *East–West Synthesis*; Porter, *Ideographia*, pp. 80–132; and Po-Chia Hsia, *A Jesuit in the Forbidden City*. For impact of Confucian ideas on Europe, see Lach, *Asia in the Making of Europe* and *China in the Eyes of Europe*; Clarke, *Oriental Enlightenment*; and Rowbotham, "The impact of Confucianism," 224–42. See also Lundbaek, "The First Translation from a Confucian Classic in Europe," 1–11. For a Saidian reading of the orientalising processes of Western sinology, see Chan, *Orientalism in Sinology*.

6 Originally, Ricci and his collaborator Ruggieri adopted the style and dress of Buddhist monks in an effort to assimilate into China. See Po-Chia Hsia, *Jesuit in the Forbidden City*, pp. 90–96, 135–40; Jensen, *Manufacturing Confucianism*, pp. 43–48, 55.

7 Quoted in Rule, *K'ung-tzu or CONFUCIUS?*, p. 1.

8 Po-hia Hsia, *A Jesuit in the Forbidden City*, p. 225; Peterson, "Learning from Heaven: the Introduction of Christianity and Other Western Religions into Late Ming China," in *China and Maritime Europe*, ed. Wills, Jr., pp. 78–134; Gernet, *China and the Christian Impact*.

9 Barrett, "Chinese Religion in English Guise," 514.

10 Mungello, *The Great Encounter*, p. 62; and "Sinological Torque", 123–41.

11 The conversion of ordinary Chinese was still very much a part of the mission, as Brockey (*Journey to the East*) demonstrates. By 1800 there were *c.* 300,000 Chinese Catholic Christians.

12 Porter, *Ideographia*, p. 81.

13 *Les Journal des Savans* 40 (Dec. 6, 1700), pp. 472–73; quoted in Porter, *Ideographia*, p. 111.

14 Longxi, *Mighty Opposites*, pp. 109, 84–116.

15 Cranmer-Byng, "First English Sinologists," pp. 247–60.

16 For St. André, Percy "was not a sinologist." See "Modern Translation Theory and Past Translation Practice," pp. 39–67 (48). Ballaster, *Fabulous Orients*, p. 241. The new and substantially growing critical literature on Percy and China includes: Porter, *Chinese Taste*, pp. 154–83; Watt, "Thomas Percy, China, and the Gothic," 95–109; Min, "Thomas Percy's *Chinese Miscellanies*," 307–24. Older studies include: Qian, "China in the English Literature of the Eighteenth Century," in Hsai (ed.), *The Vision of China*, pp. 117–21 (189); Ch'en, "Thomas Percy and his Chinese Studies," in *Visions of China*, ed. Hsia, pp. 301–24; Barry, "A Note on the Early Literary Relations," 125; Powell, "*Hau Kiou Choaan*," 446–55; Ogburn, "The Wilkinson MSS and Percy's Chinese Books," 30–36; and Fan, "Percy's *Hau Kiou Choann*," 125.

17 Min, "Percy's *Chinese Miscellanies*," 308; St. André, "Modern Translation Theory," pp. 47–48.

18 Porter, *Chinese Taste*, pp. 154–55.

19 McMahon, *Casualty and Containment*, pp. 131–32; Lu, *A Brief History*, pp. 245–56, 251–53; Huang, *Desire and Fictional Narrative*, p. 229; Mair

(ed.), *The Columbia History*, pp. 666–67; Hegel, *The Novel in Seventeenth Century China*; Levy and Ninenhauser, *Chinese Literature*; Cheung, *Theme of Chastity*; Liu, *Chinese Popular Fiction*.

20 See Cheung, *Theme of Chastity*, p. 29.

21 Davis, *Thomas Percy a Scholar-Critic*, 69–71; and Groom, *The Making of Percy's* Reliques, pp. 209–11.

22 See Chen, "Thomas Percy," 310–24; St. André, "Modern Translation Theory"; Cheung, "The *Haoqiu zhuan*," in Chan (ed.), *One into Many*, pp. 29–38.

23 Chen, "Percy's Chinese Studies," pp. 310–24; Fan, "Percy and Du Halde," 326–29.

24 For Psalmanazar, see Keevak, *The Pretended Asian*.

25 The status of this second edition has been disputed by Powell, "*Hau Kiou Choaan*," 252, and Milner-Barry "A Further," 215, 217n. Both Qian, "China in the English Literature of the Eighteenth Century," and St. André, "Modern Translation," argue that it was published (42).

26 Powell, "*Hau Kiou Choaan*," 451–52; Min, "Percy's *Chinese Miscellanies*," 311–12, 320n.

27 Staunton, *Ta Tsing Leu Lee*, p. 107.

28 Morrison, *A View of China*, p. 120. See Lehner, "From Enlightenment to Sinology." Staunton gave similar advice in 1822; see Cheung, "*Haoqiu zhuan*," p. 30.

29 Cheung, "*Haoqiu zhuan*," pp. 29–37; St. André, "Modern Translation Theory," pp. 42–43; See also Wylie, *Notes on Chinese Literature*, p. xxiii.

30 St. André, "Modern Translation Theory," pp. 42–44.

31 Percy, *Hau Kiou Choaan*, 4.226. Further references to this edition are contained in the text and cited by volume and page number.

32 Huang, *Desire and Fictional Narrative*, pp. 206–35; McMahon, *Causality and Containment*, p. 131; Lu, *Brief History*, pp. 245–46, 251–53.

33 Davis pointed out that the Chinese possess neither pens nor penknives but write with brushes. Davis, *Hao Ch'iu Chuan*, 1.ix.

34 Levy, *Chinese Literature, Ancient and Classical*, p. 132.

35 Porter, *Chinese Taste*, p. 158.

36 Percy to Shenstone, June 2 (1761), and July 16 (1761). Quoted in Powell, "*Hau Kiou Choaan*," 449.

37 See St. André's "Modern Translation Theory" for a discussion of Saidian approaches to Percy and Davis's translations.

38 St. André, "Modern Translation Theory," p. 44.

39 Fan, "Percy's *Hau Kiou Choann*," p. 125; Porter, *Chinese Taste*.

40 Porter, *Ideographia*, pp. 90–93.

41 Thomas, *Colonialism's Culture*.

42 Porter, *Ideographia*, p. 16.

43 *Ibid.*, p. 76.

44 See Kitson, *Romantic Literature, Race, and Colonial Encounter*, pp. 143–213; and Keevak, *Becoming Yellow*.

45 Min, "Thomas Percy's *Chinese Miscellanies*," 317.

2 "A WONDERFUL STATELINESS": WILLIAM JONES, JOSHUA
MARSHMAN, AND THE BENGAL SCHOOL OF SINOLOGY

1 The most recent study of Jones is Franklin, *Orientalist Jones.*

2 Hevia, *Cherishing Men From Afar*, pp. 62–77; Jones knew Macartney when he was governor of Madras and later as part of Elizabeth Montagu's blue-stocking circle. Franklin, *Orientalist Jones*, pp. 8, 76. For Macartney's intellectual and social background, see Roebuck (ed.), *Macartney of Lissanoure.*

3 Jones, "On the Second Classical Book of the Chinese," in *Works of Sir William Jones* (1799), 1.101–2.

4 For Jones, see Fan, "William Jones's Chinese Studies," in Hsai (ed.), *Vision of China*, pp. 325–37; Waley, "Sir William Jones as Sinologue," 842; Cannon, *The Life and Mind of Oriental Jones*, pp. 318–19.

5 Shore, *Memoirs of William Jones*, pp. 78–79.

6 Fan, "William Jones's Chinese Studies," p. 326; Jones, *Letters*, 1.36, 36n.

7 Jones, *Letters*, 1.59–60.

8 Fan, "William Jones's Chinese Studies," pp. 277–328; Jones, *Works*, 2.350–51.

9 Jones, *Works*, 6.453.

10 Jones, *Works*, 1.158. Jones was given a 488-page "Chinese Alphabetical Dictionary with an Index of the Characters arranged under the 214 Keys." Cannon, *Life and Mind*, p. 319; Jones, *Works*, 13.416.

11 Jones, *Letters*, 1.79; 2.684. Fan, "William Jones's Chinese Studies," p. 328. For Chitqua, see Appleton, *Cycle of Cathay*, pp. 121–39; and Clarke, "Chitqua's English Adventure," 47–58. Chitqua appears in Johann Zoffany's celebrated portrait of the academicians. See Fenton, *School of Genius.*

12 Pan, *Sons of the Yellow Emperor*; Auerbach, *Race, Law and "The Chinese Puzzle*," p. 146; and Foxcroft, *The Making of Addiction*, p. 65.

13 Keevak, *Becoming Yellow*, pp. 66–69; *Anthropological Treatises of Blumenbach*, p. 119.

14 de Bruijn, "A Chinese Celebrity at Knole."

15 Weston, *Ly Tang*, p. 1.

16 The portrait of a Chinese man that is a part of the collection of John Hunter the anatomist, displayed in the Hunterian Museum and previously identified as Huang ("Quang-at-Tong") is now believed to be a portrait of Chitqua by John Hamilton Mortimer. Chaplin, "Putting a name to a face," 11–12.

17 Keevak, *Becoming Yellow*, pp. 66–69; Seng Ong, "Whang-y-Tong," 17; Clarke, "An Encounter with Chinese Music," 543–58.

18 Jones, "On the Second Classical Book of the Chinese," *Asiatick Researches* (1790), 2.203

19 Jones, *Works*, 1.100.

20 Huang Ya Dong's letter was printed in *Asiatick Researches* (1790), 2.204, as "A Letter to the President from a Young Chinese." See Jones, *Letters*, 2.684, 684n.

21 A small Chinese community in Bengal dates back to the 1770s and 1780s. In 1819 it was estimated at 414; see Chatterjee, "The Chinese Community in Calcutta," pp. 55–65.

22 Smith, "The Sing-Song Trade," 629–58; Pointon, "Dealer in Magic"; Vincent and Leopold, "James Cox"; Altick, *The Shows of London*, pp. 69–72.
23 See Needham, Wang, De Solla Price, *Heavenly Clockwork*, p. 150; Pagani, "*Eastern Magnificence and European Ingenuity*," pp. 100–24; Schaffer, "Enlightened Automata," pp. 126–68.
24 Eur MSS C864. W. Jones to [Charles Grant], Calcutta (Feb. 27, 1785). I am indebted to Michael Franklin for this reference.
25 Jones, *Letters*, 2.732–33.
26 *Asiatick Researches*, 2.203.
27 Franklin, "I burn with a desire of seeing Shiraz," pp. 749–57.
28 Jones, *Works*, 1.366–67.
29 *Ibid.*, 1.367.
30 Chan, *Chinese Philosophy*, p. 88. Percy's and Jones's translations of the ode are contained in Minford and Lau (eds.), *Anthology of Translations*, pp. 116–18. A modern translation is contained in *Book of Poetry*, trans Xu, pp. 55–56.
31 Jones, *Works*, 1.370; Chan, *Chinese Philosophy*, p. 92; *Book of Poetry*, pp. 6–7.
32 Barrow, *Travels in China*, p. 279.
33 Fan, "Jones's Chinese studies," p. 332.
34 Spence, *The Chan's Great Continent*, pp. 168–77; Qian, *Orientalism and Modernism* and *The Modernist Response to Chinese Art*.
35 Cranmer-Byng, "First English Sinologists," p. 249.
36 Jones, *Works* 1.96–97.
37 *Ibid.*, 1.101.
38 *Ibid.*, 1.97–107.
39 Jones, *Letters*, 1.59–60
40 The Catalogue of manuscripts and books gifted to the Royal Society by Jones includes several volumes of works by Confucius and the *Shijing* and *Lunyu* supplied by Huang, as well as an MS Chinese and Latin Dictionary. Jones, *Works*, 6.452–53.
41 Fan, "Jones's Chinese Studies," p. 326.
42 Jones, *Memoirs*, 1.177–78; see also 1.78–79; 163–65; 170–80, 487–9; Fan, "Jones's Chinese Studies," pp. 325–57.
43 Fan, "Jones's Chinese Studies," p. 327; Hillemann, *Asian Empire and British Knowledge*, pp. 58–60.
44 Jones, *Memoirs* 1.179.
45 Franklin, *Orientalist Jones*, p. 20.
46 *Diary and Letters of Madame D'Arblay*. 2.393–4.
47 Liu (ed.), "Introduction," in *Tokens of Exchange*, p. 1.
48 For the Serampore Mission, see Chatterjee, *William Carey and Serampore*; Frykenberg, *Christians and Missionaries in India*; Dasgupta, *The Bengal Renaissance*; Sivasundaram, "'A Christian Benares': Orientalism, Science and the Serampore Mission of Bengal."
49 See Latour, *Science in Action*, pp. 215–57.
50 Morrison held classes in Chinese at the London Oriental Institution in Barrett's Buildings between 1825 and 1828. See Barrett, *Singular Listlessness*.

For Serampore Chinese studies, see Marshman, *Proposals*; Cutts, "Chinese Studies in Bengal," 171–74. For the methods of printing used at Malacca, see Milne, *Retrospect*, pp. 129–30, 237–67.

51 See Stifler, "Language Students," 46–83.

52 Marshman, *Elements of Chinese Grammar*, pp. 119–20; Cutts, "Political Implications," 152–63; Hillemann, *Asian Empire and British Knowledge*, pp. 119–20.

53 Marshman, *Confucius*, pp. ii. Further references to this edition are cited in the text by page number.

54 John Clark Marshman, *Life and Times of Carey, Marshman and Ward*. 1.390–91.

55 Cutts, "Political Implications in Chinese studies," 152–63; Kopf, *British Orientalism and the Bengal Renaissance*, pp. 71–80.

56 Liu, *The Clash of Empires*, p. 169; Smith, *Chinese Christians*, pp. 52–54; Hanan, "Chinese Christian Literature," pp. 260–83. Marshman claimed that Lasser employed eight Chinese assistants in 1806. See Zetzsche, "The Missionary and the Chinese 'Helper,'" 5–20 and his *History of the Union Version*. Morrison, established at Guangzhou since 1807, sent Marshman a Chinese tutor in 1811. For Marshman's and Morrison's translations of the Bible and the resulting controversies, see Bridgeman, "Chinese Versions of the Bible," 249–60.

57 See Chatterjee, "The Chinese Community in Calcutta," pp. 59–60 (pp. 55–65).

58 Marshman, *Elements*, ii. Further references to this edition are cited in the text by page number. In a letter of 1806 he would claim that Lasser spoke Armenian, Portuguese, English, and Hindi fluently. Letter to Baptist Missionary Society August 20, 1806; quoted Zetzsche, "Chinese Helper," 16.

59 Marshman, *Elements*, i–iii. For Rodriguez and Manning, see Stifler, *Language Students*, 55–60.

60 For an account of this debate, see *Christian Researches* (1857); Zetzsche, *History of the Union Version*, pp. 45–58.

61 Marshman, *Confucius*, pp. xxxiii, 2. For the process of printing see John Clark Marshman, *The Life and Labours*, 1.388. Zhu Xi's *Sishu jizhu*, or the *Collected Annotations on the Four Books*, tends to be the main source for Marshman's interpretations.

62 It is not actually clear which other commentaries Marshman's team employed, but in addition to Zhu Xi's neo-Confucian gloss they appear to have consulted commentaries by Wang Su, Fan Ziyu, Yang Shi, and Zheng Xuan (Cheng Hsüan), as well as an unidentified "much more modern, as well as copious" commentary which "appears to be the work of several hands."

63 For an account of High Qing intellectual culture, see Naquin and Rawski, *Chinese Society in the Eighteenth Century*, pp. 55–94; Guy, *The Emperor's Four Treasuries*; and Rowe, *China's Last Empire*, pp. 81–89.

64 See Rowe, *Last Empire*, pp. 86–87; Gardner, *Zhu Xi's Reading of the Analects*.

65 Pfister, *Striving For "The Whole Duty Of Man,"* pp. 14–15.

66 Confucius, *Analects* (trans.), Lau, p. 63.

67 *Ibid.*, p. 63.

68 Chan, *Chinese Philosophy*, p. 22.

69 Chan, *Orientalism in Sinology*, pp. 13–15, 56–57; and Roger T. Ames, "Translating Chinese Philosophy," pp. 741–44.

70 Confucius, *Analects* (trans.), Lau, p. 69.

71 Legge, *Chinese Classics*, p. 130.

72 Confucius, *Analects* (trans.), Lau, p. 135.

73 Schott's plagiarism was exposed by Klaproth. See *Foreign Quarterly Review* 3 (1829), 690.

74 *Quarterly Review* 11 (1814), 336.

75 *Ibid.*, 336–37.

76 Chan, *Chinese Philosophy*, pp. 84–85; Fung, *Short History of Chinese Philosophy*, pp. 43–44.

77 Marshman, *Elements of Chinese Grammar*, pp. v, ii, xv. Further references to this edition are cited in the text by page number.

3   "THEY THOUGHT THAT JESUS AND CONFUCIUS WERE ALIKE": ROBERT MORRISON, MALACCA, AND THE MISSIONARY READING OF CHINA

1 Wang, *Anglo-Chinese Encounters*, p. 8.

2 Honey, *Incense at the Altar*, pp. 36–37.

3 See Hillemann, *Asian Empire*; St. André, "The Development of British Sinology," 3–42.

4 See Honey, *Incense at the Altar*, pp. v, 26, 167–77; Schafer, "What and How Is sinology?" 23–44.

5 Davis, *Chinese Novels*, pp. 5–6.

6 St. André, "Travelling Toward True Translation," 1–22; Barrett, "Chinese Religion," 509–33; Reinders, *Borrowed Gods*, p. 1; See also Cheung, *Christianity in Modern China*; and Xi, *Redeemed by Fire*.

7 Morrison, *Memoirs*, 1.512–3; Harrison, *Waiting for China*; Bassnett and Fairbank (eds.), *Christianity in China*.

8 Barrett, "A Singular listlessness," pp. 69–72; Twitchett, *Land Tenure and the Social Order*, pp. 3–4.

9 Staunton, *Memoirs*, pp. 206–9.

10 For Legge see Girardot, *Victorian Translation of China*; Pfister, *Striving for "The Whole Duty Of Man."*

11 Hevia, *English Lessons*, pp. 130, 130–35.

12 For Wade and Giles, see Hevia, *English Lessons*, pp. 125–57.

13 For Canton and the East India Company see Davis, *The Chinese* (1851), 1.56–33; 2, 100–125; Hunter, *The "Fan Kwae" at Canton*; Morse, *Chronicles*, especially volume 2; Pritchard, *Anglo-Chinese Relations*; Greenberg, *British Trade and the Opening of China*; Phillips, *The East India Company*; Wang, *Anglo-Chinese*

Encounters Since 1800, pp. 43–74, 107–36; Van Dyke, *The Canton Trade*; Bickers, *The Scramble for China*; Cranmer-Byng and Wills, Jr., "Trade and Diplomacy," pp. 222–51. For an evocative account of life in the factories, see Spence, *God's Chinese Son*, pp. 1–22.

14 See Fromer, "Deeply indebted to the Tea-Plant," 531–47.

15 Wakeman, "Canton Trade," pp. 162–212.

16 *Ibid.*, p. 173.

17 Rowe, *China's Last Empire*, pp. 141–44.

18 Hobson, *Eastern Origins*, p. 77.

19 Cranmer-Byng and Wills, Jr., "Trade and Diplomacy," p. 183. The literature on the tea trade is substantial. The following are especially important: Ukers, *All About Tea*; Forrest, *Tea for the British*; Chaudhuri, *Trading World of Asia*; Morse, *Chronicles*; Mui and Mui, *Management of Monopoly*; Walvin, *Fruits of Empire*; Gardella, *Harvesting the Mountains*; Bowen, "Tea, Tribute and the East India Company"; Moxham, *Tea: Addiction, Exploitation and Empire*; Fromer, *A Necessary Luxury*; Rose, *For All the Tea in China*; Ellis, *et al.*, *Tea and the Tea-Table*.

20 Ukers, *All About Tea*, 1.130; Gardella, *Harvesting the Mountains*.

21 Wakeman, "Canton Trade," p. 173.

22 Ellis, *et al.*, *Tea and the Tea Table*, 3.179.

23 *Ibid.*, 1.ix; *Ibid.*, 1.xix; 2.vii.

24 See Lin, *China Upside Down*.

25 Hayter's *Opium and the Romantic Imagination* remains the classic account. See also Booth, *Opium*; Berridge and Edwards, *Opium and the People*; Milligan, *Pleasures and Pains*, pp. 3–30; Dormandy, *Opium: Reality's Dark Dream*.

26 Wakeman, "Canton Trade," p. 172.

27 This account of the opium trade is derived from Wakeman, "The Canton Trade," pp. 163–212; Chang, *Commissioner Lin and the Opium War*, pp. 1–84; Fay, *Opium War*, pp. 1–53; Milligan, *Pleasures and Pains*, pp. 3–30; Cranmer-Byng and Wills, Jr., "Trade and Diplomacy," pp. 183–254; Zhuang, *"Tea, Silver, Opium and War"*; and Lovell, *Opium War*, pp. 17–38. See also Waley, *Opium War*; and Trocki, *Opium, Empire and the Global Political Economy*. The impact of the flow of silver bullion on China is discussed by Lin, *China Upside Down*. For opium and Chinese culture, see Zheng, *Social Life of Opium*.

28 Lovell, *Opium War*, p. 25.

29 Morrison, *Memoirs* 2.131.

30 Hancock, *Robert Morrison* p. 1; Barrett, *Singular Listlessness*, p. 63; Cranmer-Byng, "The First English Sinologists," pp. 247–60.

31 Hillemann, *Asian Empire*, pp. 34–105. For Canton and the East India Company see note 13.

32 See ODNB; Cuninghame, "Part of Two Letters to the Publisher from Mr. James Cunningham F.R.S. and Physician to the English at Chusan in China" (1707); Cunningham, "Observations During a Residence in the Island of

Chusan, in 1701," in Robert Kerr (ed.), *A General History and Collection of Voyages and Travels*, 9.549–62. Bretschneider, *History of European Botanical Discoveries in China*, 1.31–32; Cox, *Plant Hunting in China*, 39–42; Coulton (ed.), *Tea in Natural History and Medical Writing*, 10.87–89.

33 Ghosh, *River of Smoke*, pp. 129–31.

34 Morse, *Chronicles*, 1.301–5; 5.75–84; 4.317–20.

35 Stifler, "Language Students," 50.

36 See Van Dyke, *Canton Trade*, pp. 77–93; Clarke, "Chitqua's English Adventure," 47–58.

37 Van Dyke, *Canton Trade*, p. 81.

38 Staunton, *An Authentic Account*, 1.38.

39 Cranmer-Byng (ed.), *An Embassy to China*, p. 210.

40 Teele, *Through a Glass Darkly*, p. 44.

41 Davis, *The Chinese* (1851), 1.610–11; See Lundbaek, "Une grammaire espangnole de la langue chinoise au XVIIIe siècle," 259–69.

42 Needham and Harbsmeier, *Science and Civilisation in China*, 7.1, pp.16–17; Davis, *Chinese Miscellanies*, p. 53; Davis, *The Chinese*, 2.173.

43 Markham, *Narratives*, p. 42. Markham indicates that Manning sent a "long and interesting account of his expedition" to Marshman at Serampore, but this does not appear to have survived (p. clxii). Manning's Chinese dictionaries are held in the archives of the Royal Asiatic Society of which he became the Honorary Chinese Librarian. See Beckingham, "History of the Royal Asiatic Society, 1823–1973," in Simmonds and Digby (eds.), *The Royal Asiatic Society*, pp. 1–77.

44 Stifler, "Language Students," 56–57.

45 *Ibid.*, 67–69.

46 Morrison, *Horae Sinicae*, p. v.

47 Yong might also have tutored Thomas Manning about this time. Markham indicates that Manning was taught "with the aid of a Chinese" in London. Markham, *Narratives*, p. clx.

48 *Memoirs* 1.79, 80–81; Stifler, "Language Students," 58; Moseley, *Origin of the First Protestant Mission to China*, pp. 82–87; Hancock, *Robert Morrison*, pp. 25–27.

49 The MS is now attributed to Jean Bassett. Hancock, *Robert Morrison*, p. 22; Zetzsche, *History of the Union Version*, pp. 28ff.

50 Morrison, *Memoirs* 1.163, 168; Strandenaes, "Anonymous Bible Translations," in Baralden, Cann, and Dean (eds.), *Sowing the Word*, pp. 120–21; Hancock, *Robert Morrison*, p. 45.

51 Hanan, "Chinese Christian Literature," 270; Morrison, *Memoirs* 1.274.

52 For translating the Bible see, Hanan, "Chinese Christian Literature"; Strandenaes, "Anonymous Bible Translations," pp. 121–28; Zetzsche, "Missionary and the Chinese 'Helper,'" pp. 301–16.

53 Staunton, *Memoir*, 1.101.

54 Liu, *Translingual Practice*. See Shi, *The Lure of the Modern*, pp. 1–48; Liu, *Tokens of Exchange*, pp. 1–12.

55 See Stifler "Language Students," 63; and Hillemann, *Asian Empire*, pp. 56–60; Cohn, *Colonialism and the Forms of Knowledge*.
56 Morrison, *A View of China*, p. 121.
57 Morrison, *Memoirs* 2.381.
58 Porter, *Religion Versus Empire?*, pp. 15–38; For the London Missionary Society, see Wilson, *This Island Race*. For the history of the Protestant Missionaries in China, see Cohen, "Christian Missions and their Impact to 1900," in Fairbank (ed.), *The Cambridge History of China*, 10.1, *Part I*, pp. 543–90; Bays, *New History of Christianity in China*, pp. 41–65; Rubinstein, *Origins of the Anglo-American Missionary Enterprise*; Bassnett and Fairbank (eds.), *Christianity in China*; Bays (ed.), *Christianity in China*; Latourette, *A History of Christian Missions in China*; Uhalley, Jr., and Wu (eds.), *China and Christianity*. For Morrison, see Ride, *Robert Morrison*; Rubinstein, *Origins*, pp. 83–87, 92; Daily, "From Gosport to Canton".
59 Milne, *The Sacred Edict*.
60 Chang, "Converting Chinese Eyes," in Kerr (ed.), *A Century of Travels in China*.
61 Morrison, *Memoirs* 2.360; Milne, *Memoirs*, 2.152.
62 Gutzlaff, *Journal of Three Voyages*, p. 151.
63 Harrison, *Waiting for China*, p. 109; Porter, *Religion Versus Empire*, pp. 11, 116–17, 316–30; Hillemann, *Asian Empire*, pp. 64–75. See also Thorne, *Congregational Missions*, pp. 36–44, 73–79.
64 Morrison, *Memoirs*, 2.219.
65 Morrison, "The Missionary Rehearsal," in *A Parting Memorial*, p. 106.
66 Morrison, *Memoirs*, 1.136.
67 For Morrison's relationship with the EIC see Stifler, "Language Students."
68 Hancock, *Robert Morrison*, pp. 31–50.
69 Morrison, *Memoirs*, 2.542–46.
70 Quoted in Hibbert, *The Dragon Wakes*, p. 84. Morrison, *Memoirs*, 2.360–61, 203; See Rubinstein, "The Wars They Wanted," 271–82; Lovell, *The Opium War*, pp. 4–5.
71 Harrison, *Waiting for China*, p. 43.
72 P.P. [Peter Perring] Thoms invented a new process of printing Chinese characters in moveable metal type for the *Dictionary*. He translated the first Chinese verse novel into English as *Hwa Tsëen. A Chinese Tale*. See Harrison, *Waiting for China*, p. 57; Morrison, *Parting Memorial*, p. 110; Milne, *A Retrospect of the First Ten Years*, p. 130; and Teele, *Through a Glass Darkly*, pp. 50–51.
73 Hancock, *Robert Morrison*, pp. 214–17, 236–37.
74 Morrison, *Memoirs*, 1.61.
75 Morrison, *Parting Memorial*, p. 199.
76 *Ibid.*, p. 170
77 Quoted in Harrison, *Waiting for China*, p. i.
78 Reinders, *Borrowed Gods*, pp. 23–24; Barrett, "Chinese Religion," p. 515
79 Morrison, *A View of China*, p. 113.
80 Giradot, *Victorian Translation of China*.
81 Hevia, *English Lessons*.

82 Chan, *Orientalism in Sinology*, pp. 10–14.

83 Morrison, *Memoirs*, 1.353.

84 *Ibid.*, 1.228.

85 *Ibid.*, 1.207–08.

86 *Ibid.*, 1.232.

87 *Ibid.*, 1.231.

88 *Ibid.*, 1.229.

89 Morrison, *View*, p. 124.

90 Morrison, *Chinese Miscellany*, p. 34.

91 *Ibid.*, p. 40.

92 *Ibid.*, pp. 41–42.

93 Morrison, *Memoirs*, 1.274.

94 *Indo-Chinese Gleaner* (July 9, 1819), 149. Scholars have generally argued that Chinese civilization does not possess an originating or creation myth. See Mote, *The Intellectual Foundations of China*.

95 Milne, *Retrospect*, pp. 25–27.

96 Morrison, *Chinese Miscellany*, p. 43.

97 *Indo-Chinese Gleaner* (July 9, 1819), 145.

98 In *Horae Sinicae*, Morrison published a "literal translation" of the *Daxue*, or *Great Learning*. His comments on the work are minimal. Morrison, *Horae Sinicae*, p. 20.

99 Morrison, *View*, p. 21.

100 Chan, *Orientalism in Sinology*, pp. 1–54.

4 "FRUITS OF THE HIGHEST CULTURE MAY BE IMPROVED AND
VARIED BY FOREIGN GRAFTS": THE CANTON SCHOOL OF
ROMANTIC SINOLOGY – STAUNTON AND DAVIS

1 See Hillemann, *Asian Empire*, for the Canton and South Asian network.

2 Davis, *Chinese Novels*, p. 24.

3 *Quarterly Review* (1815), 409.

4 The estate is now known as Staunton Country Park; see Gladwyn, *Leigh Park*, pp. 29, 66–68, 72–73, 119–28.

5 See Cranmer-Byng, "First English Sinologists," p. 255. Staunton presented the Society with 2610 volumes containing 136 Chinese works. The Society's Chinese books were transferred to the University of Leeds. He also presented the Society with the Jade sceptre presented to him by the Qianlong emperor at his audience at Jehol. See Beckingham, "A History of the Royal Asiatic Society, 1823–1973," pp. 1–3, 40, 46, 58–59.

6 Cranmer-Byng, "First English Sinologists"; St. André, "'But do they have a notion of Justice?'" 1–31; Brook, Bourgon, and Blue, *Death by a Thousand Cuts*, pp. 25–26, 176–76, 182, 185.

7 Southey also possessed a copy of Staunton's *Narrative of the Tourgouth Tartars* (1821). *Catalogue of the Valuable Library*, lots 586, 2842.

8 Jones, *The Great Qing Code*, p. v. See St. André, "'But do they have a notion of Justice?'" 1–32 (2); Brook, Bourgon and Blue, *Death by a Thousand Cuts*, pp. 174–78.

9 Cranmer-Byng and Wills, Jr., "Trade and Diplomacy," pp. 234–54.

10 Morse, *Chronicles*, 2.332–35; Matlak, *Deep Distresses*, p. 48.

11 See Wills, "Trade and Diplomacy," pp. 239–45. See Morse, *Chronicles*, 2.93–109; Fu, *A Documentary Chronicle*, pp. 297–98.

12 See Nokes, *Jane Austen: A Life*, pp. 371–72; Hubback, *Jane Austen's Sailor Brothers*.

13 Staunton, *Ta Tsing Leu Lee*, p. xxiv. Further references to this edition are cited in the text by page number.

14 St. André, "'But do they have a notion of Justice?'" 4–6, 23.

15 Mason, *The Punishments of China*. See Brook, Bourgon, and Blue, *Death by a Thousand Cuts*, pp. 25, 171–80 for Staunton's response to Mason. Mason's text is examined by Hayot in the *Hypothetical Mandarin*, pp. 60–94.

16 Brook, Bourgon and Blue, *Death by a Thousand Cuts*, p. 68.

17 This subject is extensively explored by Brook, Bourgon and Blue, *Death by a Thousand Cuts* (pp. 162–69) and Hayot, *Hypothetical Mandarin* (*passim*).

18 *Edinburgh Review* 26 (1810), 481–82.

19 Brook, Bourgon and Blue, *Death by a Thousand Cuts*, pp. 68.176–77.

20 *Quarterly Review* 3 (1810), 294, 303, 309, 315–17.

21 Morrison, *Memoirs*, 1.138.

22 St. André, "Modern Translation Theory," 51; Teele, *Through a Glass Darkly*, pp. 44, 51–55.

23 Davis, *Chinese Novels*, p. 9.

24 *Ibid.*, 2–3.

25 Davis, "Eugraphia Sinensis," 306–7.

26 For Davis, see ODNB; Morse, *Chronicles*, 1.146; Hsü, *The Rise of Modern China*, pp. 174–76, 199–202; Chang, *Commissioner Lin and the Opium War*, pp. 62–63. Sieber, *Theatres of Desire*, pp. xiii, xxi, 2, 11–13, 15, 17–18, 160, 172, 178; St. André, "The Development of British Sinology," 3–42.

27 Beckingham, "History of the Royal Asiatic Society," p. 17.

28 Davis, *Laou-Seng-Urh*, pp. iii–iv.

29 Davis, *Chinese Miscellanies*, p. 91.

30 St. André "Modern Translation Theory," p. 55, and "Development of British Sinology," 12.

31 Davis, *Chinese* (1836), 2.184.

32 Davis, *Laou-seng-urg*, ix–x, xxi, xliii–xliv. Further references to this work are cited in the text by page number.

33 Davis, *Chinese* (1836), 2.173; Sieber, *Theaters of Desire*, pp. xiii–xv; Aldridge, "First Chinese Drama," pp. 185–92.

34 Zhang, *Unexpected Affinities*.

35 *The Letters of John Keats*, ed. Rollins, 1.184–86.

36 A modern translation of *Autumn in the Palace of Han* is contained in Liu (trans.), *Six Yüan Plays*, pp. 182–224. For an introduction to the play see

Liu, *Six Yüan Plays*, pp. 32–34; Mair, *Columbia History of Chinese Literature*, pp. 814–15.

37 Zhang, *Unexpected Affinities*, p. 46.

38 For the notion of tragedy as applied to Chinese dramas, see Sieber, *Theaters of Desire*, pp. 15–27.

39 Published in *Transactions of the Royal Asiatic Society*, 2.393–461. Further references to this work are cited in the text by page number. See also Teele, *Through a Glass Darkly*, p. 52.

40 Davis, *The Chinese* (1836), 2.202.

41 Legge, *The She King*, Part I, in *The Chinese Classics*, 4.21. Teele, *Through a Glass Darkly*, pp. 54–55.

42 *Quarterly Review*, 16 (1816–17), 399–400.

43 I am indebted to Professor Zeng Li for sharing with me his analysis of the Chinese version of this poem.

44 Davis, *Laou seng urg*, pp. v–vi.

45 In addition to Davis's translations, the Company printer, P. P. [Peter Perring] Thoms translated the long verse romance, *Chinese Courtship in Verse* (1824), and in 1827 Abel-Rémusat's French version, *Iu-kaio-l or, the Two fair Cousins: A Chinese Novel* was translated into English. Stephen Weston translated *Fan-hy-cheu: a tale, in Chinese and English* in 1814. In 1842 "Tkin Shen," a student of Legge's, published a translation of the novel, *The Rambles of the Emperor Ching Tih in Këang Nan: A Chinese tale*.

46 For Li Yü, see Yenna Wu, "Vernacular Stories," in *Columbia History*, ed. Mair, pp. 613–17; and Hanan, *The Invention of Li Yü*. The Egyptologist Samuel Birch, who had wished as a young man to study China, published another tale from the *Shier lou* as *Yin Seaon low, or the Lost Child. A Chinese Tale* in 1841.

47 Davis first translated this tale as "San-Yu-Low; or the Three Dedicated Rooms" in 1815. The tale was published in *Translations from the Original Chinese* (1816). The translation was heavily revised for publication in 1822. See St. André, "Development of British Sinology," pp. 11–17.

48 Davis, *Chinese Novels*, pp. 12–13.

49 *Ibid.*, p. 16.

50 Mair, *Columbia History* p. 615.

51 Davis, *The Fortunate Union*, 1.vii, xiv–xv. Further references are cited by volume and page number in the text.

52 Reeves (1774–1856) was appointed Inspector of Tea for the Company in 1808 and travelled to China in 1812. See Fan, "Reeves, John," ODNB and *British Naturalists in Qing China*; Whitehead, *Chinese Natural History Drawings*; Bretschneider, *History of European Botanical Discoveries*; Cox, *Plant Hunting in China*; Coats, *The Quest for Plants*.

53 The detail is mentioned in Ellis, *Journal*, p. 420

54 See St. André, "Development of British sinology," pp. 9–10.

55 For an overview of the controversy with Klaproth see Thoms, "Mr. Klaproth's Attack upon Dr. Morrison," 201–6.

56 Davis, *The Chinese* (1851), 1, v. Further references to this edition are contained in the text and cited by volume and page number.
57 Davis, *China During the War*, 1.viii, 1–3, 19, 33, 39; 2.45, 101.

5   ESTABLISHING THE "GREAT DIVIDE": SCIENTIFIC
    EXCHANGE, TRADE, AND THE MACARTNEY EMBASSY

1 The standard accounts of the embassy include: Cranmer-Byng, "Lord Macartney's Embassy to Peking in 1793," 117–87; Roebuck (ed.), *Macartney of Lissanoure*; Singer, *The Lion & the Dragon*; Peyrefitte, *The Collison of Two Civilisations*; Bickers (ed.), *Ritual and Diplomacy*; Hevia, *Cherishing Men from Afar*.
2 Pritchard, "The Kowtow in the Macartney Embassy in 1793," 190–94; Cranmer-Byng, "Lord Macartney's Embassy", 117–86; Cranmer-Byng and Wills, Jr., "Trade and Diplomacy," pp. 243–52; Hevia, *Cherishing Men*, pp. 167–76.
3 Barrow, *Travels*, 82.
4 Leask, *Curiosity and the Aesthetics of Travel Writing*, pp. 15–53.
5 Adas, *Machines as the Measure of Men*, pp. 34, 177–98.
6 See Min, "Narrating the Far East," 160–80.
7 Hostetler, *Qing Colonial Enterprise*, pp. 103, 25–32.
8 See Porter, *Ideographia*, pp. 193–240 and Hevia, *Cherishing Men*; for European universalism, see Wallerstein, *European Universalism the Rhetoric of Power*.
9 Davis, *Chinese Novels*, pp. 3–4.
10 *Quarterly Review*, 36 (1827), 496–97
11 Peyrefitte, *Collision*, p. 540.
12 Hevia, *Cherishing Men*, pp. 25–26, 28, 72, 230–31, 242. For responses to Hevia, see Crossley's review in *Harvard Journal of Asiatic Studies*, 57 (1997), 597–611 and the more caustic exchanges between Hevia and Esherick in *Modern China*, 24 (1997), 135–61, 319–27; see also, Perdue, "Boundaries and Trade."
13 Horace Walpole to Lady Ossory, August 3, 1794. *Walpole's Correspondence*, 34.201.
14 Adas, *Machines and the Measure of Men*.
15 For a summary and critique of this argument, see Shapin, *Scientific Revolution*.
16 Cranmer-Byng and Wills, "Trade and Diplomacy," p. 222.
17 See Rowe, *China's Last Empire*, pp. 149–74.
18 Needham, *The Grand Titration*, p. 15; *Science and Civilisation in China*, 3.154. For a critique of Needham, see Sivin, *Science in Ancient China*.
19 Needham, *Grand Titration*, p. 34.
20 Basalla, "The Spread of Western Science," 611–22.
21 See Bodde, *Chinese Thought*; Huff, *Early Modern Science*.

22 Huff, *Early Modern Science*, pp. 262, 279, 318, 292–305; Bodde, *Chinese Thought*, pp. 90–92, 94.

23 Adorno and Horkheimer, *Dialetik des Aufklarung*.

24 Latour, *We Have Never Been Modern*, p. 179.

25 *Ibid.*, pp. 97–103, 112, 117.

26 Hobson, *Eastern Origins*, pp. 5–6.

27 Raj, *Relocating Modern Science*, pp. 7–9; See Golinski, *Making Natural Knowledge*; and Sudan, "Mud, Mortar, and Other Technologies of Empire," 147–69.

28 Hostetler, *Qing Colonial Enterprise*, p. 2, 2n, 15–16; See Subrahmanyam, "Connected Histories," 737; Goldstone, "The Problem of the Early Modern World," 249–84.

29 Elman, *On Their Own Terms*; and *A Cultural History of Modern Science in China*, pp. 100–132.

30 Waley-Cohen, *Sextants of Beijing*, pp. 24–28.

31 *Ibid.*, p. 128.

32 Fan, *British Naturalists*, p. 38.

33 *Ibid.*, p. 59.

34 Miller and Reill (eds.), *Visions of Empire*, pp. 30–33, 109; Carter, *Sir Joseph Banks*, pp. 290–91, 407, 440–41; Gascoigne, *Joseph Banks and the English Enlightenment*, pp. 179–81, 214; Gascoigne, *Science in the Service of Empire*, pp. 140–42; Métailié, "Sir Joseph Banks – An Asian Policy?" pp. 157–69.

35 Gascoigne, *Science in the Service of Empire*, p. 112.

36 Fan, *British Naturalists*, p. 38. See Thomas, "The Establishment of Calcutta Botanic Garden," 168; Sharma, "British Science, Chinese Skill and Assam Tea: Making Empire's Garden," 429–55; McCracken, *Gardens of Empire*.

37 Biswas, *Original Correspondence of Sir Joseph Banks*, pp. 185–236.

38 Banks to Sir George Yonge, May 15, 1787, *Indian and Pacific Correspondence*, 2.190–92. Quoted Thomas, "Calcutta Botanic Garden," 169.

39 Thomas, "Calcutta Botanic Garden," 173.

40 Bretschneider, *European Botanical Discoveries*, 1.203–5.

41 Fan, *British Naturalists*, pp. 38.

42 Banks to Macartney, January 22, 1792, *Indian and Pacific Correspondence*, 3.330.

43 *Ibid.*, 2.330–32.

44 See Chambers, "General Introduction," in *Indian and Pacific Correspondence*, 1.xxxiii–xlii.

45 Banks to Josiah Wedgwood, February 6, 1792, *Indian and Pacific Correspondence*, 3.337–38; Banks to Percival, February 7 and February 13, 1792, *Indian and Pacific Correspondence*, 3.338–39; 3.341–42.

46 Staunton, *Account*, 1.37; 2.165, 274, 435, 524.

47 "Hints on the subject of gardening suggested to the Gentlemen who attend the Embassy to China," f1, f2, f19; reprinted in *Indian and Pacific Correspondence*, 3.412–24.

48 Fan, *British Naturalists*, pp. 46–47.

49 Staunton, *Account*, 2.165, 274, 435, 524; Bretschneider, *European Botanical Discoveries*, 1.156–83; Macartney, *Journal*, p. 318.

50 Banks to Staunton, January 23, 1796. *Indian and Pacific Correspondence*, 4.358.

51 "The three sorts of Tea commonly carry'd to England are all from the same Plant, only the Season of the Year, and the Soil, makes the difference," 93–94. James Cuninghame, "Part of Two Letters to the Publisher from Mr. James Cunningham F.R.S. and Physician to the English at Chusan in China" (1707), reprinted in *Tea in Natural History*, ed. Richard Coulton, pp. 91–96 (93–94).

52 "Memorial dated 27 Dec. 1788, by Sir Joseph Banks, sent to the Chairman of the East India Company on the Possibility of Introducing Tea Cultivation into India," December 27, 1788, BL OIOC, MSS. Eur. D 993.

53 This "discovery" formed the basis of the first Indian tea to be marketed in London from 1839 onwards. See Ukers, *All About Tea*; Forrest, *Tea for the British*; Chaudhuri, *The Trading World of Asia*; Hoh-Cheung Mui and Lorna H. Mui, *The Management of Monopoly*; Gardella, *Harvesting the Mountains*; Rose, *For All the Tea in China*; Ellis, Coulton, Dew, and Mauger (eds), *Tea and the Tea-Table in Eighteenth-Century England*.

54 "Note relative to the method of bringing to England seeds from China and Japan in a state of vegetation," Macartney, *Journal*, pp. 318–19.

55 Macartney, *Journal*, p. 182, 374–75.

56 Proudfoot, *Biographical Memoir*, pp. 69–71, 132.

57 See Sharma, "British Science," 432.

58 Banks to Staunton, November 22, 1795, *Indian and Pacific Correspondence*, 4.332.

59 Banks to Staunton, December 26, 1795, *Indian and Pacific Correspondence*, 3.342.

60 Staunton to Banks, January 24, 1796, *Indian and Pacific Correspondence*, 3.359.

61 Abel, *Narrative*, pp. vii–viii.

62 Sharma, "British Science," 433–34.

63 *Ibid.*, pp. 444–45.

64 *Ibid.*, p. 454.

65 Zionkowski and Klekar (eds.), *Culture of the Gift*, p. 2; Mauss, *The Gift*.

66 Klekar, "Prisoners", 84–105; See Keogh, "Oriental Translations," pp. 171–91.

67 Klekar, "Prisoners," 84–86; Porter, *Ideographia*, p. 198.

68 Markley, "Anson at Canton," pp. 220, 227, 230

69 Klekar, "Prisoners," pp. 92, 97

70 Macartney, *Journal*, pp. 264–66, 270. Gillan's account of Chinese medicine is printed in Macartney, *Journal*, pp. 279–303.

71 See Peyrefitte, *Collision*, pp. 77–78, 102–4; 150; Hevia, *Cherishing Men*, pp. 102–8; Cranmer-Byng and Levere, "Case Study in Cultural Collision," 503–25.

72 "Catalogue of presents sent by His Britannic Majesty to the Emperor of China," Vol. 8, Doc. 350. Quoted in Cranmer-Byng and Levere, "Case Study in Cultural Collision," 523.

73 Macartney to Dundas, November 9, 1793. IOR G/12/92. Quoted in Schaffer, "Instruments as Cargo in the China Trade," 217–46.

74 Staunton, *Account*, 1.42–43.

75 See Berg, "Britain, industry and perceptions of China," pp. 269–88; "Britain's Asian Century," in *The Birth of Modern Europe*, pp. 133–56.

76 Hevia, *Cherishing Men*, pp. 127, 128–29.

77 Macartney, *Journal*, pp. 122–23; Peyrefitte, *Collision of Civilizations*, pp. 537–53.

78 Macartney, *Journal*, p. 96; Hevia, *Cherishing Men*, p. 104.

79 For Dinwiddie, see Proudfoot, *Biographical Memior of James Dinwiddie*; Macartney, *Journal*, pp. 310–11.

80 For Gillan, see Macartney, *Journal*, p. 311. Bivins, "Expectations and Expertise," 459–89; and *Acupuncture, expertise, and cross-cultural Medicine*.

81 Quoted, Wakeman, "The Canton Trade and the Opium War," in Fairbank (ed.), *The Cambridge History of China*, 10.1, pp. 163–212 (173).

82 John Barrow to the Earl of Buckinghamshire, President of the Board of Control, February 14, 1815. Quoted in Staunton, *Notes of Proceedings and Occurrences*, p. ix.

83 Berg, "Britain, industry and perceptions of China."

84 Quoted Berg, *Luxury and Pleasure*, p. 81.

85 Macartney, *Journal*, pp. 260, 310–11.

86 Berg, "Britain, industry and perceptions of China," 282–83

87 Staunton, *Account*, 1, p. 43.

88 Schaffer, "Instruments as Cargo," 217–46

89 Cranmer-Byng and Levere, "Case Study in Cultural Collision," 513.

90 Proudfoot, *Biographical Memoir*, p. 26; Peyrefitte, *Collision of Civlizations*, pp. 139–41; 537–42, 575; Cranmer-Byng and Levere, "Case Study in Cultural Collision," 512ff.

91 Hevia, *Cherishing Men*, pp. 78–79.

92 Schaffer, "Instruments as Cargo," 220.

93 Macartney, *Journal*, p. 96.

94 Barrow, *Travels*, pp. 112–13.

95 Macartney, *Journal*, p. 146; Hevia, *Cherishing Men*, pp. 92, 149–54.

96 Macartney, *Journal*, pp. 125–26; this part of Macartney's *Journal* is quoted by Barrow, *Travels*, p. 129; Hevia, *Cherishing Men*, pp. 178–80.

97 Proudfoot, *Biographical Memoir*, pp. 4, 10.

98 *Ibid.*, pp. 11, 46–47. In Barrow's version the emperor comments that he fancies the machines are "meant as playthings for some of my grandchildren." *Travels*, p. 312.

99 Hevia's translation in *Cherishing Men*, p. 188.

100 Barrow, *Travels*, pp. 215, 343.

101 Davis, *The Chinese* (1851), 1.36.

6 "YOU WILL BE TAKING A TRIP INTO CHINA, I SUPPOSE":
KOWTOWS, TEACUPS, AND THE EVASIONS OF BRITISH
ROMANTIC WRITING ON CHINA

1 Chang, *Britain's Chinese Eye*, pp. 3, 71–110.
2 Porter, *Chinese Taste*, pp. 1–14.
3 Volney, *Ruins of Empires*, p. 119.
4 Quoted in Gelber, *Dragon and the Foreign Devils*, p. 188
5 Hevia "'Ultimate Gesture," 212–34.
6 *Ibid.*, 220.
7 Liu, *Clash of Empires*, p. 217.
8 Hevia, "Ultimate Gesture," 227
9 Macartney, *Journal*, pp. 84, 85, 100.
10 *Ibid.*, p. 119.
11 Staunton, *Account*, 2.129–30.
12 *Ibid.*, 2.130–37.
13 Barrow, *Travels*, p. 24.
14 Pritchard, "Kowtow," 173–74
15 Staunton, *Notes of Proceedings*, p. xx
16 Ellis, *Journal*, p. 151.
17 Staunton, *Notes of Proceedings*, pp. 51–53.
18 Markham, ed. *Narrative*, pp. 258–59.
19 *Edinburgh Review*, 29 (February 1818), 436–7.
20 George, *Catalogue of political and personal satires*, 6.926–7; For Hüttner and
    Gillray, see Burwick, "James Gillray and the Aporia of Visual Hermeneutics,"
    pp. 85–103.
21 Quoted, Donald, *Age of Caricature*, p. 42.
22 Coleridge, *Lectures 1795*, p. 294.
23 "Religious Musings," lines. 280–82; *Coleridge's Poetry and Prose*, p. 29.
24 *Shelley's Poetry and Prose*, p. 431
25 *Ibid.*, p. 318.
26 Byron, *Complete Poetical Works*, 4, p. 80. Further references to this edition
    are contained within the text.
27 Said, *Culture and Imperialism*, pp. 95–116.
28 Hubback and Hubback, *Jane Austen's Sailor Brothers*, p. 219.
29 *Ibid.*, pp. 28, 218–20.
30 Nokes, *Jane Austen: A Life*, pp. 361–62, 367.
31 *Austen Letters*, ed. Deirdre Le Faye, pp. 175–78.
32 Knox-Shaw, "Fanny Price Refuses to Kowtow," 212–17 (215).
33 Lew, "'That Abominable Traffic,'" pp. 271–300; Susan Allen Ford, "Fanny's
    'Great Book.'"
34 Austen, *Mansfield Park*, p. 123.
35 *Ibid.*, p. 142.
36 Southey, *Thalaba*, p. 94.
37 *Ibid.*, p. 252; Percy, *Hau Kiou Choann*, 2, pp. 214–55.
38 Southey, *Life and Correspondence*, 3.191–92.

39 Percy, *Hau Kiou Choann*, 4.143–44.

40 Southey, *Letters to Charles Butler*, p. 7

41 Southey, *New Letters*, 1.476.

42 *Catalogue of the Valuable Library of the Late Robert Southey.*

43 Southey, "Travels in China," 69–83 (69–71). Further references to this are cited in the text by page number.

44 *Ibid.*, p. 82.

45 See Chang, *Britain's Chinese Eye*, pp. 71–110; Yang, *Performing China*.

46 Porter, *Chinese Taste*, pp. 133, 27–29.

47 Jordain and Jenyns, *Chinese Export Art in the Eighteenth Century*; Emerson, Chen, and Gates, *Porcelain Stories: From China to Europe*; Haddad, "Imagined Journeys to Distant Cathay," 53–80. O'Hara, "'The Willow Pattern That We Knew,'" 421–42; Carswell, *Blue and White*; Copeland, *Spode's Willow Pattern*.

48 Baillie, *Fugitive Verses*, pp. 161–62.

49 Southey, *Letters from England*, pp. 191–92.

50 Chang, *Britain's Chinese Eye*, pp. 6, 73–74.

51 Lamb, *Elia and the Last Essays of Elia*, pp. 120–21. Further references to this edition are cited in the text by page number.

52 James, "Thomas Manning," 21–36; Leask, *Curiosity and the Aesthetics of Travel Writing*, pp. 54–101; Lamb, *Preserving the Self*.

53 Lamb, *Elia and the Last Essays of Elia*, pp. 123. Further references to this edition are cited in the text by page number.

54 Fang, *Romantic Writing*, pp. 60–64.

55 James, "Thomas Manning," 30–33.

56 Chang, *Britain's Chinese Eye*, p. 1; Porter, *Chinese Taste*, p. 133.

57 Fang, *Romantic Writing*, pp. 60–64; Chang, *Britain's Chinese Eye*, pp. 71–81

58 Samuel Ball, an expert on tea cultivation, worked at Canton between 1804 and 1826 and was the author of *An account of the cultivation and manufacture of tea in China* (1848). Davis reports that Manning and Ball were great friends and companions, Markham, *Narrative*, p. clxiv.

59 Porter, *Chinese Taste*, p. 3

60 *Letters of Charles and Mary Lamb*, 2.15. Further references to this edition are contained in the text.

61 Chang, *Britain's Chinese Eye*, p. 83.

62 For Manning see Markham, *Narrative*, pp. clix–clxv; James, "Thomas Manning"; McMillin, *English in Tibet*, pp. 55–70.

63 Markham, *Narrative*, p. cl

64 Manning to Joseph Banks, April 16, 1807.

65 Manning to Joseph Banks, January 5, 1808.

66 Manning, *Letters*, pp. 106, 109.

67 Manning to Joseph Banks, August 27, 1811.

68 Manning to Joseph Banks, September 6, 1811.

69 Markham, *Narrative*, p. 218

70 Staunton, *Notes*, pp. 8–10.

71 Markham, *Narrative*, p. lxiv.
72 Manning's Chinese dictionaries are held in the archives of the Royal Asiatic Society of which he became the Honorary Chinese Librarian. See Beckingham, "A History of the Royal Asiatic Society, 1823–1973," p. 40.
73 *Literary Gazette*, 1264 (1841), 236.
74 Markham, *Narrative*, p. 280. Further references to this edition are cited in the text by page number.
75 Manning, "Chinese Jests," *New Monthly Magazine and Literary Journal*, 280–84, 386–92, 573–75 (282).
76 Hunt, *Leigh Hunt's Dramatic Criticism, 1808–1831*, pp. 154–55.
77 Hunt, "Domestic News from China," 213–7 (213).
78 *Ibid.*, 214.
79 Hunt, "The Subject of Breakfast Continued," 113–14.

7   CHINESE GARDENS, CONFUCIUS, AND *THE PRELUDE*

1 Lovejoy, "The Chinese Origin," 99–135.
2 Leask, "Kubla Khan and Orientalism," 1–21; Liu, *Seeds of a Different Eden*; Porter, *Chinese Taste*, pp. 37–54, 115–30; Chang, *Britain's Chinese Eye*, pp. 23–70.
3 *The World*, 12 (1753), pp. 67–72 (72). Bending, "Horace Walpole," 209–26; Porter, *Chinese Taste*, pp. 115–30; Watt, "Thomas Percy," 95–109; Kitson, "'Reason in China,'" pp. 9–21.
4 Walpole, *Anecdotes of Painting*, 4.284; Lovejoy, "Chinese Origins," p. 134n.
5 Thomas, "Yuanming Yuan/Versailles," 115–43 (130).
6 Dixon Hunt, *The Picturesque Garden*, pp. 54–56, 94–95, 147–49; Sirén, *China and the Gardens of Europe*; Fan, "China's Garden Architecture," 21–34; Honour, *Chinoiserie*, pp. 143–74; Ge, "Eighteenth-century Misreading," 106–26; Chen, "Chinese Garden in Eighteenth Century England," pp. 339–58; Qingxi Lou, *Chinese Gardens*; Gray, "Lord Burlington," 40–43; Conner, "China and the Landscape Garden," 429–40; Jacques, "On the supposed Chineseness," 180–91; Brown "Joseph Addison and the Pleasures of *Sharawadgi*," 171–93.
7 Chang, *Britain's Chinese Eye*, p. 23.
8 Walpole, Anecdotes of Painting, 4, 267–71; see Mowl's review of Liu in *American Historical Review*, 115 (2010), 192; Dixon Hunt, *Picturesque Garden*, p. 36.
9 Attiret's letter was printed in the *Lettres edifiantes et curieuse* in 1749, an English version was printed in Joseph Spence's *A Particular Account of the Emperor of China's Gardens Near Pekin* (London, 1752), and extracts were printed in the *Monthly Review* and elsewhere. The letter was subsequently reprinted by Chambers and Percy. See Jacques, "Supposed Chineseness" and Conner, "China and the Landscape Garden."
10 Thomas, "Yuanming Yuan/Versailles", 127.
11 See Barmé, "The Garden of Perfect Brightness," 111–58.
12 Thomas, "Yuanming Yuan/Versailles," 127.
13 Aravamudan, *Enlightenment Orientalism*, pp. 3, 5, 8, 74, 202, 223; see Dirlik, "Chinese History," 96–118.

14 Thomas, "Yuanming Yuan/Versailles," 115–43.
15 Harris and Snodin (eds.), *Sir William Chambers*; Bald, "Sir William Chambers and the Chinese Garden," 287–320; Porter, *Chinese Taste*, pp. 37–54; Chang, *Britain's Chinese Eye*, 28–37.
16 Bending, "A Natural Revolution?" pp. 241–66; Barrell, *Idea of Landscape* and *English Literature in History*; Everett, *Tory View of Landscape*; Daniel, *Field of Vision*; Fulford, *Landscape, Liberty, and Authority*.
17 Davis, *The Chinese* (1851), 2.55.
18 Chambers, *Dissertation on Oriental Gardening*, pp. v, vii, 12, 18–19.
19 Porter, *Chinese Taste*, pp. 37–54 (43–44), 189.
20 Chambers, *Dissertation*, pp. 27–29, 37.
21 Leask, "Kubla Khan and Orientalism"; Bending, "A Natural Revolution?" pp. 245–57.
22 Walpole to William Mason, May 25, 1772, *Walpole's Correspondence*, 28.34.
23 Chase, "William Mason and Sir William Chambers," 517–29; Bending, "A Natural Revolution?"; Leask, "Kubla Khan and Orientalism"; Porter, *Chinese Taste*, pp. 122–25; Chang, *Britain's Chinese Eye*, pp. 34–36.
24 Mason, *Satirical Poems*, pp. 44–5.
25 Bending, "A Natural Revolution?" p. 256
26 Kitson, *Romantic Literature*, pp. 195–203.
27 "Kubla Khan," lines 249–52; Coleridge, *Poetry and Prose*, pp. 182–83.
28 Wordsworth, *Home at Grasmere*, lines 654–55.
29 Hayter, *Wreck of the Abergavenny*, pp. 29, 35.
30 *Letters of John Wordsworth*, pp. 74, 77.
31 *Ibid.*, pp. 12–13
32 On his second voyage to China, John's log for May 30 describes how he had a dozen lashes administered to "one of the Chinese … for attempting to stab with a knife one of the boatswain's mates." Quoted in *Letters of John Wordsworth*, pp. 37–38.
33 *Ibid.*; Hayter, *Wreck of the Abergavenny*, p. 176.
34 *Letters of John Wordsworth*, p. 138.
35 Matlak, *Deep Distresses*, pp. 36, 34–38.
36 *Ibid.*, p. 51.
37 *Letters of John Wordsworth*, pp. 83, 93, 97–98.
38 *Ibid.*, pp. 137, 139; Gill, *William Wordsworth: A Life*, pp. 210, 213; Matlak, *Deep Distresses*, pp. 64–69.
39 *Letters of John Wordsworth*, p. 143.
40 *Ibid.*, p. 155.
41 Johnston, *Hidden Wordsworth*, p. 584.
42 *Letters of John Wordsworth*, pp. 148, 149–50, 155.
43 Hayter, *Wreck of the Abergavenny*, p. 35.
44 *Letters of William and Dorothy Wordsworth*, p. 563.
45 *Letters of John Wordsworth*, p. 116.
46 Johnston, *Hidden Wordsworth*, p. 584.
47 Hobhouse, *Diary*, Sunday, May 23, 1819.

48 *Quarterly Review*, 1 (1814), 340.
49 See Adas, *Machines as the Measure of Men*, pp. 178–92. For Barrow, see his *Autobiographical Memoir*; Lloyd, *Mr. Barrow*; Fleming, *Barrow's Boys*.
50 Elman, *Cultural History of Civil Examinations*. See also Huff, *Rise of Early Modern Science*, pp. 277–87.
51 Barrow, *Travels in China*, pp. 259–63.
52 *Quarterly Review*, 14 (1817), 397.
53 Morrison, *Memoirs*, 2.60, 61, 62, 64; Hancock, *Morrison*, pp. 138–40.
54 Hancock, *Morrison*, p. 145.
55 "Travels in China," 77–78.
56 *Diary and Letters of Madame D'Arblay*, 2.393–94; Ribeiro (ed.), *Letters of Burney. Volume I, 1751–1784*, pp. 231–5; see Clarke, "An encounter with Chinese," 543–57.
57 See Gill, *William Wordsworth: A Life*, pp. 233–44; Townsend, "John Wordsworth and his Brother's Poetic Development," 70–78.
58 Dove Cottage MS 26, 16v–17v. See Wu, *Wordsworth's Reading*; Chang, *Britain's Chinese Eye*, pp. 37–39.
59 *The Thirteen-Book Prelude*, 1.167; (5.206–8). All references to the poem are to this edition and cited by book and line number in the text.
60 *Thirteen-Book Prelude*, 2.84. This reference was drawn to my attention by Bruce Graver.
61 Coleridge, *Collected Letters*, 1.354. See Nussbaum and Makdisi (eds.), *Arabian Nights in Historical Context*.
62 For an overview of this practice see Richardson, *Literature, Education, and Romanticism*.
63 *Journals and Miscellaneous Notebooks of Emerson*, 5, pp. 120–22.
64 Bate, *Romantic Ecology*, pp. 19–35.
65 See Keswick, *Chinese Garden*, pp. 45–72; Barmé, "The Garden of Perfect Brightness," 111–58; Qingxi Lou, *Chinese Gardens*, pp. 79–133; Ringmar, *Liberal Barbarism*; Wong, *A Paradise Lost*.
66 For Chengde see Forêt, *Mapping Chengde*, and "The intended perception," 343–63; Hevia, *Cherishing Men*, pp. 3–56; Millward, *et al.* (eds.), *New Qing Imperial History*.
67 Hevia, "World Heritage," 219–43.
68 Thomas, "Yuanming Yuan/Versailles."
69 Chang, *Britain's Chinese Eye*, p. 23
70 Rather than the successful displacements that McGann, Liu, and others find in Wordsworth's poetry, my reading highlights, like Simpson's the conscious "transcriptions of conflict" in Wordsworth's mind and in society. Simpson, *Wordsworth's Historical Imagination*, pp. 185–208.
71 See Gill, *William Wordsworth*, pp. 233–44; Townsend, "John Wordsworth," 70–78.
72 The influence of Chinese notions of gardening on "Kubla Khan" is explored in Leask's "Kubla Khan and Orientalism," 1–21, and Kitson, *Romantic Literature*, pp. 195–203; Porter, *Chinese Taste*, pp. 37–54.

73 Chang, *Britain's Chinese Eye*, pp. 37–56.
74 Staunton, *Account*, 2, p. 303.
75 Chang, *Britain's Chinese Eye*, p. 50.
76 For the embellishments Alexander added to the scene, see Chang, *Britain's Chinese Eye*, pp. 45–47.
77 *Macartney of Lissanoure*, ed. Roebuck, pp. 139–44.
78 Barrow, *Travels*, p. 126.
79 Davis, *The History of Luton*, pp. 16–21.
80 Buchanan, *Wordsworth's Gardens*.
81 *Macartney of Lissanoure 1737–1806*, ed. Roebuck, pp. 139–44.
82 Bonsall, *Sir James Lowther*, pp. vi, 89–105
83 Macartney, *Journal*, p. 370n.

8 "NOT A BIT LIKE THE CHINESE FIGURES THAT ADORN OUR CHIMNEY-PIECES": ORPHANS AND TRAVELLERS – CHINA ON STAGE

1 Said, *Orientalism*, p. 109.
2 O'Quinn, *Staging Governance*, pp. 1–7, 28; and *Entertaining Crisis*; Nussbaum, *The Limits of the Human*; Worrall, *Harlequin Empire*. See also Orr, *Empire on the English Stage*; Barbour, *Before Orientalism*; Mackenzie, *Orientalism*, pp. 176–207; Witchard, *Thomas Burke's Dark Chinoiserie*, pp. 23–78.
3 Recent exceptions to this are Yang, *Performing China* and Dalporto, "Succession Crisis." See also Appleton, *Cycle of Cathay*, pp. 65–89; Clarke, *Oriental England*; Ward, *Pagodas in Play*; Nicoll, *A History of Late Eighteenth-century Drama 1750–1800*.
4 Worrall, *Harlequin Empire*, p. 1.
5 Yang, *Performing China*, pp. 1–31.
6 Ward, *Pagodas in Play*, p. 15.
7 O'Quinn, *Staging Governance*, pp. 1–7, 28
8 Yang, *Performing China*, pp. 4–5, 10.
9 See Holder, "Melodrama, realism and empire of the British Stage," in Bratton, *et al.* (eds.), *Acts of Supremacy*, p. 129
10 Nussbaum, *Limits of the Human*, pp. 219, 230.
11 Bratton, *Acts of Supremacy*, p. 4.
12 For Yuan theatre, see Dolby, *History of Chinese Drama*; Crump, *Chinese Theater in the Days of Kublai Khan*; Mackerras (ed.), *Chinese Theater*; West and Idema, *Monks, Bandits, Lovers and Immortals*; Fu, *Chinese Theatre*; For *Orphan* plays see Liu, "The Original Orphan of China," 193–12; Appleton, *Cycle of Cathay*, pp. 81–89; Liu, "Introduction," *Six Yüan Plays*, pp. 7–35; Mair (ed.), *Columbia History*, pp. 802–5; Idema, "The Many Shapes of Medieval Chinese Plays," 320–34 and "The Orphan of Zhao," 159–90; Yang, *Performing China*, pp. 148–83.
13 Sieber, *Theaters of Desire*, pp. xiii–xv, xv; Mair (ed.), *Columbia History*, pp. 785–847.
14 See Idema, "Medieval Chinese Plays," 323–30

15 *Ibid.*, 321.
16 Julien, *Tchao-chi-koi-eul, ou L'Orphelin de la chine.*
17 Liu, "Original Orphan," p. 196.
18 See Mair, *Columbia History*, p. 803.
19 See Lundbaek, *Joseph de Prémare*, p. 64, Liu, "Original Orphan," 202.
20 Chen, "The Chinese Orphan: A Yuan Play," pp. 359–83; Ballaster, *Fabulous Orients*, pp. 208–18. See Lopez, *Chinese Drama*, pp. 363–66; Sieber, *Theatres of Desire*, pp. xiii–xxi.
21 Sieber, *Theaters of Desire*, pp. 3–4, 15, 37–44; Liu, "Original Orphan," 205–6.
22 See Kitson, *Romantic Literature*, pp. 175–214.
23 Hatchett, *The Chinese Orphan*, p. vi; Liu, "Original Orphan," 203–5; Ballaster, *Fabulous Orients*, pp. 10–12.
24 Liu, "Original Orphan," 205–6; Ward, *Pagodas in Play*, pp. 98–118.
25 Quoted in Sieber, *Theaters of Desire*, p. 370.
26 Chen, "Chinese Orphan," 371–72; Ballaster, *Fabulous Orients*, p. 213.
27 Bruce, *Voltaire on the English Stage*, p. 70.
28 Murphy, *Life of Garrick*, 1.320–30; Dunbar, *Dramatic Career of Arthur Murphy*, pp. 51–65.
29 Appleton, *Cycle of Cathay*, pp. 77–78; O'Brien, *Harlequin in Britain*, pp. 243–44.
30 Lynham, *The Chevalier Noverre*; Kirstein, *Four Centuries of Ballet*, 110–14; for the fetes, see Ou, "David Garrick's Reaction against French Chinoiserie in *The Orphan of China*," 25–42, and "The Chinese Festival and the Eighteenth-Century London Audience," 31–52; Ward, *Pagodas in Play*, pp. 69–71.
31 Kirstein, *Four Centuries of Ballet*, p. 111.
32 See McPherson, "Theatrical Riots and Cultural Politics in Eighteenth-Century London," 236–52, 237–8.
33 Ou, "Garrick's Reaction," 25.
34 *An Account of the New Tragedy of the Orphan of China*, pp. 11–12.
35 Murphy, *Life of Garrick*, I. 338
36 Oliver Goldsmith, "The Orphan of China," in *Collected Works of Oliver Goldsmith*, 6 vols., ed. Arthur Friedman, 1.170–79.
37 Yang, *Performing China*, p. 149
38 Dunbar, *Arthur Murphy*, pp. 54–55.
39 Murphy, *The Orphan of China*, p. 95. Further references are cited in the text by page number.
40 Yang, *Performing China*, p. 154.
41 Review Art 24. "The Orphan of China," 575, quoted Yang, *Performing China*, p. 149.
42 For the stage history of the play, see Dunbar, *Arthur Murphy*, pp. 68–70.
43 Du Halde's original version was adapted in Germany by Christoph Wieland, and translated complete in 1774 as *Der Chineser oder die Gerechtigkeit des Schicksals.*
44 Li Jueben, *Zhaoshi gu 'er*; Hsia, "The Orphan of the House of Zhao in French, English, German, and Hong Kong Literature," p. 394.

45 For Mason and Alexander, see Hayot, *Hypothetical Mandarin*, pp. 60–94; Mayer, *Harlequin in his Element*, pp. 139–64.

46 Clunas, *Chinese Export Watercolours*, p. 25; see also Grossman, *China Trade*.

47 For chinoiserie see Porter, *Ideographia*, pp. 133–92; and *Chinese Taste*, pp. 17–36; Honour, *Chinoiserie: the Vision of Cathay*; Jacobson, *Chinoiserie*; Beever (ed.), *Chinese Whispers*.

48 Porter *Ideographia*, p. 134; *Chinese Taste*, pp. 17–36.

49 Clunas, *Chinese Export Watercolours*, p. 116; Porter, *Chinese Taste*, pp. 27–29.

50 Hayot, *Hypothetical Mandarin*, pp. 79–85.

51 Alexander, "Journal of a Voyage to Pekin in China on board the Hindostan E I M," f33–f35.

52 Beever (ed.), *Chinese Whispers*, p. 67. See Clunas (ed.), *Chinese Export Art and Design*; Conner, *The China Trade 1600-1860*.

53 Clunas, *Chinese Export Watercolours*, p. 11.

54 Beever (ed.), *Chinese Whispers*, pp. 68–69. For the changes in the early nineteenth-century chinoiserie, see Jacobson, *Chinoiserie*, pp. 171–212.

55 Quoted, Morley, *The Making of the Royal Pavilion*, p. 25.

56 George, *Catalogue of political and personal satires*, 9.1949; Roberts, *History of the Royal Pavilion Brighton*, pp. 45, 51, 52–5.

57 *The parliamentary debates from the year 1803 to the present time*, 31, p. 201

58 Quennell (ed.), *Private Letters of Princess Lieven*, p. 150.

59 Mayer, *Harlequin in his Element*, p.140.

60 *Harlequin harmonist; or, a Trip to Japan a New Pantomime* (1813); Nicoll, *Early Nineteenth century Drama*, p. 286.

61 Mayer, *Harlequin in His Element*, pp. 144–45; Ward, *Pagodas in Play*, p. 179. Moon, *Yellowface*. Other Harlequin plays and spectacles set in China include: John Cross's *The Eclipse; or, Harlequin In China* (Royal Circus, 1801); a ballet, *The Chinese Divertisement* (Drury Lane, 1824); and the "spectacular" *Chinese Wonders; or, The Five Days Fete of Pekin* (Royal Amphitheatre 1833); Nicoll, *Early Nineteenth Century Drama*, pp. 286, 442.

62 Reeve and Bate, *Harlequin Mungo; or, a Peep into the Tower*, p. 11; Worrall, *Politics*, pp. 69, 98–100.

63 *Ibid.*, p. 16.

64 O'Keefe, *Aladdin and the Wonderful Lamp* (1788), quoted in Witchard, *Burke's Dark Chinoiserie*, p. 37.

65 Larpent, 1623; Witchard, *Burke's Dark Chinoiserie*, p. 38.

66 Dibdin, *The Chinese Sorceror*, f. 17, 23.

67 *The Witch of the Desert*, ff. 763

68 Witchard, *Burke's Dark Chinoiserie*, p. 9.

69 Knight, "Andrew Cherry," rev. Wells, *ODNB*; "Memoirs of the late Mr. Andrew Cherry," 294–95. For the Irish presence in the British theatre, see Cave, "Staging the Irishman," in *Acts of Supremacy*, ed. Bratton, pp. 62–128.

70 *The European Magazine and London Review* (March 1806), 169

71 Appleton, *Cycle of Cathay*, pp. 88–89

72 Roberts, *Memoirs of John Bannister, Comedian*, 2, pp. 139–40.

73 Gay, *Jane Austen and the Theatre*, pp. (19), 7–19; Austen, *Letters*, pp. 257–58.

74 For Braham, see Burwick, *Romantic Drama: Acting and Reacting*, pp. 18, 19, 33, 148, 190–92, 201, 218, and his "The Jew on the Romantic Stage," pp. 111–19.

75 The *Critical Review* judged that "'put money in your purse,' as Iago says, seems to have been his motive for publishing this farrago, of which the public have already swallowed eight does" (8 [1806], 99). The drama was satirized in Barron Field's "La Ciriegia, an austere Imitation of Milton's L' Allegro." *The News* (March 20, 1807), p. 103.

76 Cherry, *The Travellers*, p. 13. Further references to this edition are cited by page number in the text.

77 See Cave, *Staging the Irishman*, pp. 79–83.

78 Bratton, "Introduction," *Acts of Supremacy*, p. 5.

79 Larpent 1189; *Airs, Duets, and Chorusses*, pp. 8, 13, 14–16.

80 Larpent 772. f. 8.

81 Worrall, "Chinese Indians," 105–12.

82 There is no evidence that yellow facial make up was used in the portrayal of Chinese characters at this time, although blackface was common. Worrall, *Harlequin Empire*, p. 1. Moon, *Yellow-Face*.

83 Mayer, *Harlequin in His Element*, p. 297.

84 Cohen, "British Performances of Java, 1811–1822," 87–110.

85 Holder, "Melodrama," in Bratton (ed.), *Acts of Supremacy*, pp. 129–49 (130).

86 Larpent 2290; Colman, *The Law of Java*, p. 12. Further references are cited in the text by page number.

87 Quoted Mayer, *Harlequin in His Element*, p. 297.

88 Somerset, "Wars in China or the Battles of Chinghae and Amoy," ff. 1033 (f. 618).

89 For Lin Xexu, see Chang, *Commissioner Lin and the Opium Wars*.

90 Holder, "Melodrama," p. 133.

Bibliography

PRIMARY SOURCES

MANUSCRIPTS

Angus Library, Regent's Park College, Oxford

Box IN19: Journals and Correspondence, Joshua Marshman. 1799–1837.
Box IN20: Joshua and Hannah Marshman. 1799–1837.
Boxes IN21 and IN22: Carey, Marshman, and Ward, combined correspondence. 1799–1827.
Joshua Marshman. Bound Volume. Miscellaneous Correspondence. 1799–1826.

British Library, London (BL)

Add MS 33981: Thomas Manning to Joseph Banks, 16th April 1807; Thomas Manning to Joseph Banks, 5th January 1808.
Add MS 35174: William Alexander, "Journal of a Voyage to Pekin in China on board the Hindostan E I M Which Accompanied Lord Macartney on His Embassy to the Emperor." British Library. n.d.
Add. MSS 42975. Lord Chamberlain's Plays. Vol. 110: C. A. Somerset, "Wars in China or the Battles of Chinghae and Amoy" ("The Chinese War or the Conquest of Amoy by British Arms" (April–June 1844).
Add. MSS 2915. Lord Chamberlain's Plays. Vol. 501: "The Witch of the Desert; or, the Chinese Pedlar Boy" (March–April, 1832).
Add MSS 42980. Lord Chamberlain's Plays. Vol. 116: "The Chinese Exhibition or the Feast of Lanterns" (1844).
Add. MSS. 42982. Lord Chamberlain's Plays. Vol. 118: "Shadows on the Water or the Cleverest Lad in China" (1845).
Add MSS 42990. Lord Chamberlain's Plays. Vol. 126: "Chachechichochu and Wanky Twanky Fum or Harlequin in China" (1845).
Asia, Pacific and Africa Collections (APAC), formerly Oriental and India Office Collections (OIOC). MSS. Eur. D 993: "Memorial dated 27 Dec. 1788 by Sir Joseph Banks, sent to the Chairman of the East India Company on the Possibility of Introducing Tea Cultivation into India," 27th December 1788.
Eur MSS C864: William Jones to Charles Grant, 27th February 1785.

Huntington Library, San Marino, CA: John Larpent Collection

227: Edward Topham's "Bonds without Judgment; or, The Loves of Bengal" (1787).

1623: John O'Keefe, "Aladdin and the Wonderful Lamp" (1788).

1790: Thomas John Dibdin, "Harlequin Harmonist; or, a Trip to Japan a New Pantomime" ("Harlequin Harper; or, A Jump from Japan") (1813).

1189: James C. Cross, "Harlequin and Quixote; or, The Magic Arm" (1797).

1623: "Aladdin; or, The Wonderful Lamp" (Norwich, 1810).

1695: George Male, "Tartar's Tartar'd" ("One Foot by Land and One Foot by Sea; or, The Tartar's Tartar'd!" (1811).

1758: Arthur Murphy, "The Orphan of China" (1759).

1893: "Harlequin and Fortunio; or, The Treasures of China" ("Harlequin and Fortunio; or, Shing-Moo and Thun-Ton") (1815).

2164: "Whang Fong; or, How Remarkable" (1820).

2290: George Colman, "The Law of Java." (1822).

2344: Thomas John Dibdin, "Whang Fong" ("The Chinese Sorceror; or, the Emperor and His Three Sons" (1823).

Linnaean Society, London

MS no. 115, f1-fl19: Joseph Banks, "Hints on the subject of gardening suggested to the Gentlemen who attend the Embassy to China"; Letter Banks to Sir George Leonard Staunton, 18th August, 1792.

School of Oriental and African Studies (SOAS), University of London

Council for World Mission/London Missionary Society [CWM/LMS]: China, Personal: Robert Morrison Papers. Boxes 1–3.

State Library of New South Wales

Papers of Joseph Banks. Series 20.39–20.40: Thomas Manning to Joseph Banks, 27th August 1811; Thomas Manning to Joseph Banks, 6th September 1811. www2.sl.nsw.gov.au/banks/ <accessed 28/09/2012.>

University of Washington

Wason Collection. Vol. 8. Doc. 350. "Catalogue of presents sent by His Britannic Majesty to the Emperor of China."

PERIODICALS

Annual Review
The Asiatic Journal
The Chinese Repository

The Canton Register
The Critical Review
Edinburgh Review
The European Magazine and London Review
Indo-Chinese Gleaner
The Literary Gazette and Journal of the Belles Arts, Sciences &c
The Parliamentary Debates from the Year 1803 to the Present Time. Vol. 31
Quarterly Review
Transactions of the Royal Asiatic Society
The World

PRINTED BOOKS

Abel, Clarke, *Narrative of a Journey in the Interior of China* (London: Longman, 1818).
Abel-Remusat, Jean-Pierre, *Iu-kaio-l or, the Two Fair Cousins. A Chinese Novel. From the French version of M. A. Remusat* (London: Hunt & Clark, 1827).
Airs, Duets, and Chorusses in a New pantomime Called Harlequin and Quixotte; or, the Magic Arm (London: T. Woodfall, 1797).
Alexander, William, *The Costume of China* (London: William Miller, 1805).
An Account of the New Tragedy of the Orphan of China, and its Representation (London: J. Coote, 1759).
Auber, Peter, *China. An Outline of its Government, Laws, and Policy and of the British and Foreign Embassies to, and Intercourse with, that Empire* (London: Parbury, Allen and Co, 1834).
Austen, Jane, *Jane Austen Letters*, ed. Deirdre Le Faye (Oxford University Press, 1995).
Mansfield Park, ed. Jane Stabler (Oxford: World's Classics, 2003).
Baillie, Joanna, *Fugitive Verses* (London: Moxon, 1840).
Ball, Samuel, *An account of the cultivation and manufacture of tea in China* (London: Longman, 1848).
Banks, Sir Joseph, *The Indian and Pacific Correspondence of Sir Joseph Banks, 1768–1820*, ed. Neil Chambers. 5 vols. (London: Pickering and Chatto, 2008–12).
The Original Correspondence of Sir Joseph Banks Relating to the Foundation of the Royal Botanic Gardens, ed. Kalipada Biswas (Calcutta, 1950).
Barrow, John, *An Autobiographical Memoir of Sir John Barrow* (London: John Murray, 1847).
Some Account of the Public Life of the Earl of Macartney Travels in China (London: T. Cadell & W. Davies, 1804).
Travels in China (London: T. Cadell & W. Davies, 1804).
A Voyage to Cochinchina in the years 1792 and 1793 (London: Cadell & Davies, 1806).
The Bonze, or Chinese Anchorite, an oriental epic novel (London: Dodsley, 1769).
Blumenbach, J. F. *The Anthropological Treatises of Johann Friedrich Blumenbach*, trans. and ed. Thomas Bendysse (London: Longman, 1865).
Book of Poetry, trans. Xu Yuanchong (Beijing: China Translation & Publishing Corp, 2009).

Bridgeman, Elijah Coleman, "Chinese Versions of the Bible," *Chinese Repository*, 4.vi (October, 1835), 249–60.

Burney, Fanny, *Diary and Letters of Madame D'Arblay, … Edited by her Niece. Vol II: 1781–1786* (London: Henry Colburn, 1842).

Burney, Charles, A. Ribeiro (ed.), *The Letters of Dr Charles Burney. Volume I, 1751–1784* (Oxford University Press, 1991).

Byron, George Gordon, *The Complete Poetical Works*, ed. Jerome J. McGann. 7 vols. (Oxford University Press, 1980–93).

Cannon, Garland (ed.), *The Letters of Sir William Jones.* 2 vols. (Oxford: Clarendon, 1970).

Catalogue of the Valuable Library of the Late Robert Southey (London: Compton and Ritchie, 1844).

Chambers, William, *Designs of Chinese Buildings* (London: 1757).

A Dissertation on Oriental Gardening (London: W. Griffin, 1779).

Chang, Elizabeth Hope (ed.), *British Travel Writing from China, 1798–1901.* 5 vols. (London: Pickering and Chatto, 2010).

Cherry, Andrew, *The Travellers; or, Music's Fascination: An Opera in Five Acts* (London: Richard Phillips, 1806).

Coleridge, S. T., *Coleridge's Poetry and Prose*, ed. Nicholas Halmi, Paul Magnuson, and Raimondo Modiano (New York: W. W. Norton, 2004).

Collected Letters of Samuel Taylor Coleridge, ed. Earl Leslie Griggs. 6 vols. (Clarendon Press, Oxford, 1956-).

Lectures 1795: On Politics and Religion, ed. Lewis Patton and Peter Mann (Princeton University Press, 1972).

Collie, David (trans.), *The Chinese Classical Work commonly called the Four Books* (Malacca: Mission Press, 1828).

Colman, George, *The Law of Java. A Play in Three Acts* (London: W. Simpkin and R. Marshall, 1822).

Confucius, *The Analects*, trans. and ed. D. C. Lau (Harmondsworth: Penguin, 1979).

Analects: With Selections from Traditional Commentaries, trans. and ed. Edward Slingerland (London: Hackett Publishing, 2010).

Confucius Sinarum Philosophus, sive Sinensis (Paris, 1687)

Cranmer-Byng, J. L. (ed.), *An Embassy to China. Being the Journal kept by Lord Macartney during his embassy to the Emperor Ch'ien lung, 1793–1794* (London: Longman, 1962).

Cunningham (Cuninghame), James, "Observations During a Residence in the Island of Chusan, in 1701, by Doctor James Cunningham," in Robert Kerr (ed.), *A General History and Collection of Voyages and Travels.* 18 vols. (Edinburgh: William Blackwood, 1811–24), 9.549–62.

"Part of Two Letters to the Publisher from Mr. James Cunningham F.R.S. and Physician to the English at Chusan in China" (1707).

Davis, John Francis, *China during the War and Since the Peace.* 2 vols. (London: Longman, 1852).

The Chinese: A General Description of the Empire of China and its Inhabitants. 2 vols. (London: Charles Knight, 1836).

The Chinese: A General Description of the Empire of China and its Inhabitants. 3 vols. (London: C. Cox, 1851).

Chinese Miscellanies: A Collection of Essays and Notes (London: John Murray, 1865).

Chinese Novels translated from the originals (London: John Murray, 1822).

"Eugraphia Sinensis," Transactions of the Royal Asiatic Society, (1826), 304–12.

Han Koong Tsew or the Sorrows of Han (London: John Murray, 1829).

Hao Ch'iu Chuan. The Fortunate Union; a romance, translated from the Chinese original, with notes and illustrations. 2 vols. (London: John Murray, 1829).

Hien Wu Shoo. Chinese Moral Maxims (London: John Murray, 1823).

Laou-Seng-Urh; or, "An Heir in his Old Age." A Chinese Drama (London: John Murray, 1817).

Poeseos Sinensis commentarii: on the Poetry of the Chinese (London: Asher and Co., 1829).

San-Yu-Low; or, the Three Dedicated Rooms (Canton: EIC, 1815).

Sketches of China (London: Charles Knight, 1841).

Vocabulary, containing Chinese words and phrases peculiar to Canton and Macao (Macao: Mission Press, 1824)

Davis, John Francis (with Robert Morrison), *Translations from the Original Chinese* (Canton: EIC, 1816).

Davis, Frederick, *The History of Luton* (Luton, 1855).

Du Halde, Jean-Baptiste, *A Description of the Empire of China and Chinese-Tartary, Together With the Kingdoms of Korea, and Tibet.* 2 vols. (London: T. Gardner for E. Cave, 1738–41).

Ellis, Sir Henry, *Journal of the Proceedings of the Late Embassy to China* (London: John Murray, 1817).

Ellis, Markman, Richard Coulton, Ben Dew, and Matthew Mauger (eds.), *Tea and the Tea-Table in Eighteenth-Century England.* 4 vols. (London: Pickering and Chatto, 2010).

Emerson, Ralph Waldo, *The Journals and Miscellaneous Notebooks of Ralph Waldo Emerson* (eds.), William H. Gilman, *et al.* 10 vols. (Boston: Houghton Mifflin, 1909–14).

Farley, Charles, *The New Pantomime of Harlequin and Fortunio; or, Shing-Moo and Thun-Ton* (London: J. Miller, 1815).

Field, Barron, "La Ciriegia, an austere Imitation of Milton's L' Allegro," *The News* (March 20, 1807), p. 103.

Fu Lo-Shu (ed.), *A Documentary Chronicle of Sino-Western Relations, 1644–1820* (Tucson: University of Arizona Press, 1956).

Ghosh, Armitav, *River of Smoke* (London: John Murray, 2011).

Sea of Poppies (London: John Murray, 2008).

Goldsmith, Oliver, *Collected Works of Oliver Goldsmith*, ed. Arthur Friedman. 6 vols. (Oxford: Clarendon Press, 1966).

Grosier, Jean-Baptiste, *A General Description of China* (London: G.G.J. and J. Robinson, 1788).

Gutzlaff, Karl, *Journal of Three Voyages along the Coast of China* (New York, 1833).

Hatchett, William, *The Chinese Orphan* (London, 1741).

Hobhouse, John Cam, *Diary*, Sunday, May 23, 1819.

Huang Ya Dong, "A Letter to the President from a Young Chinese." *Asiatick Researches* (1790), 2.204.

Hunt, Leigh, "Domestic News from China," *The Companion*, 16 (1828), 213–7 (213).

    Leigh Hunt's Dramatic Criticism, 1808–1831 ed. Lawrence Huston Houtchens and Carolyn Washburn Houtchens (New York: Columbia University Press, 1949).

    "The Subject of Breakfast Continued – Tea-drinking." *London Journal*, 9 (1834), 113–14.

Hunter, William C., *The "Fan Kwae" at Canton Before the Treaty Days, 1825–1844, by an Old Hand* (London: Kegan Paul, 1882).

Jones, William, *Memoirs of the life, writings and correspondence of Sir William Jones*, ed. Sir John Shore (London: Hatchard, 1804).

    "On the Second Classical Book of the Chinese." *Asiatick Researches* (1790). In *The Works of Sir William Jones*. 2 vols. (London: G. G. and J. Robinson and R. H. Evans, 1799).

    The Works of Sir William Jones. 13 vols. (London: J. Stockdale, 1807).

Jones, William C. (ed.), *The Great Qing Code* (Oxford University Press, 1994).

Julien, Stanislas, *Tchao-chi-koi-eul, ou L 'Orphelin de la chine, drame en prose et en verse, accompagné des pieces historique qui en on fourni le subject* (Paris: Le Moutardier, 1834).

Keats, John. *The Letters of John Keats*, ed. H. E. Rollins. 2 vols. (Cambridge, MA: Harvard University Press, 1958).

Lamb, Charles, in *Elia and the Last Essays of Elia*, ed. Jonathan Bate (Oxford University Press, 1987).

Lamb, Charles and Mary. *The Letters of Charles and Mary Lamb*, ed. Edwin W. Marrs. 3 vols. (Ithaca: Cornell University Press, 1975–78).

Legge, James (trans), *The She King*, Part I, in *The Chinese Classics* (London: Trübner and Co, 1871).

Li Jueben, *Zhaoshi gu 'er* (Hong Kong: Huqiao xiju chubanshe, 1970).

Liu Jung-en (trans.), *Six Yüan Plays* (Harmondsworth: Penguin Books, 1972).

Manning, Thomas, "Chinese Jests," *New Monthly Magazine and Literary Journal*, 11 (1826), 280–84, 386–92, 573–75 (282).

    The Letters of Thomas Manning to Charles Lamb (London: Martin Secker, 1925).

Markham, Clements R (ed.), *Narratives of the Mission of Georges Bogle to Tibet and of the Journey of Thomas Manning to Lhasa* (Trübner, 1876 [New Delhi: Cosmo Publications, 1910]).

Marshman, John Clark, *The Life and Labours of Carey, Marshman and Ward*. 2 vols. (Longman, Brown, Green, Longmans & Roberts, 1859).

Marshman, Joshua, *Clavis Sinica* (Serampore: Mission Press, 1814).

    Dissertation on the Chinese Characters (Serampore: Mission Press, 1814).

Dissertation on the Sounds of the Chinese Language (Serampore: Mission Press, 1810).

Elements of Chinese Grammar, with a Preliminary Dissertation on the Colloquial Medium of the Chinese (Serampore: Mission Press, 1814).

Proposals for a Subscription for Translating the Holy Scriptures into the Following Oriental Languages (Serampore: Mission Press, 1806).

The Works of Confucius; containing the original text, with a translation. Vol. i. To which is prefixed a dissertation on the Chinese language and character (Serampore: Mission Press, 1809).

Mason, George Henry, *The Costume of China* (London: William Miller, 1800).

The Punishments of China, Illustrated by Twenty-Two Engravings with Explanations in English and French (London: Bulmer and Co., 1801).

Mason, William, *Satirical Poems* (ed.), Paget Toynbee (Oxford: Clarendon, 1926).

Medhurst, Walter, H., *Ancient China: The Shoo-king, or, the Historical Classic* (Shanghai: Mission Press, 1846).

China: its State and Prospects (London: John Snow, 1838).

Chinese and English Dictionary; containing all the words in the Chinese Imperial Dictionary, arranged according to the radicals. 2 vols. (Batavia: Parapattan Press, 1842–43).

A Dictionary of the Hok-këen Dialect of the Chinese Language (Parapattan Press, 1832).

An English and Japanese and Japanese and English Vocabulary (Batavia: Parapattan Press, 1830).

A Glance at the Interior of China (Shanghai: Mission Press, 1845).

A Translation of a Comparative Vocabulary of the Chinese, Corean, and Japanese Languages (Batavia: Parapattan Press, 1835).

"Memoirs of the late Mr. Andrew Cherry," *Gentleman's Magazine*, 82.1 (1812), 294–95.

Milne, William, *A Retrospect of the First Ten Years of the Protestant Mission to China* (Malacca: Mission Press, 1820).

The Sacred Edict containing the Sixteen Maxims of the Emperor Kang-He, amplified by His Son, the Emperor Yoong-Ching (Malacca: Mission Press, 1817).

Minford, John and Joseph M. Lau, *An Anthology of Translations: Chinese Classical Literature* (New York: Columbia University Press, 2002).

Morrison, Eliza, *Memoirs of the Life and Labours of Robert Morrison, D.D. … compiled by his widow.* 2 vols. (London: Longman, 1839).

Morrison, Robert, *Chinese Miscellany; consisting of original extracts from Chinese authors, in the native character; with translations and philological remarks* (Malacca: London Missionary Society, 1825), p. 34.

Dictionary of the Chinese Language A dictionary of the Chinese language in three parts (Macao: EIC, 1815–22).

A Grammar of the Chinese Language (Macao: EIC, 1815).

Horae Sinicae: Translations from the Popular Literature of the Chinese (London: Black and Parry, 1812).

Memoirs of the Rev. William Milne, D.D., late Missionary to China (Malacca: Mission Press, 1824).

A Parting Memorial, consisting of miscellaneous discourses, written and preached in China; at Singapore (London: W. Simpkin & R. Marshall, 1826).

Translations from the original Chinese with Notes (Canton: EIC, 1815).

A View of China, for philological purposes; containing a sketch of Chinese chronology, geography, government, religion and customs (Malacca: Mission Press, 1817).

Murphy, Arthur, *The Orphan of China. A Tragedy* (London: P. Valliant, 1759).

Percy, Thomas, *Hau Kiou Choaan; or, the Pleasing History; A translation [by J. Wilkinson] from the Chinese ... To which are added, I. The Argument or story of a Chinese Play; II. A Collection of Chinese Proverbs; and III. Fragments of Chinese Poetry.* 4 vols. (London: R&J Dodsley, 1761).

Miscellaneous Pieces Relating to China (London: R&J Dodsley, 1762).

Proudfoot, William Jardine, *Biographical Memoir of James Dinwiddie, L.L.D., Astronomer in the British Embassy to China, 1792, '3, '4* (Liverpool: Edward Howell, 1868).

Quennell M. P. (ed.), *The Private Letters of Princess Lieven to Prince Metternich, 1820–1826* (New York: Dutton, 1938).

Reeve, William, and William Bate, *Harlequin Mungo; or, a Peep into the Tower* (London: J. Skirven, 1789).

Roberts, Thomas Pachall, *Memoirs of John Bannister, Comedian*, 2 vols. (London: Richard Bentley, 1839).

Shelley, Percy, *Shelley's Poetry and Prose* (New York: W. W. Norton, 2002).

Shore, John, *Memoirs of the Life, Writings and Correspondence of Sir William Jones* (Hatchard, 1804), pp. 78–79.

Smith, Adam, *An Inquiry into the Nature and Causes of the Wealth of Nations*, ed. R. H. Campbell and A. S. Skinner. 2 vols. (Oxford University Press, 1976).

Southey, Robert, *Letters from England*, ed. Jack Simmons (London: Cresset, 1951).

Letters to Charles Butler (London: Longman, 1826).

The Life and Correspondence of Robert Southey, ed. C.C. Southey. 6 vols. (London: John Murray, 1849–50).

New Letters of Robert Southey, ed. Kenneth Curry. 2 vols. (New York: Columbia University Press, 1965).

Thalaba the Destroyer, ed. Tim Fulford. Vol. 3 of *Robert Southey: Poetical Works, 1793–1810*. Gen. ed. Lynda Pratt. 5 vols. (London: Pickering and Chatto, 2004).

"Travels in China" [Review]. In *The Annual Review, and History of Literature for 1804*, 3 (1805), 69–83.

Spence, Joseph, *A Particular Account of the Emperor of China's Gardens Near Pekin* (London: R. Dodsley, 1752).

Staunton, George Leonard, *An Authentic Account of an Embassy from the King of Great Britain to the Emperor of China* (London: G. Nichol, 1797).

Staunton, George Thomas. *Memoirs of the chief incidents of the public life of Sir G. T. Staunton* (London: L. Boot, 1856).

Miscellaneous Notes Relating to China and our Commercial Intercourse with that Country (London: John Murray, 1822).

Narrative of the Chinese Embassy to the Khan of the Tourgouth Tartars (London: John Murray, 1821).

Notes of Proceedings and Occurrences during the British Embassy to Pekin in 1816, ed. Patrick J. Tuck, *Volume 10, Britain and the China Trade 1635–1842* (London: Routledge, 2000).

Ta Tsing Leu Lee: being the fundamental laws, and a selection from the supplementary statutes, of the penal code of China (London: Cadell & W. Davies, 1810).

Tela, Joseph, *The Life and Morals of Confucius … Reprinted from the edition of 1691* (London: J. Souter, 1818).

Thoms, P. P. [Peter Perring], *The Affectionate Pair, or the History of Sung-Kin* (London: Black, Kingsbury, Parbury and Allen, 1820).

Chinese Courtship in Verse (London: Black, Kingsbury, Parbury and Allen, 1824)

A Dissertation on the Ancient Chinese Vases of the Shang Dynasty (London: James Gilbert, 1851).

"Mr. Klaproth's Attack upon Dr Morrison," *The Asiatic Journal*, 2 (1830), 201–6.

Volney, Constantin, *The Ruins or a Survey of the Revolutions of Empire* (London: J. Johnson, 1792).

Walpole, Horace, *Anecdotes of Painting in England*. 4 vols. (London: J. Dodsley, 1786).

The Yale Edition of Horace Walpole's Correspondence, ed. W. S. Lewis (New Haven: Yale University Press, 1937–74).

West, Stephen H. and Wilt L. Idema, *Monks, Bandits, Lovers and Immortals: Eleven Early Chinese Plays* (London: Hackett Publishing, 2010).

Weston, Stephen, *A Chinese Poem, inscribed on porcelain, in the thirty-third year of the cycle, A.D. 1776* (London: C&R Baldwin, 1816).

Ly Tang, An Imperial Poem, in Chinese, by Kien Lung with a translation and notes by Stephen Weston, FRS. FSA (London: C&R Baldwin, 1809).

Wilkinson, George, *Sketches Of Chinese Customs & Manners in 1811–12* (Bath: Browne, 1814).

Winterbotham, William, *An historical, geographical, and philosophical view of the Chinese Empire* (London: 1795).

Wordsworth, John, *The Letters of John Wordsworth*, ed. Carl H. Ketcham (Cornell University Press, 1969).

Wordsworth, William, *Home at Grasmere. Part First, Book First of the "Recluse"*, ed. Beth Darlington (Ithaca: Cornell University Press, 1977).

The Thirteen-Book Prelude by William Wordsworth, ed. Mark L. Reed. 2 vols. (Ithaca: Cornell University Press, 1991).

Wordsworth, William and Dorothy Wordsworth, *The Letters of William and Dorothy Wordsworth. Volume One. The Early Years 1787–1805* (Oxford: Clarendon, 1967).

SECONDARY SOURCES

Abu-Lughod, Janet, *Before European Hegemony* (Oxford University Press, 1989).

Adas, Michael, *Machines as the Measure of Men: Science, Technology, and Ideologies of Western Dominance* (New York: Cornell University Press, 1989).

Adorno, Theodor W. and Max Horkheimer, *Dialetik des Aufklarung. Philosophische Fragmente* (Amsterdam: Querido, 1947).

Aldridge, A. Owen, "The Perception of China in English Literature of the Enlightenment," *Asian Culture Quarterly*, 14 (1986), 1–26.

"The First Chinese Drama in English Translation," in Yun-tong Ruk (ed.), *Studies in Chinese-Western Comparative Drama* (Hong Kong: Chinese University Press, 1990), pp. 185–92.

Altick, Richard D., *The Shows of London* (Cambridge, MA: Harvard University Press, 1978).

Ames, Roger T., "Translating Chinese Philosophy," in Chan Sin-wai and David E. Pollard (ed.), *An Encyclopaedia of Translation: Chinese–English/English–Chinese* (Hong Kong: The Chinese University Press, 1995).

Amin, Samir, *Eurocentrism* (Zed Books, 1989).

Appleton, William, *A Cycle of Cathay: The Chinese Vogue in England during the Seventeenth and Eighteenth Centuries* (New York: Columbia University Press, 1951).

Aravamudan, Srinivas, *Enlightenment Orientalism: Resisting the Rise of the Novel* (University of Chicago Press, 2012).

Tropicopolitans: Colonialism and Agency 1688–1804 (Durham, NC, and London: Duke University Press, 1999).

Arrighi, Giovanni, *Adam Smith in Beijing* (London: Verso, 2007).

The Geometry of Imperialism (London: New Left Books, 1978).

The Long Twentieth Century (London: Verso, 1994).

Arrighi, Giovanni, Takeshi Hamashita, and Mark Selden, *The Resurgence of East Asia: 500, 150 and 50 Year Perspectives* (London: Routledge, 2003).

Auerbach, Sascha, *Race, Law and "The Chinese Puzzle" in Imperial Britain* (New York: Palgrave Macmillan, 2009).

Bald, R. C., "Sir William Chambers and the Chinese Garden," *Journal of the History of Ideas*, 11 (1950), 287–320;

Ballaster, Ros, *Fabulous Orients: Fictions of the East in England 1662–1785* (Oxford University Press, 2005).

Barbour, Richard, *Before Orientalism: London's Theatre of the East, 1576–1626* (Cambridge University Press, 2003).

Barmé, Geremie R., "The Garden of Perfect Brightness, A Life in Ruins," *East Asian History*, 11 (1996), 111–58.

Barrell, John, *English Literature in History: An Equal, Wide Survey* (London: Hutchinson, 1983).

The Idea of Landscape and the Sense of Place (Cambridge University Press, 1972).

The Infection of Thomas De Quincey: A Psychopathology of Imperialism (New Haven: Yale University Press, 1991).

Barrett, T. H., "Chinese Religion in English Guise: The History of an Illusion," *Modern Asian Studies*, 39.3 (2005), 509–33.

Singular Listlessness: A Short History of Chinese Books and British Scholars (London: Wellsweep Press, 1989).

Basalla, George, "The Spread of Western Science," *Science*, no. 156 (1967), 611–22.

Bassnett, Suzanne W. and John K. Fairbank (eds.), *Christianity in China: Early Protestant Missionary Writings* (Cambridge, MA: Harvard University Press, 1985);

Bate, Jonathan, *Romantic Ecology: Wordsworth and the Environmental Tradition* (New York: Routledge, 1991).

Bays, Daniel H. (ed.), *Christianity in China from the Eighteenth Century to the Present* (Stanford University Press, 1996).

A New History of Christianity in China (Oxford: Wiley-Blackwell, 2012).

Beckingham, C. F. "A History of the Royal Asiatic Society, 1823–1973," in Stuart Simmonds and Simon Digby (eds.), *The Royal Asiatic Society: its History and Treasures* (London: Routledge, 2002).

Beever, David (ed.), *Chinese Whispers: Chinoiserie in Britain 1650–1930* (Brighton & Hove: Royal Pavilion & Museums, 2008).

Bending, Stephen, "Horace Walpole and eighteenth-century garden history," *Journal of the Warburg and Courtauld Institutes*, 57 (1994), 209–26.

"A Natural Revolution? Garden Politics in Eighteenth-Century England," in Kevin Sharpe and Stephen Zwicker (eds.), *Refiguring Revolutions: Aesthetics and Politics from the English Revolution to the Romantic Revolution* (Berkeley: University of California Press, 1998), pp. 241–66.

Berg, Maxine, "Britain, industry and perceptions of China: Matthew Boulton, 'Useful knowledge' and the Macartney Embassy to China," *Journal of Global History*, 1.2 (2006), 269–88;

"Britain's Asian Century: Porcelain and Global History in the Long Eighteenth Century," in *The Birth of Modern Europe: Culture and Economy, 1400–1840* (Leiden: Brill, 2010), pp. 133–56.

Luxury and Pleasure in Eighteenth-Century Britain (Oxford University Press, 2007).

Bernal, Martin, *Black Athena. Volume 1* (London: Vintage, 1991).

Berridge, Victoria, and Griffith Edwards, *Opium and the People: Opiate Use in Nineteenth-Century England* (London: Allen Lane, 1987).

Bickers, Robert A. (ed.), *Ritual and Diplomacy: The Macartney Mission to China 1792–94* (London: British Association for Chinese Studies/Wellsweep, 1993).

The Scramble for China: Foreign Devils in the Qing Empire, 1832–1914 (London: Allen Lane, 2011).

Bivins, Roberta, "Expectations and Expertise: early British responses to Chinese Medicine," *History of Science*, 37 (1999), 459–89;

Acupuncture, expertise, and cross-cultural Medicine (Basingstoke: Palgrave, 2000).

Blaut, J. M., *The Colonizer's Model of the World: Geological Diffusionism and Eurocentric History* (New York: Guildford Press, 1993).

Bodde, Derek, *Chinese Thought, Society, and Science: The Intellectual and Social Background of Science and Technology in Pre-Modern China* (Honolulu: University of Hawaii Press, 1991).

Bonsall, Brian, *Sir James Lowther and Cumberland and Westmorland Elections 1754–1775* (Manchester University Press, 1960).

Booth, Martin, *Opium A History* (New York: St. Martins Press, 1996).

Bowen, H. V., "Tea, Tribute and the East India Company *c.* 1750–*c.* 1775," in *Hanoverian Britain and Empire: Essays in Memory of Philip Lawson*, ed. Stephen Taylor, Richard Connors, and Clive Jones (Woodbridge: Brewer, 1998), pp. 466–86.

Bratton J. S., Richard Allen Cave, Breandon Gregory, Heidi J. Holder, and Michael Pickering, *Acts of Supremacy: The British Empire and the Stage, 1790–1930* (Manchester University Press, 1991).

Bretschneider, Emile, *History of European Botanical Discoveries in China.* 2 vols. (London: Sampson Low, 1898).

Brockey, Liam Matthew, *Journey to the East: The Jesuit Mission to China, 1579–1724.* (Cambridge, MA: The Belknap Press of Harvard University Press, 2007).

Brook, Timothy, *The Confusions of Pleasure: Commerce and Culture in Ming China* (Berkeley: University of California Press, 1999).

Brook, Timothy, Jerome Bourgon, and Timothy Blue, *Death by a Thousand Cuts* (Cambridge, MA: Harvard University Press, 2008).

Brown, Laura, *Ends of Empire: Women and Ideology in Early Eighteenth-Century English Literature* (Ithaca: Cornell University Press, 1993).

Brown, Tony C., "Joseph Addison and the Pleasures of *Sharawadgi*," *ELH*, 74.1 (2007), 171–93.

Bruce, Harold Lawton, *Voltaire on the English Stage* (Berkeley: University of California Press, 1918).

Buchanan, Carol, *Wordsworth's Gardens* (Lubbock TX: Texas Tech University Press, 2001).

Burwick, Frederick, "James Gillray and the Aporia of Visual Hermeneutics," in *Romantic Explorations. Studien zur Englischen Romantik*, vol. 6, ed. Michael Meyer (Trier: Wissenschaftlicher Verlag Trier), pp. 85–103.

"The Jew on the Romantic Stage," in *Romanticism/Judaica: A Convergence of Cultures*, ed. Sheila Spector (Farnham: Ashgate, 2011), pp. 111–19.

Romantic Drama: Acting and Reacting (Cambridge University Press, 2011).

Callahan, William A., *China the Pessoptimist Nation* (Oxford University Press, 2010).

Cameron, Nigel, *Barbarians & Mandarins: Thirteen Centuries of Western Travellers in China* (New York: Wetherill, 1970).

Cannon, Garland, *The Life and Mind of Oriental Jones: Sir William Jones, the Father of Modern Linguistics* (Cambridge University Press, 2006).

Carey, D. and L. Festa (eds.), *The Postcolonial Enlightenment: Eighteenth-Century Colonialism and Postcolonial Theory* (Oxford University Press, 2009).

Carswell, John, *Blue and White: Chinese Porcelain and its Impact on the Western World* (University of Chicago Press, 1985).

Carter, Harold B., *Sir Joseph Banks, 1743–1820* (London: British Museum, 1988).

Casanova, Pascale, *The World Republic of Letters* (Cambridge MA: Harvard University Press, 2007).

Cave, Richard Allen, "Staging the Irishman," in *Acts of Supremacy*, ed. Bratton, pp. 62–128.

Chakrabarty, Dipresh, *Provincializing Europe: Postcolonial Thought and Historical Difference* (Princeton University Press, 2000).

Chan, Adrian, *Orientalism in Sinology* (Dublin: Academica Press, 2010).

Chan, Leo Tak-hung (ed.), *One into Many: Translation and the Dissemination of Classical Chinese Studies* (Amsterdam: B.V. Rodopi, 2003).

Chan, Wing-Tsit, *A Source Book in Chinese Philosophy* (Princeton University Press, 1963).

Chang, Elizabeth Hope, *Britain's Chinese Eye: Literature, Empire, and Aesthetics in Nineteenth-Century Britain* (Stanford University Press, 2010), pp. 27–38.

"Converting Chinese Eyes: Rev. W. H. Medhurst, 'Passing', and the Victorian Vision of China," in Douglas Kerr (ed.), *A Century of Travels in China: Critical Essays on Travel Writing from the 1840s to the 1940s* (Hong Kong University Press, 2007).

Chang, Hsin-pao, *Commissioner Lin and the Opium War* (New York: W.W. Norton, 1960).

Chaplin, Simon, "Putting a name to a face: the portrait of a 'Chinese Mandarin,'" *The Hunterian Museum Volunteers Newsletter*, 3 (Spring, 2007), 11–12.

Chase, Isabel, "William Mason and Sir William Chambers' *Dissertation on Oriental Gardening*," *Journal of English and Germanic Philology*, 35 (1936), 517–29.

Chatterjee, Ramarkrishna, "The Chinese Community in Calcutta: their Early Settlement and Migration," in *India and China in the Colonial World*, ed. Madhavi Thampi (New Delhi: Social Science Press and Orient Black Swan, 2005), pp. 59–60.

Chatterjee, Sunil Kumar, *William Carey and Serampore*. 3rd edn. (Serampore, 2008).

Chaudhuri, K. N., *Asia before Europe: Economy and Civilisation of the Indian Ocean from the Rise of Islam to 1750* (Cambridge University Press, 1990).

The Trading World of Asia and the East India Company (Cambridge University Press, 1978).

Chen, Jeng-Guo, "The British View of Chinese Civilization and the Emergence of Class Consciousness," *The Eighteenth Century: Theory and Interpretation*, 45 (2004), 193–205.

Ch'en, Jerome, *China and the West: Society and Culture 1815–1937* (London: Hutchinson, 1979).

Chen Shouyi, "The Chinese Garden in Eighteenth Century England," in Hsai (ed.), *Vision of China*, pp. 339–58.

"The Chinese Orphan: A Yuan Play: Its Influence on European Drama of the Eighteenth Century," in Hsai (ed.), *Vision of China*, pp. 359–83.

"Thomas Percy and his Chinese Studies," in Hsai (ed.), *Vision of China*, pp. 301–24.

Chen, Xiaomei, *Occidentalism: A Theory of Counter-discourse in Post-Mao China.* 2nd edn. (London: Rowman & Littlefield, 2002).

Cheung, David, *Christianity in Modern China: The Making of the First Native Protestant Church* (Leiden and Boston: Brill, 2004).

Cheung, Kai-chiong, "The *Haoqiu zhuan*, the First Chinese Novel Translated in Europe: With Special Reference to Percy's and Davis's Renditions," in Chan (ed.), *One into Many*, pp. 29–38.

The Theme of Chastity in Hau ch'iu chuan and Parallel Western Fiction (Bern: Peter Lang, 1994).

Ching, Julia and Willard G. Oxtoby (eds.), *Discovering China: European Interpretations in the Enlightenment* (New York: University of Rochester Press, 1992).

Chung-shu, Ch'ien "China in the English Literature of the Eighteenth Century," *Quarterly Bulletin of Chinese Bibliography*, 2 (1941), i–ii, 7–48

Clarke, Blake, *Oriental England: A Study of Oriental Influences in Eighteenth-century England as Reflected in the Drama* (Shanghai: Kelly & Walsh, 1939).

Clarke, David J., "Chitqua's English Adventure: An Eighteenth Century Source for the Study of China Coast Pidgin and Early Chinese," *Hong Kong Journal of Applied Linguistics*, 10.i (2005), 47–58.

"An Encounter with Chinese Music in Mid-eighteenth-century London," *Early Music*, 38.4 (2010), 543–58.

Clarke, J. J., *Oriental Enlightenment: The Encounter Between Asian and Western Thought* (London and New York: Routledge, 1997).

Clunas, Craig, *Chinese Export Watercolours* (London: V&A Museum, 1984).

Clunas, Craig (ed.), *Chinese Export Art and Design* (London: V&A Museum, 1987).

Coats, Alice M., *The Quest for Plants: A History of the Horticultural Explorers* (London: Studio Vista, 1969).

Cohen, Matthew, "British Performances of Java, 1811–1822," *South East Asia Research*, 17, 1 (2009), 87–110.

Cohen, Paul A., "Christian Missions and their Impact to 1900," in John K. Fairbank (ed.), *The Cambridge History of China. Vol 10: Late Ch'ing, 1800–1911, Part I* (Cambridge University Press, 1978), pp. 543–90.

Discovering History in China (New York: Columbia University Press, 1984).

Cohn, Bernard S., *Colonialism and the Forms of Knowledge* (Princeton University Press, 1996).

Colley, Linda, *Britons: Forging the Nation, 1707–1837* (London: Pimlico, 1994, 2009).

Captives: Britain, Empire and the World 1600–1850 (London: Pimlico, 2003).

Conner, Patrick, "China and the Landscape Garden: Reports, Engravings and Misconceptions," *Art History*, 2 (1979), 429–40.

The China Trade l600-l860 (Brighton: The Royal Pavilion, Art Gallery and Museums, 1986).

Copeland, Robert, *Spode's Willow Pattern and Other Designs after the Chinese* (London: Cassell, 1980).

Coulton, Robert (ed.), *Tea in Natural History and Medical Writing* (London: Pickering and Chatto, 2010).

Cox, E. H. M., *Plant Hunting in China* (London: Scientific Book Guild, 1945);

Cranmer-Byng, J. L., "The First English Sinologists: Sir George Staunton and the Reverend Robert Morrison," in F. S Drake (ed.), *Symposium on Historical Archaeological and Linguistic Studies on Southern China, Southeast Asia and the Hong Kong Region* (University of Hong Kong Press, 1967), pp. 247–60.

"Lord Macartney's Embassy to Peking in 1793, from Official Chinese Documents," *Journal of Oriental Studies*, 4 (1957–58), 1–2, 117–87.

Cranmer-Byng, J. L. and Trevor H. Levere, "A Case Study in Cultural Collision: Scientific Apparatus in the Macartney Embassy to China, 1793," *Annals of Science*, 38 (1981), 503–25.

Cranmer-Byng, J. L. and John E. Wills, Jr., "Trade and Diplomacy with Maritime Europe, 1644–c.1800," in John E. Wills, Jr. (ed.), *China and Maritime Europe 1500–1800* (Cambridge University Press, 2011).

Crossley, Pamela Kyle, *Orphan Warriors: Three Manchu generations and the end of the Qing World* (Princeton University Press, 1991).

A Translucent Mirror: History and Identity in Qing Imperial Mythology (Berkeley: University of California Press, 1999).

Crump, J. I. *Chinese Theater in the Days of Kublai Khan* (Tucson: University of Arizona Press, 1989).

Cutts, Elmer. H., "Chinese Studies in Bengal," *Journal of the American Oriental Society*, 62 (1942), 171–74.

"Political Implications in Chinese studies in Bengal, 1800–1823," *Indian Historical Quarterly*, 34 (1958), 152–63.

Daily, Christopher Allen, "From Gosport to Canton: A New Approach to Robert Morrison and the Beginnings of Protestant Missions in China" (unpublished PhD thesis, University of London, 2010).

Dalporto, Jeannie, "The Succession Crisis and Elkanah Settle's 'The Conquest of China by the Tartars,'" *The Eighteenth Century: Theory and Interpretation*, 45 (2004), 131–46.

Damrosch, David, *What is World Literature?* (Princeton University Press, 2003).

Daniel, Stephen, *Field of Vision: Landscape Imagery and National Identity* (London: Polity, 1992).

Dasgupta, Subrata, *The Bengal Renaissance: Identity and Creativity from Rammohan Roy to Rabindranath Tagore* (London: Permanent Black, 2006).

Davis, Bertram, *Thomas Percy a Scholar-Critic in the Age of Johnson* (Philadelphia: University of Pennsylvania Press, 1989).

Dawson, Raymond, *The Chinese Chameleon: An Analysis of European Conceptions of Chinese Civilization* (New York: Oxford University Press, 1967).

de Bruijn, Emile. "A Chinese Celebrity at Knole," *Treasure Hunt* (National Trust) http://nttreasurehunt.wordpress.com/2011/05/13/a-chinese-celebrity-at-knole/ accessed 07/12/11.

Dirlik, Arif, "Chinese History and the Question of Orientalism," *History and Theory*, 35 (1996), 96–118.

Dixon Hunt, John, *The Picturesque Garden in Europe* (London: Thames and Hudson, 2003).

Dolby, William, *A History of Chinese Drama* (London: HarperCollins, 1976).

Donald, Diana, *The Age of Caricature Satirical Prints in the Reign of George III* (New Haven: Yale University Press, 1996).

Dormandy, Thomas, *Opium Reality's Dark Dream* (New Haven: Yale University Press, 2012).

Dunbar, Howard, *The Dramatic Career of Arthur Murphy* (New York, 1947).

Elliot, Mark C., *The Manchu Way: The Eight Banners and Ethnic Identity in Late Imperial China* (Stanford University Press, 2001).

Elman, Benjamin A., *A Cultural History of Civil Examinations in Late Imperial China* (Berkeley: University of California Press, 2000).

   A Cultural History of Modern Science in China (Cambridge, MA: Harvard University Press, 2009).

   On Their Own Terms: Science in China (Cambridge, MA: Harvard University Press, 2005).

Emerson, Julie, Jennifer Chen, and Mimi Gardner Gates, *Porcelain Stories: From China to Europe* (Seattle: University of Washington Press, 2000).

Everett, Nigel, *The Tory View of Landscape* (New Haven; Yale University Press, 1994).

Fairbank, John K., *Discovering History in China* (New York: Columbia University Press, 1984).

Fan, Cunzhong (T.C. Fan), "Anti-Walpole Journalism," in Hsai (ed.), *Vision of China*, pp. 251–52.

   "China's Garden Architecture and the Tides of English Taste in the 18th Century," *Cowrie*, 1 (1948), 21–34.

   "Dr Johnson and Chinese Culture," in Hsai (ed.), *Vision of China*, pp. 266–69.

   "Percy and Du Halde," *Review of English Studies*, 84 (1945), 326–29.

   "Percy's *Hau Kiou Choann*," *Review of English Studies*, 22 (1946), 125.

   "William Jones's Chinese Studies," in Hsai (ed.), *Vision of China*, pp. 325–37.

Fan, Fa-ti, *British Naturalists in Qing China: Science, Empire, and Cultural Encounter* (Cambridge, MA: Harvard University Press, 2004).

   "Reeves, John (1774–1856)," *Oxford Dictionary of National Biography* (2004) www.oxforddnb.com/index/101023307/John-Reeves (accessed January 2012).

Fang, Karen, *Romantic Writing and the Empire of Signs: Periodical Culture and Post-Napoleonic Authorship* (University of Virginia Press, 2010).

Fay, Peter Ward, *The Opium War 1840–42* (New York: W.W. Norton, 1975).

Fenton, James, *School of Genius: A History of the Royal Academy of Arts* (London: Royal Academy, 2006).

Fleming, Fergus, *Barrow's Boys* (London: Granta, 1998).

Ford, Susan Allen (2008), "Fanny's 'Great Book': Macartney's Embassy to China and *Mansfield Park*," *Persuasions On-Line* 28.2. www.jasna.org/persuasions/on-line/vol228no2/ford.htm

Forêt, Philippe, "The intended perception of the Imperial Gardens at Chengde in 1780," *Studies in the History of Gardens & Designed Landscapes*, 19 (1999), 343–63.

Mapping Chengde: The Qing Landscape Enterprise (Honolulu: University of Hawaii Press, 2000).

Forrest, Dennis, *Tea for the British: The Social and Economic History of a Famous Trade* (London: Chatto and Windus, 1973).

Foxcroft, Louise, *The Making of Addiction: The "Use and Abuse" of Opium in Nineteenth-Century Britain* (Farnham: Ashgate, 2007).

Frank, André Gunder, *ReOrient: Global Economy in the Asian Age* (Berkeley: University of California Press, 1998).

Frank, Caroline, *Objectifying China, Imagining America: Chinese Commodities in Early America* (University of Chicago Press, 2011).

Franklin, Michael J., "'I burn with a desire of seeing Shiraz': A New Letter from Sir William Jones to Harford Jones," *Review of English Studies*, 56 (2005), 749–57.

Orientalist Jones: Sir William Jones Poet, Lawyer and Linguist (Oxford University Press, 2011).

Fromer, Julie, E, "'Deeply Indebted to the Tea-Plant': Representations of English National Identity in Victorian Histories of Tea," *Victorian Literature and Culture*, 36 (2008), 531–47.

A Necessary Luxury: Tea in Victorian Britain (Athens, OH: Ohio University Press, 2008).

Frykenberg, Robert, *Christians and Missionaries in India: Cross-Cultural Communication since 1500* (London: Routledge Curzon, 2003);

Fu Jin, *Chinese Theatre* (Cambridge University Press, 2012).

Fu Lo-Shu, *A Documentary Chronicle of Sino-Western Relations, 1644–1820* (Tucson: University of Arizona Press, 1956).

Fulford, Tim, *Landscape, Liberty, and Authority: Liberty and Authority: Poetry, Criticism, and Politics from Thomson to Wordsworth* (Cambridge University Press, 1998).

Fulford, Tim, and Peter J. Kitson (eds.), *Romanticism and Colonialism: Writing and Empire, 1780–1830* (Cambridge University Press, 1998).

Fulford, Tim, Peter J. Kitson, and Debbie Lee, *Romantic Literature, Science and Exploration: Bodies of Knowledge* (Cambridge University Press, 2004).

Fung, Ho-fung, "Orientalist Knowledge and Social Theories: China and the European Conceptions of East-West Differences from 1600 to 1900," *Sociological Theory*, 21 (2003), 254–80.

Fung, Yu-Lan, *A Short History of Chinese Philosophy* (New York: Free Press, 1997).

Gardella, Robert, *Harvesting the Mountains: Fujian and the China Tea Trade, 1757–1937* (Berkeley: University of California Press, 1994).

Gardner, Daniel K., *Zhu Xi's Reading of the* Analects (New York: Columbia University Press, 2003).

Gascoigne, John, *Joseph Banks and the English Enlightenment: Useful Knowledge and Polite Culture* (Cambridge University Press, 1994).

Science in the Service of Empire: Joseph Banks, the British State and the Uses of Science in the Age of Revolution (Cambridge University Press, 1998).

Gay, Penny, *Jane Austen and the Theatre* (Cambridge University Press, 2002).

Ge, Lingyan "On the Eighteenth-century Misreading of the Chinese Garden," *Comparative Civilization Review*, 27 (1992), 106–26.

Gelber, Harry G., *The Dragon and the Foreign Devils* (London: Bloomsbury, 2007).

George, Dorothy M., *Catalogue of political and personal satires, preserved in the Department of Prints and Drawings in the British Museum*. Vol. 6, 1784–1792 (London: British Museum, 1938).

Gernet, Jacques, *China and the Christian Impact: A Conflict of Cultures* (Cambridge University Press, 1985).

Gill, Stephen, *William Wordsworth. A Life* (Oxford University Press, 1990).

Giradot, Norman J., *The Victorian Translation of China: James Legge's Oriental Pilgrimage* (Berkeley: University of California Press, 2001).

Gladwyn, Derek, *Leigh Park a 19th Century Pleasure Ground* (London: Middleton Press, 1992).

Goldstone, Jack, "The Problem of the Early Modern World," *Journal of the Economic and Social; History of the Orient*, 41 (1998), 249–84.

Golinski, Jan, *Making Natural Knowledge: Constructivism and the History of Science* (Cambridge University Press, 1998).

Goody, Jack, *The East in the West* (Cambridge University Press, 1996).

Gray, Basil, "Lord Burlington and Father Ripa's Chinese engravings," *The British Museum Quarterly*, 22.1/2 (1960), 40–43.

Greenberg, Michael, *British Trade and the Opening of China*, 1800–42 (Cambridge University Press, 1951).

Gregory, John S., *The West and China since 1500* (Basingstoke: Palgrave, 2003).

Groom, Nick, *The Making of Percy's* Reliques (Oxford: Clarendon, 1999).

Grossman, Carl, *The China Trade: Export Paintings, Furniture, Silver and Other Objects* (Princeton University Press, 1972).

Gunn, Geoffrey C., *First Globalization: The Eurasian Exchange 1500–1800* (London: Rowman and Littlefield, 2003).

Guy, R. Kent., *The Emperor's Four Treasuries: Scholars and the State in the Late Ch'ien-Lung Era* (Cambridge, MA: Harvard University Press, 1987).

Haddad, John R., "Imagined Journeys to Distant Cathay: Constructing China with Ceramics, 1780–1920," in *Winterthur Portfolio*, 41.1 (2007), pp. 53–80.

Hanan, Patrick, "Chinese Christian Literature: the Writing Process," in *Treasures of the Yenching*, ed. Patrick Hanan (Cambridge, MA: Harvard-Yenching Library, 2003), pp. 260–83.

The Invention of Li Yü (Cambridge, MA: Harvard University Press, 1988).

Hancock, Christopher, *Robert Morrison and the Birth of Chinese Protestantism* (London: T&T Clark, 2008).

Harris, John, and Michael Snodin (eds.), *Sir William Chambers, Architect to George III* (New Haven: Yale University Press, 1996).

Harrison, Brian, *Waiting for China: The Anglo-Chinese College at Malacca 1818–1843, and Early Nineteenth-century Missions* (Hong Kong: University Press, 1979).

Hayot, Eric, *The Hypothetical Mandarin: Sympathy, Modernity, and Chinese Pain* (Oxford University Press, 2009).

Hayot, Eric, Haun Saussy, and Steven G. Yao (eds.), *Sinographies: Writing China* (Minneapolis: University of Minnesota Press, 2008).

Hayter, Alethea, *Opium and the Romantic Imagination* (London: Faber & Faber, 1968).

The Wreck of the Abergavenny: The Wordsworths and Catastrophe (Basingstoke: Macmillan, 2002; Pan Books, 2003).

Hegel, Robert E. *The Novel in Seventeenth Century China* (New York: Columbia University Press, 1981).

Hevia, James L., *Cherishing Men From Afar: Qing Guest Ritual and the Macartney Embassy* (Durham, NC: Duke University Press, 1995).

English Lessons: The Pedagogy of Imperialism in Nineteenth-Century China (Durham, NC, and London: Duke University Press, 2004).

The Imperial Security State: British Colonial Knowledge and Empire Building in Asia (Cambridge University Press, 2012).

'"The Ultimate Gesture of Deference and Debasement": Kowtowing in China.' *Past and Present*, 203 (2009), 212–34.

"World Heritage, National Culture, and the Restoration of Chengde," *Positions: East Asia Cultures Critique*, 9 (2001), 219–43.

Hibbert, Christopher, *The Dragon Wakes: China and the West 1793–1911* (Harlow: Longman, 1970).

Hillemann, Ulrike, *Asian Empire and British Knowledge: China and the Networks of British Imperial Expansion* (Basingstoke: Palgrave Macmillan, 2009).

Hobson, John M., *The Eastern Origins of Western Civilisation* (Cambridge University Press, 2004).

Holder, Heidi J., "Melodrama," in Bratton (ed.), *Acts of Supremacy: Realism and Empire on the British Stage*, pp. 129–49.

Honey, David B., *Incense at the Altar: Pioneering Sinologists and the Development of Classical Chinese Philology* (New Haven, CT: American Oriental Society, 2001).

Honour, Hugh, *Chinoiserie: A Vision of Cathay* (London: John Murray, 1961).

Hostetler, Laura, *Qing Colonial Enterprise: Ethnography and Cartography in Early Modern China* (University of Chicago Press, 2005).

Hsia, Adrian, *Chinesia: The European Construction of China in the Literature of the 17th and 18th Centuries* (Tubingen: Max Niemeyer Verlag, 1998).

"*The Orphan of the House of Zhao* in French, English, German, and Hong Kong Literature," in Hsia (ed.), *Vision of China*, pp. 383–400.

Hsia, Adrian (ed.), *The Vision of China in the English Literature of the Seventeenth and Eighteenth Centuries* (Hong Kong: Chinese University Press, 1998).

Hsin-pao Chang, *Commissioner Lin and the Opium War* (New York: W.W. Norton, 1960).

Hsü, Immanuel C. Y., *The Rise of Modern China* (Oxford University Press, 1970).

Huang, Martin W., *Desire and Fictional Narrative in Late Imperial China* (Cambridge, MA: Harvard University Press, 2001).

Hubback, J. H. and Edith C. Hubback, *Jane Austen's Sailor Brothers: Being the Adventures of Sir Francis Austen, G.C.B.* (London: John Lane, 1906).

Huff, Toby E., *The Rise of Early Modern Science: Islam, China and the West* (Cambridge University Press, 1993).

Idema, Wilt L., "The Many Shapes of Medieval Chinese Plays: How Texts are Transformed to Meet the Needs of Actors, Spectators, Censors, and Readers," *Oral Tradition*, 20 (2005), 320–34.

"The Orphan of Zhao: Self-Sacrifice, Tragic Choice, and the Confucianization of Mongol Drama at the Ming Court," *Cina*, 21 (1988), 159–90.

Jacobson, Dawn, *Chinoiserie* (London: Phaidon, 1993).

Jacques, David, "On the supposed Chineseness of the English Landscape Garden," *Garden History*, 18.2 (1990), 180–91.

Jacques, Martin, *When China Rules the World: The Rise of the Middle Kingdom and the End of the Western World* (London: Allen Lane, 2009).

James, Felicity, "Thomas Manning, Charles Lamb, and Oriental Encounters," *Poetica*, 76 (2011), 21–36.

Jensen, Lionel M., *Manufacturing Confucius: Chinese Traditions and Universal Civilization* (Durham, NC, and London: Duke University Press, 1997).

Johnston, Kenneth R., *The Hidden Wordsworth: Poet, Lover, Rebel, Spy* (New York: W.W. Norton, 1998).

Jordain, Margaret and R. Soame Jenyns, *Chinese Export Art in the Eighteenth Century* (Feltham: Middlesex, 1967).

Joseph, Betty, *Reading the East India Company 1720–1840* (University of Chicago Press, 2003).

Kaul, Suvir, *Eighteenth-Century Literature and Postcolonial Studies* (Edinburgh University Press, 2009).

Poems of Nation, Anthems of Empire: English Verse in the Long Eighteenth Century (Charlottesville and London: University Press of Virginia, 2000).

Keevak, Michael, *Becoming Yellow: A Short History of Racial Thinking* (Princeton University Press, 2011).

The Pretended Asian: George Psalmanazar's Eighteenth-century Formosan Hoax (Detroit: Wayne State University Press, 2004).

Keogh, Annette, "Oriental Translations: Linguistic Explorations into the Closed Nation of Japan," *The Eighteenth Century: Theory and Interpretation*, 45 (2004), 171–91.

Keswick, Maggie, *The Chinese Garden* (London: Academy Editions, 1978).

Kirstein, Lionel, *Four Centuries of Ballet: Fifty Masterworks* (London: Dover, 1985).

Kitson, Peter J., "'Reason in China is not Reason in England': Walpole's Chinese Writings and Arthur Murphy's *The Orphan of China*," in *Romantic Adaptations*, ed. Cian Duffy (Aldershot: Ashgate, 2013), pp. 9–21.

Romantic Literature, Race and Colonial Encounter, 1760–1830 (New York: Palgrave Macmillan, 2007).

Klekar, Cynthia, "'Prisoners in Silken Bonds': Obligation, Trade, and Diplomacy in English Voyages to Japan and China," *Journal of Early Modern Cultural History*, 2 (2006), 84–105.

"'Sweetness and Courtesie': Benevolence, Civility, and China in the Making of European Modernity," *Eighteenth-Century Studies*, 43 (2010), 357–69.

Knight, Joseph, "Cherry, Andrew (1762–1812)," rev. John Wells, *ODNB* (Oxford University Press, 2004).

Knox-Shaw, Peter, "Fanny Price Refuses to Kowtow," *Review of English Studies*, 47 (1996), 212–17.

Koerner, Lisbet, *Linnaeus: Nature and Nation* (Cambridge, MA: Harvard University Press, , 2001).

Kopf, David, *British Orientalism and the Bengal Renaissance* (Berkeley: University of California Press, 1969).

Lach, Donald F., *Asia in the Making of Europe*. 3 vols. (University of Chicago Press, 1965–93).

China in the Eyes of Europe: The Sixteenth Century (University of Chicago Press).

Lamb, Jonathan, *Preserving the Self in the South Seas* (University of Chicago Press, 2001).

Latour, Bruno, *Science In Action: How to Follow Scientists and Engineers Through Society* (Cambridge, MA: Harvard University Press, 1987).

We Have Never Been Modern (Cambridge, MA: Harvard University Press, 1993).

Latourette, Kenneth Scott, *A History of Christian Missions in China* (London: SPCK, 1929).

Leask, Nigel, *British Romantic Writers and the East: Anxieties of Empire* (Cambridge University Press, 1992).

Curiosity and the Aesthetics of Travel Writing 1770–1840 (Oxford University Press, 2002).

"Kubla Khan and Orientalism: The Road to Xanadu Revisited," *Romanticism*, 4 (1998), 1–21.

Lehner, Georg, "From Enlightenment to Sinology: Early European Suggestions on How to Learn Chinese, 1770–1840," in *Asian Literary Voices: From Marginal to Mainstream*, ed. Philip F. Williams (Amsterdam University Press, 2010).

Levy, André and William H. Ninenhauser, *Chinese Literature, Ancient and Classical* (Bloomington: Indiana University Press, 2007).

Lew, Joseph H., "'That Abominable Traffic': *Mansfield Park* and the Dynamics of Slavery," in Beth Fowkes Tobin (ed.), *History, Gender and Eighteenth-Century Literature* (Athens, GA: University of Georgia Press, 1994), pp. 271–300.

Lin, Man-houng, *China Upside Down: Currency, Society and Ideologies, 1808–1856* (Cambridge, MA: Harvard University Press, 2006).

Liu, Lydia H., *The Clash of Civilizations: The Invention of China in Modern World Making* (Cambridge, MA: Harvard University Press, 2004).

"Robinson Crusoe's Earthenware Pot," *Critical Enquiry*, 25 (1999), pp. 730–48.

Translingual Practice: Literature, National Culture, and Translated Modernity-China 1900–1937 (Stanford University Press, 1995).

(ed.), *Tokens of Exchange: The Problem of Translation in Global Civilization* (Durham, NC, and London: Duke University Press, 1999).

Liu, Ts'un-yan, *Chinese Popular Fiction in Two London Libraries* (Hong Kong: Longmen shuju, 1967).

Liu, Wu-chi, "The Original Orphan of China," *Comparative Literature*, 3 (1953), 193–212.

Liu, Yu, *Seeds of a Different Eden: Chinese Gardening Ideas and a New English Aesthetic Ideal* (Columbia, SC: University of South Carolina Press, 2008).

Lloyd, Christopher, *Mr. Barrow of the Admiralty: A Life of Sir John Barrow* (London: Collins, 1970).

Lopez, Manuel D., *Chinese Drama: An Annotated Bibliography of Commentary, Criticism, and plays in English Translation* (Metuchen, NJ & London: Scarecrow Press, 1991).

Lovejoy, A. O., "The Chinese Origin of A Romanticism," in *Essays in the History of Ideas* (New York: George Braziller, 1955).

Lovell, Julia, *The Opium War: Drugs, Dreams and the Making of China* (London: Picador, 2011).

Lu Hsun (Lu Xun), *A Brief History of Chinese Fiction*, trans. Yang Hsien-yi and Gladys Yang (Peking: Foreign Language Press, 1959).

Lundbaek, Knud, "The Establishment of European Sinology 1801–1815," in *The Chinese Rites Controversy: Its History and Meaning*, ed. David E. Mungello (Monumenta Serica Monograph Series 33, 1994), pp. 129–45.

"The First Translation from a Confucian Classic in Europe," *China Mission Studies Bulletin*, 1 (1979), 1–11.

Joseph de Prémare (1666–1736), S.J. Chinese Philology and Figurism. Acta Jutlandica, LXVI: 2 (Aarhus: Aarhus University Press, 1991).

T.S. Bayer (1694–1738). Pioneer Sinologist (Scandinavian Institute of Asian Studies Monograph Series 54, 1986).

"Une grammaire espagnole de la langue chinoise au XVIIIe siècle," *Actes du IIe Colloque International de Sinologie* (Paris, 1980), 259–69.

Lutz, Jessie G., *Opening China: Karl F.A. Gutzlaff and Sino-Western Relations, 1822–1852* (Grand Rapid, MI: William B. Eerdmans Publishing, 2008).

Lynham, Deryck, *The Chevalier Noverre: Father of Modern Ballet* (London: Dance Books, 1972).

McCracken, Donal, *Gardens of Empire: Botanical Institutions of the Victorian British Empire* (Leicester University Press, 1997).

Mackenzie, John M., *Orientalism: History, Theory and the Arts* (Manchester University Press, 1995).

Mackerras, Colin, *Western Images of China* (Hong Kong and Oxford: Oxford University Press, 1989).

(ed.), *Chinese Theater From its Origins to the Present Day* (Honolulu: University of Hawai'ii Press, 1983).

McMahon, Keith, *Casualty and Containment in Seventeenth Century Chinese Fiction* (Leiden: Brill, 1998).

McMillin, Laurie Hovell, *English in Tibet, Tibet in English: Self-Presentation in Tibet and the Diaspora* (Basingstoke: Palgrave, 2002).

McPherson, Heather, "Theatrical Riots and Cultural Politics in Eighteenth-Century London," *The Eighteenth Century*, 43.iv (2002), 236–52.

Mair, Victor H. (ed.), *The Columbia History of Chinese Literature* (New York: Columbia University Press, 2010).

Makdisi, Saree, *Romantic Imperialism: Universal Empire and the Culture of Modernity* (Cambridge University Press, 1998).

Markley, Robert, "Anson at Canton, 1743: Obligation, Exchange, and Ritual Passage in Edward Page's 'Secret History,'" in Zionkowski and Klekar (eds), *Culture of the Gift*, pp. 215–34.

The Far East and the English Imagination, 1600–1730 (Cambridge University Press, 2006).

"Introduction: Europe and East Asia in the Eighteenth Century," in *The Eighteenth Century: Theory and Interpretation*, 45 (2004), 111–14.

(ed.), "China and the Making of Global Modernity," *Eighteenth-Century Studies*, 43 (2010).

Marshall, P. J. and Glyndwr Williams, *The Great Map of Mankind: British Perceptions of the World in the Age of Enlightenment* (London: Dent, 1982).

Matlak, Richard, *Deep Distresses: William Wordsworth, John Wordsworth, Sir George Beaumont* (Newark: University of Delaware Press, 2003).

Mauss, Marcel, *The Gift: Forms and Functions of Exchange in Archaic Societies* (London: Martino Books, 2011).

Mayer, David, III, *Harlequin in his Element: The English Pantomime, 1806–1836* (Cambridge, MA: Harvard University Press, 1969).

Métailié, Georges "Sir Joseph Banks – An Asian Policy?" in *Sir Joseph Banks: A Global Perspective*, ed. R. E. R. Banks, B. Elliot, J. G. Hawkes, D. King-Hele, and G. L. Lucas (London: Kew Royal Botanic Gardens, 1994), pp. 157–69.

Miller, David Philip, and Peter Hans Reill (eds.), *Visions of Empire: Voyages, Botany, and Representations of Nature* (Cambridge University Press, 1999).

Milligan, Barry, *Pleasures and Pains: Opium and the Orient in 19th-Century British Culture* (Charlottesville: University of Virginia Press, 1995).

Millward, James A., Ruth W. Dunnell, Mark C. Elliot, and Philippe Forêt (eds.), *New Qing Imperial History: The Making of Inner Asian Empire at Qing Chengde* (London: Routledge Curzon, 2004).

Milner-Barry, Ada, "A Note on the Early Literary Relations of Oliver Goldsmith and Thomas Percy," *Review of English Studies*, 2 (1925), 125.

"A Further Note on *Hau Kiou Choann*," *Review of English Studies* 3 (1927), 214–17.

Min, Eun Kyung, "China between the Ancients and the Moderns," *The Eighteenth Century: Theory and Interpretation*, 45 (2004), 115–29.

"Narrating the Far East: Commerce, Civility and Ceremony in the Amherst Embassy to China 1816–17," *Studies on Voltaire and the Eighteenth Century,* 9 (2004), 160–80.

"Thomas Percy's *Chinese Miscellanies* and the *Reliques of Ancient English Poetry* (1765)," *Eighteenth-Century Studies,* 43 (2010), 307–24.

Minimika, George, *The Chinese Rites Controversy from its Beginning to Modern Times* (Chicago: Loyola Press, 1985).

Moon, Krystyn R., *Yellowface: Creating the Chinese in American Popular Music and Performance* (New York: Rutgers, 2005).

Moretti, Franco, *Graphs, Maps, Trees* (London: Verso, 2005).

Morley, John, *The Making of the Royal Pavilion, Brighton Designs and Drawing* (London: CHP Editions, 1984).

Morse, H. B. *The Chronicles of the East India Company trading to China, 1634–1834.* 5 vols. (Oxford: Clarendon Press, 1926).

Moseley, William Willis, *The Origin of the First Protestant Mission to China* (1842).

Mote, F. W., *Imperial China 900–1800* (Cambridge, MA: Harvard University Press, 1999).

The Intellectual Foundations of China (New York: A. A. Kopf, 1971).

Moxham, Roy, *Tea: Addiction, Exploitation and Empire* (London: Constable, 2003).

Mui, Hoh-Cheung, and Lorna H. Mui, *The Management of Monopoly: A Study of the East India Company's Conduct of its Tea Trade, 1784–1833* (Vancouver: University of British Columbia Press, 1984).

Mungello, David E. (ed.), *The Chinese Rites Controversy: Its History and Meaning* (Chicago: Loyola Press, 1994).

Curious Land: Jesuit Accommodation and the Origins of Sinology (Honolulu: University of Hawaii Press, 1985).

The Great Encounter of China and the West, 1500–1800 (London: Rowman & Littlefield, 2012).

"Sinological Torque," *Philosophy East and West,* 28 (1978), 123–41.

Murphy, Arthur, *Life of Garrick.* 2 vols. (London: J. Wright, 1801).

Naquin, Susan and Evelyn S. Rawski, *Chinese Society in the Eighteenth Century* (New Haven: Yale University Press, 1989).

Needham, Joseph, *The Grand Titration: Science and Society in East and West* (London: Allen and Unwin, 1969).

Needham, Joseph and Christopher Harbsmeier, *Science and Civilisation in China,* vol. 7: Part 1 (Cambridge University Press, 1998).

Needham, Joseph, Ling Wang and Derek J. De Solla Price, *Heavenly Clockwork: The Great Astronomical Clocks of Medieval China* (Cambridge University Press, 2008).

Nicoll, Allardyce, *A History of English Drama, 1660–1900. Vol 4: Early Nineteenth-century Drama, 1750–1800* (Cambridge University Press, 1955).

A History of Late Eighteenth-century Drama 1750–1800 (Cambridge University Press, 1929).

Niranjana, Tejaswini, *Siting Translation: History, Post-Structuralism, and the Colonial Context* (Berkeley: University of California Press, 1992).

Nokes, David, *Jane Austen: A Life* (London: Fourth Estate, 1997).

Nussbaum, Felicity A., *The Limits of the Human: Fictions of Anomaly, Race, and Gender in the Long Eighteenth Century* (Cambridge University Press, 2003).

Torrid Zones: Maternity, Sexuality, and Empire in Eighteenth-Century English Narratives (Baltimore: Johns Hopkins University Press, 1995).

(ed.), *The Global Eighteenth Century* (Baltimore: Johns Hopkins University Press, 2003).

Nussbaum, Felicity A. and Saree Makdisi (eds.), *The Arabian Nights in Historical Context* (Oxford University Press, 2009).

O'Brien, John, *Harlequin in Britain: Pantomime and Entertainment, 1690–1750* (Baltimore: Johns Hopkins University Press, 2004).

Ogburn, Vincent H., "The Wilkinson MSS and Percy's Chinese Books," *Review of English Studies*, 9 (1933), 30–36.

O'Hara, Patricia, " 'The Willow Pattern That We Knew': The Victorian Literature of Blue Willow," *Victorian Studies*, 36 (1993), 421–42.

Orr, Bridget, *Empire on the English Stage 1660–1714* (Cambridge University Press, 2007).

O'Quinn, Daniel, *Entertaining Crisis in the Atlantic Imperium, 1770–1790* (Baltimore: Johns Hopkins University Press, 2011).

Staging Governance: Theatrical Imperialism in London, 1770–1800 (Baltimore: Johns Hopkins University Press, 2005).

Ou, Hsin-yun, "The Chinese Festival and the Eighteenth-Century London Audience, *The Wenshan Review of Literature and Culture*, 2.i (2008), 31–52.

"David Garrick's Reaction against French Chinoiserie in *The Orphan of China*," *Studies in Theatre and Performance*, 27.i (2007), 25–42.

Owen, Stephen, "Poetry in the Chinese Tradition," in *Heritage of China: Contemporary Perspectives on Chinese Civilization*, ed. Paul S. Ropp (Berkeley: University of California Press, 1992).

Pagani, Catherine, *"Eastern Magnificence and European Ingenuity": Clocks of Late Imperial China* (Ann Arbor: University of Michigan Press, 2001).

Pan, Lynn, *Sons of the Yellow Emperor: A History of the Chinese Diaspora* (New York: Kodansha International, 1990).

Park, Y and R. J. Rajan (eds.), *The Postcolonial Jane Austen* (London and New York: Routledge, 2000).

Parthasarathi, Prasannan, *Why Europe Grew Rich and Asia Did Not: Global Economic Divergence, 1600–1850* (Cambridge University Press, 2011).

Perdue, Peter C., "Boundaries and Trade in the Early Modern World: Negotiations at Nerchinsk and Beijing," *Eighteenth Century Studies*, 43 (2010), 341–56.

China Marches West: The Qing Conquest of Central Eurasia (Cambridge, MA: Harvard University Press, 2005).

Perlin, Frank, *Unbroken Landscape* (Aldershot: Variorum, 1994).

Petersen, Willard J., "Learning from Heaven: the Introduction of Christianity and Other Western Religions into Late Ming China," in John E. Wills, Jr. (ed.), *China and Maritime Europe, 1500–1800*, pp. 78–134

Peyrefitte, Alain, *The Collision of Two Civilisations: The British Expedition to China 1792–4* (London: Harvill/HarperCollins, 1993).

Pfister, Lauren F., *Striving For "The Whole Duty Of Man": James Legge and the Scottish Protestant Encounter With China* (Berlin: Peter Lang, 2003).

Phillips, C. H., *The East India Company, 1784–1834* (Manchester University Press, 1940).

Po-Chia Hsia, R., *A Jesuit in the Forbidden City: Matteo Ricci 1552–1610* (Oxford University Press, 2010).

Pointon, Marcia. "Dealer in Magic: James Cox's Jewelry Museum and the Economics of Luxurious Spectacle in Late-Eighteenth-Century London," in Neil De Marchi Craufurd and D. W. Goodwin (eds.), *Economic Engagements with Art* (Durham, NC: Duke University Press, 1999).

Pomeranz, Kenneth, *The Great Divergence: China, Europe and the Making of the Modern World Economy* (Princeton University Press, 2000).

Porter, Andrew, *Religion Versus Empire?: British Protestant Missionaries and Overseas Expansion, 1700–1914* (Manchester University Press, 2004).

Porter, David, *The Chinese Taste in Eighteenth-Century England* (Cambridge University Press, 2010).

  Ideographia: The Chinese Cipher in Early Modern Europe. (Stanford University Press, 2001).

  "Sinicizing Early Modernity: The Imperatives of Historical Cosmopolitanism," *Eighteenth-Century Studies*, 43 (2010), 299–306

Powell, L. F., "*Hau Kiou Choaan*," *Review of English Studies*, 2 (1926), 446–55.

Pratt, Mary Louise, *Imperial Eyes: Travel Writing and Transculturation* (New York and London: Routledge, 1992).

Pritchard, E. H., *Anglo-Chinese Relations during the Seventeenth and Eighteenth Centuries* (Urbana: University of Illinois Press, 1929).

  The Crucial Years of Early Anglo-Chinese Relations, 1750–1800 (Washington: Pullman, 1936).

  "The Kowtow in the Macartney Embassy in 1793," *Far East Quarterly*, 2.2 (1943), 163–203.

Qian, Zhaoming, *Orientalism and Modernism* (Durham, NC and London: Duke University Press, 1995).

  The Modernist Response to Chinese Art: Pound, Moore, Stevens (Charlottesville: Virginia, 2003).

Qian, Zhongshu, "China in the English Literature of the Eighteenth Century," in *The Vision of China in the English Literature of the Seventeenth and Eighteenth Centuries*, ed. Hsia, pp. 117–21

Qingxi Lou, *Chinese Gardens* (Cambridge University Press, 2011).

Qiong, Zhong, "Demystifying Qi: The Politics of Cultural Translation and Interpretation in the Early Jesuit Mission to China," in Liu (ed.), *Tokens of Exchange*, pp. 74–106.

Raj, Kapil, *Relocating Modern Science: Circulation and the Construction of Knowledge in South Asia and Europe, 1650–1900* (Basingstoke: Palgrave Macmillan, 2007).

Rawski, Evelyn, *The Last Emperors: A Social History of the Qing Imperial Institutions* (Berkeley and Los Angeles: University of California Press, 1998).

Reinders, Eric Roberts, *Borrowed Gods and Foreign Bodies: Christian Missionaries Imagine Chinese Religion* (Berkeley: University of California Press, 2004).

Richardson, Alan, *Literature, Education, and Romanticism: Reading as Social Practice, 1780–1832* (Cambridge University Press, 1994).

Ride, Lindsay, *Robert Morrison: The Scholar and the Man* (Hong Kong University Press, 1957).

Ringmar, Erik, *Liberal Barbarism: The European Destruction of the Emperor's Summer Palace* (Basingstoke: Palgrave Macmillan, 2012).

Roberts, Henry David, *History of the Royal Pavilion Brighton* (London: Country Life, 1939).

Rochwein, Adolf, *China and Europe: Intellectual and Artistic Contacts in the Eighteenth Century*, trans. J. C. Powell (New York: A. A. Kopf, 1925).

Roebuck, Peter (ed.), *Macartney of Lissanoure: 1737–1806: Essays in Biography* (Belfast: Ulster Historical Association, 1983).

Rose, Sarah, *For All the Tea in China* (London: Hutchinson, 2009).

Rowbotham, Arnold, "The impact of Confucianism in seventeenth century Europe," *Far Eastern Quarterly*, 4 (1945), 224–42.

Missionary and Mandarin: The Jesuits at the Court of China (Berkeley: University of California Press, 1942).

Rowe, William T., *China's Last Empire: The Great Qing* (Cambridge, MA: Harvard University Press, 2009).

Rubinstein, Murray A., *The Origins of the Anglo-American Missionary Enterprise in China, 1807–1840* (London: Scarecrow Press, 1996).

"The Wars They Wanted: American Missionaries' Use of *The Chinese Repository* Before the Opium War," *American Neptune*, 48 (1988), 271–82.

Rule, Paul A., *K'ung-tzu or CONFUCIUS? The Jesuit Interpretation of Confucianism* (Sydney: Allen and Unwin, 1986).

Said, Edward W., *Culture and Imperialism* (London: Vintage, 1994).

Orientalism (Harmondsworth: Penguin, 1978).

St. André, James G., "'But do they have a notion of Justice?': Staunton's 1810 Translation of the Great Qing Code," *The Translator*, 10.1 (2004), 1–31.

"The Development of British Sinology and Changes in Translation Practice: The Case of Sir John Francis Davis (1795–1890)," *Translation and Interpreting Studies*, 2.ii (2007), 3–42.

"Modern Translation Theory and Past Translation Practice: European Translations of the *Haoqiu zhuan*," in Chan (ed.), *One into Many*, pp. 39–66.

"Travelling Toward True Translation: The First Generation of Sino-English Translators," *The Translator*, 12.2 (2006), 1–22.

Saussy, Haun, *Great Walls of Discourse and Other Adventures in Cultural China* (Cambridge, MA: Harvard University Press, 2002).

The Problem of a Chinese Aesthetic (Stanford University Press, 1995).

Schafer, Edward H., "What and How Is sinology?" *T'ang Studies*, 8–9 (1990–91), 23–44.

Schaffer, Simon, "Enlightened Automata," in William Clark, Jan Golinski, and Simon Schaffer (eds.), *The Sciences in Enlightened Europe* (University of Chicago Press, 1999), pp. 126–68.

"Instruments as Cargo in the China Trade," *History of Science*, 44 (2006), 217–46.

Seng Ong, "Whang-y-Tong," *Old Sennockian Newsletter* (Easter, 2006).

Shapin, Steven, *The Scientific Revolution* (University of Chicago Press, 1996).

Sharma, Jayeeta, "British Science, Chinese Skill and Assam Tea: Making Empire's Garden," *Indian Economic and Social History Review*, 43, 4 (2006), 429–55.

Shi, Shu-mei, *The Lure of the Modern: Writing Modernism in China, 1917–1937* (Berkeley: University of California Press, 2001).

Sieber, Patricia, *Theatres of Desire: Authors, Readers, and the Reproduction of early Chinese Song-drama, 1300–2000* (Basingstoke: Palgrave Macmillan, 2003).

Simpson, David, *Wordsworth's Historical Imagination* (London: Routledge, 1987).

Singer, Aubrey, *The Lion & the Dragon: The Story of the First British Embassy to the Court of the Emperor Qianlong in Peking 1792–94* (London: Barrie and Jenkins, 1992).

Sirén, Osvald, *China and the Gardens of Europe of the Eighteenth Century* (1937; Dumbarton Oaks: Harvard University Press, 1990).

Sivasundaram, Sujit, "'A Christian Benares': Orientalism, Science and the Serampore Mission of Bengal," *Indian Economic and Social History Review*, 44 (2007), 111–45.

Sivin, Nathan, *Science in Ancient China: Researches and Reflections* (Aldershot: Ashgate, 1995).

Smith, Carl T., *Chinese Christians: Elites, Middlemen, and the Church in Hong Kong* (Hong Kong University Press, 2005).

Smith, Roger, "The Sing-Song Trade: Exporting Clocks to China in the Eighteenth Century," *Antiquarian Horology*, 30 (2008), 629–58.

Spence, Jonathan D., *The Chan's Great Continent: China in Western Minds* (London: Allen Lane Penguin Press, 1999).

God's Chinese Son: The Taiping Heavenly Kingdom of Hong Xiuquan (New York: W.W. Norton, c. 1996).

The Search for Modern China (New York: W.W. Norton, 1990).

Standaert, Nicolas, *Handbook of Christianity in China. Volume One: 635–1800* (Leiden: Brill, 2000).

Stifler, Susan Reed, "The Language Students of the East India Company's Canton Factory," *Journal of the North China Royal Asiatic Society*, 69 (1938), 46–83.

Strandenaes, Thor, "Anonymous Bible Translations: Native Literati and the Translation of the Bible into Chinese," in Stephen Baralden, Kathleen Cann, and John Dean (eds.), *Sowing the Word: The Cultural Impact of the British and Foreign Bible Society* (Sheffield Phoenix Press, 2004), pp. 120–21.

Subrahmanyam, Sanjay, "Connected Histories: Notes towards a Reconfiguration of Early Modern Eurasia," *Modern Asian Studies*, 31.3 (1997).

Sudan, Rajani, *Fair Exotics: Xenophobic Subjects in English Literature, 1720–1850* (Philadelphia: University of Pennsylvania Press, 2002).

"Mud, Mortar, and Other Technologies of Empire," *The Eighteenth Century: Theory and Interpretation*, 45 (2004), 147–69.

Tao, Zhijian, *Drawing the Dragon: The Western Reinvention of China* (Frankfurt: Rodopi, 2009).

Teele, Roy E., *Through a Glass Darkly: A Study of English Translations of Chinese Poetry* (Ann Arbor: UMI, 1949).

Teltscher, Kate, *The High Road to China: George Bogle, the Panchen Lama and the First British Expedition to Tibet* (London: Bloomsbury, 2006).

Thomas, Adrian P., "The Establishment of Calcutta Botanic Garden: Plant Transfer, Science and the East India Company, 1786–1806," *Journal of the Royal Asiatic Society*, 16 (2006), 165–77.

Thomas, Greg M., "Yuanming Yuan/Versailles: Intercultural Interactions between Chinese and European Palace Cultures," *Art History*, 32 (2009), 115–43.

Thomas, Nicholas, *Colonialism's Culture: Anthropology, Travel, and Government* (Princeton University Press, 2004).

Thompson, Carl, *The Suffering Traveller and the Romantic Imagination* (Oxford: Clarendon. 2007).

Thorne, Susan, *Congregational Missions and the Making of an Imperial Culture in Nineteenth-Century England* (Stanford University Press, 1999).

Townsend, R. C., "John Wordsworth and his Brother's Poetic Development," *PMLA*, 81.1 (1966), 70–78.

Trocki, Carl A., *Opium, Empire and the Global Political Economy: A Study of the Asian Opium Trade 1750–1950* (London: Routledge, 1990).

Twitchett, D. C., *Land Tenure and the Social Order in T'ang and Sung China* (London: SOAS, 1962).

Uhalley, Stephen and Xiaxin Wu (eds.), *China and Christianity* (London: Sharpe, 2001).

Ukers, William Harrison, *All About Tea*. 2 vols. (New York: Tea and Coffee Trade Journals, 1935).

Van Dyke, Paul A., *The Canton Trade: Life and Enterprise on the China Coast, 1700–1845* (Hong Kong University Press, 2007).

Venuti, Lawrence, *The Translator's Invisibility: A History of Translation* (London and New York: Routledge, 1995).

Vincent, Clare, and J. H. Leopold, "James Cox (ca. 1723–1800): Goldsmith and Entrepreneur," in *Heilbrunn Timeline of Art History* (New York: Metropolitan Museum of Art, 2000–), www.metmuseum.org/toah/hd/jcox/hd_jcox.htm (accessed November 2011).

Wahrman, Dror, *The Making of the Modern Self: Identity and Culture in Eighteenth-Century England* (New Haven: Yale University Press, 2004).

Wakeman Jr., Frederic, "The Canton Trade and the Opium War," in J. K. Fairbank (ed.), *The Cambridge History of China. Vol 10: Late Ch'ing, 1800–1911, Part 1* (Cambridge University Press, 1978), pp. 163–212.

The Great Enterprise: The Manchu Reconstruction of Imperial Order in Seventeenth-Century China. 2 vols. (Berkeley: University of California Press, 1985).

Waley, Arthur D., "Sir William Jones as Sinologue" *BSOAS*, 11 (1946), 842.

The Opium War Through Chinese Eyes (London: Allen and Unwin, 1958).

Waley-Cohen, Joanna, *The Sextants of Beijing: Global Currents in Chinese History* (New York: W.W. Norton, 1999).

Wallerstein, Immanuel, *European Universalism the Rhetoric of Power* (London: New Press, 2006).

Walwin, James, *Fruits of Empire: Exotic Produce and British Taste, 1660–1800* (London: Macmillan, 1997).

Wang, Gungwu, *Anglo-Chinese Encounters since 1800* (Cambridge University Press, 2003).

Wang, Hui and Ye Mamei, "A Comparison of Robert Morrison's and Joshua Marshman's Translations of the *Daxue*," *Journal of Chinese Studies*, 49 (2009), 413–26.

Wang, Ning, *Globalization and Cultural Translation* (London: Marshall Cavendish Academic, 2004).

"Orientalism versus Occidentalism?: *New Literary History*, 28 (1992), 57–67.

Wang, Ning, and Sun Yifeng (eds.), *Translation, Globalisation and Localisation: A Chinese Perspective* (Toronto: Multilingual Matters, 2008).

Ward, Adrienne, *Pagodas in Play: China on the Eighteenth-Century Italian Opera Stage* (Lewisburg: Bucknell University Press, 2010).

Watt, James, "Thomas Percy, China, and the Gothic," *The Eighteenth Century: Theory and Interpretation*, 48 (2007), 95–109.

Wheeler, Roxann, *The Complexion of Race: Categories of Difference in Eighteenth-Century British Culture* (Philadelphia: University of Pennsylvania Press, 2000).

Whitehead, Peter J. P., *Chinese Natural History Drawings selected from the Reeves Collection in the British Museum* (London: British Museum, 1974).

Wills Jr, John E. (ed.), *China and Maritime Europe 1500–1800: Trade, Settlement, Diplomacy and Missions* (Cambridge University Press, 2011).

Wilson, Kathleen (ed.), *A New Imperial History: Culture, Identity and Modernity in Britain and the Empire 1660–1840* (Cambridge University Press, 2003).

This Island Race: Englishness, Empire and Gender in the Eighteenth Century (London and New York: Routledge, 2003).

Wilson, Ming, and John Cayley (eds.), *Europe Studies China: Papers from an International Conference in European Sinology* (London: Floating World Editions, 2005).

Witchard, Anne Veronica, *Thomas Burke's Dark Chinoiserie: Limehouse Nights and the Queer Spell of Chinatown* (Aldershot: Ashgate, 2009).

Witek, John W. S.J., "Catholic Missions and the Expansion of Christianity, 1644–c.1800," in John E. Wills, Jr. (ed.), *China and Maritime Europe*, pp. 135–82.

Wong, R. Bin, *China Transformed* (New York, Cornell University Press, 1997).

Wong, Young-tsu, *A Paradise Lost: The Imperial Garden Yuanming Yuan* (Honolulu: University of Hawai'i Press, 2011).

Worrall, David, "Chinese Indians: A James Gillray print, Covent Garden's 'The Loves of Bengal,' and the eighteenth-century Asian Economic Ascendancy," *European Romantic Review*, 19 (2008), 105–12.

Harlequin Empire Race, Ethnicity and the Drama of the Popular Enlightenment (London: Pickering and Chatto, 2007).

Wu, Duncan, *Wordsworth's Reading 1800–1815* (Cambridge University Press, 2007).

Wylie, Alexander, *Notes on Chinese Literature* (London: Trübner, 1867).

Xi, Lian, *Redeemed by Fire: The Making of the First Native Protestant Church* (New Haven: Yale University Press, 2010).

Yang, Chi-ming, *Performing China, Virtue, Commerce, and Orientalism in Eighteenth-century England 1660–1760* (Baltimore: Johns Hopkins University Press, 2010).

Yao, Xinzhong, *An Introduction to Confucianism* (Cambridge University Press, 2000).

Young, John D., *East-West Synthesis: Matteo Ricci and Confucianism* (Hong Kong: Centre of Asian Studies, 1980).

Zetzsche, Oliver Jost, *History of the Union Version: The Culmination of Protestant Missionary Bible Translation in China* (Nettetal: Monumenta Serica, 1999).

"The Missionary and the Chinese 'Helper': A Reappraisal of the Chinese Role in the Case of the Bible Translation in China," *Journal of the History of Christianity in Modern China*, 3 (2000), 5–20.

Zhang, Longxi, *Allegoresis: Reading Canonical Literature East and West* (Ithaca: Cornell University Press, 2005).

Mighty Opposites: From Dichotomies to Differences in the Comparative Study of China (Stanford University Press, 1999).

The Tao and the Logos: Literary Hermeneutics, East and West (Durham, NC: Duke University Press, 1992).

Unexpected Affinities: Reading Across Cultures (University of Toronto Press, 2007).

Zheng, Yangwen, *The Social Life of Opium in China* (Cambridge University Press, 2005).

Zhou, Xiaoyi and Q. S. Tong, "Comparative Literature in China," CLCWeb: Comparative Literature and Culture, 2.iv (2000), 1–11.

Zhuang, Guotu, "Tea, Silver, Opium and War: From Commercial Expansion to Military Invasion," *Itinerario*, 17 (1993), 10–36.

Zionkowski, Linda and Cynthia Klekar (eds.), *The Culture of the Gift in Eighteenth-Century England* (New York: Palgrave Macmillan, 2009).

Zurndorfer, Harriet T., *China Bibliography: A Research Guide to Reference Works about China Past and Present* (Leiden: Brill, 1995).

Index

Index

CAMBRIDGE STUDIES IN ROMANTICISM

General Editor
James Chandler, University of Chicago